Rebekah Rousi · Catharina von Koskull ·
Virpi Roto
Editors

Humane Autonomous Technology

Re-thinking Experience with and in Intelligent Systems

Editors
Rebekah Rousi
University of Vaasa
Vaasa, Finland

Catharina von Koskull
University of Vaasa
Vaasa, Finland

Virpi Roto
Aalto University
Espoo, Finland

ISBN 978-3-031-66527-1   ISBN 978-3-031-66528-8 (eBook)
https://doi.org/10.1007/978-3-031-66528-8

This Palgrave Macmillan imprint is published by the registered company Springer Nature Switzerland AG
The registered company address is: Gewerbestrasse 11, 6330 Cham, Switzerland

If disposing of this product, please recycle the paper.

PREFACE

Humane Autonomous Technology - Re-thinking Experience with and in Intelligent Systems is a book representing multidisciplinary perspectives and insight into issues of human-centred and ethical autonomous technological development. This edited volume presents empirical studies and theoretical discussions alike that aim to probe contemporary understandings of human experience in relation to a range of technology in the autonomous domain, including artificial intelligence (AI) and its related forms (e.g., generative AI), robotics and autonomous vehicles. The book engages with emerging discussions in human-AI co-work and collaboration, the ethical issues arising in AI-enabled service, design, information technology, art and aesthetics. The book is a timely contribution to a growing body of technology ethics-related scholarship, with highlights that include:

- Critical multidisciplinary perspectives on topical ethical issues pertaining to AI;
- Empirical and conceptual studies advancing the understanding of the implications of AI;
- Challenging commonly held public views of AI and its output in terms of industry, labour, originality, intellectual property rights and creativity;
- Raising the flag for concerns pertaining to human traits within the systems, i.e., lying, imperfection, bias, identity and social emotions.

Contributions embody industrial, cognitive, design, art and creativity, service and collaborative labour perspectives. The topics covered in this volume are highly relevant for contemporary professional practitioners, researchers and students across several fields including: design, service design, creative art, sociology, communication studies, information systems, work studies and consumer studies. Readers are challenged to think about the presented topics and cases on an all-encompassing and profound systemic level that establishes a platform for future sociotechnical discussions and initiatives to engrain the humane in a multidimensional humanistic way.

Vaasa, Finland   Rebekah Rousi
Vaasa, Finland   Catharina von Koskull
Espoo, Finland   Virpi Roto

Acknowledgements

The editors and authors would like to express their gratitude to a number of organisations and parties that enabled the featured research and current book to materialise. The editors' and researchers' own universities, the University of Vaasa (School of Marketing and Communication, Finland), Aalto University (Department of Design, and Department of Art and Media, Finland), the University of Jyväskylä (Faculty of Information Technology, Finland), Carnegie Mellon University (Human-Computer Interaction Institute, United States of America, USA), University of Texas at Austin (Moody College of Communication, USA), Edith Cowan University (School of Arts and Humanities, Australia), Penn State College of Arts and Architecture (USA).

Funding bodies and projects supporting these research endeavours include: the Research Council of Finland (BUGGED project, decision number 348391; and SYNTHETICA, decision number 358714); Business Finland (DIMECC Sea4Value, grant 81/31/2020); Tiina and Antti Herlin Foundation; Maj and Tor Nessling Foundation; Japan Society for the Promotion of Science (JSPS, Kakenhi research grant), and Kongsberg Maritime Finland Oy. Other organizations to whom we are grateful include the VR Group, Tampere Regional Transport Bysse, WSP Finland Oy, Idis Design Oy, Villivisio Oy.

CONTENTS

Notes on Contributors

About the Editors

Rebekah Rousi is an Associate Professor (Tenure Track) of Communication and Digital Economy, at the School of Marketing and Communication, University of Vaasa, Finland. Rousi holds a Ph.D. in Cognitive Science and has specialised in researching human experience via embodied cognition and semiotics in relation to diverse forms of technology. Rousi has a professional background as a contemporary performance artist, with research experience in cultural studies, and particularly postcolonial theory. Her research interests mainly focus on human-robot and human-artificial intelligence interaction, embodied emotional experience, posthumanism, ethics, and issues of trust and privacy.

Catharina von Koskull is an Associate Professor of Marketing at the School of Marketing and Communication and the multidisciplinary Digital Economy Platform, University of Vaasa, Finland. Her research background lies within service marketing and management and particularly service innovation. More recently, her work has moved towards Transformative Consumer Research where she focuses on consumer wellbeing (i.e. agency, privacy and dignity) related to ageing and digital technology. She is experienced in traditional ethnography and is passionate about inclusive, participatory outreach methods such as Art-based methodologies and ethnodrama.

Virpi Roto is a Senior University Lecturer at the Department of Design, Aalto University, Finland. She has worked for 15 years at Nokia Research Center, where she studied human-centred design and user experience. During the last 10 years at Aalto University, she has acted as Professor of Practice in Experience Design and led the Aalto team of designers in several research projects related to work automation with industry partners. She is thus familiar both with the research and practice of Industry 4.0, and her current research focus is on human-centred design of the work tools for Industry 5.0.

Contributors

Hanna-Kaisa Alanen (MA) is a designer completing her Ph.D. in Cognitive Science at the University of Jyväskylä. Her research explores individual and socio-emotional dimensions of Human-Technology Interaction in everyday life conditions, using fashion as a lens. Alanen is a project researcher in a Research Council of Finland project BUGGED, Emotional Experience of Privacy and Ethics in Everyday Pervasive Systems (University of Vaasa). She is a member of the Science Attic at Puistokatu 4, a joint initiative of the Tiina and Antti Herlin Foundation and Maj and Tor Nessling Foundation, dedicated to promoting a sustainable way of life within planetary boundaries.

Martina Čaić is an Assistant Professor in Strategic Service Design at the Department of Design, School of Arts, Design and Architecture, Aalto University (Finland). She studies interactions between AI-powered agents and humans in diverse service settings focusing on value creation, beneficiaries' well-being, ethical implications, and organizational transformation.

Giuseppe Chiorazzo is a leader with expertise in marketing and transformative digital experiences. He assists industrial companies in harnessing digital marketing technologies. Guided by human-centric ethos and passionate about digital technologies, he is interested in their impact on customer experience, user interaction, employee performance, and societal dynamics

Robert Ciuchita is an Associate Professor in the Department of Marketing at Hanken School of Economics (Finland) and the director of Hanken's Bachelor (BSc) in Business programme. His research and teaching interests lie in the areas of service management, digital marketing, innovation management, and emerging technologies.

Nils Ehrenberg is a postdoctoral researcher in the Department of Design at Aalto University, Finland. He recently defended his doctoral dissertation, titled "Panopticons of Convenience: The Internal Politics of the Smart Home". His research explores issues of civic engagement, smart technologies, and how these topics intersect with justice and power relations.

Rolf Findsrud is a postdoctoral researcher at CREDS – Center for Research on Digitalization and Sustainability. Findsrud holds a Ph.D. in service innovation from Inland Norway University of Applied Sciences, Norway. His research interests include resource integration through a service lens, motivation, service innovation, digitalization, artificial intelligence, and sustainability.

Sarah E. Fox is an Assistant Professor at Carnegie Mellon University in the Human-Computer Interaction Institute, where she directs the Tech Solidarity Lab. Her work examines how the deployment of AI within essential sectors reshapes existing work practices, with a focus on developing systems that centre workers' needs and expertise.

Paul Haimes is an artist/designer living in Kyoto, Japan. He is currently an Associate Professor of design at Ritsumeikan University. His main interests are in the aesthetics of Japanese art and design.

Jo Jung is a Lecturer in Design at Edith Cowan University, Australia, specialising in user experience design (UX). With a keen focus on enhancing user interactions, Jo has contributed significantly to various projects, including the development of food and nutrition curriculum support materials for the WA Healthy Children Program. This extensive project, spanning from 2013 to 2022, received funding from the Department of Health WA. Jo's teaching endeavours centre on integrating UX principles into higher education and fostering collaboration with industry partners empower students to create intuitive and engaging user experiences in various design contexts.

Aaron Knochel completed his doctorate in Art Education (Ohio State University, 2011) on critical media literacy, software studies, and art education. He has worked in visual arts learning spaces including schools, museums, and community arts programmes both domestically and internationally. Dr. Knochel is currently an Embedded Researcher in the Art & Design Research Incubator, at the College of Arts & Architecture. His research focuses on the intersections between art education, social theory, and software studies. From community-based media production to engaging digital visual culture in the K-12 art classroom, his interests follow the complexities of civic engagement through the arts and network connectivity.

Stuart Medley is a researcher at UNIDCOM, IADE, Portugal, and Associate Professor of design at Edith Cowan University, Australia. He has worked as a visual communication designer and illustrator for thirty years, and is the author of the book, The Picture in Design. He is a co-founder of the Perth Comic Arts Festival and heads the Applied Comics for Law Think Tank at the University of Western Australia. He is Art Director for Hidden Shoal Recordings, a record label with clients including the Australian Broadcasting Corporation, the BBC and Showtime.

Jonas Oppenlaender is a postdoctoral researcher with a focus on applying generative artificial intelligence for practical applications in creative and technological domains. With a Ph.D. in Computer Science from the University of Oulu, Finland, his expertise extends to the development and study of generative artificial intelligence within the context of text-to-image generation. He is the author of research papers, including "The Creativity of Text-to-Image Generation" and "Prompting AI Art: An Investigation into the Creative Skill of Prompt Engineering," which explore the intersection of generative AI technology and creative processes. Jonas contributes to the ongoing dialogue on the potential and challenges of AI in fostering innovative creative practices.

Samantha Shorey is an Assistant Professor at the University of Texas at Austin in the Moody College of Communication. She is a design researcher who studies how communication about innovation shapes technology culture and technology labour.

Tomi Slotte Dufva (Doctor of Art) works as a Senior University Lecturer at Aalto University, School of Arts, Design, and Architecture, in the Department of Art and Media. Slotte Dufva's artistic work focuses primarily on the intersections between art, technology and science. He is the co-founder of art & craft school Robotti, which combines technology and art. Slotte Dufva's research revolves around post-digital culture and art education, embodied digitality, art and tech, and societal, philosophical and cultural issues within AI and digitality.

Hannah Snyder is an Associate Professor at the Department of Marketing, BI - Norwegian School of Business. Her research interest relates to service innovation, sustainability, lying behaviour and business models. She has published in journals such as Journal of Service Research, Journal of Business Research, and European Journal of Marketing.

Bård Tronvoll is a Professor at Inland Norway University of Applied Sciences, Norway, and director of the Center for Research on Digitalization and Sustainability (CREDS). He is also a Professor at the CTF-Service Research Center at Karlstad University, Sweden. Tronvoll focuses on value co-creation through a service perspective, focusing on digitalization, sustainability, and service innovation.

Lars Witell is a Professor of Marketing at Linköping University, Sweden. His research interests concern ethics, service innovation, service infusion and customer experience. He has published about 80 papers in scholarly journals such as Journal of the Academy of Marketing Science, Journal of Retailing and Journal of Service Research.

LIST OF FIGURES

LIST OF TABLES

CHAPTER 1

Introduction

Rebekah Rousi, Catharina von Koskull, and Virpi Roto

INTRODUCTION

We are now living in an era where century-long dreams of independently moving and seemingly thinking machines are becoming a reality. From robots and self-driving vehicles, to personal assistants embedded within our word processing tools, art and design generators, as well as artificial companions, all enabled by machine learning (ML). Perhaps, more aptly put, there is no sector within modern societies in which AI has not been ideated and conceptualised, developed for, and/or implemented. It is indeed becoming the 'new electricity' of the twenty-first century, empowered by the groundwork of the contemporary landscape of global connectivity and the Internet.

R. Rousi (✉) · C. von Koskull
University of Vaasa, Vaasa, Finland
e-mail: rebekah.rousi@uwasa.fi

C. von Koskull
e-mail: catharina.von.koskull@uwasa.fi

V. Roto
Aalto University, Espoo, Finland
e-mail: virpi.roto@aalto.fi

R. Rousi et al. (eds.), *Humane Autonomous Technology*,
https://doi.org/10.1007/978-3-031-66528-8_1

Despite the excitement of bountiful opportunities arising from the developments, launches of AI-based innovations have been met with scepticism, worry, and outright horror when new solutions for old problems bring with them, new problems in themselves. To illustrate, one of the attractions behind self-driving vehicles is that of reducing uncertainty induced by varying skill levels in human drivers. In other words, on the roads, some people are better at handling fast moving vehicles than others. In March 2018, belief in the integrity of self-driving vehicle safety was desecrated when a self-driving car, supervised by a 'safety driver', hit and killed a pedestrian (Elish, 2019). The physical accident itself gave rise to a number of dynamic factors that need to be considered when implementing autonomous technology such as: the human dimension— how to ensure humans maintain oversight of unfolding events; as well as accountability and responsibility—when incidents occur who should be made responsible and accountable if a machine makes decisions that are erroneous or harmful. These types of incidents, as well as other unfolding scenarios such as gender bias in AI-driven recruitment tools as well as racial bias in law enforcement technology are a part of a growing ecosystem of AI-related ethical concerns that perhaps not so much invent new dilemmas, but rather, amplify old ones.

Newer examples can be seen in the rising amount of scandals specifically related to generative artificial intelligence (GenAI) such as the *Sports Illustrated* incident in which Chief Executive Officer Ross Levinsohn was fired after using GenAI to produce stories and generated false biographies (Goldman, 2023). Another incident saw a financial official pay 25 million US dollars after engaging in a video call with a deep fake impersonating his organisation's chief financial officer (Chen & Magramo, 2024). On an increasingly personal and sensitive side of human integrity, there have been increasing accounts of deep fake porn and AI-enabled sextortian (Satter, 2023; Singer, 2024). These incidents have seen a greater number of female targets, and particularly, underage female targets (Rousay, 2023). On the flip side, ethical concerns have also caused overreactions in the systems, witnessing 'reverse biases' in output such as seen in the recent Gemini.AI case in which the AI-image generator refused to produce 'white' subjects in artistic images. This occurrence entailed visualised over-compensatory phenomena such as culturally diverse Nazi-era soldiers (see Heath, 2024). Thus, the linguistic and representational nature of our current AI-landscape is transforming tangible and physical ethical issues into cultural, sociological and psychological ones.

While the obvious catastrophes are noted and mediated, the subtler effects of how humans live with, are affected by, and in turn affect intelligent technology remain under the radar. There is no doubt that notice has been given to conditions such as the 'Google Effect', or degenerated memory (short-term, working and long-term) based on the convenience of the Google search - removing the need for memorization and thus decreasing cognitive training in humans (Sparrow et al., 2011). Social media addiction (Sun & Zhang, 2021) is another phenomenon much discussed among psychologists and sociologists linked to theories of hyper presentation and framing of self (Maddox, 2017), fear of missing out (FOMO, Oberst et al., 2017), and privacy paradox (from the data privacy perspective, see e.g., Waldman, 2020). The problem is that all of these current conditions are connected to present concerns linked to the recent infiltration of AI throughout our global society. Google feeds AI and is AI. Human memory loss is Google's gain. Thanks to AI algorithms, social media gives us what we want—and a lot of it. AI reminds us when we are missing out, and despite the warnings (General Data Protection Regulation, GDPR), we would still rather be in the domains, feeding our data, than being excluded from the rest of the post-post-industrial human kingdom. Moreover, as critical as we are of the new hit, Generative AI (GenAI— ChatGPT, Midjourney, Nightcafe, DALL E 2, Stable Diffusion, etc.), for all the above-mentioned reasons, many (if not most of us) love to use it for its output and convenience.

More problems are rearing their ugly heads, such as digital sweatshops in South-East Asia and Sub-Saharan Africa (again old wine in a new bottle in the Global South) to power OpenAI's 'ethical AI' data supplier Sama (Jason, 2023). Workers labouring on a menial wage with appalling conditions, scan labelled data of all kinds of dark content (child pornography, torture, incest, etc.) to train the language models to detect and filter before reaching the users of the Global North (see also Nyabola, 2023). All of these dilemmas stem from and revolve around profoundly human afflictions. As Sam Altman (OpenAI's founder) states, 'AI will probably most likely lead to the end of the world, but in the meantime, there'll be great companies' (cited in Jason, 2023), seeing that money wins over the logic of life. The question and trajectory of AI in itself—the re-creation or mimicry of human thought to replace and surpass humans in a variety of tasks—is characteristic of the human condition in which through pride, demonstration of prowess, control and dominance, we are willing to outsource ourselves. This particularly holds for an era in which not only our technologies become ever more autonomous while ironically being connected, but our lives become ever more disconnected from one another—while ironically *being connected*.

Humaness and Ethics

The term 'humane' conjures many ideas of benevolence and compassion between human beings as well as from human beings towards other beings. Ultimately, humane is applied to describe actions and decisions that exhibit empathy and promote wellbeing towards others. It can be considered a proponent of *ethics* and morality in terms of behaving according to conceptualisations of right and wrong. It can also be understood as the act and agenda of putting others' best interests and values first—i.e., not prioritising profit over human and environmental wellbeing. Paul Goodman (1969) in his essay, 'Can Technology Be Humane?' explains human commitment to technology. Reflecting on the historical Hiroshima bombing (1945), Goodman emphasises the commitment human societies give towards technology as if it were a religion. Technology as truth—a product of objective science enabling objective and accurate observations and results, and a means of semantic distinction (i.e., social connection to technology and products seen in brand identification, etc.)—is a silent chant that has characterised the modern era (see Danaher & Saetra, 2022; Drew, 2016).

Goodwin (1969) argued that people need 'meaning systems' in which to believe, yet already during the 1960s technology in its entirety, or technological determinism as a means of *definition*, had already overtaken the human and the spiritual. This can be seen as one of the current 'sore points' of current ethical AI dilemmas, for we know through, e.g., GenAI that the phenomena we relate to via the technology, and often the technology itself, is not what we think it is (i.e., deepfakes, hallucinations and blackboxes). Thus, in his foresight, Goodman argued for a cybernetic approach towards techno-societal development in which technology would be studied and developed with humans and their values in mind.

Ethics is a broad philosophical field that deliberates questions of good and evil, right and wrong (see e.g., Saariluoma & Rousi, 2020). It relates to morality, moral behaviour and moral decision-making, that either: (a) is used descriptively to indicate particular codes of conduct that are promoted by societies or communities, as well as individually; or (b) normativity, to indicate codes of conduct that are promoted universally on the basis of rationality (Gert & Gert, 2020). Ethical considerations refer to sets of principles and values that pertain to matters of good or bad in relation to humans and their actions (Reeve, 2014).

Ethical considerations when deliberating social-technological concepts is one step towards transforming the human to the *humane* (compassion and benevolence). It is the humane, and what we term 'humane-centred design' that we focus on in this edited book. The book features the thoughts and studies from prominent international scholars, who from their own positioning, case and context, approach the *humane* and its potentialities in autonomous technology. The featured chapters dance across disciplinary boundaries to provide deeper, systemic insight into the factors, states, challenges and opportunities of AI and related autonomous technology in a variety of domains.

As editors, we have striven to select authors and studies that encompass the complex ramifications that technology of this nature (information-intensive, so-called self-learning technology) have on human life and experience, and how these technologies in turn, reflect the deeper darker workings of human cognition and values. Contributors represent a broad range of disciplines: consumer studies, marketing, design (service, user experience and interaction design, industrial design, illustration and game design), art (conceptual, drawing, performance, print-making, community and participatory), software engineering, sociology, cognitive science and communication studies. This broad range of disciplinary thinking is condensed into three distinct sections of the book (see Fig. 1.1).

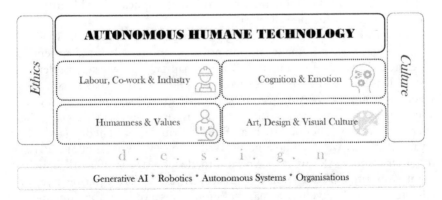

Fig. 1.1 Structure of the book

Structure of the Book

The book is divided into four themes (see Fig. 1.1): (1) Labour, co-work and industry; (2) Cognition and emotion; (3) Humanness and values; and (4) Art, design and visual culture (see Fig. 1.1). The themes capture the diverse areas of scholarship represented by the book, and highlight the ways in which AI-related phenomena are streaming through all sectors and disciplines of society. The AI revolution at workplaces has started, and we need to rethink how work with autonomous systems should be organised. Likewise, the nature of knowledge work and indeed understanding of creativity (in work, art and design) are being twisted by what we witness in the GenAI era.

Theme 1 focuses on various aspects of this workplace revolution that ever increasingly sees humans and AI as co-workers. In Chapter 2, Martina Čaić, Robert Ciuchita and Giuseppe Chiorazzo take a look at the dynamics and complexities of expert co-work between humans and chatbots. In their chapter, 'Help me help you: The dilemma of collaboration between expert employees and chatbots' Čaić and colleagues describe an illustrative case study in which semi-structured interviews were used to observe changes to human roles in B2B knowledge work. The chapter delves into the heart of current developments in the human-AI field, observing not simply an appropriation of traditionally considered *human qualities* in task distribution, but a more profound pondering of the evolution of human engagement in work, afforded by the AI systems. Yet, other factors arise that challenge us to critically evaluate the current and unfolding states of human-AI co-work that implicate our identities as human beings, including self-worth.

In contrast to passive monitoring of automation, in Chapter 3, Virpi Roto suggests that humane autonomous technology has the potential to enrich the work for humans. Roto's chapter, 'Co-worker, butler or coach? Designing automation for work enrichment', forces us to consider whether or not we want our AI to be designed to behave like a colleague, a butler serving us, or a coach that helps us grow as a people. The chapter draws on theories such as Self-Determination Theory (Deci & Ryan, 1985) as well as Eudaimonic Well-being (Waterman et al., 2010) to observe how AI can take workers to deeper stages of work enrichment over time. From another human-centred co-work perspective, in Chapter 4, Sarah Fox and Samantha Shorey observe how the implementation of AI affects the tasks and routines of janitorial staff and recycling sorters. Their findings indicate a shift in tasks that transform practical workers into machine supervisors and technology trouble-shooters. On the basis of these empirical findings, they propose recommendations on how AI should be installed, evaluated and maintained in co-work environments.

Theme 2 of the book focuses on 'Cognition and Emotions'. The represented chapters apply understandings of cognition and emotions from the perspectives of: embodied technology design experience; human embodied expert cognition and the Most Advanced Yet Acceptable theory; and dual process theory within the context of technology-enabled services. Hanna-Kaisa Alanen and Rebekah Rousi's Chapter 5, 'Moving spaces—the affective embodied self in tram design and the autonomous imaginary' looks at current experiences of the emerging present—a newly established tramway in the city of Tampere, and how this is intertwined with the imagined future of autonomous transport. A symbolic inter-actionist (Blumer, 1980) approach is taken towards understanding how experience is formed across the dimensions of the material and imma-terial in relation to self, identification of self and distinction (Bourdieu, 1979, 1996). Here, experience is formed in relation to the design and *others* as well as within the design. This notion of being 'within design' is taken up in Chapter 6 by Rousi who conceptually examines the Most Advanced Yet Acceptable (MAYA) theory (Loewy, 1951) in relation to disruptive autonomous maritime technology. Rousi focuses on the role of expert mental models and embodied cognition in ascertaining '*Whose MAYA*' is at play in popular perceptions of autonomous maritime vehicles and disruptive design developments.

Rolf Findrud and Bård Tronvoll examine human cognition in the unfolding era of human–machine co-work. By applying dual process theory to explore cognitive processes in the moments of, and in relation to, co-work with intelligent machines, Findrud and Tronvoll formulate a framework of human–machine symbiosis that incorporates necessary adaptation between human and machine 'thinking'. There is a rela-tionship between Chapter 7 and Chapter 6 (Rousi) that see cognition, embodied affective processes, and the inner workings of human–machine synthesis as an integrated whole. In this integrated whole there is no superficial separation between humans and technology—they are intrinsi-cally connected to one another, and in order to forge an effective and humane future, need to be developed in a way that compliments the various qualities presented by the organic and artificial actors.

This relationship is teased out further in the theme focusing on 'Humanness and values'. In Chapter 8, "Smart home technologies: convenience and control," Nils Ehrenberg elaborates on the nature of smart homes from the perspective of power. The chapter presents empirical findings that highlight the dynamics not simply between humans and their smart environments, but also in relation to circumstantial factors such as home renting versus ownership. This aspect is widely overlooked in the fields of human–computer interaction and computer science (Internet of Things), yet have severe ethical implications from a range of perspectives, none-the-least privacy. Ehrenberg applies a Foucaultian lens in what he describes as 'Panopticons of convenience' in which individual homeowners trade-off privacy for the perceived benefits of services, albeit 'autonomous' systems in the home (robot vacuum cleaners, mops, Alexa, etc.). The chapter challenges who the *actual users* are of the smart home, whether they are in the house or not. Users are subsequently divided into various types that once more instils a power structure that rests both between humans and technology, as well as between humans according to their role in the technology utilisation process.

In Chapter 9, 'Social robot design and the aesthetics of imperfection', Rousi and Paul Haimes explore the aesthetic possibilities of disrupting perfection. Where one technological trajectory has been that of human enhancement—the quest towards *human perfection*—Rousi and Haimes draw on the Japanese *Wabi-Sabi* and Christian philosophy to understand the *humaness* of the 'glitch'. They reach beyond the pragmatic to understand a social and psychological role of robotics that can only be satisfied through design that goes beyond skin deep. We all know how it feels to be lied to. On the topic of imperfection and then, potential deviance, Lars Witell and Hannah Snyder's Chapter 10, 'Dishonesty through AI: can robots engage in lying behavior?' draws on recent developments such as those seen in generative AI, in which the systems can be perceived as 'lying' to us. They refer to the inaccuracies and hallucinatory effects established when humans cannot rely on the algorithms they have created. More pertinently, the chapter focuses on the business and organisational context in which the ripple effects of content falsification (mis or dis-information) can be catastrophic. This particularly holds from the customer point of view in which trust is the maker or breaker of any individual-organisational relationship. Here, emphasis is placed on lying behavior in service encounters.

Four chapters on the theme Art, Design and Visual Culture constitute the final section of the book. First out, in Chapter 11 'Grasping AI entanglements—digital feminism and generative AI,' Tomi Slotte Dufva makes way for discussions on art and creativity. Slotte Dufva applies feminist phenomenology to analyse machine learning models and how they manifest predominant ideologies in AI-generated imagery. Moving beyond mere discussions on bias in the algorithms, Slotte Dufva challenges the reader to consider the broader implications of engaging with the technology from ecological, political and ideological standpoints. The author observes changes of discourse and roles in creative practices. In particular, he emphasises the dynamics of positioning humans in creative processes—from mark maker, image taker (photographer), image creator to 'prompt engineer'. Assemblage theory and entanglement are applied to understand the interrelationships and fragile dependencies between humans and technology in image production and subsequent interpretation. Prompt engineering in itself is textually and linguistically intensive, rendering a major level of abstraction from the output produced. Thus, the fabrics in between intention, input and output comprise intricate components of a larger assemblage that is ever more exposed to mathematical calculation and probabilities.

Aaron Knochel, in Chapter 12, 'Scribbles, spirographs, and AI, oh my!' advances this discussion by re-framing mark-making practices through graphicality, socio-materiality, meaning and participatory cultural engagement. Once more, Assemblage Theory (Delanda, 2006) is used to understand the social ontology of creative artistic practice, and practices of graphicality, yet this time in light of the *more-than-human*. It is a re-defining of autonomous technology through something that goes beyond ourselves. The chapter presents an alternative view on the potentials of creative production and human–machine symbiosis that is not rigidly tied to current developments in AI. However, with this said, the chapter aids in the pondering of what AI means to art practice, creative expression and human–human (multi-people collaboration) as well as human-non-human creation—as a tool and as an actor. 'Mr Fusion and Johnny 5? Visual rhetoric of AI design' (Chapter 13) by Stuart Medley and Jo Jung, takes us on a ride through time, popular culture and Modernism to discover 'the language of AI' in design. The chapter observes the human dimensions of trust and control in AI through visual aesthetics and rhetorical use of Modernist style. Modernism is examined as a stylistic metaphor used strategically in communication design related to and created from

AI and its generative AI counterparts. To illustrate this argument Medley and Jung analyse the design of several digital products, which harness the Modernist design philosophy of clarity, simplicity and understatement. Modernist design philosophy connects with historical movements attempting to unify through design, as a sign of progress and expression of 'honesty'—*form follows function* (Crouch, 1998). Historically, some notable moments of Modernist design history such as those seen in Scandinavian and Nordic design—post-world war two—correspond with critical advancements in AI development and conceptualisation. This particularly stands for major steps in the scholarship of cognitive science. As we see however, Modernism as a style or philosophy, can be seen as a smokescreen for complexity, manipulation and hypocrisy.

Finally, Chapter 14, 'The cultivated practices of text-to-image generation' by Jonas Oppenlaender, sees critical issues raised relating to the recent rise in popularity of AI image generation software. Oppenlaender closely scrutinises the co-creative ecosystem of humans and text-to-image generators by highlighting controversies such as intellectual property issues and the problems of rapid utilisation and spreading of synthetic data. The chapter is a gripping end to this edited book that has covered the opportunities and the potential ethical pitfalls of AI and autonomous systems becoming a normal part of our everyday lives. The aim has been to assemble the expertise and insight of scholars across the disciplines from service design, human–computer interaction, computer science, cognitive science, communication studies, visual art, and design in order to re-frame the significance of AI in our emerging culture. We have used these contributions as an opportunity to grasp the complexity and steer future AI design development towards one that embraces human values, and overall humaness—benevolence, empathy and care. Our intention is to move forward in a world where AI is a co-inhabitant. Yet, at the same time, our goal is to ensure that the co-inhabitant is designed and developed in a way that places people first.

REFERENCES

Blumer, H. (1980). Mead and Blumer: *The convergent methodological perspectives of social behaviorism and symbolic interactionism* (pp. 409–419). *American Sociological Review*. https://www.jstor.org/stable/2095174

Bourdieu, P. (1979/1996). *Distinction: A social critique of the judgement of taste* (8th printing). Harvard University.

Chen, H., & Magramo, K. (2024). *Finance worker pays out $25 million after video call with deepfake 'Chief Financial Officer'*. https://edition.cnn.com/2024/02/04/asia/deepfake-cfo-scam-hong-kong-intl-hnk/index.html

Crouch, C. (1998). *Modernism in art, design and architecture*. Bloomsbury Publishing.

Danaher, J., & Saetra, H. S. (2022). Technology and moral change: The transformation of truth and trust. *Ethics and Information Technology, 24*(3), 35.

Deci, E. L., & Ryan, R. M. (1985). *Intrinsic motivation and self-determination in human behavior*. Plenum.

Delanda, M. (2006). *A new philosophy of society: Assemblage theory and social complexity*. Bloomsburg.

Drew, R. (2016). Technological determinism. In G. Burns (Ed.), *A companion to popular culture* (pp. 165–183). Wiley Blackwell.

Elish, M. C. (2019). *Moral crumple zones: Cautionary tales in human-robot interaction* (pre-print). Engaging Science, Technology, and Society (pre-print).

Gert, B. & Gert, J. (2020). The Definition of Morality. In Edward N. Zalta (Ed.), *The Stanford Encyclopedia of Philosophy (Fall 2020 Edition)*. https://plato.stanford.edu/archives/fall2020/entries/morality-definition/

Goldman, J. (2023). *2023 saw a number of AI scandals, demonstrating the need for clearer guidelines for brands and publishers*. https://www.emarketer.com/content/2023-saw-number-of-ai-scandals-demonstrating-need-clearer-guidelines-brands-publishers

Goodman, P. (1969). Can technology be humane? *The New York Review of Books, 13*(20), 199–215.

Heath, A. (2024). *Google CEO says Gemini AI diversity errors are 'completely unacceptable'*. https://www.theverge.com/2024/2/28/24085445/google-ceo-gemini-ai-diversity-scandal-employee-memo

Jason, P. R. (2023). *Digital sweatshops and dirty AI* . https://jasoninstitute.com/digital-sweatshops-and-dirty-ai/

Loewy, R. (1951). *Never leave well enough alone*. John Hopkins University Press.

Maddox, J. (2017). "Guns don't kill people... Selfies do": Rethinking narcissism as exhibitionism in selfie-related deaths. *Critical Studies in Media Communication, 34*(3), 193–205.

Nyabola, N. (2023). *ChatGPT and the sweatshops powering the digital age* . https://www.aljazeera.com/opinions/2023/1/23/sweatshops-are-making-our-digital-age-work

Oberst, U., Wegmann, E., Stodt, B., Brand, M., & Chamarro, A. (2017). Negative consequences from heavy social networking in adolescents: The mediating role of fear of missing out. *Journal of Adolescence, 55*, 51–60.

Reeve, C. D. C. (2014). *Nicomachean ethics*. Hackett Publishing Co.

Rousay, V. (2023). *Sexual deepfakes and image-based sexual abuse: Victim-survivor experiences and embodied harms* (Doctoral dissertation). Harvard University.

Saariluoma, P., & Rousi, R. (2020). Emotions and technoethics. *Emotions in Technology Design: From Experience to Ethics*, 167–189.

Satter, R. (2023). *FBI says artificial intelligence being used for 'sextortion' and harassment* . https://www.reuters.com/world/us/fbi-says-artificial-intelligence-being-used-sextortion-harassment-2023-06-07/

Singer, N. (2024). *Teen girls confront an epidemic of deepfake nudes in schools* . https://www.nytimes.com/2024/04/08/technology/deepfake-ai-nudes-westfield-high-school.html

Sparrow, B., Liu, J., & Wegner, D. M. (2011). Google effects on memory: Cognitive consequences of having information at our fingertips. *Science, 333*(6043), 776–778.

Sun, Y., & Zhang, Y. (2021). A review of theories and models applied in studies of social media addiction and implications for future research. *Addictive Behaviors, 114*, 106699.

Waldman, A. E. (2020). Cognitive biases, dark patterns, and the 'privacy paradox.' *Current Opinion in Psychology, 31*, 105–109.

Waterman, A. S., Schwartz, S. J., Zamboanga, B. L., Ravert, R. D., Williams, M. K., Bede Agocha, V., Yeong Kim S., & Brent Donnellan, M. (2010). The questionnaire for eudaimonic well-being: Psychometric properties, demographic comparisons, and evidence of validity. *The Journal of Positive Psychology, 5*(1), 41–61.

PART I

Labour, Co-Work and Industry

Help Me Help You: The Dilemma of Collaboration Between Expert Employees and Chatbots

Martina Čaić◉, Robert Ciuchita◉, and Giuseppe Chiorazzo

INTRODUCTION

Research and managerial interest in chatbots, conversational agents that enable interaction between humans and machines through natural language, has rapidly increased since 2010 (Rapp et al., 2021). A Research and Markets (2023) report estimates that the global chatbot market will reach around $1.25 billion in 2025, an over sixfold increase compared

M. Čaić (✉)
Department of Design, School of Arts, Design and Architecture, Aalto University, Espoo, Finland
e-mail: martina.caic@aalto.fi

R. Ciuchita
Department of Marketing, Hanken School of Economics, Helsinki, Finland
e-mail: robert.ciuchita@hanken.fi

G. Chiorazzo
Wirepas Ltd, Tampere, Finland
e-mail: giuseppe.chiorazzo@gmail.com

© The Author(s) 2024
R. Rousi et al. (eds.), *Humane Autonomous Technology*,
https://doi.org/10.1007/978-3-031-66528-8_2

to 2016, when it amounted to $190.8 million. In 2020, the technological research and consulting company Gartner assessed that chatbots have passed the peak of inflated expectations in their hype cycle for artificial intelligence (AI) (Goasduff, 2020). This analysis implies that by 2025 chatbots will reach the plateau of productivity (i.e., the technology will have broad market applicability and relevance) (Gartner n.d.).

While other conversational technologies fueled by AI developments seem to be scaling back (e.g., voice assistants; Latham, 2023), text-based chatbots seem to proliferate. An illustrative example is ChatGPT, the text-based, AI-powered chatbot that has been making headlines since its introduction in November 2022 (Sundar, 2023). Microsoft (2023) announced it was making a multiyear, multibillion-dollar continuation of its investment in OpenAI, the developer of ChatGPT. Amazon will also invest up to $4 billion in Anthropic, a generative AI start-up that operates the chatbot Claude (Satariano & Metz, 2023).

In this research we focus on text-based chatbots which have become objects of study in different business and management fields, including marketing (e.g., Crolic et al., 2022), information systems (e.g., Ashfaq et al., 2020), human–computer-interaction (e.g., Nguyen et al., 2022), and service management (e.g., Sands et al., 2021). Our review of the business and management literature, mirrored by efforts from other disciplines (see e.g., Rapp et al., 2021 for a systematic literature review with a human–computer interaction focus) shows a concentration on interactions with chatbots in business-to-consumer (B2C) settings and a great focus on technology and its features. However, fewer studies have examined chatbots in business-to-business (B2B) settings (see Kushwaha et al., 2021 and Lin et al., 2022 for notable exceptions) and especially in complex, knowledge-based contexts such as industrial equipment development and manufacturing. Such research is warranted, as illustrated by a recent event study of how investors respond to companies introducing AI chatbots which concludes that B2B companies have more to gain from implementing AI chatbot customer service compared to B2C companies (Fotheringham & Wiles, 2023).

The purpose of this research is to examine the introduction of an AI-powered chatbot in a B2B context through the lens of the People–Process–Technology (PPT; Leavitt, 1964; Schneier, 2009) organization change management framework. This is a parsimonious, yet comprehensive framework that has been employed to study technology deployment in different fields including customer relationship management (e.g.,

Chen & Popovich, 2003), information systems (e.g., Maruping et al., 2019) and tourism (e.g., Chen et al., 2021). We draw on semi-structured interviews with expert employees and business customers who are users of the chatbot. Our qualitative results show two emerging People roles (i.e., *knowledge experts* and *content curators*), two key Processes (i.e., *human-chatbot collaboration* and *efficiency gains*), and two Technology themes (i.e., *troubleshooting tool* and *competence requirement*). In the following, we present a brief literature review of empirical chatbot studies in business and management literature, followed by a presentation of our method, our findings, and a conclusion.

Literature Review

In business and management literature, empirical studies have primarily focused on interactions with chatbots in B2C settings, including online retail (e.g., Li & Wang, 2023; Pizzi et al., 2021; Roy & Naidoo, 2021; Sands et al., 2021), financial services (Adam et al., 2021; Luo et al., 2019), travel and tourism services (e.g., Nguyen et al., 2022; Sheehan et al., 2020), telecommunication services (e.g., Crolic et al., 2022) or transportation services (e.g., Fan et al., 2023). Most of these studies focus on customer (self) service interactions with text-based chatbots (Luo et al., 2019 is an exception focusing on voice-based chatbots making outbound sales calls). Table 2.1 provides an overview of extant literature and highlights empirical contexts, theoretical background, methods, and contributions.

Only a few studies focus on chatbots in B2B contexts. Kushwaha et al. (2021) draw on B2B enterprise social media data to investigate the factors that impact customer experience (CX) in AI-driven chatbot-based interactions. They identify a series of factors relating to, amongst others, flow, system design, privacy/safety, transparency, and trust. Lin et al. (2022) focus on employees who use chatbots to interact with customers in B2B companies and their evaluations of chatbot technology features. Through a survey, they identify the affordances of automatability and personalization influence perceptions of chatbot effectiveness, while null decision-making (i.e., the chatbot's inability to make decisions) leads to discomfort with using chatbots.

While few studies draw on field experiments (e.g., Crolic et al., 2022; Fan, et al., 2023; Luo et al., 2019) most studies employ experimental designs (e.g., Araujo, 2018; Kull et al., 2021; Mozafari et al., 2021) or

Table 2.1 Overview of chatbot-focused empirical studies in business and management literature

Authors	Chatbot	Context	Theoretical background	Method	Contributions
Araujo (2018)	Virtual agent in Facebook Messenger	Online retail (flowers purchase)	Anthropomorphism; Social presence; Service encounters	Experimental study (students and MTurk workers)	This research contributes to research on anthropomorphic design cues for conversational agents. Results show that using human-like cues (e.g., saying "hello" and "good-bye" and having a human name) had an influence on the emotional connection that consumers feel with the company. Human-like language or names were enough to increase the perception of the virtual agent as being human-like, in terms of both mindless (i.e., attribution of human characteristics to something that is not human) and mindful (i.e., conscious evaluations of being human- or machine-like) anthropomorphism. Finally, adopting an intelligent frame (i.e., a virtual agent powered by artificial intelligence) did not reduce perceptions of mindless anthropomorphism for machine-like agents (i.e., when human-like cues were absent).
Ashfaq et al. (2020)	Text-based chatbot for customer service	Various customer service experiences	Expectation-confirmation model (ECM); Information system success (ISS) model; Technology acceptance model (TAM); Need for interaction with a service employee (NFI-SE)	Cross-sectional survey (MTurk workers who had interacted with a text-based chatbot)	This study contributes to chatbot acceptance and continuance literature by combining elements from different models (i.e., technology acceptance, information system success, and expectation-confirmation) to examine drivers of user satisfaction. Results show that information quality and service quality positively influence users' satisfaction, while the need for interaction with an employee moderates the effects of perceived ease of use and perceived usefulness on user satisfaction.

Authors	Chatbot	Context	Theoretical background	Method	Contributions
Chen et al. (2022)	Artificial intelligence (AI) chatbot	Various industries (e.g., hospitality, financial services, healthcare, consulting, retailing, entertainment, and education)	Service quality	Mixed methods for scale development (interviews with managers and consumers and surveys with online platform users)	This research contributes to service quality and information systems success literature by defining the dimensions of AI chatbot service quality (AICSQ) and developing a measurement scale including seven second-order and 18 first-order constructs. The second-order dimensions of AICSQ include semantic understanding, close human-AI collaboration, human-like, continuous improvement, personalization, culture adaption, and efficiency.
Chung et al. (2020)	Chatbot for the luxury brand Burberry	Online retail (luxury fashion)	Service encounters; e-service quality	Cross-sectional survey (students)	This study contributes to e-service agents and luxury fashion literature by showing that consumer perceptions of a chatbot's marketing efforts in a luxury brand context are affected by the convenience and quality of communication offered by the chatbot.
Crolic et al. (2022)	Text-based chatbot driven by natural language processing (NLP)	Telecommunications and online retail (camera purchase)	Anthropomorphism; Expectancy violation; Customer anger	Five studies (one field study and four experimental studies)	This research contributes to anthropomorphism literature by demonstrating the negative effects of anthropomorphism in a customer service setting. Results show that anthropomorphic chatbots can harm firms (in terms of customer satisfaction with the service encounter, overall evaluation of the firm, and subsequent purchase intentions) when customers interact with them while in an angry emotional state. The explanation for this negative effect is that anthropomorphism may inflate pre-interaction expectations of chatbot efficiency and if those expectations are disconfirmed, an expectancy violation occurs. The implications are that when serving angry customers, it is best to downplay the anthropomorphic chatbots' capabilities.

(continued)

Table 2.1 (continued)

Authors	Chatbot	Context	Theoretical background	Method	Contributions
Fan et al. (2023)	Artificial intelligence (AI) customer service and cross-selling chatbot	Transportation services (e-bike sharing)	Ambidexterity; Dual process models; Customer experience	Mixed methods (survey of users of the mobile app, secondary data on conversations with the chatbot and purchase behavior)	This research contributes to literature on AI services and customer experience by examining how different configurations of ambidexterity impact smart experiences and customer patronage. A wider range of ambidexterity is considered (service sales, efficiency-flexibility, and existing-new product selling) and the results suggest that chatbot ambidexterity is not always beneficial for smart experiences. Specifically, a chatbot's ability to provide frontline services that are both efficient and flexible (i.e., efficiency-flexibility ambidexterity) benefits smart experiences and customer patronage. However, a chatbot's ability to provide both customer service and selling (i.e., service-sales ambidexterity) is detrimental to the creation of smart experiences.
Fotheringham and Wiles (2023)	Artificial intelligence (AI) customer service chatbots	Firms of various size, R&D intensity, advertising intensity (pharmaceutical and financial services)	Market-based asset theory	Event study, experimental study (MTurk Prime workers) and cross-sectional survey (MTurk Prime workers)	This research contributes to AI marketing literature by examining the effect of launching an AI customer service chatbot on firm value. The results provide evidence that investors respond positively to customer-centric AI implementations that may strengthen customer-firm relationships. Furthermore, differences between B2B vs. B2C service contexts emerge: B2B firms have more to gain from implementing AI chatbot customer service. In addition, examining the interaction between chatbot anthropomorphism and customer type (B2B vs. B2C) shows that investors respond less (more) favorably to anthropomorphized chatbots used in B2B (B2C) customer service roles.
Kull et al. (2021)	Chatbots operating in a mobile setting	Hospitality and financial services	Social categorization; Stereotype content model (warmth and competence); Brand-self distance	Experimental studies (MTurk workers)	This research contributes to AI marketing literature by examining how the tone (warm VS. competent) of the initial message sent by a brand's chatbot impacts consumer-brand connection and engagement. Results show that a chatbot's warm (vs. competent) initial message may bring consumers closer to the brand on whose behalf the chatbot communicates which in turn may increase consumers' motivations to learn more about the brand. However, this effect does not apply to brands that customers have a negative association with.

Authors	Chatbot	Context	Theoretical background	Method	Contributions
Kushwaha et al. (2021)	Artificial intelligence (AI) chatbots on social media	User generated content (UGC) from social media	Flow; Information systems success (ISS) model; Diffusion of innovation (DOI) theory;	Content analysis	This study contributes to customer experience and chatbot design literature by examining the influencing factors of AI-based chatbots for B2B firms. Results show that the customer experience of using an AI-based chatbot is influenced by a series of factors relating to flow, touchpoints, system design and privacy/safety, transparency, and customer trust.
Li and Wang (2023)	Text-based chatbot for customer service	Online retail (return policies)	Language expectancy theory; Parasocial interaction; Brand affiliation	Experimental studies (members of an online survey platform)	This research contributes to chatbot literature by examining how variations in language style (formal vs. informal) impact customer responses. The results show that using an informal language style makes chatbot messages seem more natural which eventually leads to positive service outcomes. That is because an informal language style fosters parasocial interaction which can improve chatbot continuance intentions and brand attitude. Brand affiliation serves a boundary condition: the effect of informal language style on continuance intentions through parasocial interaction was weaker for customers who did not have an affiliation with the brand.
Lin et al. (2022)	Chatbot for customer service in B2B	Various industries (manufacturing, banking/finance, and retail)	Technology affordances and disaffordances;	Cross-sectional survey (panel of marketing employees who use chatbots to interact with their customers in B2B companies)	This study contributes to customer service literature in B2B by examining how technology affordances and disaffordances impact employees' psychological perceptions of and their attitudes toward chatbots. Results show that the technology affordances of automatability and personalization can enhance employee perceptions of chatbot effectiveness, the former stronger for small firms and the latter stronger for medium-to-large firms. Results also show that the technology disaffordances of null decision-making can result in employee perceptions of discomfort with using chatbots, an effect that is stronger for small firms. Finally, results show that both chatbot employee perceptions of effectiveness and discomfort with using chatbots affect employees' attitudes toward the chatbots.

(continued)

Table 2.1 (continued)

Authors	Chatbot	Context	Theoretical background	Method	Contributions
Luo et al. (2019)	Voice-based chatbot making outbound sales calls	Financial services (loan renewal)	Not applicable	Field experiment and cross-sectional survey (customers who have interacted with the bot)	This study contributes to the literature on AI chatbots by examining how the disclosure of a chatbot's machine identity impacts real-life consumer purchases. The results suggest that chatbots that do not disclose they are machines are as effective as proficient workers and four times more effective than inexperienced workers in engendering customer purchases. However, if chatbots disclose their machine identity before the conversation, the purchase rates drop by close to 80%. The consumer behavioral mechanisms that may explain these results include perceiving the disclosed chatbot as less knowledgeable and less empathetic despite the chatbot's objective competence.
Mostafa and Kasamani (2022)	Chatbots in e-commerce	Online retail (various)	Diffusion of innovation (DOI) theory; Theory of acceptance and use of technology (UTAUT); Technology acceptance model (TAM); Trust	Cross sectional survey (individuals familiar with chatbots)	This study contributes to chatbot literature by examining the antecedents of initial chatbot trust through the combined lenses of the theory of acceptance and use of technology, diffusion of innovation and technology acceptance model. The results show that compatibility, perceived ease of use and social influence drive customers to form an initial trust toward chatbots. In turn, initial trust in chatbots enhances the intention to use the chatbots and encourages customer engagement.
Mozafari et al. (2021)	Text-based chatbot for customer service	Energy services	Attribution theory; Trust; Service criticality; Service outcomes	Experimental studies (members of an online panel)	This research contributes to chatbot-based service delivery literature by examining how consumers react to chatbot disclosure in different types of frontline service settings. The results show that when services are critical for the customer, even if the chatbot can solve the customer's issue, disclosure will negatively impact customer trust. When services are less critical, chatbot disclosure does not impact trust. Importantly, when the customer's issue cannot be resolved, the negative failure effect may be mitigated by chatbot disclosure which acts as an apology. Furthermore, three trust dimensions are examined with the results showing that lower perceptions of the conversational partner's competence and benevolence lead to a loss of trust.

Authors	Chatbot	Context	Theoretical background	Method	Contributions
Nguyen et al. (2022)	Text-based chatbot driven by natural language processing (NLP) (Hello Hipmunk)	Hospitality services (travel planning)	Self-determination theory	Experimental study (students)	This study contributes to information systems research by examining how AI chatbot capabilities implemented in a user interface impact user outcomes. The results show that compared with users interacting with a menu-based interface, users interacting with chatbots with a natural language processing (NLP) interface showed lower levels of perceived autonomy and higher cognitive load, in turn resulting in lower user satisfaction. Furthermore, the effect of perceived autonomy on perceived competence was found to be stronger in the chatbot interface compared to the menu-based interface.
Pizzi et al. (2021)	Artificial intelligence (AI) customer service chatbots	Telecommunications (mobile plan purchase) and transportation (rent a car) services	Reactance theory; Digital service assistance; Anthropomorphism	Experimental studies (market research company panel)	This research contributes to AI acceptance and service-dominant logic literature by examining how consumers react to distinct characteristics of digital assistants. These results show that initiation interacts with anthropomorphism so that if a customer activates a human-like digital assistant reactance is minimized, whereas when a non-human-like assistant activates automatically, reactance is maximized. Reactance in turn triggers a series of consumer evaluations in the decision-making progress eventually leading to satisfaction.
Roy and Naidoo (2021)	Text-based chatbot for customer service	Hospitality services (hotel room booking) and online retail (smartphone and business suit purchases)	Anthropomorphism; Social judgment (warmth and competence); Time orientation	Experimental studies (students)	This research contributes to the literature on anthropomorphic design cues by examining design discourse and chatbot conversational styles that may enhance the humanness of chatbots. Results show that when the conversation styles of chat agents were presented as warm (vs. competent), consumers evaluated chatbot interactions as they would personal interactions. However, consumers' temporal orientation is a boundary condition: while present-oriented consumers are more favorable to warm chatbots, future-oriented consumers are more favorable to competent chatbots. Results also suggest a carry-over effect of warmth or competence traits from the chatbot to the brand.

(continued)

Table 2.1 (continued)

Authors	Chatbot	Context	Theoretical background	Method	Contributions
Sands et al. (2021)	Text-based chatbot for customer service	Online retail (laptop purchase)	Social impact theory; Service interactions; Service scripts	Experimental study (MTurk workers)	This study contributes to service scripts literature by examining the role of physical distance in frontline service employee (FSE-) VS. chatbot-customer interactions. Results indicate that when an educational script is employed (e.g., encouraging learning, product information, or information seeking) satisfaction and purchase intentions are higher in customer interactions with FSEs (compared to chatbots). This is explained through the bonds developed through close proximity to a human service agent due to emotion and rapport. However, when an entertaining script is employed (e.g., encouraging playfulness and fun), there are no differences between an FSE and a chatbot regarding outcomes.
Sheehan et al. (2020)	Text-based chatbot for customer service (FlowXO)	Hospitality (hotel room booking) and transportation (travel pass purchase) services	Anthropomorphism; Self-service technologies	Experimental studies (MTurk workers)	This research contributes to chatbot adoption literature by examining the role of chatbot (mis)communication in driving adoption intent. The results suggest that a chatbot that is humanlike enough to identify potential miscommunication performs as well as a completely error-free chatbot and is better than a chatbot that has no contextual awareness of errors. These results are explained by elicited agent knowledge, an antecedent of anthropomorphism. Furthermore, anthropomorphism is more positively related to adoption when the consumer's need for human interaction is high.
This study	Text-based chatbot for B2B customer service	Industrial equipment (Heat, ventilation, and air conditioning [HVAC] applications)	People – Process – Technology framework	Semi-structured interviews (expert employees and business customers)	This research contributes to B2B customer service literature by examining the employee perspective when a chatbot is introduced as a new customer support channel. The results show that organizational actors are seen as knowledge experts and content curators, while the non-human actor (i.e., the chatbot) is perceived as a troubleshooting tool that must be competent rather than warm. Expert employees realize the relevance of human-chatbot collaboration for both AI advancement and improved organizational efficiency, however, they worry about how the reliance on a chatbot may erode their sense of worth and identity as knowledge gatekeepers.

cross-sectional surveys (e.g., Ashfaq et al., 2020; Mostafa & Kasamani, 2022) to collect data. Some studies focus solely on chatbot interactions: e.g., Crolic et al. (2022) show that when customers enter a chatbot interaction in an angry emotional state, chatbot anthropomorphism (i.e., a human-looking avatar with a name and personal information) has a negative effect on the customers' satisfaction with the service encounter. Other studies focus on comparing chatbot interactions with human interactions: e.g., Sands et al. (2021) find that chatbots should engage with customers in an entertaining manner, while engaging in an educational manner should be left to human customer service agents. A few studies (e.g., Luo et al., 2019; Mozafari et al., 2021) examine chatbot disclosure, or the extent to which companies should specify that the chat customer service agent is not human. For example, Luo et al. (2019) find that, while chatbots perform better than inexperienced workers in a sales context, chatbot disclosure may reduce purchase rates by almost 80%.

One of the main topics of chatbot interaction studied empirically is the extent to which chatbots or specific chatbot features are perceived to have humanlike characteristics (i.e., *anthropomorphism*; Araujo, 2018; Crolic et al., 2022; Pizzi et al., 2021; Roy & Naidoo, 2021; Sheehan et al., 2020). Characteristics that are typically examined include the extent to which the chatbot (feature) is perceived as *competent* and/or *warm* (e.g., Kull et al., 2021; Nguyen et al., 2022), is worthy of *trust* (e.g., Mostafa & Kasamani, 2022; Mozafari et al., 2021) or has *social presence* (e.g., Adam et al., 2021; Araujo, 2018). Kull et al. (2021) for instance study how chatbots initiate conversations on a mobile travel application and respectively a bank's website. They show that when a chatbot employs a warm (as opposed to a competent) initial message, consumer–brand connections and ultimately engagement may be fostered. Mozafari et al. (2021), find that for services that are subjectively determined as very important by the recipient (i.e., highly critical services), chatbot disclosure will negatively impact customer trust even though the chatbot is able to solve the customer's issue. However, when the chatbot fails to deliver the expected service, chatbot disclosure can enhance overall trust. Finally, Adam et al. (2021) show that in a financial service setting, social presence mediates the impact on anthropomorphic design cues (e.g., identity, small talk, and empathy) on user compliance.

Another important topic studied empirically is chatbot acceptance or adoption, with studies drawing on one or multiple dimensions of innovation diffusion theory (DOI; Rogers, 2005), the technology acceptance model (TAM; Davis, 1989), or the unified theory of acceptance and use of technology (UTAUT; Venkatesh et al., 2012) (e.g., Ashfaq et al., 2020; Kushwaha et al., 2021; Mostafa & Kasamani, 2022). For example, Mostafa and Kasamani (2022) study chatbot e-commerce interactions in a Middle Eastern country and show that compatibility (from DOI), perceived ease of use (from TAM), and social influence (from UTAUT) drive customers to form an initial trust toward chatbots which in turn may drive usage intentions and engagement.

Other topics in extant literature include scale development (e.g., Chen et al., 2021 developed an AI chatbot service quality measurement), chatbot language use (e.g., Li & Wang, 2023 show that an informal chatbot language style in an e-commerce setting nurtures the feeling of parasocial interaction, which may lead to higher continued chatbot usage intentions) or chatbot ambidexterity (e.g., Fan et al., 2023 examined the impact of different configurations of chatbot ambidexterity, e.g., pursuing service and sales at the same time, on customer smart experiences, with mixed results).

Method

This study leverages a qualitative approach to explore the changes brought by AI-powered chatbots in a B2B context. In this study, through semi-structured interviews, we employ the PPT framework (Leavitt, 1964; Schneier, 2009) to investigate (1) the changing roles of people, (2) the effects AI-powered chatbots have on the customer-service process and (3) the (dis)empowering role of technology. Qualitative methods were deemed appropriate for gathering informants' data-rich stories aimed at a better understanding of this rather novel phenomenon (Patton, 2014).

Context

The study zooms in on HVAC, a pseudonym for a European developer and manufacturer of equipment for heat, ventilation, and air conditioning industrial applications. The company has been operating for close to a century and currently employs over 40,000 people and does business in more than one hundred countries. HVAC primarily serves original equipment manufacturers (OEMs), distributors and system integrators, but also installers, and end-users.

Table 2.2 Overview of informants

Code	Organizational function	Selection criteria	Gender
E1	Sales Engineer	HVAC employee	Male
E2	Service Technician	HVAC employee	Male
E3	Continuous Improvement Manager	HVAC employee	Female
E4	Customer Service Supervisor	HVAC employee	Male
E5	Internal Technical Support	HVAC employee	Male
C1	Projects Engineer	Business customer	Male
C2	Technical Manager	Business customer	Male
C3	Internal Sales and Technical Support	Business customer	Male
C4	Sales Support Engineer	Business customer	Male

HVAC was a suitable study object for three main reasons. First, HVAC has embarked on a journey to become more customer-centric in its operations. Second, HVAC aims to enhance customer and employee satisfaction by developing and providing advanced digital solutions. Third, HVAC utilizes an AI-powered chatbot aimed at improving customer support on the group's corporate website. The chatbot troubleshoots alarms or fault codes queried by HVAC clients and provides them with the relevant possible causes and remedy steps. When the chatbot is unable to help, it directs its users to their closest HVAC sales and service touchpoint.

Sample

The sampling included the identification of two groups of purposefully selected people: (1) HVAC customer support agents and (2) HVAC business customers experienced in using the chatbot. We employed snowball sampling and asked informants to identify other potential participants fulfilling the criteria to be part of our study (Patton, 2014). The final sample includes nine informants, five HVAC employees, and four HVAC customers (for more details, please see Table 2.2).

Interview Guide

The interview guide was developed to serve as a topic checklist while allowing for flexibility and probing for new directions. One pilot interview was conducted to gather feedback on (a) question clarity, (b) question sequence, and (c) time management. The final guide contained four main sections. The first section collected general job-related information (e.g., "What falls under your current job role?") and aimed at gathering a base understanding of the informant's daily activities, needs, and digital tools used. This section aimed at gaining knowledge about the current support process. In the second section, informants were encouraged to share their experience with the chatbot (e.g., their usage, perceptions, and satisfaction). In the third section, interviewees reflected on the human-chatbot interplay (e.g., "When could chatbots be preferred to humans and vice versa?", "How can humans and chatbots together improve customer experience?"). Finally, the fourth section focused on future expectations (e.g., the role of chatbots in organization transformation, opportunities, and challenges related to evolving job roles).

Data Analysis

The interviews were collected via Microsoft Teams video calls and lasted an average of 35 minutes. With permission from the informants, all the interviews were recorded and later transcribed verbatim. The data were analyzed using thematic analysis following a process of identifying, analyzing, and reporting repeated patterns (Braun & Clarke, 2006). The thematic analysis was appropriate and well-fitted to use since we were seeking to understand informants' experiences, thoughts, and behaviors across the data set (Braun & Clarke, 2012). Two authors read and coded the verbatim transcripts independently, following the six steps of thematic analysis (Clarke & Braun, 2017; Kiger & Varpio, 2020), including (i) familiarization with the data, (ii) generating initial codes, (iii) searching for themes, (iv) reviewing themes, (v) defining and naming themes, and (vi) producing the report/manuscript. Throughout the process, the authors had several joint analysis sessions in which they aggregated and further fine-tuned the codes into themes.

FINDINGS

Following the coding process, two themes emerged under each of the elements in the PPT framework. Figure 2.1 depicts the actors in the B2B context (i.e., organizational employees, business customers, end-customers, and the non-human actor–chatbot), as well as the emerging themes under the people, process, and technology pillars. As suggested in

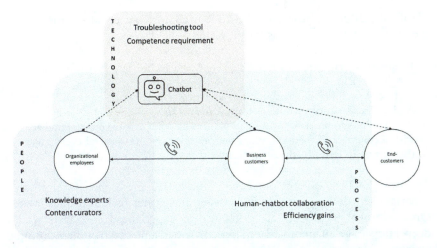

Fig. 2.1 Qualitative analysis themes in the PPT framework

the figure, the chatbot can be utilized by any of the B2B actors, either as a replacement for a phone call or an augmented knowledge base during a phone call with a customer. In this section we elaborate on the emerging themes, starting with the *people* element comprising two roles knowledge experts and content curators; the *process* element including human-chatbot collaboration and efficiency gains; and the *technology* element including troubleshooting tool and competence requirement themes.

People

Under the People component, our analysis uncovers elements affecting people's readiness to collaborate with a chatbot, as well as employees' new organizational roles.

Knowledge Experts

With this theme, we capture the commonly shared views by the organizational employees that they are the knowledge experts, that they have the information "in their heads" and there is no need to rely on a chatbot to help their customers with technical issues. Being both knowledge experts and knowledge keepers is part of their organizational role identity

(Ashforth, 2000; Ashforth et al., 2008). Hence, the collaboration with the chatbot is almost seen as losing professional face.

> I support my customer with my **expertise as a technician**, that's my main task here. (E1)
>
> I have used it [the chatbot], but as I told you, it is not my daily tool. And **I already know what is covered in it.** (E5)
>
> I would recommend it [the chatbot] to a customer that is not so familiar with technical stuff, you know maybe some farmers... in general every guy that is **not in daily business in technical stuff**. (E2)

From the business customer side, there is a preference for human experts when dealing with difficult issues and rather technical questions. Organizational employees are perceived as experienced specialists with deep knowledge of potential equipment issues and the troubleshooting process. This finding is in line with previous research (e.g., Larkin et al., 2022) suggesting that people prefer receiving medical and financial risk management advice from their fellow humans rather than AI.

> I would say only a little bit [would he use the chatbot] because I've got these engineers who **have the answers up in their heads**. (C2)
>
> I need that little **extra 10% that the real experts have**. So, that's where I need to talk to the experts at the organization. (C2)
>
> If we're physically on site and there's an issue, then I'd **definitely prefer having a person** there rather than just a chatbot [...] because we have come across a problem or a situation that we're not able to solve and it'd have to be a **fairly technically difficult situation**. So, it's unlikely that a chatbot would be able to provide the solution, although, we can be surprised. (C3)

Due to their strong identification with the role of knowledge experts, organizational employees express low levels of readiness to collaborate with the chatbot. They further emphasize that the chatbot might be for less technical, less experienced, and less skilled staff members or end-customers. There is a prevailing stance among both groups of informants that the chatbot is "not for me but for someone else."

> **Mostly the end customers** that are not so technical, **not so familiar with the technical stuff.** This could be a place where the chatbot could assist. (E2)

> [...] **for service guys** it [the chatbot] would be a very helpful tool. (E1)
>
> At the moment it would be more **for a basic service engineer**. Or the motor guy who doesn't deal with the organization on an everyday basis. They're the ones who I think would benefit the most. (C2)
>
> I think for **someone who doesn't have quite a lot of support experience**, it is a reasonably good solution. [...] I think from that point of view, it is pretty good for customers to use it. (C3)

Content Curators

The employees are experiencing certain changes to their organizational roles due to the introduction of the chatbot. They are observing a potential transformation toward the role of content curator for the chatbot which requires human-chatbot collaboration (discussed more under the process theme). New tasks that employees are taking over include, for example, training the algorithm by adding technical depth to the chatbot content and continuous updates to and monitoring of the chatbot's database.

> I think we need to **update the bot with the right information all the time.** We also need resources, [...] someone needs to take care that **the quality of the bot is insured** because otherwise the customers are getting frustrated so, that needs to be done from our side. (E3)
>
> **We can help with how you have to ask the questions.** So, I think it's difficult to ask the chatbot the right questions. Maybe it needs a technician to type in or to store the right questions inside the chatbot because if you don't type the right questions to get in, you don't get the correct answers. (E1)
>
> If a customer calls me and he asks for some information **I will write those questions down and send them to a chatbot improvement team**, so they can add that information in the chatbot. So, if there are similar questions coming in the future the chatbot can help them. (E2)

This new role of content curators moves the organizational employees from the frontline to the back office of customer support. It also opens the question of the future role of human actors in AI-powered customer service (e.g., Will organizational employees become AI supervisors rather than the first line of customer support?).

Process

It is crucial that people understand how they fit within the new organizational process and how they can contribute to achieving organizational goals (Sarker & Sarker, 2009). The process is where people and technology come together. Under the process component, the two emerging themes are human-chatbot collaboration and efficiency gains.

Human-chatbot Collaboration

As organizational employees start sharing the customer service frontline with AI-powered agents, human-chatbot collaboration becomes crucial. The emergence of the new organizational role of chatbot content curator calls for process integration and cross-departmental efforts to improve the chatbot quality for enhanced customer experience. As emphasized by E2, there is a need for "*a chatbot improvement team*" in order to keep the content up-to-date and aligned with the organizational mission. Such a team should also cross departmental boundaries, as pointed out in the following quote.

> I'm in sales. The guys in service are having different questions than I have. Maybe we have to **join together and see how to make the chatbot better.** (E1)

Business customers also express the need for human-chatbot collaboration for the algorithm to improve and ultimately be adapted by various user groups. This could be achieved through activities such as (i) teaching the chatbot users how to phrase the questions (i.e., prompts), and (ii) relying on a chatbot's help rather than calling customer service.

> [...] if this was a situation where I was talking to a [HVAC] technician over the phone, and they had access to chatbot themselves. [...] they might be able to phrase the questions to the chatbot better than I can. They have previous experience finding the information in the chatbot, so **they know exactly how to phrase the question to a chatbot.** (C3)
>
> Situations where I'm on the phone with a customer, and unable to answer their question and need to find a solution very quickly. It's a critical situation for the customer. If I was then unable to get onto the help desk or any of the customer support team locally, then **the chatbot would be very useful in finding the information.** Even just **sparing the customer**

support team locally from contacting them—not using up their time, which they could be using to support customers who were not able to find the solution in the chatbot. So yeah, another level for finding the information that you're looking for. **I'm trying to alleviate some of the pressure on the local support team** (C3)

How can **both [the chatbot and employees] complement each other?** Maybe use the same knowledge base so that all the information is coming from one tool. Instead of getting different answers from different sources. (C1)

This collaborative approach assumes co-working with AI-powered agents, rather than being fully replaced by AI (Sowa et al., 2021). Through interactions with the chatbot and utilizing its support, organizational actors enhance the value of AI-powered support.

Efficiency Gains

There is a shared belief among the informants that the organizational processes would be streamlined if the chatbot would be utilized for troubleshooting in less complicated cases. This would improve efficiency both on the employee and business customer side. As emphasized by the employee group, they would have more time to focus on difficult issues and more complicated questions, be more available to help, and overall be more efficient in their job.

So, I guess if chatbot would improve a little bit further, it could be a nice tool to make it **more efficient to work with the customer.** (E1)

I would say it will reduce the number of phone calls. If the customer is using the chatbot for some easy questions that they called us in the past, the chatbot can easily answer. I would say that the easy questions, so uh the chatbot could be **useful to help my daily business.** (E2)

In my job, it [the chatbot] would be useful because if our end-customer could get good answers from the chatbot, it helps me, and **I can take more important and more complicated cases.** (E5)

The customer group perceives efficiency stemming from both their knowledge augmentation and end-customers being able to help themselves without calling for support.

It is just efficient. That is key for efficiency... just knowledge. Like, if you're just curious about how something works instead of trying to figure out where it is in the manual you can throw it up at the chatbot and get some answers quickly. (C1)

It's going to be **fewer calls for us**, I noticed that means that I can focus on other things instead of, you know, having troubleshooting phone calls. (C4)

It [the role of chatbot] could be twofold. It could mean that I have quicker access to a greater knowledge base than what I have available at the moment. So, it could mean that **I can support my customers a lot quicker and more effectively with that greater knowledge base.** From a customer's point of view, it could mean that it could **save them a phone** call having to contact us to find the information. it could mean that they, rather than coming to us for information could quickly look it up in the chatbot. (C3)

By helping the chatbot improve, through continuous updates, resource integration, and monitoring of the quality of provided answers, organizational actors support the realization of efficiency gains in their own customer support processes. These efficiencies are expected from reduced times spent on calls with customers, as well as less frequent calls from customers dealing with simple technical issues.

Technology

Finally, we focus on the technology element, which is the initiator of organizational transformation. While the extant chatbot literature discusses AI-powered technologies as more than just a tool, even suggesting the role of a colleague (Huang & Rust, 2022; Luo et al., 2019), our analysis reveals that the value of the technology in the B2B context comes mainly from its guiding and troubleshooting roles. The two emerging themes under the technology component are Troubleshooting tool and Competence requirement.

Troubleshooting Tool

The main purpose of the studied chatbot is to troubleshoot alarms or fault codes of a product (e.g., the device that controls the speed of an air conditioning motor), and therefore to provide its users with the possible causes

and remedy steps. Our informants propose several elements that constitute the "backbone" of their user experience with the chatbot, including
speed (e.g., immediate answers), availability (e.g., available 24/7), and
efficiency (e.g., it does its job). From the employee group, the helpfulness
of the tool is highlighted through its guiding capabilities which warrant
its role as the first touchpoint in the customer troubleshooting journey.

> I think it's really a **helpful tool,** especially when you have an error with
> a number. Let's say, when the product tells you I have whatever failure
> number and then you type it in and then you get a little bit more detailed
> description of what is the failure about so you can help yourself a little bit
> easier instead of calling us all the time. (E3)
>
> Let's say um if you have simple questions. For instance, where to find
> what's on our web pages like documents, catalogs, drawings, [...] and then
> the bot could easily **guide.** (E3)
>
> I'd tell them [the customers] that they can't always reach me, that I
> am not always free. If you want **answers at once**, please use the chatbot.
> (E5)
>
> It's just like normally the customer has some office hours where they
> just can reach some support and the chatbot could **help them 24/7**, so
> this could be a big advantage and improve the customer loyalty. (E2)

In addition to the elements proposed by the employee group, the business customers point out the chatbot's role in knowledge augmentation.

> Yeah, mainly its fault finding or like **programming query that I don't
> quite know how to solve.** I'll go and ask it [the chatbot] if there's another
> way. [...] because manuals are thick, and they can take you ages just to find
> your way through it and find what you're looking for. While in the chatbot
> you can just put a couple of keywords in, and you'll find it straight away.
> (C1)
>
> If I can't get hold of anyone at the organization or I'm in the office
> and I can't get answers, everyone's busy here and I haven't got anyone
> I can ask. Having that chatbot there is **just another lifeline.** It's another
> avenue to explore. (C1)
>
> It's **the speed** at which you can get your answers from it, which seems
> to be quicker than having to rifle through a lot of different manuals and
> catalogs and brochures on and on... grabbing the wrong manual to get the
> dimensions, for example. So, when you multiply that by the 25 product
> ranges that the organization has, it gets quite frustrating. It would make
> my life a little **quicker and easier.** (C2)

I would love to have a tool like that. I can just type something and **get the information straight away**. So, it would be quicker if I had a tool like that. It would **guide me specifically**… what to look at, what to tell the customer to check, what to expect, what to measure, what to read, what parameter to look for, you know, those sort of things… **guide me.** And actually, I could give the customer more ideas […] So, it's either waiting or having something that guides me and that makes a huge difference. (C4)

Even though not all the informants acknowledge the value of a troubleshooting chatbot in its current state, they envision a future in which AI-powered agents will have a more prominent role and enhanced capabilities.

Competence Requirement

While B2C literature suggests that chatbot's warmth (e.g., characteristics such as sociable, humorous, and warm; Fiske et al., 2007) plays an important role in chatbot's evaluations, our findings suggest the primacy of the competence component (e.g., skillful, intelligent, and practical; Fiske et al., 2007). For example, business customers favor chatbot's direct answers with no space left for chitchat. Furthermore, they appreciate the consistency in the support quality, which is independent of individual employees' skillfulness.

I think it's great, so far, the way it answers is it just comes up with your answer. I don't feel that I need much more interaction with it apart from I need this answer and it says, hey, here's **a black and white answer** … is that what you're looking for? Brilliant. Thanks very much. (C1)

I think it's more than the knowledge that the chatbot is 24/7 and he's kind of independent of whom you talk to. So, you're getting, you should be getting **a best-in-class response independent of when it is or whom you're talking to**. You know, it's, it's, there are a couple of guys down at [HVAC] and if you get them, you're going to get a brilliant answer. But if they're not there, then maybe the answer is going to be a little bit less than brilliant sort of thing. So yeah, **consistency,** I guess. (C2)

Quick access to **support information or even critical information.** (C3)

On the other hand, warmth on top of competence is expected from the organizational employees, as they indicate themselves:

I just try **to calm them down by talking to them** and explaining what the next steps are and what our process looks like. (E1)

I give them an overview on how the process looks like and to **avoid any confusion.** (E2)

CONCLUSION

The present research explored how expert employees and business customers in a B2B company react to the introduction of an AI-powered chatbot. We use the PPT framework to analyze and present qualitative findings from semi-structured interviews with these two groups of informants. Table 2.3 includes the emerging themes within the PPT framework across the two informant groups. Our findings show that the people see themselves as knowledge experts and content curators, while the technology is seen as little more than a troubleshooting tool that must be competent, rather than warm. Using the chatbot can lead to efficiency improvements that may spill-over to the end customer, but collaboration between the human employees and the chatbot is still a work-in-progress process.

These findings reflect the specifics of the B2B context that warrant additional research on chatbots beyond the evaluation of technology features (Rapp et al., 2021). Most of the empirical work on humans interacting with chatbots has focused on the consumer or end-user perspective and on comparing chatbot agents with human agents. Very few studies (e.g., Lin et al., 2022) have offered an employee perspective. Our research extends this work in a setting where the employees are technical experts and naturally wary of the chatbot's competence. Moreover, the business customers are technical experts in their own rights and the type of requests they have of customer service are somewhat more complex than the product information searches in B2C studies.

Whether they are aware of it or not, the expert employees find themselves faced with a dilemma. On the one hand, the chatbot can lead to improved efficiency. It may help business customers navigate through simpler issues while allowing expert customer service employees to focus on more serious, complicated, or urgent matters. To facilitate this process, the expert employees can help the business customers formulate better

Table 2.3 Overview of findings

Organizational Roles	PPT framework					
	People		Process		Technology	
	Knowledge experts	*Content curators*	*Human-chatbot collaboration*	*Efficiency gains*	*Troubleshooting tool*	*Competence requirement*
Organizational employees	- Addressing customer queries via phone - Supporting business customers with their technical expertise - Knowledge gatekeepers - Providing a personalized and emphatic approach - Low readiness for collaborating with a chatbot	- New organizational role - Training the algorithm - Feeding the chatbot with the data - Continuous updates and monitoring of the chatbot"s database - Moving from the frontline to the back office of customer support	- A need for process integration and cross-departmental efforts to improve the chatbot's quality - Helping AI-powered chatbots improve, leads to enhanced organizational efficiency	- Allowing the chatbot to take over less complicated troubleshooting queries, enables human employees more time for critical and complicated issues - Improves employee's efficiency in customer support efforts	- The chatbot is perceived as a tool rather than a colleague - Main benefits derive from its guiding capability, availability, speed, and competence	- Primacy of competence over warmth (emotional sensitivity is reserved for human customer service) - Standardization of customer service (homogeneity in replies)

Organizational Roles	PPT framework					Competence requirement
	People		Process		Technology	
	Knowledge experts	Content curators	Human-chatbot collaboration	Efficiency gains	Troubleshooting tool	
Business customers	- Contacting customer service (i.e.. knowledge experts) when faced with difficult technical issues - Preference for human (knowledge experts) over AI-powered support - Trust in human expertise (years of troubleshooting experience, existing rapport, specialized knowledge)	- Providing feedback to the customer service representatives	- Teaching the end customers how to ask a chatbot for help (i.e.. writing effective prompts) - Relying on the chatbot's help rather than calling customer support (i.e., knowledge experts)	- End customers relying on self-service through AI-powered chatbots reduces the amounts of calls to handle - Knowledge augmentation by AI reduces the time spent with each customer request	- Knowledge augmentation - The chatbot can help with addressing issues where they lack technical knowledge and expertise - The chatbot can guide them in difficult situations and acts as another lifeline (e.g. when human customer service cannot be reached)	- Quick reaction in critical - Responses independent of the customer support channel (homogeneity in replies)

prompts or can provide feedback to the chatbot trainers to ensure the appropriate answers are available. In doing so however, they help the chatbot become a knowledge expert and, given the AI technology advancements, it is only a matter of time before the chatbot evolves from a troubleshooting tool into a competent curator of knowledge. In essence, by collaborating with the chatbot they may in the short-run be eroding their job-related sense of worth (e.g., by actively using the chatbot they signal they are less competent and skilled because that is whom the chatbot is meant for), while in the long-run they may be eroding their role identity as knowledge gatekeepers.

References

Adam, M., Wessel, M., & Benlian, A. (2021). AI-based chatbots in customer service and their effects on user compliance. *Electronic Markets, 31*(2), 427–445.

Araujo, T. (2018). Living up to the chatbot hype: The influence of anthropomorphic design cues and communicative agency framing on conversational agent and company perceptions. *Computers in Human Behavior, 85*, 183–189.

Ashfaq, M., Yun, J., Yu, S., & Loureiro, S. M. C. (2020). I, Chatbot: Modeling the determinants of users' satisfaction and continuance intention of AI-powered service agents. *Telematics and Informatics, 54*, 101473.

Ashforth, B. (2000). *Role transitions in organizational life: An identity-based perspective*. Routledge.

Ashforth, B. E., Harrison, S. H., & Corley, K. G. (2008). Identification in organizations: An examination of four fundamental questions. *Journal of Management, 34*(3), 325–374.

Braun, V., & Clarke, V. (2006). Using thematic analysis in psychology. *Qualitative Research in Psychology, 3*(2), 77–101.

Braun, V., & Clarke V. (2012). Thematic analysis. In H. Cooper (Ed.), *APA handbook of research methods in psychology*. Vol. 2, research designs. American Psychological Association.

Chen, I. J., & Popovich, K. (2003). Understanding customer relationship management (CRM): People, process and technology. *Business Process Management Journal, 9*(5), 672–688.

Chen, Z., Chan, I. C. C., Mehraliyev, F., Law, R., & Choi, Y. (2021). Typology of people–process–technology framework in refining smart tourism from the perspective of tourism academic experts. *Tourism Recreation Research*, 1–13.

Chen, Q., Gong, Y., Lu, Y., & Tang, J. (2022). Classifying and measuring the service quality of AI chatbot in frontline service. *Journal of Business Research, 145*, 552–568.

Chung, M., Ko, E., Joung, H., & Kim, S. J. (2020). Chatbot e-service and customer satisfaction regarding luxury brands. *Journal of Business Research, 117*, 587–595.

Clarke, V., & Braun, V. (2017). Commentary: Thematic analysis. *Journal of Positive Psychology, 12*(3), 297–298.

Crolic, C., Thomaz, F., Hadi, R., & Stephen, A. T. (2022). Blame the bot: Anthropomorphism and anger in customer—chatbot interactions. *Journal of Marketing, 86*(1), 132–148.

Davis, F. D. (1989). Perceived usefulness, perceived ease of use, and user acceptance of information technology. *MIS Quarterly, 13*(3), 319–340.

Fan, H., Gao, W., & Han, B. (2023). Are AI chatbots a cure-all? The relative effectiveness of chatbot ambidexterity in crafting hedonic and cognitive smart experiences. *Journal of Business Research, 156*, 113526.

Fiske, S. T., Cuddy, A. J., & Glick, P. (2007). Universal dimensions of social cognition: Warmth and competence. *Trends in Cognitive Sciences, 11*(2), 77–83.

Fotheringham, D., & Wiles, M. A. (2023). The effect of implementing chatbot customer service on stock returns: An event study analysis. *Journal of the Academy of Marketing Science, 51*(4), 802–822.

Gartner (n.d.). *Gartner Hype Cycle. Interpreting technology hype.* https://www.gartner.com/en/research/methodologies/gartner-hype-cycle, Accessed 19 March 2023.

Goasduff, L. (2020). *2 Megatrends Dominate the Gartner Hype Cycle for Artificial Intelligence*, https://www.gartner.com.au/en/articles/2-megatrends-dominate-the-gartner-hype-cycle-for-artificial-intelligence-2020, Accessed 19th March 2023.

Huang, M. H., & Rust, R. T. (2022). A framework for collaborative artificial intelligence in marketing. *Journal of Retailing, 98*(2), 209–223.

Kiger, M. E., & Varpio, L. (2020). Thematic analysis of qualitative data: AMEE Guide No. 131. *Medical Teacher, 42*(8), 846–854.

Kull, A. J., Romero, M., & Monahan, L. (2021). How may I help you? Driving brand engagement through the warmth of an initial chatbot message. *Journal of Business Research, 135*, 840–850.

Kushwaha, A. K., Kumar, P., & Kar, A. K. (2021). What impacts customer experience for B2B enterprises on using AI-enabled chatbots? Insights from Big data analytics. *Industrial Marketing Management, 98*, 207–221.

Larkin, C., Drummond Otten, C., & Árvai, J. (2022). Paging Dr. JARVIS! Will people accept advice from artificial intelligence for consequential risk management decisions?. *Journal of Risk Research, 25*(4), 407–422.

Latham, K. (2023). *Have we fallen out of love with voice assistants?* https://www.bbc.com/news/business-64371426, Accessed 19th March 2023.

Leavitt, H. J. (1964). Applied organization change in industry: Structural, technical and human approaches. In W. W. Cooper & H. J. L. M. W. Shelly (Eds.), *New perspectives in organization research journal* (pp. 55–71). John Wiley & Sons.

Li, M., & Wang, R. (2023). Chatbots in e-commerce: The effect of chatbot language style on customers' continuance usage intention and attitude toward brand. *Journal of Retailing and Consumer Services, 71*, 103209.

Lin, X., Shao, B., & Wang, X. (2022). Employees' perceptions of chatbots in B2B marketing: Affordances vs. disaffordances. *Industrial Marketing Management, 101*, 45–56.

Luo, X., Tong, S., Fang, Z., & Qu, Z. (2019). Frontiers: Machines vs. humans: The impact of artificial intelligence chatbot disclosure on customer purchases. *Marketing Science, 38*(6), 937–947.

Maruping, L. M., Venkatesh, V., Thong, J. Y., & Zhang, X. (2019). A risk mitigation framework for information technology projects: A cultural contingency perspective. *Journal of Management Information Systems, 36*(1), 120–157.

Microsoft. (2023). *Microsoft and OpenAI extend partnership*. https://blogs.microsoft.com/blog/2023/01/23/microsoftandopenaiextendpartnership/, Accessed 19th March 2023.

Mostafa, R. B., & Kasamani, T. (2022). Antecedents and consequences of chatbot initial trust. *European Journal of Marketing, 56*(6), 1748–1771.

Mozafari, N., Weiger, W. H., & Hammerschmidt, M. (2021). Trust me, I'm a bot–repercussions of chatbot disclosure in different service frontline settings. *Journal of Service Management, 33*(2), 221–245.

Nguyen, Q. N., Sidorova, A., & Torres, R. (2022). User interactions with chatbot interfaces vs. Menu-based interfaces: An empirical study. *Computers in Human Behavior, 128*, 107093.

Patton, M. Q. (2014). *Qualitative research & evaluation methods: Integrating theory and practice*. Sage publications.

Pizzi, G., Scarpi, D., & Pantano, E. (2021). Artificial intelligence and the new forms of interaction: Who has the control when interacting with a chatbot? *Journal of Business Research, 129*, 878–890.

Rapp, A., Curti, L., & Boldi, A. (2021). The human side of human-chatbot interaction: A systematic literature review of ten years of research on text-based chatbots. *International Journal of Human-Computer Studies, 151*, 102630.

Research and Markets. (2023). *Chatbot market, by product type, by application, by function, by end-use, and by region forecast to 2030*. https://tinyurl.com/2k3st263, Accessed 19th March 2023.

Rogers, E. M. (2005). *Diffusion of innovations. 4th Edition*. Simon and Schuster.

Roy, R., & Naidoo, V. (2021). Enhancing chatbot effectiveness: The role of anthropomorphic conversational styles and time orientation. *Journal of Business Research, 126*, 23–34.

Sands, S., Ferraro, C., Campbell, C., & Tsao, H. Y. (2021). Managing the human–chatbot divide: How service scripts influence service experience. *Journal of Service Management, 32*(2), 246–264.

Sarker, S., & Sarker, S. (2009). Exploring agility in distributed information systems development teams: An interpretive study in an offshoring context. *Information Systems Research, 20*(3), 440–461.

Satariano, A., & Metz, C. (2023). *Amazon takes a big stake in the A.I. Start-up anthropic.* https://www.nytimes.com/2023/09/25/technology/amazon-ant hropic-ai-deal.html, Accessed 28th September 2023.

Schneier, B. (2009). *Schneier on security.* John Wiley & Sons.

Sheehan, B., Jin, H. S., & Gottlieb, U. (2020). Customer service chatbots: Anthropomorphism and adoption. *Journal of Business Research, 115*, 14–24.

Sowa, K., Przegalinska, A., & Ciechanowski, L. (2021). Cobots in knowledge work: Human–AI collaboration in managerial professions. *Journal of Business Research, 125*, 135–142.

Sundar, S. (2023). *If you still aren't sure what ChatGPT is, this is your guide to the viral chatbot that everyone is talking about.* https://www.businessinsider.com/everything-you-need-to-know-about-chat-gpt-2023-1?r=US&IR=T, Accessed 19th March 2023.

Venkatesh, V., Thong, J. Y., & Xu, X. (2012). Consumer acceptance and use of information technology: Extending the unified theory of acceptance and use of technology. *MIS Quarterly, 36*(1), 157–178.

CHAPTER 3

Co-worker, Butler, or Coach? Designing Automation for Work Enrichment

Virpi Roto

INTRODUCTION

Work is transforming. The future of work is affected by macro trends of digitalization, globalization, demographic change, education, migration, and the transformation of people's values and preferences (BMAS, 2017). Of these trends, digitalization and the transformation of people's values and preferences are most relevant to the theme of this book and this chapter. One of the megatrends in digitalization is the increasing use of artificial intelligence (AI) in automating work tasks and work processes, leading to the dismissal of entire job roles. While automation has been changing job roles since the 1800s, the magnitude of the work transformation with AI is expected to exceed all prior industrial revolutions.

When automation becomes autonomous, able to run all needed tasks without a human, there is an economical desire to establish black box factories—fully automated factories that take in material and output products without human help, with no humans inside. While the early vision

V. Roto (✉)
Department of Design, Aalto University, Espoo, Finland
e-mail: virpi.roto@aalto.fi

45

of automation saw machines doing all the work and people could just relax, research has proven it is not that simple. A black box factory is not only a safety and resiliency problem but also a societal problem. If there is little work for people to earn a wage for living, the capitalist society needs to rethink the ways people can earn their living. Philosophers and economists have produced several proposals on the new order of society (see e.g. Spencer, 2023 for a summary), and this chapter will not argue which of them is the best solution. In the long run, however, it seems likely that the role of work in people's lives will change, and we will have more freedom to choose how much we want to work. If work automation reaches the level where people need to work less or not at all, the dreams of more free time and focus on creativity rather than productivity may be finally realized.

This chapter targets a future where people are working with highly automated systems. As autonomous systems can take care of production, the work largely consists of passive monitoring of automation. Work enrichment is proposed as a central concept in designing Humane Autonomous Technology that improves employee experience through meaningful interactions and activities.

Waves of Human–Computer Interaction Research Repeat

The humane aspects of digital systems have been widely studied in Human–Computer Interaction (HCI). When computers became more commonplace in workplaces in the 1980s, HCI research started by investigating human factors related to human interaction with computers. The user interface was based on "arcane commands and system dialogs" and interaction means were still cumbersome for laymen to understand (Carroll, 2013). In the 1990s, HCI moved from human factors to human actors (Bannon, 1995), i.e., the role of humans as error-prone helpers of computers shifted toward actors with their own needs. In other words, the mindset of humans as servants of obscure computers changed to user-friendly computers serving people. The new millennium brought up the next mindset change to HCI, where the usability of the system was not the only important topic in HCI. Both industry and academia noticed that people may have a love relationship with certain digital services and the emotional aspects can and should be considered in design. User experience (UX) was an important keyword of this third wave of HCI, and designing engaging user experiences was an important design goal.

During the second decade of this millennium, HCI research found the dark side of designing engaging systems, e.g., the addiction to social media. To address these challenges, during the 2010s, the focus of HCI research was increasingly on the ethical and human well-being aspects of digital systems, and the main design goal was rather human well-being than maximum engagement with the websites and apps.

The 2020s introduced an AI wave to HCI. Interaction with AI is changing the 60-year-old command-based interaction paradigm to an intent-based interaction paradigm (Nielsen, 2023), which means we see the HCI waves starting from the beginning. The AI systems of today are as difficult to understand and interact with as the computers of the 1980s, and it will require much work to take the AI-enabled automation systems through the four waves: first making them usable, then engaging, and finally improving human wellbeing. So far, HCI research has investigated AI interactions on lower levels of automation, such as with chatbots and other conversational agents (Level 2 on Parasuraman & Sheridan, 2000 model), recommender systems (Level 3), and human-AI teaming (Levels 4-). The higher levels of automation have not been interesting to HCI researchers, since interaction between people and highly autonomous systems is expected to be minimal (Level 10 ignores the human). However, due to the problematic consequences of interactions with high levels of automation, HCI expertise is needed more than ever to work on solutions that avoid the human role as a servant of automation. Therefore, this chapter aims to find means to improve employee experience at work with intelligent automation. This approach requires us to shift the focus from rationalistic human factors research to a humanistic design research approach.

Humane Work with Automation

When the artists of the early 1900s envisioned the world in the year 2000, they predicted work that included human control, a concrete view of what automation does, and outdoor work continuing in the fresh air (Fig. 3.1).

The agricultural automation reality of today is sitting in front of monitors in a dark room, trying to verify that the highly automated systems work correctly (Fig. 3.2). Is this kind of work something we would design today if we were tasked to design humane work with automation? Instead of having automation systems at the center of automation

A Very Busy Farmer

Fig. 3.1   An early vision of agricultural work automation[1]

design, I suggest we rethink working with highly automated systems from a human-centered and user experience perspective.

When studying the literature on user experiences at work, Simsek et al. (2021) found many studies on pragmatic, performance-related topics, but few studies on the effect of the tools used at work on employees' emotional experiences. Considering the increasing amount of time spent daily with digital work tools, this is a surprising gap in research. It seems HCI researchers have treated employees as rational actors who behave optimally when they have the relevant information available to conduct their work. However, it is the meaningful and inspiring experiences that make life worth living, and the work context is not an exception. Now that we are discussing the design of autonomous systems, it is important to highlight the important role of these systems in creating work satisfaction.

Several international organizations are calling for a humane approach to both the future of work and AI. The International Labor Organization chose a "human-centered approach for the future of work" as a

[1] Unknown artist: A Very Busy Farmer. En L'An 2000 series, 1899. ©BnF.

Fig. 3.2 How agricultural automation has turned out to be[2] ⊜

central theme of their centenary year (ILO, 2019). In 2021, the European Commission called for the fifth industrial revolution, Industry 5.0, to bring a more sustainable, human-centric, and resilient industry to Europe, and to place the wellbeing of the industry worker at the center of the production process (EC, 2021). As an example of this future, Noble et al. (2022) suggest that "harmonious human–machine collaborations" lead to the well-being of multiple stakeholders in the 5th industrial revolution.

As the initial step toward humane autonomous technology, several ethical guidelines for the design of intelligent systems have been published. All such guidelines want to prevent AI systems from harming people, and in that sense, they are human-centered. However, removing the violations of basic human rights is not enough to address the values and preferences of modern people. The Ethically Aligned Design guideline by IEEE (2019) goes radically beyond prevention of harm by "prioritizing human wellbeing with autonomous and intelligent systems". Although the difference between the prevention of harm and human well-being may seem thin, there is a remarkable difference from a design perspective. It is comparable to the influential Positive Psychology movement, where healing a mental illness focuses on the negative while improving well-being focuses on the positive: what makes a person flourish (Seligman, 2000). The same ideology is adopted in Positive

---

[2] https://www.flickr.com/photos/usdagov/50996477916/in/photostream.

Design (Desmet & Pohlmeyer, 2013). While the focus on pain points is prevalent in interaction design, Positive Design focuses on the means of maximizing human well-being and flourishing. This is a worthy attitude also in designing work automation systems.

This chapter on designing automation for work enrichment is targeted at employee-centered designers and developers of highly automated work systems. After introducing why passive monitoring work is an unpreferred future of work, the chapter proposes designing automation for work enrichment as a solution toward more humane autonomous technology. The main research contributions to this end are a redefined concept of work enrichment and three levels of work enrichment through automation design.

CRITIQUE ON MONITORING WORK

For decades, control rooms have been the workplace for employees who have moved from field to office to monitor and control how automation executes the tasks that employees used to do. Control rooms are pervading new industry sectors, such as logistics centers with autonomous cranes and vehicles, marine industry with autonomous ships, or autonomous construction of building units in factories. Control rooms are likely to also reach consumer services, such as restaurant kitchens, hotels, delivery services, and hospitals.

With the increasing levels of automation in control rooms and human-automation interaction in general, the interaction paradigm evolves from commanding to approving and then to monitoring. The first two paradigms are commonplace and thoroughly discussed in human–computer interaction research, but the monitoring paradigm introduces many unsolved challenges and thus deserves more attention.

Let us imagine Jake, a truck driver, whose driving work has changed along the increasing levels of automation. Now the trucks are unmanned and Jake is assigned to monitor one or more autonomous, unmanned trucks in a control room. Jake had chosen the truck job because he felt he was good at driving and enjoyed controlling such massive vehicles. Now that the driving tasks are automated, his work no longer supports those competencies and experiences.

On one hand, assigning the driving task to the AI system is work simplification, as most of the driving tasks are automated and thus Jake's tasks are narrowed down. On the other hand, the challenges in his work become higher: he needs to follow several videos per truck to get situational awareness of all sides of the truck, especially on a multi-lane road. He needs to follow the status of the overall trip, the steering response (e.g., on icy roads), cargo movements, and other truck-specific aspects. When on the truck, Jake simply senses these qualities, but more attention is required when following these aspects from the control room screens, especially if he has several trucks to be monitored.

What today is a meaningful, active job role for an expert is likely to be reduced into a job where the expert passively monitors that automation works correctly. When automation works as it should, the job includes few tasks for the expert, but the human is still needed to monitor and be ready to help automation in case unexpected situations emerge. With increasing levels of automation, control rooms are turning into monitoring centers. The remaining task for people in monitoring centers is to monitor the alarm systems and take action when the automation needs help.

A profound challenge with the increasing share of work turning to monitoring is that humans are not made for monitoring work. When automation works fine for hours, days, or even months, employees lose their interest in keeping themselves alert and can no longer act quickly when a problem arises due to lost situational awareness and erosion of skills. Would Jake, the remote truck driver, be able to take over an autonomous truck when there is a sudden unexpected event on the road, such as a ball bouncing from someone's yard onto the street? Is there enough time to react, and does the remote driver still have the skills to act in such a surprising situation? Still, it is probably Jake and not the AI system who realizes that children may run to the street soon after the ball.

Assigning employees a passive supervisory role leads to a plethora of unsolved challenges in human-automation interaction, such as understandability, predictability, and reversibility, not to mention the long-term effects such as employees' complacency, boredom, and erosion of competence (Wiener & Curry, 1980, p.13). The main human factors questions on automation monitoring work include how to keep the operators alert in highly automated environments (operator vigilance), how to make automation understandable (transparency, explainability), and how the human and automation could best work together (function allocation, human-automation interaction). Unfortunately, the evergreen human factors challenges of loss of situational awareness, operator complacency, monitoring inefficiency, and deskilling of employees remain still unsolved (Janssen et al., 2019; Mouloua et al., 2019). If decades of human factors research have not been able to find solutions to these challenges, it is likely they will never be solved (Mouloua et al., 2019). Therefore, it is time to rethink the approach to designing work with automated systems.

Work Enrichment

This section introduces a central concept of work enrichment, which guides the design of humane autonomous technology. First, seminal works related to work enrichment and related concepts are introduced, followed by the status of automation work enrichment research in automation monitoring contexts. Based on the related research and the future of work with humane autonomous technology, a renewed definition is provided for work enrichment.

Previous Research on Work Enrichment and Related Concepts

There are several well-studied concepts related to work enrichment such as employee motivation, job enrichment, job enlargement, and work-family enrichment. The Motivation-Hygiene Theory by Frederick Herzberg (1966) is a pioneering theory addressing work enrichment. It posits that if an organization wants to improve employees' motivation, performance, and satisfaction, the managers should enrich the work rather than make it simpler. Herzberg argued that to enrich work, management should give them opportunities for psychological growth: interesting work, increasing responsibility, and challenges to solve. The Motivation-Hygiene Theory introduced work enrichment as a means to increase employee motivation, which has been an important topic in management research for decades.

Two concepts targeting improved employee motivation are very close to work enrichment. First, Job Enrichment works vertically by introducing tasks that increase responsibility, personal growth, and recognition, such as managerial tasks (Herzberg, 1968). Second, Job Enlargement works horizontally; rather than doing a fraction of a bigger work unit, the job can be enlarged to cover a larger part of the same unit (Chung & Ross, 1977). For example, a car repairman may specialize in the steering and propulsion system, but after some time, the repairman might be motivated to learn to repair other parts of the car as well.

More recent research on work enrichment studies the broader needs and impacts of work enrichment. For example, Wood and Wall (2007) saw work enrichment as a central way of increasing organizational employee involvement, which in turn means "opportunities to make decisions concerning the conduct of their jobs and to participate in the business as a whole". Another example of a broader scale is the many publications on work-family enrichment, i.e., "the extent to which experiences in one role [work] improve the quality of life in another role [family]" (Greenhaus & Powell, 2006, p. 73), and thus it is close to this chapter's interest in enriching work as an important part of living a good life. The topics in work-family enrichment literature are mainly about work culture, work context, work role, and workload (ibid.), which the management in the workplace can influence. of which automation design can influence the workload.

Research on Enrichment of Automation Monitoring Work

The context of automation monitoring work differs from the work contexts studied in work enrichment research so far. In the work enrichment publications, the employees are expected to be active and execute the needed tasks to produce good-quality results. This is no longer the case when active work transforms into passive monitoring of highly automated systems. Therefore, I wanted to see how previous research has approached work enrichment in automation monitoring work.

Surprisingly, I did not manage to find any studies on work enrichment or job enrichment in the context of automation monitoring work. This is alarming since there seems to be an obvious need to enrich the passive job of monitoring highly autonomous systems, which seems to be the future of work in so many sectors. Even management research, which seems the forerunner field in studying employees' emotions at work, has overlooked the role of tools as the source of work satisfaction. I would not like to make a conclusion that management research has no interest in employees after automation arrives and takes over the work. I rather believe that management research is still unsure of the consequences of autonomous systems on the work of employees and managers.

Redefining Work Enrichment

Work has changed a lot since the early ideas of work enrichment. Now that work seems to transform toward automation monitoring, work may become too simple and monotonous, and enrichment of work becomes increasingly important.

The concept of "work enrichment" seems not to be in active use, and it is not clearly defined. Instead, there is research on "job enrichment," which refers to a job design process where management aims to improve the efficiency of organizational operations and improve employees' motivation by changing the job content, e.g., from repetitive tasks to varied tasks, or involving the employees to managerial roles (Alias et al., 2018). Job design by the management is not the only way to enrich work, since also intelligent systems at work can provide new opportunities for work enrichment.

I approach work enrichment from the perspective of designing humane highly automated work systems that could enrich passive monitoring work or downtime at work. I suggest using the term work enrichment to refer to *activities introduced to or requested by employees to address their timely pragmatic and/or psychological needs.* Work enrichment can take place when there are few other activities at work.

When monitoring work is passive and boring, employees may appreciate activities that fill the time with something meaningful, fulfilling, fun, and/or inspiring. For example, designers of intelligent automation systems could make the automation system provide stimuli to activate the employee with activities that make work more meaningful, fulfilling, and inspiring. Periodically, on request, or when the system notices an employee's vigilance decreasing, the intelligent system could suggest interesting activities, such as learning more about the autonomous system, physical or mental exercises, entertainment, or discussions between the system and the employee(s). The stimuli provided by the intelligent system should be personalized, i.e., based on the preferences of an individual employee. The stimuli can include a selection of activities and allow the employee to choose one. The selection of activities should be such that the employee can get back to monitoring work when needed. These activities should not take the employee's full attention for long periods, in case there becomes some "real" work that requires action. Work enrichment differs from job enrichment, as it is not driven by management but built in the interactive tools that employees use, and it is not a long-term change of one's duties but momentary.

Levels of Designing Automation
for Work Enrichment

Traditionally, most benefits of automation are seen to relate to more efficient operations and the safety of employees. This chapter approaches automation from a humanistic design research perspective and contributes to automation design research and practice. Even if autonomous systems might not need people for months, human-centric systems can provide future employees a chance to interact with them.

An important functionality automation developers should enable for enriching work is an adaptable level of automation, which enables the operator to adjust the level of automation for selected tasks (Chavaillaz et al., 2019). So, even when the system is highly autonomous, the employee can choose a more active role and lower the level of automation for the tasks to work on. When ready to do so, the employee can change back to the higher level of automation. This will add a much-needed feeling of control to automation work.

A framework of the Levels of Work Enrichment for Automation Design is presented in Table 3.1. The framework suggests three ways in which humans and automation can work together, and the level of work enrichment increases through the levels. The levels of work enrichment should not be mixed with the levels of automation, although the level of automation can grow through the levels. It is more important to provide adaptable automation, i.e., the employee can adapt the level of automation on all levels.

The levels of work enrichment are seen to emerge sequentially over time. In the mid-2020s, we see early phases of Level 1 realizing, while the next levels are further in the future. Level 3 is the most futuristic, requiring much development of AI technologies, workplaces, and the society in which they can exist. Level 3 addresses the utopia of a human-centric future of work where people can choose how much they want to work.

The three levels of work enrichment can be best characterized by the three roles that automation has in enriching the work of employees: Co-worker, Butler, and Coach, each of which is explained in the next subchapters. The main differences between the three levels address the roles between automation and employee, the benefit for the employee, and the broader benefit for business and society.

Table 3.1 Levels of work enrichment through automation design

Work enrichment	Level 1	Level 2	Level 3
Role of automation	Co-Worker	Butler	Coach
Theoretical grounding	Decent work	Self-Determination Theory	Eudaimonia
Experience goal	Achievement	Motivation	Flourishing
Design grounding	Pragmatic needs	Psychological needs	Virtue
Design approach	Human-Centered Design	Positive Design	Eudaimonic Design
Employee benefit	Easier and safer work	Well-being	Good life
Broader goal	Operational efficiency	Organizational resilience	Societal resilience

Level 1: Co-worker

On the first level of the model (Table 3.1), the primary design goal is to deliver the employee an experience of Achievement. Instead of having the employee serve the autonomous system, the automation designers should design systems that provide employees responsibility for executing tasks from which to gain personal achievement experiences. Achieving together with others can be more satisfying than achieving alone, if the different skills of each contributor are utilized. Designing automation that is able to collaborate with employees follows the idea of hybrid human-AI teams where employees and AI systems collaborate as a team (see Seeber et al., 2020 for a research agenda in human–machine team collaboration). Both automation and employees do their part of the work, so both take the role of a worker, with their different skills and abilities.

A central challenge to be solved in human-AI teaming is task allocation, which would utilize the best skills of automation and humans. If optimal task allocation can be achieved, work execution becomes fluent in hybrid teams. Human-centered designers should find out which tasks are boring, difficult, error-prone, or dangerous for the employees and prioritize automation of those tasks. For example, during a night-long drive, automation can take care of trucks driving on a divided highway when the weather is good because such a task would be boring and tiring for people. People may be better than automation at driving on populated streets when it is snowing and the street borders are hardly visible. In those circumstances, the drivers may fully utilize their skills to tackle the challenges. Once complete, they are likely to experience achievement.

Optimal task allocation is not often enough, but more interaction and negotiation are needed for human-AI co-working. Akata et al. (2020) propose hybrid intelligence, where human intellect and capabilities are augmented by AI. According to them, gaining hybrid intelligence requires developing AI that is collaborative, adaptive, responsible, and explainable. For example, collaboration design could include negotiation on task allocation between Jake, the remote driver, and the truck automation system. Adaptive automation would recognize when the remote driver is tired or overloaded and take over some of their tasks, with or without negotiation. With automated task allocation, automation can be seen as a co-worker, who silently takes care of some of the work. Still, automation will need human help when an unexpected situation occurs, therefore, questions of responsibility and explainability need to be addressed (ibid). The expected benefit of improved teamwork with AI for the employees is easier and safer work, and for the company more effective and less risky operations and thereby operational efficiency.

One possible guideline, if not a theoretical grounding, for this level of design is Decent Work. It is an agenda of the International Labor Organization (ILO) targeting "productive work for women and men in conditions of freedom, equity, security, and human dignity." In line with this agenda, ILO has declared the Human-Centered Future of Work as the goal in the transformation of the world of work. Therefore, a human-centered design approach is the obvious choice for this first level of work enrichment (Table 3.1). Human-centered design is a core competence of the HCI community, and this competence will be beneficial also when designing work automation. For example, investigation of the user needs from the beginning of the design project will be the key to addressing the employees' pragmatic needs later in the design process.

Level 2: Butler

The second level of the model (Table 3.1) expands the design requirements from pragmatic needs toward employees' psychological needs. According to the Self-Determination Theory (Deci & Ryan, 1985), relatedness, competence, and autonomy are basic psychological needs that drive intrinsic motivation. All three are highly relevant also in work contexts, but when working with a high level of automation, there is a threat that the work no longer fulfills any of these basic psychological needs. Jake may be the only remote truck driver in the control room, with scarce relatedness experiences. He may feel his skills deteriorate as the system takes care of driving and he may lose the feeling of being a competent driver. Experiences of autonomy may be gone if the system does not give him any control, but only calls him for help when something fails. If the work fails to address the basic psychological needs, employees' motivation to work is low.

The design goal of Motivation refers mainly to intrinsic motivation, i.e., "doing an activity for its own sake because one finds the activity inherently interesting and satisfying" (Tremblay et al., 2009). Automation design can also trigger extrinsic motivation, i.e., "doing an activity for an instrumental reason" (ibid), by rewarding the employee. The intrinsic motivation is more interesting to discuss here since it is more complex and tends to be longer term than task-reward functionality in the automation system.

Automation does not have to be highly intelligent to be able to serve Jake's psychological needs. Jake could find his work more motivating if the tool provided a discussion channel with other remote truck drivers (relatedness). The automation system could ask if he could take over when it is snowing, which is challenging weather for both automation and a human driver, and give grateful feedback when Jake safely stops the truck at the destination (competence). The automation system could allow Jake to change the level of automation, e.g., when the truck approaches a scenic, curvy road that Jake enjoys driving (autonomy).

Compared to the equal human-automation teams in Level 1 of work enrichment, Level 2 assigns Jake more power to control the automation. On level 2, the role of automation is like a butler. It serves and supports the employees in doing their work, and also works silently in the background on the tasks that aid employees and their organization. The employee should have the autonomy to decide the allocation of tasks under his responsibility. If designing for the basic psychological needs is successful, the employees have the intrinsic motivation to excel in their work and they carry the responsibility for their actions.

Such design for Work Motivation and empowering employees with self-determination will improve organizational resilience. Resilience has been discussed as one of the threats of high levels of automation. The phenomenon is called the Lumberjack Effect: the higher the tree, the harder it falls (Onnasch et al., 2014). The more dependent an organization is on automation, the more vulnerable it becomes. If automation fails, there may not be people who can take over, and the organizational tolerance for such failures is low. When there are experts whose skills have been in use and they are satisfied with their work, they can do at least some of the work manually and keep the organization alive until automation works again.

An important difference in the design attitude between the first and second levels is a move from problem-centric to opportunity-centric design. This is a similar idea to Positive Psychology (Seligman, 2000), which has shifted the focus from healing illness to supporting well-being. Positive Design is a design approach adopting this idea and thus moving design from pain point fixing to designing for the best possible experience is a powerful method to design for Motivation. The designers using Positive Design could make automation learn each employee's work preferences and personalize the user interface accordingly. While intelligent technology cannot improve working conditions, income, or other organizational factors affecting work Motivation, it can provide performance appraisal, let the employee make decisions on the tasks they want to perform themselves, provide tools to strengthen social connections at work or other features that address the factors improving Motivation.

Level 3: Coach

This highest level of work enrichment is proposed for a future where automation and a new societal order finally provide us the freedom to choose how much we want to work. Automation is skilled, reliable, and able to handle close to all work tasks, but still, people are needed to oversee automation. Automation has the capacity not only to execute the actual work tasks but also to enrich the employee's days by acting as a coach. When employees have free time, the AI coaches them to develop themselves toward the virtues they see as admirable and worth pursuing.

On this level, work enrichment design targets an experience of Flourishing, living a more fulfilling life. One of the famous theories aiming at human flourishing over time is the Aristotelean philosophy of Eudaimonia, which can indeed be translated as Flourishing. Eudaimonia is old but gaining more and more interest, and there are several different interpretations of it. I use here one of the highly cited works, Ryff (1989), according to whom eudaimonia is about the highest human good, living a good life through the realization of one's true potential. In essence, eudaimonia refers to positive psychological functioning over a person's life span (ibid.).

Eudaimonia is a broad philosophy that deals with many aspects of a good life, and there is a good selection of literature, guidance on living according to this philosophy, and questionnaires testing one's progress on the way there. This knowledge base enables designers to design a wide range of activities, exercises, and discussion topics to offer to employees through the automation system.

The Questionnaire for Eudaimonic Well-being by Waterman et al. (2010) may concretize in a compact form the ideas of Eudaimonia. The questionnaire consists of six dimensions, around which 21 questions are formulated. The dimensions are described below, and descriptions are my summaries of longer descriptions by Waterman et al. (2010), slightly adjusted to work contexts.

1. Self-discovery: one has recognized who one really is and the suitable work roles for one.
2. Development of one's best potential: knowing one's best potential at work and developing them whenever possible.
3. A sense of purpose and meaning in life: putting one's skills and talents to use in the pursuit of personally meaningful objectives.
4. Investment of significant effort in pursuit of excellence: one enjoys spending a great deal of effort to achieve excellent work results.
5. Intense involvement in activities: subjectively experiencing flow with many tasks at work.
6. Enjoyment of activities as personally expressive: it is most important that one enjoys the work, no matter what others think.

Since the dimensions are not straightforward to implement into employees' lives, work enrichment requires intelligent, personalized algorithms to guide employees toward flourishing. While Waterman et al. (2010) did not develop their questionnaire designers in mind, the 21 questions included can be used by the coach to find out the eudaimonic status of and development areas for the employee. The vast literature on Eudaimonia can then be utilized to teach AI to take pathways in coaching the employee to improve their psychological functioning.

For example, Jake may be searching for his identity after the truck driving work changed dramatically. The AI system could have a confidential series of discussions about how he feels about the new work and if he can realize his best potential there. Then AI could help Jake find out his passions and who he really is, and help him find and utilize his strengths, both at work and in other life contexts. This kind of discussion delves into fundamental topics that, if well-designed, can enrich Jake's days in a transformational way and make him flourish.

Discussion through querying, advising, and giving feedback is something that personalized AI systems can learn to do, and these interactions would be highly useful for coaching. The AI coach could learn to use a tone that the employee finds natural for them. For employees who prefer a softer tone, the coach could act as a eudaimon, which means "a good spirit or angel" in Greek mythology (Merriam-Webster., 1995). A coach or eudaimon built into the automation system would enrich work, as every day the employee might experience positive personal growth and self-actualization. The work itself can provide the right level of challenge for one's skills, and skillful automation can take care of the easy or difficult tasks.

An important ethical aspect in designing such a coach is respect for privacy, as employers should not have access to the coaching data of the employees. It should be up to employees what they want to share with their superiors or colleagues. Not every employee may enjoy this kind of interaction at work in the first place, therefore designers must respect employees' decision to opt out of coaching. Those who take the opportunity may find their inner self and their purpose in life. If many people have such harmony in their lives, the impact may be seen as a more harmonious society. The broader benefit of successful AI coaches can thus be improved societal resilience.

CONCLUSION

Conquering the old challenges with highly automated systems requires rethinking the ways we design automation systems. After decades of rationalistic AI and automation research, there is a need for humanistic design research in this domain. This chapter introduces the concept of Work Enrichment to defend the need for meaningful and fulfilling work even with highly automated systems and provides a framework with three levels of work enrichment for automation design.

In the mid-2020s, interaction designers are exploring ways to make automation and people work together as co-workers, addressing work enrichment level 1. When successful, they have reached a point when work in hybrid teams is fluent, and working with automation can be counted as Decent Work. Level 2 enrichment addresses not only the pragmatic needs of work execution but also the basic psychological needs of employees. Designing automation to act as a helpful butler for the employees can improve their work motivation and well-being. On Level 3, automation is about enriching life both at work and outside the work through Eudaimonic Design. This level best applies to a society where people can choose how much they want to work. The intelligence of automation can be utilized for the best of employees. They can develop both their professional and virtuous abilities through discussions with automation.

This chapter has introduced the concept of work enrichment to avoid a dehumanizing future of work with highly automated systems. As the main contribution toward a human-centered future of work, the chapter provides a 3-level framework for Work Enrichment through Automation Design (Table 3.1). In the long run, automation designers should strive to design enriching automation, which can provide meaningful, fulfilling, and inspiring experiences for employees and even help them live a good life.

References

Akata, Z., Balliet, D., De Rijke, M., Dignum, F., Dignum, V., Eiben, G., & Welling, M. et al. (2020). A research agenda for hybrid intelligence: Augmenting human intellect with collaborative, adaptive, responsible, and explainable artificial intelligence. *Computer, 53*(8), 18–28.

Alias, N. E., Othman, R., Hamid, L. A., Salwey, N. S., Romaiha, N. R., Samad, K. A., & Masdek, N. R. N. (2018). Managing job design: The roles of job rotation, job enlargement and job enrichment on job satisfaction. *Journal of Economic & Management Perspectives, 12*(1), 397–401.

Bannon, L. J. (1995). From human factors to human actors: The role of psychology and human-computer interaction studies in system design. In *Readings in human–computer interaction* (pp. 205–214). Morgan Kaufmann.

BMAS. (2017). Reimagining Work: White paper work 4.0 (2017). BundesMinisterium für Arbeit und Soziales *(German Federal Ministry of Labor and Social Affairs)*. https://www.bmas.de/SharedDocs/Downloads/EN/PDF-Publikationen/a883-white-paper.pdf?__blob=publicationFile&v=3

Carroll, J. M. (2013). Human computer interaction-brief intro. *The encyclopedia of human-computer interaction, 86*.

Chavaillaz, A., Schwaninger, A., Michel, S., & Sauer, J. (2019). Work design for airport security officers: Effects of rest break schedules and adaptable automation. *Applied Ergonomics, 79*, 66–75.

Chung, K. H., & Ross, M. F. (1977). Differences in motivational properties between job enlargement and job enrichment. *Academy of Management Review, 2*(1), 113–122.

Deci, E. L., & Ryan, R. M. (1985). *Intrinsic motivation and self-determination in human behavior*. Plenum.

Desmet, P. M., & Pohlmeyer, A. E. (2013). Positive design: An introduction to design for subjective well-being. *International Journal of Design, 7*(3).

EC (European Commission), Directorate-General for research and innovation, Breque, M., De Nul, L., & Petridis, A. (2021). *Industry 5.0: Towards a sustainable, human-centric and resilient European industry*, Publications Office. https://data.europa.eu/doi/https://doi.org/10.2777/308407.

Greenhaus, J. H., & Powell, G. N. (2006). When work and family are allies: A theory of work-family enrichment. *Academy of Management Review, 31*(1), 72–92.

Herzberg, F. (1966). *The motivation-hygiene theory. Work and the nature of man*. UK.

Herzberg, F. (1968). *One more time: How do you motivate employees* (Vol. 65). Harvard Business Review.

IEEE. (2019). *Ethically aligned design: A vision for prioritizing human well-being with autonomous and intelligent systems*, First Edition. https://ethicsinaction.ieee.org/

ILO (International Labour Organization). (2019). *Work for a brighter future. Global commission on the future of work*, International Labour Organization.

Janssen, C. P., Donker, S. F., Brumby, D. P., & Kun, A. L. (2019). History and future of human-automation interaction. *International Journal of Human-Computer Studies, 131*, 99–107.

Merriam-Webster; Encyclopædia Britannica, eds. (1995). *Merriam-Webster's Encyclopedia of Literature*. Merriam-Webster. ISBN 0877790426.

Mouloua, M., Ferraro, J. C., Parasuraman, R., Molloy, R., & Hilburn, B. (2019). Human monitoring of automated systems. *Human performance in automated and autonomous systems: Emerging Issues and Practical Perspectives, Chapter 1*. CRC Press.

Nielsen, J. (2023). *AI: First New UI Paradigm in 60 Years*. Nielsen Norman group. https://www.nngroup.com/articles/ai-paradigm/

Noble, S. M., Mende, M., Grewal, D., & Parasuraman, A. (2022). The fifth industrial revolution: How harmonious human–machine collaboration is triggering a retail and service (r) evolution. *Journal of Retailing, 98*(2), 199–208.

Onnasch, L., Wickens, C. D., Li, H., & Manzey, D. (2014). Human performance consequences of stages and levels of automation: An integrated meta-analysis. *Human Factors, 56*(3), 476–488.

Parasuraman, R., Sheridan, T. B., & Wickens, C. D. (2000). A model for types and levels of human interaction with automation. *IEEE Transactions on Systems, Man, and Cybernetics-Part a: Systems and Humans, 30*(3), 286–297.

Ryff, C. D. (1989). Happiness is everything, or is it? Explorations on the meaning of psychological well-being. *Journal of Personality and Social Psychology, 57*(6), 1069–1081.

Seeber, I., Bittner, E., Briggs, R. O., De Vreede, T., De Vreede, G. J., Elkins, A., & Söllner, M. et al. (2020). Machines as teammates: A research agenda on AI in team collaboration. *Information & management, 57*(2), 103174.

Seligman, M. E., & Csikszentmihalyi, M. (2000). *Positive psychology: An introduction* (Vol. 55, No. 1, p. 5). American Psychological Association.

Simsek Caglar, P., Roto, V., & Vainio, T. (2022). User experience research in the work context: Maps, gaps and agenda. *Proceedings of the ACM on Human-Computer interaction, 6*(CSCW1), 1–28.

Spencer, D. A. (2023). Technology and work: Past lessons and future directions. *Technology in Society*, 102294.

Tremblay, M. A., Blanchard, C. M., Taylor, S., Pelletier, L. G., & Villeneuve, M. (2009). Work extrinsic and intrinsic motivation scale: Its value for organizational psychology research. *Canadian Journal of Behavioural Science/revue Canadienne Des Sciences Du Comportement, 41*(4), 213.

Waterman, A. S., Schwartz, S. J., Zamboanga, B. L., Ravert, R. D., Williams, M. K., Bede Agocha, V., Su Yeong Kim., & Brent Donnellan, M. (2010). The questionnaire for eudaimonic well-being: Psychometric properties, demographic comparisons, and evidence of validity. *The Journal of Positive Psychology, 5*(1), 41–61.

Wiener, E. L., & Curry, R. E. (1980). Flight-deck automation: Promises and problems. *Ergonomics, 23*(10), 995–1011.

Wood, S. J., & Wall, T. D. (2007). Work enrichment and employee voice in human resource management-performance studies. *The International Journal of Human Resource Management, 18*(7), 1335–1372.

CHAPTER 4

Artfully Integrating AI: Proceeding Responsibly With Worker-Centered Best Practices

Sarah E. Fox◉ *and Samantha Shorey*◉

INTRODUCTION

[The] goodness of computer systems is essentially tied to their artful integration into the sites of their use. Artful integration, in turn, requires fundamental transformations in the knowledge and working relations through which we produce new technologies. We need to begin by reexamining the dichotomy of 'designer' and 'user,' and locating ourselves instead within the extended networks of social relations and forms of work that take their place.

— Lucy Suchman (as quoted in Friedman et al., 1994)

S. E. Fox (✉)
Carnegie Mellon University, Pittsburgh, Pennsylvania, USA
e-mail: sarahfox@cmu.edu

S. Shorey
University of Pittsburgh, Pittsburgh, Pennsylvania, USA

© The Author(s) 2024
R. Rousi et al. (eds.), *Humane Autonomous Technology*,
https://doi.org/10.1007/978-3-031-66528-8_4

Popular depictions of the AI lifecycle suggest a linearity—design, test, deploy—that isn't really there. In the words of anthropologist and human–computer interaction scholar Lucy Suchman (2002a), technology production is often approached as "a series of hand-offs along a kind of multidisciplinary assembly line" (p. 141), with researchers and technologists plotting intended use, then releasing systems out into the world to be taken up as-is. Yet, decades of scholarly research on technology adoption within workplaces highlights the innovative and improvisational practices required of users to integrate and sustain technology in their deployment settings (Orr, 1996; Star & Strauss, 1999; Suchman, 1995).

The social decisions and material practices of implementation are deeply consequential, but under-considered in discussions of ethical AI (Williams et al., 2022). In the most recent edition of Stanford's 100-year study of AI, leading researchers called for a shift in thinking about AI as *integrated*, rather than deployed (Littman et al., 2021, p. 65). Deployment, they suggest, typically follows a process whereby technical systems are released into the real-world without recognition of the continued work needed to adapt them to local conditions. Design from the perspective of deployment takes on a kind of unidirectionality, where visions of a technology extend from the centerpoint of creators to the periphery of users. This narrow focus can amount to, in the words of Mateescu and Elish (2019), a "contextless dropping in" of AI, where—rather than supporting existing working relations—the technology's introduction reconfigures practices and requires those on the ground to make changes to accommodate the system.

In this chapter, we examine key tensions and compromises around implementation that emerged across a study on the rapid introduction of AI within essential sectors over the past several years. Specifically, we draw from ethnographic observation we conducted in two locations of waste labor managing the introduction of AI during the height of the COVID-19 pandemic: (1) an international airport in the Rust Belt region of the United States, piloting a set of autonomous floor cleaning robots and (2) a single-stream recycling plant in the Southwest region of the United States, contending with the continued integration of automated sorting robots. Within each site, we observed an intensification of frontline work because the additional labor of integration was not accounted for prior to the technology being piloted or deployed.

We offer a set of recommendations toward artfully and responsibly integrating AI informed by our findings. Presented as "best practices," these recommendations are focused on the often overlooked and under-valued work of incorporating and configuring systems in context. We seek to intervene not in system design per se, but rather in the processes and policies that define how organizations manage implementation (Suchman, 2002a, p. 139). With this work we ask the following questions: (1) *What forms of integration work are necessary to accommodate AI within the material and social context of use?* (2) *What alternative organizational practices might ease the burden of implementation, and recognize the labor that is necessarily taken on in this process?* and (3) *What opportunities might there be to interrupt the asymmetry of deployment toward more worker-centered ends?*

Over the course of this chapter, we not only aim to illustrate the critical role frontline workers play in onboarding and maintaining technological infrastructures across two cases, but also seek to provide organizations and worker advocates with insights into shifts in work brought on by technology integration, considerations for supporting worker safety, and suggestions for brokering workplace conversations around automation.

Invisible Work of AI Integration

Human-fueled automation is nothing new. Mary Gray and Siddharth Suri (2019) establish how many seemingly automated digital systems rely on (unseen) human labor—what they call "ghost work." Book scanning, image tagging, and content moderation are all forms of low-wage work necessary to bridge "automation's last mile" (Gray & Suri, 2019; Williams et al., 2022). This work occupies a "hidden layer" underpinning the publicly celebrated, highly rewarded labor of designers and engineers (Irani, 2015; Roberts, 2019). Wang et al. (2022) further describe how the organizational structures and practices driving the data labeling industry can be viewed as a systematic exercise of power, whereby the need for high-quality data at a low cost outweighs annotators' aspirations for well-being.

Much like the data work that precedes it, the continued work that sustains AI on-site is undervalued and often rendered invisible (Fox et al., 2023; Star & Strauss, 1999; Suchman, 1995). Mateescu and Elish (2019), for example, examine the work necessary to "harmonize" automation technologies, despite promises of labor savings—for example, the ongoing need for retail workers to guide confused customers through the grocery self-checkout line. Technologies are placed within communities and work settings with social and political histories that meaningfully transform such interventions. As Suchman argues, the "greater the distance—geographical, economic, cultural, experiential—the greater the need for reworking is likely to be" (Suchman, 2002b, p. 139). Focusing too tightly on the feasibility of a particular technology (rather than how it fits) within a particular, local circumstance misses how a technology comes to matter and upon whose labor it depends.

Outlining Best Practices with Two Sites

The labor of integration is performed in many cases by on-the-ground, hourly employees whose activities are simulated by the technologies they are improving (Endacott & Leonardi, 2021; Moradi & Levy, 2020). In doing so, essential workers are dually impacted by AI: they are the people most likely to be tasked with managing AI's initial inadequacies and most likely to be displaced when AI's capabilities are fully realized. To gain insight into how automation is introduced and attuned to the contexts of deployment, we took a multi-sited ethnographic approach. As Abebe et al. (2020) observe, "descriptive ethnographic research is essential for understanding how social and organizational practices intersect with technical systems to produce certain outcomes" (p. 254). This type of research offers insight into the disparate impacts of computational systems which are often not just a product of system design (i.e., technical bias) but are an "aspect of the system in use" (Friedman & Nissenbaum, 1996, p. 343).

Interviews. Beginning in June 2020, we conducted twenty-two hours of interviews with eleven participants, most of whom were managers and administrative personnel. The questions outlined in our active interview guides focused conversations on the processes, procedures, and impetus for integrating automated technologies in their facilities. This conversational data in the form of interview transcripts provided in-depth information from the perspective of organizational decision-makers.

Ethnographic Observation. In-person access to research sites resumed in September 2020 (sanitation) and February 2021 (recycling). Our field visits were guided by an attention to the tasks performed by workers, the "pain points" that emerge through their interactions with technology and the solutions enacted by workers and supervisors to overcome them. Data was produced in the form of ethnographic fieldnotes which recorded the everyday work practices of waste workers and their perspectives on contending with automated machinery on the ground (Emerson et al.,

2011). Our presentation of our findings follows the format of foundational scholarship on sociotechnical labor (Orr, 1996) in which illustrative vignettes are paired with segments of analysis as an interpretive method of knowledge production (Lindlof & Taylor, 2011).

Across the sections that follow, we offer a series of observations from our fieldwork that highlight the everyday effects of AI on workplace responsibilities and working conditions, and the physical reconfigurations that elide any notion of a smooth adoption. The instances from each field site depict the critical work of AI adoption, and illustrate the critical need to shift organizational practice to better account for this too often under-recognized labor. We offer a set of responsive recommendations to help decision-makers anticipate, mitigate, or avoid the issues identified and experienced by on-the-ground workers in future AI implementation.

Inevitability of Breakdowns and Need to Offer Training

When introducing the floor cleaning robot to employees, administrators stated the purpose of the technology was to *augment* the work of janitorial staff—making it such that they could perform their regular duties of surface cleaning with the robots there to disinfect after. But it quickly became clear to those working on site that the robots were much less independent than advertised, often needing to be rebooted and tended to mid-operation. Across our observations and interviews at the airport, shift supervisors[1] played a critical role in ensuring that the floor cleaning robots remained functional on-site. They were often radioed to scenes where a cleaning robot may have stalled out to either restart the device or drive it back to storage until a field engineer could assess the issue. Though more janitors than supervisors were circulating the space and could conceivably get to the robots more quickly, they were not trained to troubleshoot or move the devices should something go wrong.

A wide variety of staff were given a demonstration when the pilot began in early 2020,[2] but—according to employees we interviewed—training on how to operate the machines was offered exclusively to

---

[1] Like janitorial staff, shift supervisors would be considered frontline workers. Often longtime staff who have been promoted, they directly oversaw cleaning for the airport and constantly circulated the space should issues arise that needed quick response.

[2] Many janitorial staff members were not present as they were furloughed at the time or not yet hired.

those in more senior positions such as shift supervisors and managers (a choice made by administrators). Long-time supervisor Antoni[3] disagreed with this decision, noting seniority did not necessarily mean one is well-positioned to take on the task of maintaining the devices. Instead, in many cases, employees who were in supervisory positions felt their time was increasingly split, in part a byproduct of the deployment. Janitorial staff, on the other hand, described a desire to be formally trained on how to operate the floor cleaning robots, believing these skills would allow them to address problems more quickly. In the words of Scott, a janitor who'd been at the airport for 5 years, such training would allow him to bypass "redundancies" he observed through his current line of work. Sending out calls for his supervisor to address every instance the robot was stopped seemed to create a bottleneck, where one or two shift supervisors were drawn away from other duties in order to tend to the machines. Instead, as he saw it, it would be more efficient for janitorial staff to be able to move or tend to the devices themselves.

Janitorial staff at the airport expressed a strong desire to be able to gauge what might be going wrong or have the ability to manage the machines should they malfunction in a way that was disruptive to the environment. In the airport, this might have looked like offering training on how to move robots out of the way in cases where they were blocking travelers or in a situation that could be potentially dangerous. For those with particular interest in learning more, there could be additional opportunities to gain knowledge on how the devices function and career ladders designed to recognize and compensate workers for this investment. Without formal pathways to train employees, staff from different levels of the organization were unsure of their intended interaction with the technology, and any associated responsibility.

Recommendation: Offer Training and Continued Dialogue

Even when AI is marketed as "labor-augmenting" (Klinova, 2022), it is often the case that training is sparse. At minimum, we recommend organizations formally introduce the system to all frontline workers as they join and offer means by which they can gain knowledge about software updates or hardware changes as they are rolled out. This more lightweight, follow-up communication might be incorporated into

---

[3] All participants' and organizations' names are pseudonyms.

regular meetings, where staff already congregate and shift supervisors share news and assignments for the day. These regular updates not only inform staff on how to operate or troubleshoot the technology, but also create opportunities for them to communicate more readily with their unions and management about expectations and disruptions brought about by the technology and how the system might be adjusted to better serve their work practices (or avoided in cases where the harm or burden outweighs the good). With AI often reconfiguring workflows in ways that invisibilize human labor (Joyce et al., 2021), it is critical that organizations invest in these continued lines of dialogue around the technology and its impact on workers.

Measure Expectations with Reality

The recycling facility where we conducted our fieldwork, Reciclo, was negotiating the integration of robotics within an organization that was actively scaling. A sustainability-focused investment firm had acquired a majority share in Reciclo in 2019, shortly before we began observation. With this influx of capital, Reciclo had recently made two acquisitions: an older facility in a nearby suburb that was "lower tech" and state-of-the-art facility in a large, neighboring state that had eight times the number of AI-powered sorting robots[4] than our site. Reciclo represented a sort of middle ground. Our gatekeeper[5] Gabriel was formerly the General Manager of the local facility, and he had been progressively promoted, moving from site-specific leadership to executive roles that had a higher-level view of various facilities throughout the company. Gabriel's experience grounded him in the realities of the recycling sorting process, and he acknowledged that the data granularity offered by the AI-robot's visioning system—while impressive—wasn't necessary on a system level. "They're really new and it remains to be seen how they'll be useful," he stated. He seemed open, even a little optimistic.

But, by the time we conducted our wrap-up interview more than a year later, Gabriel had become disillusioned with the AI-powered sorting robots. "I will never buy another one again," he said, later stating "If

---

[4] We use the general descriptor "AI-powered sorting robots" rather than the branded name for the machines we observed in the facility.

[5] In ethnography, a "gatekeeper" grants access to a field site and gives researchers permission to gather observational data (Lindlof & Taylor, 2011, p. 98).

I could put them on the curb, I would." Their status going forward in the organization was unclear: Reciclo might move them to the smaller suburban facility, or sell them. At the highly automated facility they were planning a full retrofit, to remove the robots there all together. The pair of robots at our fieldsite were still in operation, for now. A sorter was regularly stationed next to the machines to grab all the valuable plastic they missed. Recounting the manufacturer's value propositions, Gabriel stated that the robots were supposed to be "faster, better, and more accurate" than existing technologies. But, the sorting process had only gotten *more expensive* since they'd been implemented, not cheaper. Cecilia, a sorting supervisor, substantiated Gabriel's evaluation. She said "You know, they brought in these machines because they didn't want to pay all of these ladies to sort there anymore. But, they ended up paying for a really expensive machine. And, we still need a lady there."

Recommendation: Benchmark Adoption Decisions

Rather than fully buying-in to an emerging technology, we recommend facilities create benchmarked integration plans. These plans should have scheduled assessment points, in which multiple stakeholders in the facility—including those working alongside machines—can measure claims against practical outcomes. This will help facilities avoid situations in which workers have to compensate for the failings of AI machines, in addition to their previous duties, because the "sunk costs" are too great to change direction. Large-scale organizational decisions that rearrange worker routines and physical infrastructure to prioritize unproven technology should be avoided. Gradual adoption will require facilities to resist pervasive, industry-level narratives around "future proofing" (Hsiao & Shorey, 2023). Technology companies use logics of competition to impel adoption, leveraging facilities' fear that they will fall behind new industry standards (Vinsel & Russell, 2020).

Recommendation: Develop Internal Methods to Judge Efficacy

A primary selling point of AI-powered technologies is a reduction to the cost of labor. Implied by these claims is the ability of robots (who, of course, don't need to be paid an hourly wage) to perform equal to or better than human workers. Facilities will typically assess these claims by closely monitoring output. While even simple metrics—like how often receptacles fill—can reveal if robots are falling short, they can also conceal the ad hoc and collaborative nature of robots' achievements. A receptacle might be filled by the activities of AI-powered sorting robots. Or, it might be filled by the activities of sorting robots and a human sorter stationed alongside them. Though some instantiations would be organizationally evident through daily role assignments, we also witnessed as supervisors would sort there briefly, in between other duties. "Flex sorters" would sometimes occupy the position for less than an hour, moving when they were needed elsewhere in the facility. These forms of labor are harder to account for.

Facilities should assess the claims of technology manufacturers by developing their own metrics for efficacy. Of specific importance is measuring the degree of intervention required to achieve tasks or outputs. Intervention evaluations will require detailed observation of regularly occurring processes. When a technology fails to achieve its core task, who steps in to fill the gap and keep things running as they should? Not accounting for intervention work can result in a total system shutdown when positions are reassigned or eliminated under the assumption that activities are happening "automatically." Organizations should be committed to recognizing what aspects of a process are not off-loaded by automation, and thus should continue to be compensated as aspects of workers' duties and accounted for in their time.

Acknowledge Maintenance as Vital Integration Work

Troubleshooting and responding to shortcomings of the floor cleaning robots became a constant concern of staff on-site at the airport. Supervisors, in particular, reported needing to "babysit" the robots as they stalled out frequently on the floor, creating obstacles for travelers moving quickly between gates. Even when supervisors managed to restart the robots on their path, the devices left behind a puddle of water that the janitorial staff, in turn, had to mop up. Several frontline workers expressed frustration around this point—the floor cleaning robots were marketed as autonomous, yet staff needed to clean up after them when they failed (a daily occurrence, during our fieldwork).

Though there were regular communications between managers and the robotics company representatives, there were fewer opportunities for frontline staff to be updated on the state of the machines. This disconnect became so pronounced that at one point a janitorial staff member told us he began placing a spare scrubber on top of robots in disrepair. If the scrubber was moved, he explained, they would know that the robotics company field engineer had been by to service the device. Before developing this strategy, he and other frontline staff were left uncertain about whether the robots were functioning properly and if they should be put out on the floor. In later months of fieldwork, frontline workers began to disassemble the floor cleaning robots, removing scrubbers and ceasing the practice of refilling their tanks with water. With this adaptation, they reserved the key feature of UV light disinfection, but removed the other functions of the machine prone to breakdown. In a creative effort meant to make the system work locally, janitorial staff drew on their deep knowledge of the context—spanning both material constraints and organizational motivations.

Recommendation: Recognize and Remunerate Maintenance Work

Our observations make it impossible to uphold design and development as *the* site of creativity or invention within the AI lifecycle. The essential work of integration is what ensures AI will actually perform in a particular context, and moments of breakdown reveal mismatches between designers' and technologists' visions and the actual circumstances of a deployment. It is necessary for organizations to consider the infrastructural labor workers perform in filling the gaps of AI, and to reliably communicate about the status of technology they are meant to integrate. Though repair is often overlooked in conceptions of innovation (Jackson, 2014; Vinsel & Russell, 2020), the proximity of field technicians to engineering fields earns them higher prestige and pay than many on-the-ground workers. Prevalent discourses around AI frame these technologies as an opportunity for "upskilling" and upward mobility for low-wage workers. Yet, realizing these promises is contingent upon maintenance work being recognized and compensated by employers, not just accumulated by essential workers.

Treat Workers as Domain Experts

On-site at the recycling facility, news that the robots might be decommissioned had traveled through the facility. "Word around town is, they're going to get rid of them"[6] one of the supervisors reported. The information was delivered as *chisme* (gossip), testifying to its layered truth. On the one hand, it was unconfirmed by those with the status in the organization to make the decision. But, on the other hand, it reflected a knowledge that the workers had long possessed. The technology wasn't fulfilling its promise. Lately, the robot had been overheating in the nearly 100-degree days of October in the American Southwest. The back panel door was permanently ajar even as it continued picking. Cecilia stationed a fan to blow cool air across a tangle of blue and green wires—the material guts of all that AI technology—diagnosing the problem, which was later confirmed by the manufacturers.

Many of the machines' struggles were a product of the use context. Though the digital AI-visioning system was the novel selling point for the technology, recycling sorting is a physical process. To grab objects off the conveyor belt, the robots used a suction cup gripper. "Consider the environmental conditions that a suction cup has to work in" Gabriel said, with exasperation. "Is there a chance that it will be high dust? Then the filter will get clogged. Is it possible that there will be [muck], like food, on the material? That will clog the filter too." Of course, these things would be true about a facility that sorted waste.

The supervisors and sorters who worked on the ground knew this trouble intimately. They had to do maintenance on the robot's suction cups almost every day. In our earliest visits to the facility, we observed the facility's maintenance team responded to problems identified and reported by "the ladies" who worked on the floor. When a technician arrived, he unlatched the metal grate that surrounded the robots and separated them from the rest of the facility. He removed debris or replaced the suction cup (depending on the severity), relatched the grate, logged the repair, and moved on. Over time, these crucial acts of maintenance became routines performed by the ladies themselves. When stationed next to the robots, Fernanda, a sorter, observed the machines as she was working alongside them. Briefly pausing their operation, she would open the enclosure, place her hand underneath the suction cup to check the airflow, and remove plastic wrap or other clogging material. These understated acts of care prevented more organizationally complex service

---

[6] Interviews with on-the-ground workers at Reciclo, including supervisors and sorters, were primarily conducted in Spanish and translated by the project's lead graduate research assistant.

calls to the maintenance team or the manufacturer, and kept the system running consistently.

Recommendation: Compare Ideal Conditions to Deployment Context
Facilities should perform a careful analysis of the ways in which their use context differs from ideal deployment conditions to anticipate how these dissimilarities might affect performance. As a method for accounting for this distance, Littman et al. (2021) offer the idea of "model cards" (p. 65). Originally proposed by Mitchell et al. (2019), model cards are produced by AI developers and provide documentation for the social context in which the technology is likely to perform well and the organizational processes that led to its development. Here, we suggest technology manufacturers should supply facilities with information about the material parameters a machine is designed for and tested in to support the pre-assessment process. The parameters may already be communicated, to some extent, through warranty conditions—but these stipulations do more to limit the responsibility of the manufacturer than to align expectations. When discrepancies are identified, facilities should anticipate the work that will be required to address them. This work should be assigned to specific roles and their job duties accordingly.

Of course, not all configuration labor can be anticipated pre-deployment, so facilities should also track emergent tasks once machines are running. We recommend that facilities watch for the accumulation of additional action *and* oversight. When technology recurrently malfunctions, workers must anticipate these breakdowns and deviate from other tasks when they occur. Splitting attention is a central contributor to workplace "techno-stress," causing employees to feel cognitive overload (Bucher et al., 2013).

DISCUSSION

AI and automation technologies may be marketed as "add-ons" that can be integrated into existing facilities or replace them altogether. This framing is meant to promote adoption by assuring facility owners that they can benefit from AI's capabilities without having the enormous expense of reconfiguring or building new facilities from scratch. Though depicted as an initial act of alignment through engineering, integration is a continual operation that requires the activities of essential workers. Crediting workers for these contributions is not just fundamental to ethical AI practices, but is also necessary for an accurate understanding of how systems operate (Bell, 2022; D'Ignazio & Klein, 2020; Star & Strauss, 1999).

Across this chapter, we have illustrated tensions and recommendations for organizations considering procuring and implementing AI within essential industries, as well as worker advocates who may seek to negotiate the terms of its deployment. Importantly, organizational best practices represent just one way of ensuring ethical implementation, but admittedly they are dependent on industry actors operating in good faith. To close out this chapter, we reflect on broader governance initiatives that seek to put guardrails around those who might not adhere to such principles, particularly around promotion and use of artificial intelligence within workplaces.

Communicating Limits

The hype around AI technology is a consequential aspect of AI deployment. Enthusiastic narratives can impel the adoption of technologies across an industry that are only partly capable of doing what they claim. As technology manufacturers race to improve and refine their products, the lag time is a nightmare for worker well-being. Workers are simultaneously tasked with adapting to these new technologies *and* compensating for their shortcomings, as they strive to keep facilities running.

In February 2023, the US Federal Trade Commission's Division of Advertising Practices released a set of guidelines for marketing claims about Artificial Intelligence (Atleson, 2023). Building upon previous guidelines for fairness and accountability in AI decision-making processes, this new set of directives is specifically aimed at "overpromising." AI producers must provide scientific support for their performance claims and adequate proof for their competitive claims that technologies can better non-AI counterparts. Though hype around AI seems to have proliferated unchecked for decades, the FTC reminds technology companies that "false or unsubstantiated claims about a product's efficacy" are the core interest of their commission, regardless of industry. The Department of Justice recently filed criminal charges against a cryptocurrency company that claimed it used AI-bots where none existed at all (Gilluly et al., 2023). As early as 1997, technology companies have come under scrutiny for practices like "vaporware"—in which companies market unrealized software in order to deter development by competitors (Bayus et al., 2001). In other industries, such as pharmaceuticals, overpromising is even more tightly regulated. Section 502 of the Federal Food, Drug and Cosmetics Act is focused on how products are represented and provides a potential exemplar for legal constraint. Known as "misbranding," this regulation forbids false or misleading statements on product labels and advertising. The inflated claims around AI have detrimental, material consequences for workers who are performing some of the most vital activities in our society; thus, these technologies should be evaluated for their accuracy and truth, as are other potentially harmful products.

Prioritizing Workers

The same conditions that challenged the performance of robots in our field sites—heat, dirt, unpredictability—challenge the well-being of human workers. Automated technologies are often presented as a method of addressing the issues that emerge from these conditions, such as high turnover and position vacancies (see, for example: Peters, 2019). Yet, newly integrated technologies are not a way of removing people from jobs that are "dirty, dangerous, and dull," as robots will still require people to work alongside them as they are configured and maintained. Common in technical parlance, the "3Ds of robotics" actually draw from discussions on the exploitative conditions migrant workers face—physically demanding work in unsafe conditions (Atanasoski & Vora, 2019). In these situations, humane autonomous technologies are a product of improving the environments in which human–robot collaboration takes place rather than removing the worker.

Recognizing the relay between humans and machines in automated processes is only a first step. With this recognition must come a prioritization of workers in the design of collaborative routines and infrastructure. When worker activity acts as a provisional measure to address the limitations of more rigid technologies, machines remain the central organizing principle. Claims that AI is "fully autonomous" create a vision of technology in which the experience of human workers isn't a necessary design consideration. But as our research suggests, people are very much still there, often upholding the image of autonomy through their acts of artful integration.

A commitment to ethical AI means interrogating industry practices that obscure the often low-wage work upon which it depends, and demanding better working conditions for those who occupy these positions. In European nations like France, Germany, and Sweden, board-level codetermination arrangements make way for forms of representative worker input on the procurement and adoption of workplace technologies (De Stefano, 2018; Jäger et al., 2022). Responding to the recent Blueprint for an AI Bill of Rights, senior counselor to the US Secretary of Labor Tanya Goldman argues that worker voice on the design and deployment of AI is critical to ensuring its safety and value in the workplace (Goldman, 2022). Yet, in the words of Christina J. Colclough on the circulation of principles and commitments toward more ethical futures of work, "unless we really start putting flesh to the bone, so to speak, and turning principle into practice, then they remain words of good intent" (Colclough, 2020). Across this chapter, we've sought to expound on such calls by illustrating the material impacts of AI in the present and responding with recommendations for how we might govern installation, evaluation, and maintenance across essential industries over time.

References

Abebe, R., Barocas, S., Kleinberg, J., Levy, K., Raghavan, M., & Robinson, D. G. (2020). Roles for computing in social change. In *Proceedings of the 2020 Conference on Fairness, Accountability, and Transparency*. Association for Computing Machinery, New York, NY, USA, pp. 252–260. https://doi.org/10.1145/3351095.3372871

Atanasoski, N., & Vora, K. (2019). https://read.dukeupress.edu/books/book/2553/Surrogate-HumanityRace-Robots-and-the-Politics-of

Atleson, M. (2023, February 24). Keep your AI claims in check. *Federal Trade Commission*. https://www.ftc.gov/business-guidance/blog/2023/02/keep-your-ai-claims-check

Bayus, B. L., Jain, S., & Rao, A. G. (2001). Truth or consequences: An analysis of vaporware and new product announcements. *Journal of Marketing Research, 38*(1), 3–13. https://doi.org/10.1509/jmkr.38.1.3.18834

Bell, S. A. (2022). *AI and job quality: Insights from frontline workers* (SSRN Scholarly Paper No. 4337611). https://doi.org/10.2139/ssrn.4337611

Bucher, E., Fieseler, C., & Suphan, A. (2013). The stress potential of social media in the workplace. *Information, Communication & Society, 16*(10), 1639–1667. https://doi.org/10.1080/1369118X.2012.710245

Colclough, C. J. (2020, November 13). AI as a tool for workers' empowerment, with Christina J. Colclough. *Carnegie Council for Ethics in International Affairs*. https://www.carnegiecouncil.org/media/series/aiei/20201113-ai-tool-workers-empowerment-christina-j-colclough

De Stefano, V. (2018). *Negotiating the algorithm: Automation, artificial intelligence and labour protection* (SSRN Scholarly Paper No. 3178233). https://doi.org/10.2139/ssrn.3178233

D'Ignazio, C., & Klein, L. F. (2020). *Data feminism*. The MIT Press.

Emerson, R. M., Fretz, R. I., & Shaw, L. L. (2011). *Writing ethnographic fieldnotes*. University of Chicago Press.

Endacott, C., & Leonardi, P. (2021). Identity-based motivations for providing the unpaid labor that makes AI technologies work. *Academy of Management Proceedings, 2021*(1), 12195. https://doi.org/10.5465/AMBPP.2021.12195abstract

Fox, S. E., Shorey, S., Kang, E. Y., Montiel Valle, D., & Rodriguez, E. (2023). Patchwork: The hidden, human labor of AI integration within essential work. *Proceedings of the ACM on Human-Computer Interaction, 7*(CSCW1), 81:1–81:20. https://doi.org/10.1145/3579514

Friedman, B., Leveson, N., Shneiderman, B., Suchman, L., & Winograd, T. (1994). *Beyond accuracy, reliability, and efficiency:Criteria for a good computer system*, (C. Plaisant, Ed., pp. 195–198). Association for Computing Machinery (ACM). https://doi.org/10.1145/259963.260253

Friedman, B., & Nissenbaum, H. (1996, July). Bias in computer systems. *ACM Transactions on Information Systems, 14*(3), 330–347. https://doi.org/10.1145/230538.230561

Gilluly, J., Tobey, D., & Goodlett, B. (2023, February 27). *Regulatory, litigation and disclosure considerations concerning artificial intelligence*. DLA Piper. https://www.dlapiper.com/en/insights/publications/2023/02/regulatory-litigation-and-disclosure-considerations-concerning-artificial-intelligence

Goldman, T. (2022, October 4). What the blueprint for an AI bill of rights means for workers. *U.S. Department of Labor Blog*. http://blog.dol.gov/2022/10/04/what-the-blueprint-for-an-ai-bill-of-rights-means-for-workers

Gray, M. L., & Suri, S. (2019). *Ghost work: How to stop silicon valley from building a new global underclass*. Houghton Mifflin Harcourt.

Hsiao, W. J., & Shorey, S. (2023). Machine visions: A corporate imaginary of artificial sight. *New Media & Society*. https://doi.org/10.1177/14614448231176765

Irani, L. (2015, January 15). Justice for "Data janitors." *Public Books*. https://www.publicbooks.org/justice-for-data-janitors/

Jackson, S. J. (2014). Rethinking repair. In T. Gillespie, P. J. Boczkowski & K. A. Foot (Eds.), *Media technologies: Essays on communication, materiality, and society*. https://mitpress.universitypressscholarship.com/view/10.7551/mitpress/9780262525374.001.0001/upso-9780262525374-chapter-11

Jäger, S., Noy, S., & Schoefer, B. (2022). Codetermination and power in the workplace. *Journal of Law and Political Economy, 3*(1). https://doi.org/10.5070/LP63159039

Joyce, K., Smith-Doerr, L., Alegria, S., Bell, S., Cruz, T., Hoffman, S. G., Noble, S. U., & Shestakofsky, B. (2021). Toward a sociology of artificial intelligence: a call for research on inequalities and structural change. *Socius, 7.* https://doi.org/10.1177/2378023121999581

Klinova, E. (2022). Governing AI to advance shared prosperity. In J. B. Bullock, Y. C. Chen, J. Himmelreich, V. M. Hudson, A. Korinek, M. M. Young & B. Zhang (Eds.), *The oxford handbook of AI governance.* Oxford University Press. https://doi.org/10.1093/oxfordhb/9780197579329.013.43

Lindlof, T. R., & Taylor, B. C. (2011). *Qualitative communication research methods* (3rd ed.). Sage Publications.

Littman, M. L., Ajunwa, I., Berger, G., Boutilier, C., Currie, M., Doshi-Velez, F., Hadfield, G., Horowitz, M. C., Isbell, C., Kitano, H., Levy, K., Lyons, T., Mitchell, M., Shah, J., Sloman, S., Vallor, S., & Walsh, T. (2021). *Gathering strength, gathering storms: The one hundred year study on artificial intelligence (AI100) 2021 study panel report* (pp. 1–82). Stanford University. http://ai100.stanford.edu/2021-report

Mateescu, A., & Elish, M. (2019). *AI in context: The labor of integrating new technologies* (United States of America) [Report]. Data & Society Research Institute. https://apo.org.au/node/217456

Mitchell, M., Wu, S., Zaldivar, A., Barnes, P., Vasserman, L., Hutchinson, B., Spitzer, E., Raji, D., & Gebru, T. (2019, January). Model cards for model reporting. In *Proceedings of the Conference on Fairness, Accountability, and Transparency* (pp. 220–229).

Moradi, P., & Levy, K. (2020). The future of work in the age of AI. *The oxford handbook of ethics of AI* (pp. 269–288). Oxford University Press.

Orr, J. E. (1996). *Talking about machines: An ethnography of a modern job* (1 ed.). ILR Press.

Peters, A. (2019, November 14). Meet the tireless robots that are helping to tackle the recycling crisis. *Fast Company.* https://www.fastcompany.com/90430489/meet-the-tireless-robots-that-are-helping-to-tackle-the-recycling-crisis

Roberts, S. T. (2019). *Behind the screen: Content moderation in the shadows of social media.* Yale University Press.

Star, S. L., & Strauss, A. (1999). Layers of silence, arenas of voice: The ecology of visible and invisible work. *Computer Supported Cooperative Work (CSCW), 8*(1), 9–30. https://doi.org/10.1023/A:1008651105359

Suchman, L. (1995). Making work visible. *Communications of the ACM, 38*(9), 56–64. https://doi.org/10.1145/223248.223263

Suchman, L. (2002a). Located accountabilities in technology production. *Scandinavian Journal of Information Systems, 14*(2). https://aisel.aisnet.org/sjis/vol14/iss2/7

Suchman, L. (2002b). Practice-based design of information systems: Notes from the hyperdeveloped world. *The Information Society, 18*(2), 139–144. https://doi.org/10.1080/01972240290075066

Vinsel, L., & Russell, A. L. (2020). *The innovation delusion: How our obsession with the new has disrupted the work that matters most.* Crown.

Wang, D., Prabhat, S., & Sambasivan, N. (2022). Whose AI dream? In search of the aspiration in data annotation. *Proceedings of the 2022 CHI Conference on Human Factors in Computing Systems,* 1–16. https://doi.org/10.1145/3491102.3502121

Williams, A., Miceli, M., & Gebru, T. (2022). *The exploited labor behind artificial intelligence.* https://www.noemamag.com/the-exploited-labor-behind-artificial-intelligence

PART II

Cognition and Emotion

Moving Spaces—The Affective Embodied Self in Tram Design and the Autonomous Imaginary

Hanna-Kaisa Alanen⊙ *and Rebekah Rousi*⊙

INTRODUCTION

The current climate of technological discussion is geared towards a fully immersive era of cyber, characterised by ambitious initiatives to train self-learning software (machine learning [ML] systems) with big data and developments in sub-fields of information technology (IT). While emphasis is placed on the power of digital algorithms and artificial intelligence (AI), simultaneously the physical world is being re-imagined and re-embodied. This transformation is particularly evident in growing urban areas as the majority of the world's population will live in cities

H.-K. Alanen (✉) · R. Rousi
School of Marketing and Communication, University of Vaasa, Vaasa, Finland
e-mail: hanna-kaisa.alanen@uwasa.fi; hanna-kaisa.hk.alanen@student.jyu.fi

R. Rousi
e-mail: rebekah.rousi@uwasa.fi

H.-K. Alanen
Faculty of Information Technology, University of Jyväskylä, Jyväskylä, Finland

© The Author(s) 2024   87
R. Rousi et al. (eds.), *Humane Autonomous Technology*,
https://doi.org/10.1007/978-3-031-66528-8_5

in the future (World Bank, 2023). Cities are shaped by various mobilities—social, technological, geographical, cultural, and digital—which create new forms of socio-material and cultural relations, impacting people's daily routines and practices (Freudendal-Pedersen et al., 2019). This emphasis is reflected in major infrastructural upgrades worldwide, such as hospitals, schools, and transportation systems. These infrastructures encompass emerging IT systems including AI, physical robotics, self-driving vehicles, evolving pervasive connectivity, and new, rapidly improving ways of information retrieval and display. While this is a leap into the future, some of its elements are more apparent, such as strategies like ACES (Automated, Connected, Electric, Shared), which represent ongoing developments in transportation (Adler et al., 2019). This suggests transformation in perspectives and engagement in ways people perceive, interact with, and comprehend their everyday environment. The shift in environmental experience occurs through design changes, morphing contextual circumstances, as well as shifts in understanding the relationship between physical and digital realms.

The development of IT-based systems, including sustainable mobility aspects like vehicle design, smart mobility, and infrastructure, is closely intertwined with efforts not only to achieve for example broader ecological stability, but also to enhance greater resilience in system performance encountered at a personal level within people's day-to-day existence (Herweijer & Waughray, 2018). This endeavour comprises considerations of availability, affordability, efficiency, and convenience, constituting a pivotal trend to address efficient transportation solutions in growing cities (Holden et al., 2019). Technological advancements in mobility, such as electric vehicles (EVs) and autonomous vehicles (AVs), ridesharing, and digital connectivity offer cities opportunities to create cleaner, more convenient solutions (Hannon et al., 2019). One prime example of this integration is in the public transport sector. Here, sustainability, within a broader scope, is an integral part of the value-based fabric of mass transportation, seamlessly incorporating aspects like safety, integrity, reliance, resilience, and customer service, among others (Abdallah, 2017). Despite ongoing discussions on the technological benefits of, for example, AVs, innovation diffusion and public acceptance is not always seamless; non-technological concerns often pose more significant obstacles to technology adoption (Othman, 2021). This can be seen in, e.g., safety concerns, ethical dilemmas, liability issues, and regulatory challenges.

In line with contemporary trends in infrastructure renewal and the evolution of systemic change contributing to urban revitalisation, *tramways*, and other forms of light railways, have experienced a global regeneration. Being popular internationally from the early 1800s through to the mid-1900s, tramways slowly began to be decommissioned during the 1950s, continuing until the early 1980s (Petkov, 2020). These vehicles began their history as horse-drawn carriages, gradually evolving into gas-powered machines, and finally becoming electrically powered cars. The reduction of tramway systems stemmed from the ideology of the "car society" of the era, advocating the idea of urban transformation that profoundly altered people's lifestyles. Car ownership became a symbol of modernity, individualism, and personal expression (Hård & Misa, 2008). Despite this, some cities such as Melbourne (Australia), Athens (Greece), Basel (Switzerland), and Helsinki (Finland) managed to keep their tramway systems intact. Over time, these have become beloved cultural icons that not only embody a distinct era in urban history but have also gained significant cultural recognition, serving as "prototypes"[1] for integration into smart city concepts (Rousi & Alanen, 2021).

The re-emergence of trams, labelled as the Tramway Renaissance, began in the mid-1990s and remains ongoing. This resurgence has brought a significant socio-technological upgrade that extends beyond the physical infrastructure (Petkov, 2020). This trend has also delineated a shift in the ways that people perceive mobility and conceptualise the urban environment (Moraglio, 2011; Souter, 2001). Trams serve as more than mere technical developments. Moreover, they also embody and convey a socio-cultural atmosphere within a specific temporal landscape.

This intrinsic connection is closely intertwined with the seminal nature and dynamics of *fashion*—as a universal concept that unfolds as a multi-faceted event (Entwistle, 2000). For this reason, in this context, the authors aim to present fashion as a lens (tool) and a cultural marker that captures the interaction of micro-level and macro-level socio-dynamic forces in times of change within the technological landscape (Cholachat-pinyo et al., 2002). The re-introduction of trams into urban spaces demarks engagement with global trends ingrained within the *technology-fashion* change that is also implicated with the re-definition of embodied

---

[1] Prototype, or 'prototypicality,' in accordance with Leder et al. (2004), refers to the amount to which an object is representative of a class of objects, built through experience (learned knowledge).

space sharing, social cohesion, preferable urbanity, and updating the public images of the cities themselves (Mackett & Edwards, 1998; Moraglio, 2011). From the perspective of re-thinking *space,* this has meant a reconfiguration of the travel pathways and surfaces in cities, promoting shared experiences and socially sustainable movement (Coles et al., 2023).

Motivations behind the new tramways represent a direct intersection with ideological ecological discourse. This stands particularly in relation to personal vehicle usage. Given that ethics may be considered to have affective qualities that engage specific emotional experiences (see e.g., Saariluoma & Rousi, 2020), it is worth assessing how the frame of fashion contributes to the evaluation and utilisation of the multidimensionality of the tramway and its systemic existence in users' interactive experiences. Specifically, focus is placed on how the embodied affective conceptualisation of *self* (identity and being) translates within the experience of a new tramway.

This chapter presents a study of the tram experience in Tampere, Finland, which marks the beginning of a new era in the city's history. The tram system has been implemented as part of a transformation towards sustainable and IT-based transportation systems, which is expected to significantly disrupt the way people experience and interact with urban transportation in the next decade (Baltic et al., 2019). Moreover, the technology of tramways has long been associated with the fantasy of automation and autonomisation (Petkov, 2020). The key goals of the tramway system are to improve easier and cleaner everyday life and transportation in the municipality, support urban growth and development, and enhance the city's appeal (Tampereen Ratikka, 2023).

EMBODIMENT IN SOCIO-TECHNOLOGICAL FASHION AND SYMBOLIC INTERACTIONISM

Maurice Merleau-Ponty et al. (2014) notes, "History, then is neither a perpetual novelty nor a perpetual repetition, but rather the *unique* movement that both creates stable forms and shatters them" (p. 90). As seen in the precarious history of trams, technology is tightly intertwined with social, cultural, and economic trends (Petkov, 2020). This means that in order to understand the relationship between humans and trams, or any vehicle for that matter, one must look beyond the technical and towards the dimensions that both frame and are framed by technical choices. The purpose of the fashion frame (SoTEM) we are launching, is to introduce the approach as a lens for understanding and structuring the complex connections between the different dimensions. Fashion weaves the experience of newness and meaningfulness, both as a social construct and as a socio-material phenomenon in physical objects, surpassing mere functionality (Petersen et al., 2016). Fashion, as a collective event, ultimately mirrors people's willingness to adapt to ideas and ideologies shared within society. This implies an embodied and situated social practice (Entwistle, 2000).

The cocoon of this section is characterised by the understanding that all technology, none-the-least transport-related technology, operates within social dimensions. Socio-technology, or the intersection between society and technology (Bunge, 1998), is thus referred to in order to express trams as both technical (material) and social-cultural (immaterial) technology. This means that technology operates within social plains both as a direct connector and mediator, as well as a symbolic vehicle (Nadin, 2007; Rousi, 2013a). The authors take a symbolic interactionist (Blumer, 1998; Mead, 1934) approach to illustrate and investigate a dialogical process of embodied experience of the *self* (see e.g., Rousi & Alanen, 2021). In symbolic interactionism (SI), there is an ecological understanding of the experience of self in light of and in relation to others. Through the lens of social psychology, this means that the *self* is both expressed and constructed through existence with and engagement in others (Bourdieu, 1990; Dunn, 1997; Sterne, 2003)—human and non-human.[2] When choosing to consume, engage, or participate in technologies and technology-enabled actions, humans enact their ideologically driven values (Cockton, 2017, 2020; Leikas, 2009). Technological experience is never simply an isolated engagement. Rather, it is confounded by the past, present, and what is anticipated and imagined for the future (Roto et al., 2011; Rousi, 2020; Wurhofer, 2015). This imagining of the future involves a decision on behalf of the individual to form an allegiance that once more goes beyond the material and logistic, towards the immaterial and transformational (Dunn, 1997).

---

[2] This additionally implicates the traditions of Actor Network Theory (ANT, see e.g., Latour, 2007) that views actors (human and non-human) as existing in networks in which mutual effect occurs.

Fashion, and the Socio-Technological Embodiment Model

Building upon Matteucci and Marino's (2016) view of fashion as a universal concept, part of a larger debate on its nature, fashion is extended to different cultures and societies. This perspective is influenced by classical sociologists such as Simmel (1957; 2012), who emphasised the way in which social dynamics within spatial contexts, especially in urban environments, shape human interactions, closely relating to the phenomenon of fashion (Pyyhtinen, 2020). Fashion is shaped within social meaning structures (semiotic systems, see, Peirce, 1905) as a cultural marker. It indicates the presence of certain traits or changes in a society or environment, manifesting itself temporally through places, products, systems, and experiences (König, 1973). Merleau-Ponty et al. (2014), sheds light on the adaptability of historical stereotypes (e.g., norms) within the cultural landscape, when people create a mental and practical framework as a basis for interpreting and engaging with their environment. This also characterises universal fashion as a practice. According to Merleau-Ponty, stereotypes "are not for that matter destiny, and just as clothing, jewelry and love transform the biological needs from which they are born, so too, within the cultural world, the historical *a priori* is only consistent for a given phase" (p. 90) requiring flexible responses to ever-changing cultural circumstances. However, the academic perspective on fashion is most evident in the realm of "dress,"[3] encouraging a closer examination of this field.

Mary Lynn Damhorst (2005) focuses on the psychological and communicative aspects of dress and the body. She has developed a *clothing-in-context model* as a sign system in the form of a radial chart, where each layer illustrates relationships among tangible and intangible elements, some of which may have multiple subcomponents. It begins with the basic perceptual features of clothing, such as shape, colour, lines, weight, patterns, and so on, continuing to the conditioning and treatment of materials. These are followed by layers related to the body (e.g., haptics), including its movements and situational surroundings. The model then extends outward to personal characteristics and social relationships, all governed by "grammar" and shared aesthetic rules within

---

[3] In fashion studies, the term 'dress' is used to encompass a wider spectrum than clothing, emphasising the comprehensive nature of appearance (see e.g., Kawamura, 2005; 2011).

the cultural context, contributing to the interpretations of meanings. Thus, in accordance with Damhorst, the relationship between the body and its ecological dimensions extends from the contextual and situational to the environmental and higher-level dimensions, which shape and interweave the connections between materiality (i.e., formal design features) and the human sense of self. The advantage of this contextual framework is that it illustrates the connections between individuals, society, and culture, where social-psychological processes play a role in shaping cultural change within the cultural context (Kaiser, 1997).

We demonstrate that the Damhorst's model can be adapted to encompass any socio-technological embodiment (Fig. 5.1), further reinforcing the conceptualisation of fashion as a socio-cultural manifestation that reflects and shapes social meanings and practices. This understanding of fashion enables a better comprehension of the relationships between temporality, sociality, culture, and the embodied self in any given socio-technological context. As a result, the adapted socio-technological embodiment model provides a multilayered framework for understanding the complex interactions among technology-fashion change, culture, self, and everyday contextual experiences. It further illustrates how these layers are embedded in relation to one another through dynamic and ongoing mutual processes.

As shown in *Fig. 5.1*, culture provides a broader spatio-temporal field (Bourdieu, 1996) for the interpretation of meanings (layer: *culture*), while multilayered social processes and the construction of shared meanings are created and enacted within this field (layer: *social dynamics*). In the context of our study, the tram case as an example, the city serves as a commonplace, providing scaffolding for social interactions and facilitating the cultivation of shared awareness, a sense of group belonging, and shared emotions (layer: *group association*). This framework acknowledges that the immediate embodied context and relatedness on a tram (layer: *social situation*), as well as multisensory experience of the tram environment as a dynamic and affective moving space (layer: *embodied perception*), are where the human-technology interactions occur.

The concept of embodied perception, influenced by technical (material) design entities, comprises various sublayers. In the context of a tram, these sublayers include the immediate body space, kinetic interaction, layout and accessibility, scenic perception, information communication, everyday surface aesthetics, and interior aesthetics. All of these sublayers collectively contribute to shaping the embodied experience of the self and

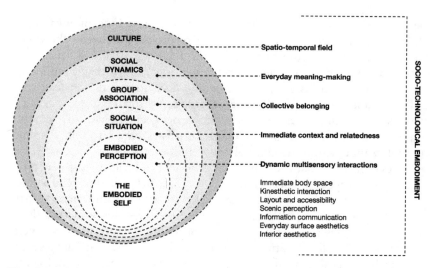

Fig. 5.1 Adaptation of a *clothing-in-context model* by Damhorst (2005) and conversion to a general *socio-technological embodiment* sign system format informing SoTEM

being. In this regard, there is a *relatedness* that is noticed in Merleau-Ponty's et al. (2014) theorisation of embodiment that sets the positioning of the body and its actions into a system of events that cause and affect the ways in which people both experience and are experienced by others (see also, Shusterman, 2005). In this sense, the adapted socio-technological embodiment model also has a connection to Merleau-Ponty's "phenomenal field," which refers to the holistic realm of sensory experiences. Embodied perception is not a passive process, but rather involves integrating various sensory inputs and contextual factors into a unified whole.

As the authors, we see the self in both its material and immaterial form—the "*me self*" (ecological self[4] positioned within the system of systems) and the "*I self*" (the reflective or internal self, somewhat abstract to the environs) (see, James, 1890). Thus, the logical progression of

---

[4] According to Neisser (1988), the ecological self is the self as directly perceived in the immediate physical environment. Today, it manifests within both natural and digitally constructed environments as part of a larger system of systems.

Damhorst's model places the self at the centre, highlighting the interplay between the embodied self in a tram and multidimensional technological experience, affecting the immediate body space. This understanding is relevant to studying how mobility systems are transformed in everyday life conditions as it sheds light on how personal values (ideology) and preferences, as well as smart technologies, influence people's response to different aspects of the tram vehicle and its related systems.

The social situation of the tram can be divided into two main domains. Firstly, interactions that occur during tram travel with others (e.g., mobile devices). Secondly, the broader social situation, extending from micro-level (family and personal circumstances) to macro-level situations (societal paradigms, social-political, environmental climate, etc.). Group association occurs with strains, communication, representations, and ideologies within the social situation as an act, or acts, of identification that actively situate the self—the *I self* and literally the *me self*—in relation to others (Blumer, 1980). *Particular others* (those who hold significance in relation to the self) and *general others* (those who are not identified as possessing significance) in turn are defined by group association. Culture frames the experience, its reading (interpretation), and how these socio-technological characteristics manifest in the first place (McCarthy & Wright, 2004; Shilling, 2004).

Embodied Semiotics—Multisensory Perception and Relatedness

The tram, and public transportation experience, are integral parts of the evolving urban landscape that go beyond the design of the tram vehicle and its infrastructure. The aesthetics of the tram connect with elements that supersede landscaping, tram stops, tram routes, street designs, movement, and other technical factors. Rather, the embodied aesthetic experience contributes to the experience of *being*—socially and culturally. It is this holistic experience of being, particularly the essence of relationality, that requires a deeper semiotic understanding that includes a rationality of its past, present, and unfolding future (Merleau-Ponty et al., 2014; Reynolds, 2020). This temporal aspect possesses an awareness (learned knowledge) of what has been, that is confounded by the identification and positioning of the individual in relation to this history. This manifests in present interactions, which are also influenced by an anticipated future (Michalco et al., 2015; Rousi, 2020). Merleau-Ponty draws parallels to this kind of temporal horizon and the way objects are perceived from different spatial perspectives, which is not limited to a single isolated moment. He further argues that the body takes herein possession of time and enables temporal horizons to exist for a present moment, thus actively "constituting time". This refers to the way people actively shape and experience time through embodied perception—rather than merely being passive recipients of "constituted time."

Design semiotics, or the study of sign systems in relation to design (Vihma, 2007; Warell, 2003), has deep roots in pragmatic philosophical traditions such as those represented by Charles Peirce (1905) and John Dewey (1908). Yet, design itself poses challenges towards understanding basic sign models such as Peirce's object, signifying element (sign or symbol), and interpretant. For, a design can be understood as both object and signifying element (Rousi, 2013a). It is on the one hand (whether artefact, system, or service) an object. Yet, on the other hand, it is a signifying element, that represents affordances and what can be achieved via the design (see e.g., Gibson, 1979). Design constitutes immaterial qualities such as symbolic values and references to other times and paradigms, as seen in activities related to sustainability and autonomous technology.

When individuals engage with trams as design objects, they undergo a transitional metamorphosis process that sees the interaction of mentally-bound information (mental content, Rousi et al., 2010) with multisensory information (Silvennoinen et al., 2015), and, in the cases of past and future, sense data (remembered sensory information, Rousi & Silvennoinen, 2018). This can be considered as *multisensory design semiosis* (Rousi, 2013b). In encounters with design objects, the multisensory experience can be broken down into three distinct yet related dimensions: (1) the formal, physical, or structural properties of the object (syntactic material dimension); (2) the expressive or semantic properties of the object (semantic dimension); and (3) the pragmatic dimension that encompasses the object's immaterial semantic qualities (pragmatic dimension) (see e.g., Vihma, 2007; Warell, 2003). These semantic properties may imbue the object with symbolic meaning and emotional significance (Fiore, 2010), and thus, also respond to concerns related to the object's experiential benefits beyond interaction (Krippendorf & Butter, 2008).

METHOD

Participants, Recruitment, and Research Ethics

The current study was conducted in collaboration with the Tramway Alliance, which includes partners such as the City of Tampere, Tampere Regional Transport (Nysse), and VR Group Plc, a Finnish state-owned company known for its passenger and logistics services. Participants were selected from a pool of about 2,000 registered candidates who had expressed interest in tram user testing during trial runs. Our research partner, Nysse, coordinated participant selection. Together with VR Group, they managed the trial run schedules and facilitated the researcher's data collection during these sessions, all of which took place during the COVID-19 pandemic.

A total of 30 participants (14 women, 15 men, and one participant identifying as "other") were recruited to participate in a two-part sequential one-to-one interview session. Participants represented five different age segments based on Nysse's classification: 17–25 years old, 26–40 years old, 41–55 years old, 56–70 years old, and over 71 years old. They were selected based on three pre-defined user groups: public transport users, public transport and car users, and car users. Nysse further categorised these groups based on different passenger (user) personalities, with group 1 comprising "saver" and "responsible" users, group 2 comprising "optimiser" and "enhancer" users, and group 3 comprising "cruiser" and "forced motorist" users. Participant representatives were chosen for each group to ensure a diversity of views and reasons for using public transportation, in alignment with Nysse's brand strategy.

As the data were collected during the test runs of the Tampere Tram in May 2021, when the tram was not yet in public use, most of the interviewees had no prior experience of travelling by the Tampere Tram. There were, however, some exceptions. Some participants had been involved in the test drives, typically taking just one trip. While participants' deeper attitudes towards the tram were unknown, their willingness to engage in these trial runs indicated a certain level of curiosity and interest in the tram project.

In alignment with ethical guidelines, participants were supplied with a Research Notification and Privacy Notice, explaining the study's broader context, procedures, fully anonymised data collection, usage and storage, and the participant's right to withdraw. Participants were also asked to sign an informed consent form in compliance with the University's ethical guidelines, Finnish National Board on Research Integrity, and General Data Protection Regulation (GDPR).

Interview Procedure

The research was conducted in Tampere over a two-and-a-half-week period. Data collection involved in-person thematic interviews, which comprised two consecutive parts. These interviews aimed to explore three key aspects: (1) socio-cultural dynamics (cultural processes); (2) tangible and intangible systems of signification (expressions); and (3) the holistic nature of the experience (social, emotional). Guided by a universal fashion perspective and in addition to the SoTEM model, the exploration was influenced by Kaiser's (1997, p. 59) contextual framework, which integrates such dimensions to enable the examination of shifts in meaning. The first part was a semi-structured interview held at a library, served to gain pre-travel insight regarding initial thoughts, expectations, and prior experiences. The second part, which forms the data and *results presented in this chapter*, occurred during the tram journey. This interview operated as a thinking aloud procedure, in which participants directly presented their experiences and thoughts as they interacted with their surroundings while moving through the city. Participants were given the opportunity to share their perceptions of the tram's design, appearance, usability, and related environmental changes. The interviewer asked open-ended questions about the participant's first impressions and their holistic experience inside the tram as a moving space. While the second interview primarily explored participants' real-time tram journey experiences, it also allowed them to supplement their responses from the first interview, though not actively encouraged. The entire journey took approximately one hour. Interviews were conducted while travelling from one end of the central city line to a suburban district. After reaching the final stop, participants changed to a returning tram. All comments were audio-recorded for verbatim transcription.

Analyses

All interviews were transcribed and analysed using ATLAS.ti software, which included coding of the data and content analysis (Carley, 1993; Hsieh & Shannon, 2005) based on three initial interview themes that encompassed the content of part 1 and part 2. From the analysis of the second part, focused on the tram journey, three key topics emerged: (1) scenic perception (through window); (2) kinesthetics (seamless movement and mobility); and (3) visual and spatial aesthetics (interior atmosphere). Results are based on a synthesised "assembly" derived from these emergent topics, which includes semiotic logic and its accompanying syntactic, semantic, pragmatic qualities, and affective dimensions. We adopt a discursive approach to report and explain themes pertaining to these topics adhering to our refined Socio-Technological Embodiment Model (SoTEM) of embodied perception. The model emphasises the multi-layered and multi-sensory nature of the tram on users' affective responses. Themes are: smooth and carefree motion (ride *comfort*); interconnected seamless mobility (*utility, convenience, and* autonomous *imaginary*); effortless, safe and inclusive transportation (*usability* and *accessibility*); speed and experience of time (*temporality*); embodied spatial aesthetics (spatial *awareness* and *being*); experiencing *urbanity* (the self, the tram and the whole in the city); appearance of a tram form (visual design and *expression*); colour co-design and shared decision-making (*inclusiveness* and *belonging*); tram as mediator in cultural significance and the city's identity (shared *values* and *memories*); socio-cultural ambivalence in colour perception (aesthetic preferences and *individuality*); and the unsettling of status quo via unsettling in colour disruption (shared *practices, norms, and values*). The themes are discussed in detail in the Results section (Sect. 5.4). Findings are presented as explanations that are accompanied by key examples extracted from the data illustrating the combined sentiments of participants.

Results

This study shows the rich multisensory interactions and socio-technological role of the tram as conveying meaning. The tram system's human interactive characteristics extend beyond its design and usability, encompassing its social and cultural presence in a specific context at a given time. Spatial aesthetic atmosphere played a crucial role in shaping participants' experiences and influencing their affective responses and embodied perception of the environment. This resonates with Merleau-Ponty's et al. (2014) notion that sensory qualities emerge in "indeterminacy," where sensory experiences lack full clarity but create an "atmosphere" through which formal design qualities gain significance. The qualities thus have an expressive value. Likewise, Spence (2020) emphasises that our interactions with the environment are influenced by all our senses, even when we are not consciously aware of their effects. This highlights the significant impact of embodied perception and atmospheric interaction on our well-being.

Tram Kinesthetics: Motion, Fluency, Stability, and Speed

The *Tram Kinesthetics* section explores the participants' embodied perceptions of the tram's unique aesthetic features, including its: (1) smooth and carefree motion; (2) fluency in seamless and interconnected mobility; (3) effortless, safe, and inclusive stability; and (4) rapid, accelerating, fleeting speed. These themes are closely tied to aspects of the tram experience such as ride comfort, utility, convenience, usability, accessibility, and the temporal dimension of the journey. This section sheds light on how these features contribute to the overall quality of the experience in relation to the embodied self.

The participants' initial impressions and perceptions of the tram journey were significantly influenced by their prior experiences of moving around the city, primarily with the public bus system. Many participants had embodied memories of their previous bus journeys, often characterised as "shaky" and "bouncy" due to the city's cobblestone streets. This comparison with previous modes of transportation revealed unique aesthetic features of the new tram system, providing valuable insights into the participants' experiences. One key aspect that was revealed was the smooth movement of the tram. This caught the attention of virtually all passengers from the start and was a recurring theme in their appraisals of the tram's competence during the journey. Compared to previous bus experiences, many participants highlighted the enhanced physical comfort and stress-free opportunities created by the smooth movement. This comfort contributed to a sense of safety, inclusiveness, and pure joy, as the effortless and seamless, yet efficient, movement of the tram provided a carefree and enjoyable experience:

> It's easy to fall asleep here because it's so steady and I don't have to worry about staying on the bench.
> (Female, 56-70 years old, public transportation user: saver)
> [...] this is soft, soft motion [...].
> (Female, 56-70 years old, public transportation and car user: optimiser)

The responses reflected sensations influenced by participants' prior embodied experiences, aligning with Merleau-Ponty et al. (2014), who posits that the body and bodily memories are integral parts of real-time lived experience. Consciousness extends throughout the body, oscillating between the present and the past. The tram was said to reduce feelings of stress, creating a space for relaxation. This was particularly true for private car drivers, who felt a positive sense of relief in being able to focus on other things besides traffic. These kinds of notions were also revealed when participants were asked about their perception of themselves travelling by tram while seeing cars driving on the road beside them. Some participants considered the tram a viable alternative option to a car, especially during their free time, offering an opportunity to rest while someone else takes care of the driving. Many perceived the tram as a convenient and easy mode of transport, especially in busy city centres where parking is a challenge:

> It feels so carefree somehow. I don't have to pay attention to anything else except staying on the bench. With this, one can have such a smooth ride [...]. I can focus on other things besides traffic. When driving a car, I have to be so careful regardless of the weather [...] the weather does not really affect this.
> (Male, over 71 years old, car user: cruiser)

Other participants expressed that the tram would provide convenience to families with two or more commuters, particularly in light of inner-city traffic. From the traffic perspective the efficiency and safety (carefree character) were emphasised. Stress and its relief via tram use was a reason for car drivers to seriously consider future tram use. The experience tended to highlight a rare moment in the everyday when one could potentially relax and enjoy. Car driving was pronounced as a risk with uncertainties about supportive infrastructure (parking) and scheduling (timetables). The tram was seen as the solution to these car-bound issues. These experiences align with Merleau-Ponty's et al. (2014) philosophical perspective on relatedness, in which the body, through its sensory experiences and spatial awareness, enables individuals to perceive the world in a holistic manner. Thus, participants' emphasis on convenience highlights the body's innate capacity to engage with the immediate environment, emphasising the significance of "here" and "now," with a focus on immediate sensory experiences and present-moment awareness.

Additionally, the notions expressed by participants expose a shift in attitudes towards the use of private cars, and the lack of any stigma associated with the use of trams. These perceptions signal a transformation and the imaginary crossroad in the realm of seamless mobility, where the boundaries between private, shared, and public transport are becoming increasingly blurred, disrupting the transportation status quo (Baltic et al., 2019). While a fully integrated IT-run mobility system is not yet widespread, participants' responses indicated the early stages of a diffusion process. This process offers a glimpse into the evolving landscape of daily mobility practices, as perceived by participants within specific contextual circumstances.

Further, many participants expressed enthusiasm about the prospect of bringing their personal bicycles or scooters onto the tram. This integration of the tram system into their daily lives represented a shift in their mobility habits, incorporating the affordances provided by the tram system. However, one participant, a male aged 26–40, particularly stood out due to his early adopter disposition towards electric vehicles (EVs). He owned an electric car, electric bike, and electric scooter, and he also expressed a keen interest in using the upcoming electric tram system in Tampere. His choice to embrace EVs was driven by ecological concerns, cost-effectiveness, and comfort. He eagerly anticipated the potential benefits that new innovations could bring to the evolving mobility landscape:

> I'm just interested in new things in general. I'm not the type of person who clings to the old, but rather looks forward to those innovations that can improve the quality of life. [...]. In the same way, I see that the tram does that.
> (Male, 26-40 years old, car user: cruiser)

He mentioned that he enjoys the convenience of being able to choose the best mode of transportation for each specific journey, and that he has used his electric bike for commuting to work. He also discussed the potential benefits of shared mobility options, such as short-term rental services for cars, and expressed a belief that car ownership will become less important in the future:

[...] car ownership will decrease for sure, if it becomes easy to rent a car for a short period. There are already those [...] Teslas and LEAFs that can be rented for short periods of time [...]
(Male, 26-40 years old, car user: cruiser)

This participant's responses suggest that a more versatile transportation system can be available for adoption, aimed at reducing people's stress in everyday life and improving overall convenience:

[...] one must be able to move around. It's just like a basic human right.
(Male, 26-40 years old, car user: cruiser)

This insight sheds light on the systemic optimism that will potentially be brought about by the trams as an interconnected facet of the larger urban mobility and lifestyle system. There is both relief and address of the changing circumstances faced by urban commuters who view the trams as an opportunity to improve overall life quality. However, as the city's tram system covers only a portion of the journey, requiring efficient feeder traffic, such as buses and cars, are also needed to ensure seamless mobility. Many participants expressed concerns about the availability and convenience of feeder traffic and the disruption to their established bus routes. Public debates had already raised questions about the future of autonomous mobility adaptation, which some participants believed to be just around the corner:

That tram is quite limited [...]. In my opinion, there is good transportation in Hervanta. However, the buses [...] will stop due to the tram. Now, they need to arrange cross-traffic [...]. People are a bit puzzled and hesitant about it, wondering how it will work and if it is a good idea. Moreover, the shuttle bus is a robot car. [...] there is a robot car coming there now...
(Female, over 71 years old, public transportation user: responsible)

The integration of autonomous mobility into the transportation system can also raise growing concerns about rapidly changing everyday practices. Moreover, interviews revealed that the appreciation of including various modes of transportation within the tram system, as part of a seamless mobility experience, applies to all users, including those with mobility aids such as rollators, wheelchairs, and strollers. This highlights the importance of accessibility and inclusivity, as these devices are essential for individuals with mobility impairments and for parents and caregivers travelling with young children. Participants praised the tram's accommodating design, which was particularly favourable for elderly passengers and those who had to stand during the journey. The tram's accessibility and inclusivity contribute not only to its functionality but also to its aesthetic appreciation. Perceived accessibility in mobility facilitates a satisfying life, increasing overall comfort and well-being (Friman et al., 2020), and plays a crucial role in how individuals encounter and experience the transportation system. With an aging population, there is a growing emphasis on inclusiveness in public transportation, especially for older individuals, who also oftentimes rely on their "cognitive age" rather than "chronological age" (Sudbury & Simcock, 2009), promoting self-fulfillment for all (Wolfe, 1997):

> It feels good, it feels like a soft ride. There are no sudden stops. This is quite important, especially if you're standing. It's not dangerous for the elderly.
> (Male, 41-55 years old, public transportation user: responsible)
> [...] it makes the transportation easier and of course elderly people, like my father who has slowed down a lot over these eighty-seven years [...] so I see it as a safety issue for these elderly people.
> (Female, 56-70 years old, public transportation user: responsible)

Participants also emphasised the low-floor design of the tram as a key feature for convenience and comfort, providing a smooth and effortless transition between the platform and tram, and the opportunity to just "walk in." The absence of stairs allowed passengers with mobility issues to access the tram with minimal to no assistance:

> When you look at it, it's easier to use with all kinds of means, wheelchairs and stuff, when there is almost no threshold...
> (Male, 26-40 years old, public transportation user: responsible)

The tram's wide doors and spacious interior were noted for their contribution to making it easier for passengers with mobility aids to move around and find a comfortable position. The designated area inside the tram, marked with a large yellow wheelchair infographic on the grey floor, provided a safe and secure place for these aids during the journey and was highly appreciated by participants:

It's a lot more spacious. Indeed, the wheelchair spot is near that [door], so you can leave easily [...] even if you have strollers at the same time.
(Male, over 71 years old, car user: cruiser)

The inclusion of various modes of transportation as part of the seamless mobility experience can be seen as an extension of users' physical capabilities. This creates a sense of extended embodiment and integration into their overall sense of self. In accordance with Merleau-Ponty et al. (2014), individuals using objects like a rollator or bicycle do not perceive these as isolated entities with specific dimensions. Instead, they consider how these items interact with the available space to function effectively, enabling them to expand their being-in-the-world, appropriate new instruments, and extend their capabilities.

Finally, the majority of participants experienced a rush of excitement from the speed and convenience during their initial ride. They enjoyed the acceleration from the city centre to 70 km/h towards a suburban district, known for its large student population and high-tech companies. The reasonable half-hour commute time from the inner city to the end of the line changed participants' perception of distance between the two places. Many noted the effectiveness of the tram's priority traffic signals and the resulting uninterrupted ride. Participants reported that "time flies" during the journey. The sense of speed seemed to affect participants' flow experiences, characterised by full attention and immersion in the activity (Csikszentmihalyi & Halton, 1981). The ride became enjoyable and absorbing:

I used to laugh about a five-minute difference, but it's not just about that, it's more of a whole feeling that it's not too cramped here, it's not too hot here, it doesn't smell bad here, and then, when it comes so briskly, the journey somehow seems to go faster, even though it's only a difference of 3-5 minutes, or even less, I don't know how much it really is [...]
(Male, 41-51 years old, public transportation and car user: optimiser)

The tram's rapid acceleration exceeded participants' current adaptation level, resulting in an intense positive response. For example, Frijda's (1988) law of change in emotions describes that emotions are not solely triggered by the presence of favourable or unfavourable conditions but by changes in these conditions, whether real or anticipated. The other design attributes of the tram also enhanced the sense of speed and satisfaction.

This reinforces the interpretation of the tram experience connecting to flow theory, as the multisensory features in themselves serve an immersive function in the experience.

Tram Perspectives on the City: Spatiality, Relatedness, and Expression

The *Tram Perspectives on the City* section explores the participants' perceptions of the tram's unique spatial perspectives and their relationality to the city's surroundings. These themes are explored through the lens of the tram's: (1) spatiality and windows as social interfaces; (2) immersive and transforming scenic views in relatedness; and (3) expression and aesthetic appreciation of the tram's form. The section sheds light on how these themes enhance the sense of being through spatial awareness, visual design, and expression. Additionally, this sense of *being* through the embodied self plays out in relation to the tram itself and the city and its urbanity.

The design of the windows in the tram aligned with Arnheim's (1977) notion of windows as interfaces and shelters, which "connected and separated creatures in their environment and related them to it" (p. 144), akin to digital user interfaces. The placement of windows also contributed to the modern and stylish appearance of the tram. Moreover, the tram's windows functioned as spatial elements that significantly impacted the overall atmosphere and illumination inside the vehicle. Many participants expressed aesthetic appreciation for how the ribbon-shaped design and infusion of natural light created a unique sense of spaciousness and openness within the tram.

Participants conveyed a sense of freedom, increased awareness, and connection to the city. For many participants, the panoramic view and amp visibility outside were significant dimensions that positively influenced aesthetic and interaction experiences. They provided a constantly changing story of the city that passengers could immerse themselves in without worrying about the journey. This was facilitated by active tram movement, which supports Arnheim's (1977) idea that spatial knowledge is best acquired through "purposeful locomotion" (p. 153) rather than stationary observation:

> [...] I get to observe the city [...]. I have time to observe the city differently than if I were driving myself, but also in comparison to walking,

because when walking you have to be careful of other pedestrians and follow traffic rules and traffic lights [...].

(Female, 41-55 years old, public transportation and car user: optimiser)

A flaneur-like experience was expressed by the participants who, while being one with the cityscape, were also removed in their "airy" mobile observation towers. Many participants were able to witness the rapidly changing landscape, offering a unique perspective on their familiar and commonplace urban environment and its transformation over time. Some expressed nostalgia for areas that were once familiar, and their tram ride prompted memories of certain buildings, places, and events. Others demonstrated excitement for the city's future and direct interest and curiosity towards it. Ironically, many gas stations were in the process of being demolished at the time of the test rides. The once indeterminate and even romantic spaces (Wilson, 2003) were now filled with buildings designed to follow the track as the tram entered the city. The journey inspired mixed feelings of a growing city. The tram was not just transportation as a means of travel through participants' commonplace, rather it provided a unique opportunity for them to connect with the transforming urban landscape:

Well, it's just nice to have something new, but I don't know if this [city] is really ready for it.

(Male, 26-40 years old, public transportation user: responsible)

These landscapes probably live in such a way that I would imagine every field will inevitably be filled with apartment buildings, but probably for places like this [where we are now], nobody can really do anything anymore.

(Female, 56-70 years old, car user: forced-motorist)

Another feature from the window was that of the green tram track. This captured the attention of almost all participants, many of whom had been following the landscape architecture in the surrounding area for some time. It was noted as a positive environmental change that improved the appearance of the street, enhancing the quality of everyday urban life. Phrases such as "boulevard", "esplanade", "park-like", or "big-city-like", reflected the transformation from an ugly road to a more elegant city boulevard, which historically has been a hallmark of sophisticated metropolitan areas (Searns, 1995). The greenery and its softening effect were described as contributing to the wellbeing of the urban environment, suggesting a level of environmental sophistication that residents were proud of. This is in line with contemporary values for liveable areas and sustainable design:

> This has become really nice now, with so much greenery, like an esplanade or boulevard. In the middle, there's a green area [...] It's definitely pleasing to the eye.
> (Female, 26-40 years old, public transportation user: responsible)

The impressions of the tram are caressed by the green-casing (grass-lined passages) of its tracks. The effects of the grassy strips ripple into the internal–external sentiments of the ride. Sustainability of the design takes on a direct reference to nature as the greenery is seen as breaking the asphalt-ridden characteristics of the old roadways. Furthermore, the participants' scenic perceptions were not confined to the external environment viewed through the windows. Rather, it also encompassed the appearance of the tram exterior. Despite being familiar with the tram after seeing it around the city for six months before the test rides, participants still perceived its appearance and design as an integral part of the surrounding urban landscape, shaping their perception of their hometown. This emphasizes the importance of understanding the tram's role in the broader perceptual field.

Almost all participants were impressed by the bow-shaped design of the tram, which features a curved front and large windshield that many found aesthetically pleasing. Comparing the form to traditional box-like trams or to the city's previous bus system, many associated it with modern and up-to-date qualifications. The tram's design was perceived as dynamic, efficient, and sleek, with participants using terms like "bullet-train-like", "shuttle-like", "fast-looking", "smooth-looking", and "streamlined". This suggests that form qualifications signified progress and forward-thinking, indicating that the tram contributed to the sense of being part of a contemporary commonplace. Their excitement and positive experience over the tram's form implies that its sleek design and modern features hold significant meaning for the participants beyond its practical function as a mode of transportation, as well as its positioning towards the systemic autonomous future:

The design of the tram is very modern. It looks fast, so to speak, with a fast design, with round shapes and angular shapes, so that it's a bit like a bullet train, even though it isn't […].

(Male, 26-40 years old, car user: cruiser)

This is more like a spaceship model. Like a shuttle […] the front, it's aerodynamic. […] it looks different from Helsinki's rickety square trams, aren't they just some straight […]. It's like a spaceship is actually going, like a future means of transport.

(Female, over 71 years old, public transportation user: responsible)

Statements of the modern aesthetics of the tram were connected to the curved nature of the front of its body. One participant emphasised the futuristic shuttle-like nature of the vehicle, comparing it to the outdated nature of other cities' trams. Another participant emphasised the temporal newness of the design which was stated to be a positive characteristic. This indicates that participants focused on the specific aesthetic qualities of the tram. Merleau-Ponty describes this as the "power of suspension," the ability to suspend or restrict one's attention within the field of perception to examine certain details.

Yet, reflections on the form were not all optimistic. Visual aesthetics are influenced by a range of factors, including previous experiences, personality factors, cultural background, and personal preferences (see e.g., Arnheim, 1974). As such, a few participants had different reactions to the same design based on these factors. One participant described the tram's bow shape as unimaginative, unaesthetic, unappealing, and unsatisfying, likening it to a "blunt-nosed caterpillar" and expressing disappointment in its impact on the surroundings and experience of the city environment. Another participant saw the tram as an "ugly grub-like creature" and was critical of its lack of aerodynamic design. They believed that a more streamlined design would have been more efficient and more pleasing:

I was looking at it from my own balcony, our balcony, when it passes here, and I think it's an ugly caterpillar, a "flat-faced caterpillar" […] it's not streamlined at all, so it consumes more electricity when it runs flat-faced, instead of being a little bit inclined […]

(Female, spouse of a man aged 56–70 years old in the same age group, car user: forced-motorist).

The aesthetics of the tram form allow it to serve as a means of self-realization. Positive reactions to the tram's design suggested that it fulfilled an aspect of participants' self-expression, while negative reactions indicated a sense of dissonance in their relationship to the surrounding urban environment. These perceptions can be associated with stylistic preferences. Merleau-Ponty et al. (2014) uses the concept of "style" to characterise the unity of the world. He compares it to recognising an individual based on their unique style of behavior or expression. This recognition of the world's unity occurs through experiences, even if a precise definition of that unity remains elusive. Merleau-Ponty acknowledges that knowledge, including our understanding of the world's style, is dynamic, evolving with time, perception, and new experiences, perspectives, and insights. He states that this evolving knowledge does not undermine the world's unity but rather reflects dynamic engagement with it.

Tram Colour and Aesthetic Preferences: Inclusiveness, Heritage, Individuality, Astonishment, and Disruption

The *Tram Colour and Aesthetic Preferences* section explores the participants' perceptions of the tram's colour. It strongly resonates with a process of citizen engagement that asked Tampere residents in earlier stages of the design process for their input into choosing the final colour of the vehicles. Several themes emerged that seemed to impact the experience of the colour. These were: (1) the colour red—as voted by the people of Tampere; (2) the industrial heritage of Tampere and its continuous historical role as an icon of modern technology; (3) personal colour perceptions and individual assertion; (4) surprise and astonishment in relation to the colour and overall visual impression of the tram system; and (5) symbol of commercialisation, contemporary brand value, and breach of cultural norms. The colour of the tram proved to be a prominent topic among the participants in the study, with many expressing strong feelings and attitudes towards its unique shade. According to Arnheim (1974), colours carry strong expression, as participants associated the colour with cultural, historical, and practical significance.

Those responsible for the tram design had previously engaged the citizens in the participation process by holding a colour vote, allowing them to have a word in the tram appearance. The participants could choose from three predetermined colours, two of which were different shades of blue and one was red. There had been a discussion about colours on social media and there were supporters for the colour pink as well, but it had not been approved as an option for the vote. Eventually, the colour red was chosen to be the colour of the tram. Many participants found the vote to be an exciting and important event, as it allowed them to feel included in the shared decision-making among the community members. Other votes were also organised during the tram's design path. One participant, who had also been involved in a special 13-person user testing group, whose members had been involved in testing the tram prototype at the beginning of its design process, described the shared intention of many participants towards the colour vote:

> I'm probably saying it for the fifth time now. This was designed by people from Tampere.
> (Female, 56–70 years old, public transportation user: saver).

Moreover, the colour red, despite varying opinions on the exact shade, was consistently associated with positive emotions and perceived as aesthetically pleasing and familiar. For most participants, the colour resembled that of old factory buildings, a nod to the city's industrial heritage. While some participants also associated the colour with the city's political and ideological roots as a working-class city which was not the primary focus for the majority. Instead, participants were more concerned with how the colour complemented the city's historically significant old factory buildings with chimneys, which have undergone adaptive reuse to new purposes. As such, the colour was seen as having cultural and historical significance and representing the city's identity. In addition to its symbolic importance, participants also noted that the colour served a practical purpose in making the tram easily recognisable and distinct from the blue buses:

> Maybe it's just because Tampere has such a red culture, that in the history of some red cities, it's still a working-class city, more of a working-class colour. [...] This is an old industrial city so I thought [brick-coloured] would be a reminder that it used to be an industrial city [...].
> (Male, 26-40 years old, public transportation user: responsible)

According to Arnheim (1974), colour perception is influenced by a range of psychological and perceptual factors in addition to physical stimuli, such as context, contrast, and the interaction of colours with each other. The Tampere Tram's colour was perceived differently by different people, with some finding it unappealing or disappointing, which highlights the subjectivity of colour perception:

> It's not a bright colour. It's a dull colour. It was a bit disappointing [...].
> (Male, 56–70 years old, car user: forced-motorist)
> It's not even a brick colour [...] we compared it to the red of bricks since Tampere is a city with a lot of brick buildings, so it would have been better. I am an aesthete [...] I am disgusted.
> (Female, spouse of a man aged 56–70 years old in the same age group, car user: forced-motorist).
> We talked about that brick red colour. I haven't seen any brick that colour [...].
> (Male, 41–55 years old, public transportation user: saver)

Furthermore, during the test drives that took place at the same time as the interviews, many participants were surprised to find that the trams in the entire system were not all the same colour. Some of the trams were a different colour than the original red that was voted on, and these trams were covered in advertisements. Some participants mentioned that there was a voting process for the original colour and expressed discomfort and confusion about the different colours of some trams, regarding the advertisements covering entire trams. Some suggested that the initial colour should still be visible which emphasised the emotional attachment to the original colour. Participants described that the primary aesthetics should be preserved and that advertisements should be well-placed, non-intrusive, and artistic. The presence of advertisements on some trams disrupted the original aesthetics and was even described as "messy" and "cheap looking." Overall, the presence of advertisements on some trams was seen as compromising the brand value and reputation of the tram system:

> In general, it has a negative appearance, [...] it does bring buses to mind if they are completely covered with some ads, but just when all trams are red or one or two are those red-black ones and then there's that LähiTapiola blue tram [...].
> (Male, 26–40 years old, public transportation user: responsible)
> To me, it's about being somehow uniform, that they are like the same, that's the feeling, but then if you start wrapping them with ads, then they're all different, and for some reason, it depends on who is advertising

and what kind of ad it is, but it does lower the value or make it feel cheaper[...].
(Male, 41–55 years old, public transportation and car user: enhancer)

This suggests that some participants perceived trams as a symbol of commercialisation and undervaluation of public space due to the changes in appearance that detract from the overall experience of a new public transportation system. This sentiment was also reflected in the tram's interior environment, which may indicate shifting values in terms of overload stimuli in people's daily lives:

I don't remember if it was certain, but I think that these were not supposed to be wrapped [...], so of course it kind of takes it in a way that they become big advertisements [...].
(Male, 41–55 years old, public transportation and car user: enhancer)

However, one male participant expressed an opposing view to the majority in terms of the aesthetics of the advertising trams. Despite his earlier aesthetic preference for the red colour, his initial preference changed due to the appearance of the advertising trams. He enthusiastically described,

Well, as soon as it got some colour, some sort of color life, it changes the whole look [better] [...] this colour thing, when we voted for it. I voted for the red one. Now that I have seen those taped blue ones [...] they are much nicer!
(Male, 26–40 years old, public transportation user: responsible)

Some participants expressed confusion about the different coloured trams in operation, which suggests that the breach of the cultural norm of community engagement created confusion. Citizens had come together with a shared intention to choose the colour of the tram, an act that also reflects collective acceptance and a shared emotional connection to the tram. Colour preferences revealed participants' varied collective and individual perceptions and emotions, largely stemming from many participants' involvement in the design process. These emotions were intertwined with the city's identity, its industrial past, shared memories, and personal preferences. Additionally, the presence of advertisements on some trams challenged cultural norms and practices. From the perspective of co-design, this also raises questions about the responsibility of considering participants' opinions.

CONCLUSION

The cultural context and dynamics of Tampere City, characterised by a unique history of academic and industrial heritage, were evident in the participants' perceptions and associations. This revealed a shared cultural perspective on their social world, urban environment, and its placement in technological discourse. According to Zerubavel (1999), cities have a tendency for creating thought communities to which individuals belong (p. 9). Simmel (1912) argues that the development of contemporary culture, seen through universal fashion, is characterised by the dominance of the objective spirit in shaping the individual's self-knowledge and personal identity. The objective spirit (or better known as objective culture) can be described as collections of tools, products, symbols, and rules that are created by humans and exist externally to any one person. Objective culture and fashion are integrated into individual identity and practices to form "subjective culture" (Nisbet, 1980).

The findings of this study are visualised in Fig. 5.2, which illustrates the atmospheric and environmental cues as described by Merleau-Ponty et al. (2014) and Spence (2020). These cues consist of three main elements: (1) scenic perception (observed through windows); (2) kinesthetics (seamless movement and mobility); and (3) visual and spatial aesthetics (interior atmosphere). The interwoven nature of the interior, along with its window-enabled connection to the surrounding urban spaces, opens a gateway to aesthetic appreciation through embodied and multisensory design semiotics, temporality (nostalgia and projection), and sustainable ideological engagement. The affective experiences of participants' embodied selves in their dynamic interactions with technology are closely connected to contextualization, allowing to examine how meanings of technology change as situations evolve within a specific spatio-temporal field.

While tramways, their design and infrastructure may be carefully documented, the systems within the systems feature a complex network of the material and immaterial that can never be fully accounted for. Some qualities came to the fore in the study when referring to the aesthetic and symbolic dimensions of the trams such as form or usage (car ownership),

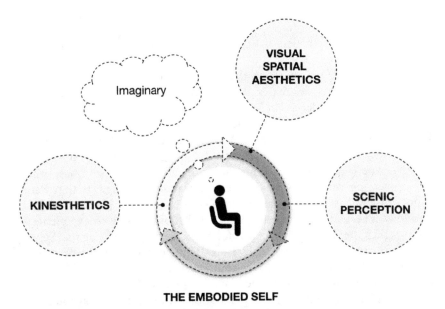

Fig. 5.2 The self in embodied multisensory tram experience

particularly in light of *self*, *identification* and *future*. The participants' perceptions and experiences of the tram journey in Tampere city were shaped by their cultural context, social and cultural presence, and prior experiences of public transportation.

Imaginings of a smart future were alluded to through the form of the chassis. Conflict arose in the responses of the participants, whereby some perceived the nose of the vehicle to be shuttle-like and aerodynamic, while others felt more tilt would have accentuated its futuristic ambitions. Sustainability and its connections to smart cities were accentuated through the greenery of the grassy track casing. Ideological dimensions included social democracy (accessibility and fairness) and decrease in car traffic. Yet, the main imaginary crossroad of the future appeared to be in people's mental image. Participants' reactions to the integration of autonomous mobility varied, with some already recognizing the need to adapt to changing habits for seamless mobility, while others expressed concerns and confusion about the future of transportation. This reveals a delicate balancing act between opposing forces such as group affiliation and individual assertion, conformity and independence, as well as dependence and freedom, which are typical of fashion changes (Shusterman, 2016).

The study lends reflection on the tram system emergence and appearance in the city, its aesthetics, experience and physical existence in a specific context and place. The study also established connections between universal fashion and embodied perception and introduced an adapted Socio-Technological Embodiment Model (SoTEM) to depict the multifaceted nature of embodied experience. According to Merleau-Ponty et al. (2014), experiences flow continuously, with each experience implicating and explicating others, using Paris as an example. He asserts that Paris is not merely a sum of separate objects or individual perceptions but embodies a certain style or sense grasped through a flow of experiences. Each explicit perception, be it a café, faces, or the bends of the Seine, contributes to the city's overall essence. Thus, objects are not perceived in isolation but as part of the overall sense that pervades a landscape or town, as is the case with the Tampere Tram. Ultimately, Merleau-Ponty emphasises that an initial perception without any background or context is inconceivable. Every perception relies on the subject's past, and the abstract function of perception involves encountering objects and implying a more underlying and implicit act by which individuals continuously shape and elaborate their perceptual milieu within a certain temporal horizon.

To draw on Juhani Pallasmaa (2012), embodied experiences may be observed through architectural sensations, as "[a]n architectural experience silences all external noise; it focuses attention on one's very existence" (p. 31). Attention is thus projected away from the building, or in this case vehicle, towards the individual and their positioning in the world. Architecture generally does not take centre stage within everyday practices. Rather, it provides the structural framework through which other encounters and interactions occur. Trams are both structures that frame other social situations, while also being structured and augmented by the surroundings (environmental, cultural, political, etc.). They present a multisensory integration of environmental and atmospheric cues that within the hussle of the everyday remain unnoticed, unless causing concern or threat. The self, from the *I self* through to the *Me self*, unravels via chains of interactions with objects and others. Pallasmaa describes how "[b]uildings and cities provide the horizon for the understanding and confronting of the human existential condition"

(p. 12). These structures serve as mental cues that trigger the imagination, inspire dreams, and fuel desire. There is no such thing as a technological structure that exists in isolation. Buildings and other structures engage consciousness in reflective states that impact one's sense of self and notions of being that are both embodied and spiritual within collective ethos of the times.

The Tampere Tramway system is not yet autonomous. It can be understood rather as a "Wizard of Oz" forerunner in a metropolitan transportation system that is intended to serve a smart city of the future. As such, this study enabled insight into the symbolic interactions that occur between the individual with the environment, technology, ideologies, past and projected future. Ideas about the future are echoed through sentiments of form, seamless mobility, and relatedness to the broader urban environment. The strongest notions reflected towards the future pertained to the changing urban environment—change the tramway and new mobility habits as a part of.

Acknowledgements The authors would like to express their gratitude to VR Group and Tampere Regional Transport Nysse for their financial support. Special thanks go to Senior Service Designer Mari Siikonen and Customer Relationship Manager Riikka Salkonen for facilitating interviews. The authors also acknowledge the valuable contributions of Pia Salmi from WSP Finland Oy, Jussi Hurskainen from Idis Design Oy, and Pasi Kuhmonen from Villivisio Oy. The collection of empirical data was made possible by the funding from the Faculty of Information Technology at the University of Jyväskylä. The authors are also grateful to the Emotional Experience of Privacy and Ethics in Pervasive Computing Systems (BUGGED) project funded by the Academy of Finland (funding no. 348391), and the University of Vaasa, School of Marketing and Communication (Digital Economy). Additionally, the authors would like to thank the Tiina and Antti Herlin Foundation and the Maj and Tor Nessling Foundation for their support through the Puistokatu 4 Science Attic.

References

Abdallah, T. (2017). *Sustainable mass transit: Challenges and opportunities in urban public transportation*. Elsevier.

Adler, M. W., Peer, S., & Sinozic, T. (2019). Autonomous, connected, electric shared vehicles (ACES) and public finance: An explorative analysis. *Transportation Research Interdisciplinary Perspectives, 2*, 100038. https://doi.org/10.1016/j.trip.2019.100038

Arnheim, R. (1974). *Art and visual perception*. University of California.

Arnheim, R. (1977). *The dynamics of architectural form: Based on the 1975 Mary Duke Biddle lectures at the cooper union* (Vol. 376). University of California.

Baltic, T., Hensley, R., & Salazar, J. (2019). The trends transforming mobility's future. *The McKinsey Quarterly*. Retrieved 20 March 2023 from https://www.mckinsey.com/~/media/mckinsey/industries/automotive%20and%20assembly/our%20insights/the%20trends%20transforming%20mobilitys%20future/the-trends-transforming-mobilitys-future-vf.pdf

Blumer, H. (1980). Mead and Blumer: The convergent methodological perspectives of social behaviorism and symbolic interactionism. *American Sociological Review*, 409–419. https://www.jstor.org/stable/2095174

Blumer, H. (1998). *Symbolic interactionism: Perspective and method*. University of California Press.

Bourdieu, P. (1990). *The logic of practice*. Trans. Richard Nice. Stanford University Press.

Bourdieu, P. (1996). *Distinction: A social critique of the judgement of taste*. (8th printing). Harvard University.

Bunge, M. (1998). Sociotechnology. In M. Bunge (Ed.), *Social science under debate: A philosophical perspective* (p. 297). University of Toronto.

Carley, K. (1993). Coding choices for textual analysis: A comparison of content analysis and map analysis. *Sociological Methodology*, 75–126.

Cholachatpinyo, A., Fletcher, B., Padgett, I., & Crocker, M. (2002). A conceptual model of the fashion process–part 1: The fashion transformation process model. *Journal of Fashion Marketing and Management: An International Journal*, 6(1), 11–23.

Cockton, G. (2020). Worth-focused Design: Approaches, contexts and case studies, Volume 2. *Synthesis lectures on human-centered informatics*, 13(2), i–203. https://link.springer.com/book/10.1007/978-3-031-02230-2

Cockton, G. (2017). New process, new vocabulary: Axiofact= a_tefact+ memoranda. In *Proceedings of the 2017 CHI Conference Extended Abstracts on Human Factors in Computing Systems* (pp. 747–757). https://doi.org/10.1145/3027063.3052755

Coles, A.-M., Clarke, I., & Piterou, A. (2023). A "poor man's carriage": System building and social interactivity in UK urban tramway development, 1860–1890. *Industrial and Corporate Change*, dtac063. https://doi.org/10.1093/icc/dtac063

Csikszentmihalyi, M., & Halton, E. (1981). *The meaning of things: Domestic symbols and the self*. Cambridge University Press.

Damhorst, M. L. (2005). Dress as nonverbal communication. In M. L. Damhorst, K. A. Miller, & S. Michelman (Eds.), *The meanings of dress* (2nd ed., pp. 78–89). Fairchild Publications.

Dewey, J. (1908). What does pragmatism mean by practical? *The Journal of Philosophy, Psychology and Scientific Mmethods, 5*(4), 85–99. https://www.jstor.org/stable/2011894

Dunn, R. G. (1997). Self, identity, and difference: Mead and the poststructuralists. *The Sociological Quarterly, 38*(4), 687–705. https://doi.org/10.1111/j.1533-8525.1997.tb00760.x

Entwistle, J. (2000). Fashion and the fleshy body: Dress as embodied practice. *Fashion Theory, 4*(3), 323–347. https://doi.org/10.2752/136270400778995471

Fiore, A.-M. (2010). *Understanding aesthetics for the merchandising and design professional*. A&C Black.

Freudendal-Pedersen, M., Kesselring, S., & Servou, E. (2019). What is smart for the future city? Mobilities and automation. *Sustainability, 11*(1), 221. https://doi.org/10.3390/su11010221

Frijda, N. H. (1988). *The Laws of Emotion. American Psychologist, 43*(5), 349–358. https://doi.org/10.1037/0003-066X.43.5.349

Friman, M., Lättman, K., & Olsson, L. E. (2020). Public transport quality, safety, and perceived accessibility. *Sustainability, 12*(9), 3563. https://doi.org/10.3390/su12093563

Gibson, J. J. (1979). The theory of affordances. *The ecological approach to visual perception* (pp. 67–82). Houghton Mifflin.

Hannon, E., Knupfer, S., Stern, S., Sumers, B., & Nijssen, J. T. (2019). *An integrated perspective on the future of mobility, part 3: Setting the direction toward seamless mobility demand*. McKinsey Center for Future Mobility. Retrieved 20 March 2023 from https://integral.ms/wp-content/uploads/2019/01/An-integrated-perspective-on-the-future-of-mobility-part-3.pdf

Herweijer, C., & Waughray, D. (2018). *Fourth industrial revolution for the earth harnessing artificial intelligence for the earth*. A report of PricewaterhouseCoopers (PwC). Retrieved 12 September 2023, from https://www.pwc.com/gx/en/sustainability/assets/ai-for-the-earth-jan-2018.pdf

Holden, E., Gilpin, G., & Banister, D. (2019). Sustainable mobility at thirty. *Sustainability, 11*(7), 1965. https://doi.org/10.3390/su11071965

Hsieh, H. F., & Shannon, S. E. (2005). Three approaches to qualitative content analysis. *Qualitative Health Research, 15*(9), 1277–1288.

Hård, M., & Misa, T. J. (Eds.). (2008). *Urban machinery: inside modern European cities*. MIT Press.

James, W. (1890). *The principles of psychology*. Henry Holt & Co.

Kaiser, S. B. (1997). *The social psychology of clothing: Symbolic appearances in context*. Second Edition. Fairchild.

Kawamura, Y. (2005). *Fashion-ology: An introduction to fashion studies*. Bloomsburg Publishing.

Kawamura, Y. (2011). *Doing research in fashion and dress: An introduction to qualitative methods*. Bloomsbury Publishing.

Krippendorff, K., & Butter, R. (2008). Semantics: Meanings and contexts of artifacts. In H. N. J. Schifferstein & P. Hekkert (Eds.), *Product Experience* (pp. 353–376). Elsevier.

König, R. (1973). *The restless image: A sociology of fashion*. Allen & Unwin.

Latour, B. (2007). *Reassembling the social: An introduction to actor-network-theory*. Oxford University Press.

Leder, H., Belke, B., Oeberst, A., & Augustin, D. (2004). A model of aesthetic appreciation and aesthetic judgments. *British Journal of Psychology, 95*(4), 489–508. https://doi.org/10.1348/0007126042369811

Leikas, J. (2009). *Life-based design: A holistic approach to designing human-technology interaction*. VTT Technical Research Centre of Finland.

Mackett, R. L., & Edwards, M. (1998). The impact of new urban public transport systems: Will the expectations be met? *Transportation Research Part a: Policy and Practice, 32*(4), 231–245. https://doi.org/10.1016/S0965-856 4(97)00041-4

Matteucci, G., & Marino, S. (Eds.). (2016). *Philosophical perspectives on fashion*. Bloomsbury Publishing.

McCarthy, J., & Wright, P. (2004). Technology as experience. *Interactions, 11*(5), 42–43. https://doi.org/10.1145/1015530.1015549

Mead, G. H. (1934). *Mind, self, and society* (Vol. 111). University of Chicago Press.

Merleau-Ponty, M., Landes, D., Carman, T., & Lefort, C. (2014). *Phenomenology of perception*. Routledge.

Michalco, J., Simonsen, J. G., & Hornbæk, K. (2015). An exploration of the relation between expectations and user experience. *International Journal of Human-Computer Interaction, 31*(9), 603–617. https://doi.org/10.1080/10447318.2015.1065696

Moraglio, M. (2011). La bataille de la route [The Battle for the Road]. *The Journal of Transport History, 32*(2), 224. Retrieved 24 March 2023, from https://www.proquest.com/openview/094d58de8c287a520d ec85d9a093ad53/1?pq-origsite=gscholar&cbl=37653

Nadin, M. (2007). Semiotic machine. *The Public Journal of Semiotics, 1*(1), 85–114. https://doi.org/10.37693/pjos.2007.1.8815

Neisser, U. (1988). Five kinds of self-knowledge. *Philosophical Psychology, 1*(1), 35–59.

Nisbet, R. (1980). *History of the idea of progress*. Basic Books.

Othman, K. (2021). Public acceptance and perception of autonomous vehicles: A comprehensive review. *AI and Ethics, 1*(3), 355–387.

Pallasmaa, J. (2012). *The eyes of the skin: Architecture and the senses*. John Wiley & Sons.

Peirce, C. S. (1905). What pragmatism is. *The Monist, 15*(2), 161–181. https://doi.org/10.5840/monist190515230

Petersen, T. B., Mackinney-Valentin, M., & Melchior, M. R. (2016). Fashion thinking. *Fashion Practice, 8*(1), 1–9. https://doi.org/10.1080/17569370.2016.1147699

Petkov, D. (2020). The emergence of the modern French tramway as a socio-technical novelty. *Tramway renaissance in Western Europe: A socio-technical analysis* (pp. 151–228). https://doi.org/10.1007/978-3-658-28879-2

Pyyhtinen, O. (2020). Simmel's resonance with contemporary sociological debates. *The Routledge international handbook of simmel studies* (pp. 33–45). Routledge.

Reynolds, J. (2020). Embodiment and emergence: Navigating an epistemic and metaphysical dilemma. *Journal of Transcendental Philosophy, 1*(1), 135–159. https://doi.org/10.1515/jtph-2019-0008

Roto, V., Law, E., Vermeeren, A. P. O. S., & Hoonhout, J. (2011). User experience white paper. Bringing clarity to the concept of user experience. Result from Dagstuhl seminar on demarcating user experience, September 15–18 (2010). *Disponible en ligne le, 22,* 06–15. Retrieved March 24, 2023, from https://drops.dagstuhl.de/opus/volltexte/2011/2949/pdf/10373_AbstractsCollection.2949.pdf

Rousi, R. (2020). That Crazy World We'll Live in—Emotions and anticipations of radical future technology design. In R. Rousi, J. Leikas, & P. Saariluoma (Eds.), *Emotions in technology design: From experience to ethics* (pp. 141–153). Springer. https://doi.org/10.1007/978-3-030-53483-7_9

Rousi, R. (2013a). From cute to content: User experience from a cognitive semiotic perspective. *Jyväskylä Studies in Computing, 171.* University of Jyväskylä.

Rousi, R. (2013b). Formidable bracelet, beautiful lantern: studying multi-sensory user experience from a semiotic perspective. In *Design Science at the Intersection of Physical and Virtual Design: 8th International Conference, DESRIST 2013, Helsinki, Finland, June 11–12, 2013. Proceedings 8* (pp. 181–196). Springer.

Rousi, R., & Alanen, H. K. (2021). Socio-emotional experience in human technology interaction design—a fashion framework proposal. In M. Rauterberg (Ed.), *Culture and Computing. Design Thinking and Cultural Computing: 9th International Conference, C&C 2021, Held as Part of the 23rd HCI International Conference, HCII 2021, Virtual Event, July 24–29, 2021, Proceedings, Part II* (pp. 131–150). Springer International Publishing. https://doi.org/10.1007/978-3-030-77431-8_8

Rousi, R., & Silvennoinen, J. (2018). Simplicity and the art of something more: A cognitive-semiotic approach to simplicity and complexity in human-technology interaction and design experience. *Human Technology*, *14*(1). https://doi.org/10.17011/ht/urn.201805242752

Rousi, R., Saariluoma, P., & Leikas, J. (2010). Mental contents in user experience. *Proceedings of MSE2010*, *2*, 204–206.

Saariluoma, P., & Rousi, R. (2020). Emotions and technoethics. In R. Rousi, J. Leikas, & P. Saariluoma (Eds.), *Emotions in technology design: From experience to ethics* (pp. 167–189). Springer Nature.

Searns, R. M. (1995). The evolution of greenways as an adaptive urban landscape form. *Landscape and Urban Planning*, *33*(1–3), 65–80.

Shilling, C. (2004). *The body in culture, technology and society*. Sage.

Shusterman, R. (2005). Pragmatism: Dewey. In B. Gout & D. McIver Lopes (Eds.), *The Routledge companion to aesthetics* (pp. 141–152). Routledge.

Shusterman, R. (2016). Fits of fashion: The somaesthetics of style. In G. Matteucci & S. Marino (Eds.), *Philosophical perspectives on fashion* (pp. 91–106). Bloomsbury Publishing.

Simmel, G. (1957). Fashion. *American Journal of Sociology*, *62*(6), 541–558.

Simmel, G. (2012). The metropolis and mental life. In J. Lin & C. Mele (Eds.), *The urban sociology reader* (pp. 37–45). Routledge.

Silvennoinen, J. M., Rousi, R., Jokinen, J. P., & Perälä, P. M. (2015). Apperception as a multisensory process in material experience. In *Proceedings of the 19th International Academic Mindtrek Conference* (pp. 144–151). https://doi.org/10.1145/2818187.2818285

Spence, C. (2020). Senses of place: Architectural design for the multisensory mind. *Cognitive Research/ Principles and Implications*, *5*(1), 46. https://doi.org/10.1186/s41235-020-00243-4

Sterne, J. (2003). Bourdieu, technique and technology. *Cultural Studies*, *17*(3–4), 367–389. https://doi.org/10.1080/0950238032000083863a

Souter, I. A. (2001). An analysis of the development of the tramway/light rail concept in the British Isles. *Proceedings of the Institution of Mechanical Engineers, Part F: Journal of Rail and Rapid Transit*, *215*(3), 157–166. https://doi.org/10.1243/0954409011531486

Sudbury, L., & Simcock, P. (2009). Understanding older consumers through cognitive age and the list of values: A UK-based perspective. *Psychology & Marketing*, *26*(1), 22–38. https://doi.org/10.1002/mar.20260

Tampereen Ratikka. (2023). *The Tampere Tramway Story*. Tampereen Ratikka. Retrieved August 24, 2023, from https://www.tampereenratikka.fi/en/the-tramway-story/

Vihma, S. (2007). Design Semiotics—Institutional experiences and an initiative for a semiotic theory of form. In R. Michel (Ed.), *Design research now* (pp. 219–232). Birkhäuser Verlag GmbH.

Wilson, E. (2003). Against Utopia: The romance of indeterminate spaces. In A. Bingaman, L. Sanders, & R. Zorach (Eds.), *Embodied Utopias* (pp. 274–280). Routledge.

Warell, A. V. (2003). *Design syntactics: A functional approach to visual product form. Theory, models, and methods* [PhD Dissertation]. Chalmers University of Technology, Gothenburg.

Wolfe, D. B. (1997). Older markets and the new marketing paradigm. *Journal of Consumer Marketing, 14*, 294–302.

Wurhofer, D. (2015). *Characterizing experiential changes—Temporal transitions of user experience* [PhD Dissertation]. University of Salzburg, Salzburg. Retrieved March 24, 2023, from https://eplus.uni-salzburg.at/obvusbhs/content/titleinfo/5015270/full.pdf

World Bank. (2023). *Urban development*. Retrieved August 24, 2023, from https://www.worldbank.org/en/topic/urbandevelopment/overview

Zerubavel, E. (1999). *Social mindscapes: An invitation to cognitive sociology.* Harvard University Press.

CHAPTER 6

Whose Mental Model? Multi-stakeholder Most Advanced Yet Acceptable (MAYA) Visions of Disruptive Autonomous Maritime Technology

Rebekah Rousi

INTRODUCTION

> We're looking for something that's disruptive but not unprecedented.
> (Gary Hamel)

On March 23rd 2021, the *Ever Given*, a massive cargo ship the length of the Empire State Building became stuck in the Suez Canal, preventing traffic by other ships through the canal (Gambrell, 2021; Stubley, 2021). While luckily no human being was injured, the incident caused great costs in global trade and logistics due to the inability of other vessels to pass through the waterways. The canal was blocked until March 29th, causing an estimated USD\$9.6 billion in loss of trade for each day it was stranded

R. Rousi (✉)
School of Marketing and Communication, University of Vaasa, Vaasa, Finland
e-mail: Rebekah.rousi@uwasa.fi

R. Rousi et al. (eds.), *Humane Autonomous Technology*,
https://doi.org/10.1007/978-3-031-66528-8_6

125

(Russon, 2021). Reasons for the occurrence were said to be high winds, with the large amount of cargo (containers) acting like a sail. Additionally, it is said that both technical and human error-based errors may also have been at play (BBC, 2021). Nonetheless, on-board the vessel there were 18,000 containers of goods that were seized with the ship over a 900,000-euro compensation dispute, causing additional delays and costs (Paris & Wang, 2021). If nothing more, this incident in the Suez Canal has served to demonstrate the ripple effects of events that occur within contemporary systems. For instance, the effects of goods withheld on the ship can be seen in delays and changes to product schedules and releases in stores such as Aldi (Doody, 2021). Moreover, substantial quantities of fuel (oil and natural gas) for instance were prevented from movement, due to the event. Interestingly, commercial pressure in itself has been identified as a risk factor for safety culture in maritime traffic (Darbra et al., 2007).

In a study of the most influential human factors contributing to maritime accidents between 2011 and 2016, Coraddu and associates (2020) observed that lack of knowledge, lack of skills, ignoring training, safety awareness and cutting corners were major reasons for cargo vessels being grounded or stranded. Devising ways to reduce risk through minimising human error is one main motivation for the drive in autonomous maritime development (Veitch & Alsos, 2022).

With approximately 90% of global trade occurring via sea, the maritime industry is one of the most complex and oldest industries in the world (Main & Chambers, 2015). People remain at the heart of the industry despite the myriad of technologies that are utilised to enable the logistics and traffic flow of insurmountable amounts of cargo and other phenomena (e.g., naval, research vessels, etc.). Sea trade and technology have played significant cultural roles throughout human history. Thus, it should be remembered that humans and their sensory perception exist in many dimensions of maritime vehicles and their movement. Humans are responsible for their conceptualisation (the ideas behind the technologies and how they will be realised), design (embodiment of these ideas through formalisation processes), engineering (calculation and actualisation of design and material properties), operation, utilisation, direction and further significance. Furthermore, in an ever increasingly autonomous maritime environment, humans are increasingly responsible for the programmed logic of the systems (Ahvenjärvi, 2016). Not only do people's ideals, beliefs and values come into play within the development of maritime technology, but so too do the biases, errors and fixations that are translated from human thought to actionable artefact, service and system.

The chapter applies the Most Advanced Yet Acceptable (MAYA) (Hekkert et al., 2003; Loewy, 1951) principle to understand the current direction and vision of autonomous maritime technology, and then challenge this vision through highlighting its design fixation (Person et al., 2008) –adherence to known imaginings and logic that have accrued through discourse and experience. The theoretical article explains the links between cognition, domain expertise and design to show that through learned knowledge various parties hold differing sets of expectations for desired design features and technological logic. Yet, within the public imagination—and subsequently prevailing technological developments—specific ideas, notably manifested through popular culture and the like, set the path for how future design developments unfold. The aim is to problematise *whose visions* are driving current developments. The chapter is an endeavour to expand future autonomous technology design directions by first highlighting the fixated nature of current visions, and then second illustrating how through re-thinking the human at the centre of the design we may enable a richer Co-human (human-artificial intelligence co-existence) that is not only efficient, but sustainable and humane.

The chapter begins with a brief history on ship piloting, in order to show how it has developed, in light of needs and knowledge. The chapter progresses by discussing human maritime factors in respect to the need for technological innovation, i.e., to increase safety and wellbeing of staff and other stakeholders, as well as to avoid potential disasters caused by incidents such as the Ever Green incident. The MAYA principle is explained, and is followed by a discussion on design fixation and how design fixation guides experiences of MAYA—defining how people recognise the qualities of design and innovation. The mental models of multiple stakeholders are considered in relation to MAYA, drawing attention to the differences of stakeholder groups. The chapter concludes by proposing a model to dismantle the 'one-logic' MAYA—Yet Unknown but Better (YUBB). The overall aim of this chapter is to take stock of the current un-human fixation there is with future maritime design and introduce a humane approach to re-plant the human in the future of the sea.

Piloting and the Human Factor in Autonomous Maritime

As a historical industry, maritime navigation and design have taken many forms and standards. Regardless of the changes in shape, speed, energy, emissions, etc., the general idea of the logistics remains the same— the construction of purpose-made sea-bound vessels that are capable of performing the tasks in question whether it be transportation of cargo, people, fishing or otherwise. The maritime has played a key cultural role throughout human history as it allowed not only travel, but the interchange between products, languages and behaviour that have set forth to shape the multisensory experience and stories of the contemporary world (Paine, 2014). The guidance of seacraft and its crew have differed through the centuries. 'Pilots' or 'guides' of ships were named as early as the sixth century and an even earlier ancestor of the pilot can be seen in literature dating back to the first century AD (FFPM, 2023). A pilot role is an individual who has extensive knowledge and experience of specific waters and terrains in which a vessel is moving, and who serves as a guide to aid its safe passage. Traditionally, due to the vast range of ship travel, captains have not possessed sufficient knowledge of the diverse waters in which they travel. Local pilots are more adept at guiding vessels through shallow and narrow passages. Pilots in this sense, can be understood as the land-sea interface of maritime navigation (Main & Chambers, 2015).

During the 1600s, Dutch pilots became a part of either the ship's crew or piloting organisations. These individuals began to systematically record the surroundings and create sea charts in order to provide guidance and documentation for others. Around the same time, Piloting Acts or national laws regulating piloting began to emerge in Europe. This gave rise to the professional status of pilots. To this day, piloting remains a prominent profession in the maritime industry and can be understood as the key human factor that connects maritime technology (vessels and other navigational equipment) and the elements with human-centred goals (Hontvedt, 2015). While pilots are the key factor in ensuring safe navigation in difficult, narrow and shallow waters, one must not forget the importance of safety for these humans. Due to the challenging conditions including varied weather conditions, long and uncomfortable work shifts, safety concerns for the pilots themselves have often been raised (Darbra et al., 2007).

Psychological and health-related research have focused on the detrimental effects of piloting on body and psyche (Chambers & Main, 2015; Tait et al., 2021). These effects include stress, hypertension and other ill-effects on physical fitness caused by factors such as inadequate exercise levels, stress eating (mental compensatory behaviour) and other unhealthy lifestyle choices (Barbarewicz et al., 2019). Yet, knowing how to address all of these issues—from vessel (s) to professional health and safety—has proved a difficult and debatable task (MacLachlan et al., 2012). One of the most obvious long-term design solutions and moves towards solving these problems has been the idea that if we remove the human element (human factor) from the piloting situation itself with the aid of artificial intelligence (AI), we will be able to remove the likelihood of human factor related accidents (see e.g., Allianz, 2015; Rolls-Royce, 2016). This idea has been in existence for a significant amount of time, and increasingly societal technological efforts have been focused on achieving this goal (Relling et al., 2018). An autonomised maritime is understood as providing the opportunity to adapt to future challenges that include both the need to meet safety and environmental standards, as well as reduce costs (Ahvenjärvi, 2016).

Future Maritime Discourse

In maritime technological discourse there are two prevailing directions through which we understand the future of shipping and piloting: (1) self-navigating vessels; and (2) remotely operated vessels (Relling et al., 2018). Within both scenarios the main aim is to reduce the presence of humans—either on the bridge or the vessel entirely. Changes in the presence of human operators will cause significant alterations in maritime traffic and logic in general. Relling et al. (2018) argue that the removal of humans from the picture of shipping is simply a reductionist idea. Through addressing safety via the removal of human factors, scientists and technologists are simplifying or trivialising complexity. While simplicity in itself can be argued as complex (Rousi & Silvennoinen, 2018), Rasmussen (1997) claims that 'all work situations leave many degrees of freedom to the actors for choice of means and time for action' (p. 187).

The human role within systems comprises an overwhelming number of dynamic dimensions that are near impossible to account for through mere implementation of AI technology. One simple example of this can be seen in self-service checkouts that demand attendance by at least one to four human staff members—shop assistants and security—for the purposes of usability assistance, alcohol purchase, discounts and theft prevention to name some. Similar to this self-service example, Relling et al. (2018) stress that the emergence of new technological systems also brings new properties and problems that did not exist earlier (i.e., bugs in the automatic piloting programme and vulnerability to cyber security issues). While safety is claimed to be an antecedent for replacing humans on ships, different forms of safety concerns also arise in interaction with the novel components (Levenson, 2004).

While vast investments are currently made into the digital transformation of global transport with the direction of AI systems still being determined, there should be active discussion and consideration for what (ethical and 'best'—efficient, effective, fruitful) direction our techno-cultural society should take. So-called visions of the future are based on established ideas that are perhaps already now outdated. Ahvenjärvi (2016) cites initiatives that began in the 1970s to establish a fully automatic offshore industry that was subsequently demonstrated by Japanese technologists in the 1980s. Fully autonomous un(hu)manned surface vessels already exist in abundance in fields such as the military, coast guards and ocean research.

Complexity of Human-Technology Relationships

There is a symbiosis that exceeds the mere ability for humans to work with technology. Rather, humans should be understood as an intricate part of the systems from logic to outlook and action. The very existence of any type of technology has been defined and created by cultural forces that render the significance of the artefacts and their function (Murphie & Potts, 2003). Technology is formed through human cognition, is an expression of human cognition, and in turn, influences human cognition (Shaffer & Clinton, 2006). With knowledge of humans, human systems and in particular, embodied cognitive-affective processes that have seemingly advanced over the last three hundred years, it would not make sense to revise our traditional views on the future and autonomy of machinery (Rousi, 2020).

Thus, already within the small scope of this current discussion there are two main questions that should be highlighted: (1) if humans are the main point of concern within the safe and efficient operation of technology, why do we need to embed the qualities of humans within its logic?; and (2) if, from what research has revealed over the last few centuries, humans are still a highly advanced psycho-physiological species in terms of their capabilities for flexible thought, problem-solving, creativity and embodied cognition (unconscious, subconscious and conscious representationalism and processing), then why are they not incorporated more—for what they are—into the design and development of emerging systems? From the outset, humans, human error and human bias cannot be separated from the logic of AI, as AI and all technology are the products of human thought (Ahvenjärvi, 2017; Belk, 2021; Relling et al., 2018; Vakkuri & Abrahamsson, 2018). Yet, failing to acknowledge this and neglect the incorporation of human strengths within the development of a new vision of maritime could prove disastrous from a number of perspectives. None the least, humans *should* be able to live in harmony with autonomous systems.

Addressing Human Factors in Autonomous Maritime Technology

It is reported that anywhere from 50–90% of maritime accidents contributing to injury or death have been caused by human error (Cockroft, 1984). From the perspective of piloting, around 90% of these incidents have occurred in confined waters. Maritime safety, health and well-being can be discussed from a number of perspectives—personal, environmental, community, economic, etc. Much of the literature focusing on the occupation of maritime piloting concerns studies relating to health factors (Main & Chambers, 2015), decision-making and safety (Hetherington et al., 2006), knowledge transfer (Tuncel et al., 2022), communication and leadership (Chauvin et al., 2013; Kim et al., 2021), mental models (Orlandi et al., 2015; Imset, M., & Øvergård, 2017) and personality (Barca, 2019). In particular, problems have been identified relating to stress, fatigue and implications on physical fitness as well as eating habits (Carotenuto et al., 2012; Main & Chambers, 2015). Some of the factors contributing to these pilot-related physiological issues can be seen in the work conditions of the pilots. These conditions can often be characterised as isolated (Darbra et al., 2005) and unfamiliar, waterways and weather conditions can be challenging (Nielsen et al., 2013), and shifts overall are often long and tiring (Main & Chambers, 2015). These are some of the factors that contribute to stress and fatigue. Other mediating factors relate to limited exercise and extended periods of attention and concentration (Cook & Shipley, 1980).

Another contributor that has been somewhat discussed pertains to the maritime pilots as people—personality traits and accessibility for studying. Personality traits can be defined as characteristics or qualities that exhibit people's outlooks, attitudes, motivations and actions (Eysenck, 1976). Often researchers have difficulties in accessing pilots to study. This may be due to a number of reasons including availability (between work shifts), as well as personality traits—both within the individual and their demeanour and/or disposition towards the research, and/or due to the psycho-physiological effects of the work itself. These effects can be described in terms of for instance burnout and over-commitment leading to social disengagement (Basinska & Gruszcynska, 2020; Lehr et al., 2010; O'Brien et al., 2004). Thus, Barbarewicz and associates (2019) highlight that there are possibilities that existing research represents biases within their results, with a tendency to focus on 'healthy workers'—those capable of and willing to engage in studies—while down-playing or under-estimating the levels of strain and stress that the maritime pilot population actually experiences overall.

The basic personality traits that are considerably desirable for the profession of maritime piloting can be seen to embody resilience and humility, goal orientation, the ability to cope with change and uncertainty, ability to take control, yet also possess high levels of empathy and intersubjective awareness. These qualities are coupled by the need to be attuned to the environment through the body and its senses, as well as to act and react in logical ways to various situations. These qualities resemble the ideal thinking-feeling autonomous system, or Emotion AI (Zhao et al., 2022). The authors of this article hold the concern that justifications for the design, development and technological road-mapping of maritime technological autonomy to date, have simply focused on the shortcomings of the human factor in maritime logistics (Porathe et al., 2018). This grossly underestimates not only the strengths and sophistication that humans as intelligent organisms in maritime traffic have for its smooth running, but also underplays the valuable role they hold for further technological development in the industry (Ahvenjärvi, 2016). Strong mental and embodied models, combined with personality traits, form a substantial organic (cognitive-affective) database from which technology developers should endeavour to mine and utilise within their design of a human-technology future.

A burning issue in the direction of future maritime technology hinges upon mental (cognitive) fixations. People from diverse fields and professional domains possess fixations, and in the case of the present article, design (idea) fixations of what the future technology should look and be like. The question is—something that is also applicable for the autonomous car industry: Whose fixation are we developing with? Are the intricacies of domain-specific maritime piloting knowledge (mental models and embodied know-how) being taken enough into consideration within the development of future, scalable autonomous technological design directions? And, could in fact, the professional maritime piloting knowledge and *body* be used to dismantle current ideas and deliver even better, unknown (unprecedented) solutions?

Here, we focus on the human role of the maritime pilot, yet in doing so, we offer a glimpse at both the complexity of the human-systems relations, as well as the ways in which we can reconfigure and redefine the parameters of the directions in which emerging maritime technologies should take shape. Psycho-physiological factors influence the ways in which maritime professionals imagine and envision the future of maritime technology and its logic. These human factor-related details affect the 'fixated' image and understandings of what maritime technology is, what it could be and what it should be. The knowledge held by maritime pilots also influences the mental models of what is *Most Advanced Yet Acceptable* (MAYA) within the visions and realisation of future maritime technology. Domain-specific knowledge held by these professionals affects what they understand as being feasible and desirable. Psycho-physiological as well as sociological factors known by maritime pilots also aid in the understanding of how the eventual technological solutions will be accepted and integrated from a multi-stakeholder and multidimensional perspective.

Design Fixation and the Challenge of Making New

Design is an apt arena for studying problem-solving as design problems are often ill-defined (Purcell & Gero, 1998). Ethical design and development (e.g., Saariluoma & Rousi, 2020; Vakkuri et al., 2020) for instance, not only face challenges in ethics and their ambiguity, but in relation to obstacles of unpredictability when conceptualising the future and its conditions. It is important to consider a non-linear and non-fixed way of shaping the future through design—harnessing temporality while abandoning it in approach. Rather than imagining wholes, we should consider the steady building blocks based on values, principles and consistencies that may be reconfigured in infinite ways depending on what opportunities and challenges emerge. Design problems, wicked, ill-defined or well-defined, always provide opportunities for creative solutions and innovations (Fahey, 2016). Similarly, these domains prove considerably 'wicked' from the perspective of design fixation.

The term 'fixation' is described by the Merriam-Webster (2023) dictionary as the act of fixing or fixating—concentrating and sticking to something. From the cognitive perspective, fixation alludes to the process of blocking the completion of certain types of cognitive processes that pertain to creative idea generation, problem-solving and even memory (Chrysikou & Weisberg, 2005; Crilly & Cardoso, 2017; Jansson & Smith, 1991; Purcell & Gero, 1998). Fixation can be both beneficial and detrimental. On the one hand, fixation can assist in concentration and the strengthening and automatisation of highly practiced activities. On the other hand, fixation may prevent one's ability for flexible and analytical thinking that allows the discovery of diverse avenues (Fig. 6.1).

Design fixation is generated through factors such as attentional blink, whereby human attention is drawn to specific characteristics based on past knowledge, experience and emotional reactions towards particular phenomena (Weingarten et al., 2016). The ways in which humans learn about phenomena and how it is framed (associated with other phenomena

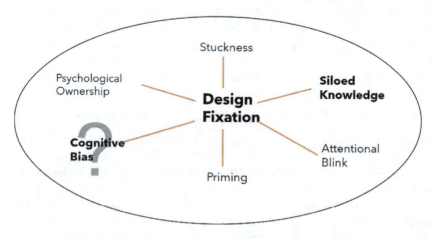

Fig. 6.1 Design fixation (adapted from Crilly & Cardoso, 2017)

and sentiments) shape how phenomena are mentally represented. Design fixation can be seen as a form of 'stuckness' in terms of how individuals understand phenomena (Crilly & Cardoso, 2017).

There is also the element of psychological ownership (PO). PO is the psychological (cognitive and emotional) bond that people have with objects, domains, places, etc. (Asatryan & Oh, 2008; Pierce et al., 2003). This type of cognitive-emotional relationship to phenomena contributes not only to a sense of expertise, or perceived authority over information pertaining to the phenomena, but also determines the commitment one has to matters related to and surrounding it (Pierce et al., 2003). PO is particularly important to remember as this article progresses as it helps explain the relationship between mental models and understandings of MAYA from an emotional perspective.

Across all fields and none the least cultural industries (i.e., art, design, music, etc.) design fixation presents challenges, particularly in terms of creative thinking and bringing designs forward to an innovative and constructive state. Purcell and Gero (1998) have examined this in the context of design sketching especially among less experienced practitioners and students. Arguably in the sketches of students when skills and ideas are still underdeveloped, design students often demonstrate a premature commitment to a solution. Rather than exploring ideas and alternative solutions through research, they often choose from known options. This is also a common problem among more experienced design professionals.

Jansson and Smith (1991) challenged mainstream design discourse by illustrating that despite the designer role of shaping the world and driving novel innovation, designers are fixated with particular ideas. Through exposing designers to images of possible design problem solutions before a design session, designers become fixated with details of the images and their overall conceptual properties. Exposure to prior ideas and conceptualisations dramatically affects the means through which designers envisage the potential design outcome. Prior exposure blocks mental access to alternative ways of solving design problems. Purcell and Gero (1998), argued that the foundations of fixation originate from the necessity to draw upon two types of mental representation of the problem itself: (1) the *conceptual space*—abstract knowledge of principles, rules and concepts that may be used as tools for problem-solving; and (2) *object space*—physical objects, elements and features that may be appropriated within the concrete design to practically solve the problem. Difficulties rest in the ability to shift from the object space to the conceptual space—that is, from looking directly at known and materialised solutions to problems towards looking at the problems and their properties in themselves, in order to discover different pathways towards the solution.

There is also a very practical cognitive explanation for the preference of object space and drawing on previously known physicalities in our problem-solving processes. This explanation rests on cognitive-affective preferences for the familiar (Monroe, 1976; Rousi & Silvennoinen, 2018). Familiarity increases processability, as repeated exposure means increased opportunities to learn the presented information, its patterns and sequences. This in turn becomes cognitively embedded, increasing processing fluency (Reber et al., 2004; Zajonc, 2001). Thus, it is little surprising that designers either consciously or subconsciously gravitate towards known solutions as this form of preference is hardwired into human cognitive-affective processing. The necessity to revert to the *conceptual space* when analysing ill-defined, wicked or perhaps any design problem regarding true innovation, demands greater levels of higher-order cognitive processing (abstract and critical thinking) (Weiss, 2003). Or, in other words, higher amounts of cognitive load.

This provides a clear hindrance in the fostering of future design directions as both designer education, and industry, rely heavily on already existing examples and visioning. Images and scenarios that are significantly old often take hold in the design ideation and processes for emerging technologies as they have become cognitively incubated through culture (Edwards, 2010). The impact of this is pronounced because the same models that are used to train or familiarise designers with particular ideas and approaches are also the ones that form the basis of the understanding within designers' minds of what the solution will be like. The role of the professional domain in shaping individuals' mental representations of phenomena, problems and their solutions is subsequently of interest for the purposes of this current article.

Conceptual Design and Disrupting Fixation

Conceptual design is a process in which ideas (concepts) are generated, deliberated, analysed, evaluated and selected generally at the beginning of a design or development process (French et al., 1985). This is considered to be a front-end process that is implemented shortly after identification of the need or problem in question (Jansson & Smith, 1991). The aim of this design phase is to set the foundation for the main technical concept of the project. While on an overall scale, the time spent in this phase is relatively short, the effects of this phase may carry major implications for the subsequent phases, direction and outcome of the process. In other words, the early conceptual development provides a critical step in any design project as it foregrounds the vision, steps and framing of not simply the output of the process but also of the conceptual contents of the design problem.

Within this phase, Jansson and Smith (1991) outlined that once again, designers and developers are engaged within two mental or cognitive spaces: (1) *the conceptual space*; and (2) *the configuration space*. While we have already briefly described the conceptual space and its function in dissecting, rearranging and analysing design problems in relation to their conceptual building blocks, the configuration space is the space in which designers actively construct alternative solutions for these problems. The configuration space is different to the physical space in that the physical space is a zone in which physical stimuli, and memories of physical stimuli inform the conceptualisation of the problem's solution. Yet, the configuration space can be seen as an area of opportunity in which the basic elements generated within the conceptual space may be configured to create something new.

Thus, the configuration space can be understood as a productive imaginary space in which information is arranged into operational solutions. This is the area in which the potential (precedented and unprecedented) physical object is mentally represented. These solutions include anything from rough sketches and names, to storyboards, narratives and the actual overall product or system itself. In order to deliberate and develop functional ideas within the configuration space, as usually happens within any design and development process, there is interaction between the configuration and conceptual spaces. The conceptual space in which understanding of the problem at hand occurs, often influences and causes changes within the configuration space. Alterations to the configuration space are motivated by changes in the levels of abstracts and mental representation of concepts. Changes can only occur within the configuration space through alterations emerging in the conceptual space (see Fig. 6.2).

There is the need to understand how to encourage design problem-solving deliberation processes towards the conceptual space rather than directly to the object space. Additionally, ease of movement and flow between the conceptual and configuration spaces should be made fluent.

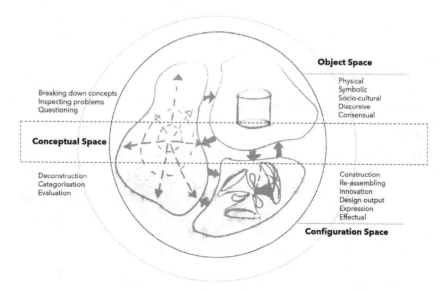

Object Space

Physical
Symbolic
Socio-cultural
Discursive
Consensual

Breaking down concepts
Inspecting problems
Questioning

Conceptual Space

Deconstruction
Categorisation
Evaluation

Construction
Re-assembling
Innovation
Design output
Expression
Effectual

Configuration Space

Fig. 6.2   Design spaces model

Obstacles that prevent the ability to understand design problems in an abstract manner, and then configure these understandings into operable compositions, then back again, should be identified and addressed. *Discovery* in the conceptual design sense means a journey in which designers identify as many alternatives and opportunities as possible, not simply for producing a solution but for uncovering the multiple facets of the problem. Design is a research process.

Through this conceptual model it is understood that there are several ways to tackle fixation and encourage movement between the mental spaces. One method to achieve this is called the Parameter Analysis (PA) in which designers and developers identify and explicate the boundaries of spaces relevant for various domains of knowledge (Jansson & Smith, 1991; Moreno et al., 2015). Not only does PA identify and separate the conceptual space into domain-specific spaces, but the identification of the relationship between the object space and the conceptual space is held vital. Unfortunately, design fixation involves a form of conceptual and configurative blindness that may confound problems rather than solve them.[1] Design fixation manifests in repetition, similarities, being 'stuck-in-a-rut' and non-explainability in designer-led decision-making.

Implicit commitment to one strain of thought is often referred to as 'mechanised thought'. This is a cognitive process that follows a previously established method of thought. Mechanised thought, or functional fixedness, is a type of long-term cognitive block that is contextually bound and situationally induced (Luchins & Luchins, 1959). When thinking of the technological future there are usually biases towards understandings of machines that will eventually function autonomously. Seeing beyond autonomy is perhaps the most challenging, yet pertinent objective that may be placed, particularly when considering the development of an ethical human technological future. Rather than turning towards previously established examples of what the future will look like, perhaps a more profound way of addressing the future through the design would be to re-focus towards the conceptual building blocks of the design problems in question (Jansson & Smith, 1991).

Most Advanced Yet Acceptable

The design fixation section focused on characterising the ways in which designers become fixed, or stuck, with previously represented ideas. Related to design fixation is the notion of Most Advanced Yet Acceptable (MAYA). MAYA was coined by futuristic designer Robert Loewy (1893–1986) to describe the way that designers should aspire to negotiate between the known and the new in order to generate designs that were both seemingly novel, yet palatable by larger groups of people (Friis Dam, 2021). The idea behind this relates to the ways people seek novelty and a sense of progression within the products they consume, particularly in light of evolving cultural and societal trends, or fashions (see e.g.,

---

[1] Consider the potential problems of dismissing humans in the development of future autonomous maritime technology—unemployment, bias and severe consequences for human safety—when all the conceptual components are not incorporated and adjusted within the configuration space. Simply stating potential, for instance, ethical implications is not enough when the execution of a design concept that precedes ethical deliberation in the conceptual space is undertaken. This will result in a double-layer (compounded) ethical dilemma within the system: (1) that the ethical considerations were not actively accommodated for within the design and development process; and (2) that it is known that ethical deliberations in the configuration space should be made during the early stages of design and development engagement.

Rousi & Alanen, 2021; Saariluoma et al., 2021), yet they prefer elements of familiarity in the designs and concepts that are emerging (Hekkert & Leder, 2008; Thurgood et al., 2014). The human mind prefers familiarity as it enables efficiency and fluency when identifying and processing information in the form of patterns (Rousi & Silvennoinen, 2018). This also enhances reactivity in relation to social-emotional cues within the designs (Rousi & Alanen, 2021).

Loewy was well known for his designs of the US postal service logo, Coca-Cola bottle, the Shell Oil logo, Greyhound bus logo, Airforce One logo and others. The challenge that Loewy identified was that although there may have been vast alternatives available for solving design problems, the adult mind draws heavily on known representational (physical or other symbolic) examples in order to identify and accept phenomena for their function and purpose. This is often referred to as typicality (Thurgood et al., 2014). Typicality increases the likelihood that mental information contents match the encountered design (Saariluoma & Rousi, 2015). As Loewy (cited in Friis Dam, 2021) argued,

> The adult public's taste is not necessarily ready to accept the logical solutions to their requirements if the solution implies too vast a departure from what they have been conditioned into accepting as the norm.

Like computers, humans are programmed—socially and culturally conditioned—to perceive, recognise, process and respond to phenomena through discrete laws of logic (Hofstede et al., 2005). Children may be seen as more open to new ideas and alternative ways of understanding phenomena, as their mental representations of how things 'should be' are not as fixed (fixated) as adults (Vygotsky, 1980). What children as socially learning (Bandura & McClelland, 1977) beings do, however, is looking towards their role models for ideas and standardisations on beliefs, behaviour and practices. This means that they learn and are conditioned into particular ways of processing information, and associate specific meanings and codes of behaviour accordingly. A solution may be preferred because it resonates physically, symbolically or behaviourally with what is already known through previous exposure (i.e., through cultural and social discourse). Yet, the contents of these cognitively established solutions that exist in the object space may not properly match or address the contents of the problem existing in the conceptual space.

Viewing future maritime technology through the lens of MAYA, it may be questioned as to whether the removal of humans from the sea vessels will eliminate incidents involving human error. Or, whether there is an entire field of issues implicated in this removal that indicates the necessity for designers and developers to re-enter the conceptual problem space of maritime design. Already at this point, issues have been raised concerning the potential exacerbation of human error through AI programming and lack of maritime expertise among developers (Ahvenjärvi, 2016). Moreover, other identified ethical problems such as the displacement of human workers, complexity of responsibility and accountability, ambiguity of logic and blurring of transparency, may be caused to not simply remove humans from maritime technological systems, but instead, revise their roles within these systems.

At this pivotal point in technological history, the point at which AI, remote, autonomous and embodied systems are becoming infiltrated in societies, the role of the human needs to be revised. There is an urgency to understand how technology and its ecosystems can best serve human and humane purposes, and can be best re-configured to address the burning issues that have inspired the now-fixated ideas. These issues include safety, accuracy, speed, efficiency, quality and sustainability (environmental, social, economic). In order to do this, there is the need to better understand how and whose ideas the design fixation has been formed upon. The following sections focus on questioning prevailing design visions on autonomous maritime technology development through examining the mental models and issues concerning maritime pilots in particular. This information is then compared to the mental models of various actors from diverse domains including designers, developers, policymakers and general public. The details affecting the ways in which maritime pilots form their mental models of the industry and its technology in addition to professional knowledge, include the professions impact on skills and embodied knowledge, responsibility, stress and physical factors.

Revising the Removal of Humans—A Quick Check

When analysing the nature of autonomous technology, we may refer to Leveson (2004) who highlighted that by establishing independence from a human operator through installing or building an automatic, or autonomous device, the risk for human error simply shifts from one player to the next. The responsibility effectively moves from the heavy machinery operator to the designers and development team. If errors are inherent within the system they devise, the result will be not simply that one vessel misbehaves, but all vessels. Particular errors would be repeated throughout the entire 'autonomous' system, which may at worst be catastrophic. When reviewing the above-mentioned causes for major maritime accidents, it should be noted that two of the primary types of faults rest in *leadership* and *supervision* as well as *organisation*. Perhaps more attention should be placed on how to utilise AI to support leadership and supervision, and even to advise on the organisation of operations—from business and society to workload.

In order to develop a more effective, safe, ethical and sustainable maritime, we should be focusing on human strengths within the industry. Afterall, logistics, sea transport and portside processes are human. They have been developed by humans for humans. As designers and builders of the sea vessels, humans provide the best interface between the ships, the natural elements, artificial elements and human systems, provided that they have enough skill, experience and the right personality traits to negotiate these high-pressure activities. Moreover, it is the minds and bodies of pilots who have interfaced sea vessels and the elements for thousands of years. These should be the informants of future maritime technology development.

One challenge for developing a highly automated, remote or autonomous maritime, is the transferral of knowledge from human experts to artefacts and systems. The reason being, is that we may consider human knowledge as an iceberg. The amount of knowledge that people can consciously explicate, or voice aloud, is a portion of what they actually know (Fig. 6.3).

As Fig. 6.3 illustrates, a significant amount of expert knowledge is implicit (Baars, 2011; Collins, 2010). One of the fundamental problems in technology development is the transfer of the *best human-based information* (data)—expert domain knowledge—into system logic. The greatest challenge with this task is posed by the quantity of tacit knowledge that is relied on in day-to-day activities. Everyday operational knowledge, with its embodied, qualitative (experiential), sensual (semi- and unconscious sensations) and automatised (expertise beyond the point of representation—disappearing 'self-talk' and engagement in the flow of the tasks through action) (see e.g., MacIntyre et al., 2014; Montero, 2016) nature is difficult if not impossible to linguistically represent.

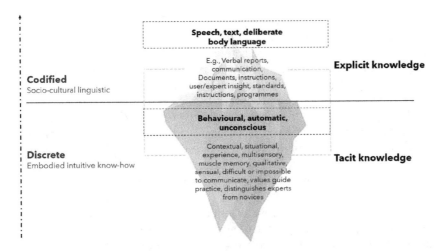

Fig. 6.3 Knowledge iceberg—Explicit versus tacit knowledge

MENTAL MODELS OF MARITIME PILOTS

The transferral of human professional maritime knowledge and logic, is to date, impossible in its entirety. Interviews, conversations and observations are limited in efforts to develop maritime systems that can compensate or even improve the performance of human pilots and crew. The major findings of De Maya et al.'s (2020) study on human-based contributions to maritime accidents were: (1) improper design, installation and working environment; (2) inadequate leadership and supervision (similar to Coraddu and colleagues (2020)); (3) inadequate safety management system—inadequate procedures or deviation from Standard Operating Procedure (SOP); (4) inadequate safety management system: substandard monitoring; (5) lack of communication and coordination; (6) lack of safety culture; (7) lack of training; (8) lack of, improper or late maintenance; and (9) unprofessional behaviour. In fact, Batalden and Sydnes (2014) also found that unsafe supervision was the main contributor to extremely serious maritime accidents in 34.7% of cases analysed in their study, while it contributed to 23.1% of serious accidents.

This type of information shifts the dynamics from an understanding of humans *in general* affecting the safety of maritime transport, to specific humans, roles and actions that have been discovered time and time again to contribute to maritime accidents. In this light, focus should be placed on elements pertaining to leadership and supervision, safety systems and culture (including attention to maintenance and the condition, as well as age of equipment, and leadership in the 'higher' executive sense that decides over resources and culture development). This entails that the ideal cognitive approach to the conceptual deliberation of future maritime technology would be an in-depth examination of the mental models, motivations and needs of top-level executives, managers and organisational designers. In other words, it is often the people determining the technology, systems, procedures and protocol that contribute more significantly to incident on the seas, than those who are on the vessels themselves.

With this said, if we move back to a more traditional sense of understanding the development of an autonomous maritime and fairway (navigable waters and channels) from the perspective of pilot cognition, we should observe the mental models of these professionals. Mental models can be described as cognitive frameworks that are generated by people to interpret phenomena in terms of purpose, form, response and other semantic contents. Mental models provide individuals with 'explanations of system functioning and observed system states, and predictions of future states' (Rouse & Morris, 1986, p. 7). Rouse and Morris (1986) also emphasise that human mental models are not necessarily computational models. Within a design context, and particularly that of future maritime design, it is useful to consider mental models as being purpose-based (see Fig. 6.4).

Through adapting Rouse and Morris' (1986) framework we can understand a mental model as one that *describes* the purpose and form, *explains* function and state, and *predicts* state. In turn, the purpose alludes to why a system exists in the first place. *Purpose* is linked to human motivation and is determined by values and basic needs either directly or indirectly (Maslow, 1958; Troland, 1928). The purpose of an autonomous maritime is stated as aiding sustainability (our physiological human need to have a healthy environmental ecosystem) as well as increasing effectiveness (accuracy and precision), safety (physiological need) and efficiency (time and money—meaning that there is greater potential profit for the companies). Autonomous technology is also experienced as a threat to employment (physiological, psychological and self-actualising needs) and even safety (threat to physiological safety through error or even take-over).

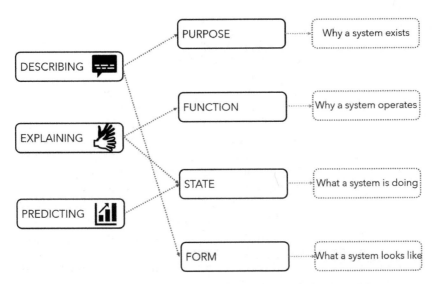

Fig. 6.4 Mental models in design (adapted from Orlandi et al., 2015; Rouse & Morris, 1986)

Some mental models are paramount for the construction and creation of a safe and effective autonomous maritime, these include pilots' abilities to predict and judge (visually, spatially, temporally) the vessel's physical dynamics in relation to manoeuvres (Orlandi et al., 2015). Parts of these mental models are about what can be expressed verbally.[2] This is also known as *perceptual access reasoning* where, through mental representation and association with linguistic and explainable constructs, individuals are about to describe what they are mentally 'seeing' (Fabricius et al., 2021; Lopes, 2000). Yet, a great proportion of knowledge and its structures that are held by domain experts and field professionals pertains to what cannot be mentally represented or verbally expressed, i.e., embodied or bodily knowledge—that which cannot be succinctly represented (Preston, 1994; Smith, 2013) inherent to tacit knowledge. Thus, speed and its management, propulsion type and manoeuvres of varying

---

[2] This is where we enter the domain of representational theory of the mind (see e.g., Fodor, 1997; Sterelny, 1990).

degrees of difficulty are processed by maritime pilots for instance, through ontologies that cannot be readily verbally expressed.

Mental models describe dynamics between abstract elements and concepts through cognitive processes such as deductive reasoning and inference (Aronson, 1997) or affective processes such as Appraisal and Core Affect (Roseman & Smith, 2001; Scherer, 1999). They are not, however, limited to an individual's mental construction, on the contrary, social interaction and social cognitive processes play a major role in how people gain particular understandings of phenomena (Augoustinos et al., 2014). That is, common understandings and specific ways of seeing systems in domains and through paradigms greatly occur via social actions such as teamwork (Banks & Millward, 2000). Planning and visioning strengthen shared understandings and thus, particular types of mental models in teams (Stout et al., 1999). They are knowledge structures, or ways of formulating and representing information, that occur through relatively stable and repetitive interactions of greatly unchanging representations (Johnson-Laird, 1983).

Conclusion—Yet Unknown But Better (YUBB).

Pertinent to remember is that it is often the people determining the technology, systems, procedures and protocol that contribute more significantly to incidents at the sea, than those on the vessels themselves. John McDermid (2020) highlights that one of the main challenges in bringing autonomous vehicles into mainstream traffic hinges upon the difficulties attaining agreement across sectors and standardisation bodies regarding algorithms, training, testing and validation. There are also problems in developing machine learning that can be deemed as safe. Hubertus Bardt (2017) emphasises the complexity of not only autonomous vehicle implementation but also production, i.e., economics (i.e., Europe and associated regulations) and the implantation of big tech in these vehicles. Again, regarding the design there is a need to understand how various levels of expertise affect mental models. These mental models are built into the logic of the AI and ML systems, while strongly affecting the human dimension and human interaction with the end products. As with the automotive industry, the maritime and its structures are highly complex. To give a simplified example of the mental model challenges faced with envisioning and developing the field of autonomous shipping and piloting, we can focus on four major stakeholder groups:

(1) the pilots and sea crews, (2) shipping engineers; (3) software engineers; and (4) general public—including some members of policymaking communities.

YUBB combines multi-professional knowledge from across stakeholder groups to go beyond MAYA (Rousi et al., 2017). YUBB invites uncertainty and ambiguity through not only combining different perspectives on the design target in question, but different types of knowledge—from the cultural-discursive through to the embodied, affective, and technical. In Fig. 6.5, we observe at least four possible MAYAs: maritime experts (engineers and seafarers), as well as software developers and the general public (policymakers and business specialists included). The cognitive dimensions of MAYA play out through the embodied, cognitive and affective relationship the diverse expert groups have with the topic of autonomous maritime. For the pilot and sea crew, mental models of the future are based on embodiment, dynamics, professional and technical knowledge. For the engineers, future potential is based on technical knowledge of the artefacts, their operation and predicted capacity as well as scientific knowledge. Software developers often possess knowledge dominated by systemic software logic and a form of technical understanding of the machinery and its conditions. The general public represents the sphere of collective imagination in which the maritime comprises cultural ideals, discursive elements (i.e., regarding the transitions in human labour, etc.), social layers (what this means for an individual through to societal livelihood and wellbeing) and the personal world of one's own imaginings.

Ahvenjärvi (2016) questions the ability of designers to anticipate the varied scenarios an autonomous ship could face. Autonomous ship traffic does not equate to un-humanned maritime. While autonomous ships may interact with one another, there is also the factor that not all ships will lack human staff. How then, will an autonomous ship interact with the deck officers on another ship? Perhaps, via ChatGPT or a similar large language model. There is still much potential that should be explored regarding how future maritime technology could be realised, not only in the most efficient way, but maybe the most imaginative. Where effectivity comes with affectivity and a complete transformation of what seafaring is about. Real-time software systems, data structures, algorithms, task priorities and self-diagnostics are just some parts of these complex systems, yet not the all-encompassing cybernetic ensemble of human-technology symbiosis.

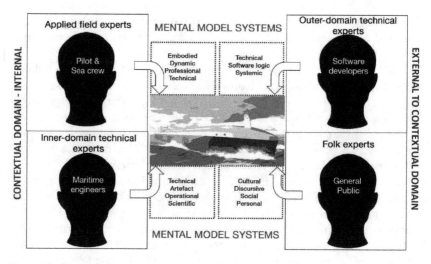

Fig. 6.5 Yet unknown but better—MAYA in multi-professional mental model systems

Rather than holding design hostage with outdated non-humanned models, multi-professional design teams should truly engage in hybrid re-imaginings of the maritime future, in which not only are the accident-prone functions of human being safety-netted through technology, but the strengths of humans are kept in synergy with the intelligent systems. Human operators possess flexibility of thought, tacit knowledge and creativity. The human ability to adapt to surprising situations has positive effects on the safety of the system, although the human ability to adapt - i.e. the ability to learn—may also be a drawback or delay. Software developers have difficulties in predicting the unpredictable outside their own knowledge domain. Human pilots and other sea crew may not have a perfect mental model of the unexpected, but what they do have is a broad set of information nodes, built of previous experience that can be drawn on like a tool kit in times of trouble—storms, fault machinery or even pirates.

REFERENCES

Ahvenjärvi, S. (2016). The human element and autonomous ships. *TransNav: International Journal on Marine Navigation and Safety of Sea Transportation, 10*(3). https://doi.org/10.12716/1001.10.03.18

Allianz. (2015). Safety and shipping review 2015, *36*. https://www.agcs.allianz.com/news-and-insights/news/safety-shipping-review-2015.html

Aronson, J. L. (1997). Mental models and deduction. *American Behavioral Scientist, 40*(6), 782–797. https://doi.org/10.1177/0002764297040006007

Asatryan, V. S., & Oh, H. (2008). Psychological ownership theory: An exploratory application in the restaurant industry. *Journal of Hospitality & Tourism Research, 32*(3), 363–386. https://doi.org/10.1177/1096348008317391

Augoustinos, M., Walker, I., & Donaghue, N. (2014). *Social cognition: An integrated introduction.* Sage.

Baars, T. (2011). Experiential science; towards an integration of implicit and reflected practitioner-expert knowledge in the scientific development of organic farming. *Journal of Agricultural and Environmental Ethics, 24*(6), 601–628. https://doi.org/10.1007/s10806-010-9281-3

Banks, A. P., & Millward, L. J. (2000). Running shared mental models as a distributed cognitive process. *British Journal of Psychology, 91*(4), 513–531. https://doi.org/10.1348/000712600161961

Bardt, H. (2017). Autonomous driving—a challenge for the automotive industry. *Intereconomics, 3.* https://www.intereconomics.eu/contents/year/2017/number/3/article/autonomous-driving-a-challenge-for-the-automotive-industry.html

Batalden, B. M., & Sydnes, A. K. (2014). Maritime safety and the ISM code: A study of investigated casualties and incidents. *WMU Journal of Maritime Affairs, 13*, 3–25. https://doi.org/10.1007/s13437-013-0051-8

Bandura, A., & McClelland, D. C. (1977). *Social learning theory* (Vol. 1). Prentice Hall.

Barbarewicz, F., Jensen, H. J., Harth, V., & Oldenburg, M. (2019). Psychophysical stress and strain of maritime pilots in Germany. A cross-sectional study. *Plos one, 14*(8), e0221269. https://doi.org/10.1371/journal.pone.0221269

Barca, T. B. (2019). *Predicting maritime pilot selection with personality traits* [Doctoral dissertation]. Walden University. Retrieved May 4, 2023, from: https://scholarworks.waldenu.edu/dissertations/7459/

Basinska, B. A., & Gruszczynska, E. (2020). Burnout as a state: Random-intercept cross-lagged relationship between exhaustion and disengagement in a 10-day study. *Psychology Research and Behavior Management, 13*, 267.

BBC. (2021). Container ship facts: Egypt's Suez Canal blocked by massive boat. Newsround. *BBC.* https://www.bbc.co.uk/newsround/56511717

Belk, R. (2021). Ethical issues in service robotics and artificial intelligence. *The Service Industries Journal, 41*(13–14), 860–876. https://doi.org/10.1080/02642069.2020.1727892

Carotenuto A., Molino I., Fasanaro A.M., & Amenta F. (2012). Psychological stress in seafarers: a review. *International Maritime Health, 63,* 188–194. https://pubmed.ncbi.nlm.nih.gov/24595974/

Chauvin, C., Lardjane, S., Morel, G., Clostermann, J. P., & Langard, B. (2013). Human and organisational factors in maritime accidents: Analysis of collisions at sea using the HFACS. *Accident Analysis & Prevention, 59,* 26–37. https://doi.org/10.1016/j.aap.2013.05.006

Chrysikou, E. G., & Weisberg, R. W. (2005). Following the wrong footsteps: Fixation effects of pictorial examples in a design problem-solving task. *Journal of Experimental Psychology: Learning, Memory, and Cognition, 31*(5), 1134. https://doi.org/10.1037/0278-7393.31.5.1134

Cockroft, A. N. (1984). Collisions at sea. *Safety at sea international.* 17–19.

Collins, H. (2010). *Tacit and explicit knowledge.* University of Chicago Press.

Coraddu, A., Oneto, L., de Maya, B. N., & Kurt, R. (2020). Determining the most influential human factors in maritime accidents: A data-driven approach. *Ocean Engineering, 211,* 107588.

Crilly, N., & Cardoso, C. (2017). Where next for research on fixation, inspiration and creativity in design? *Design Studies, 50,* 1–38. https://doi.org/10.1016/j.destud.2017.02.001

Darbra, R. M., Crawford, J. F. E., Haley, C. W., & Morrison, R. J. (2007). Safety culture and hazard risk perception of Australian and New Zealand maritime pilots. *Marine Policy, 31*(6), 736–745. https://doi.org/10.1016/j.marpol.2007.02.004

Doody, K. (2021). *Aldi reveal full list of every product shortage due to Suez Canal blockage.* Retrieved May 4, 2023, from: https://www.dailyecho.co.uk/news/19235567.aldi-reveal-full-list-every-product-shortage-due-suez-canal-blockage/

de Maya, B. N., Babaleye, A. O., & Kurt, R. E. (2020). Marine accident learning with fuzzy cognitive maps (MALFCMs) and Bayesian networks. *Safety in Extreme Environments, 2*(1), 69–78.

Edwards, D. (2010). *The lab: Creativity and culture.* Harvard University Press.

Eysenck, H. J. (1976). The measurement of personality. *University Park Press.* https://doi.org/10.1007/978-94-011-6168-8

Fabricius, W. V., Gonzales, C. R., Pesch, A., et al. (2021). Perceptual access reasoning (PAR) in developing a representational theory of mind. *Monographs of the Society for Research in Child Development, 86*(3). https://doi.org/10.1111/mono.12432

Fahey, L. (2016). John C. Camillus: discovering opportunities by exploring wicked problems. *Strategy & Leadership, 44*(5), 29–35. https://doi.org/10. 1108/SL-08-2016-0067

FFPM (2023). History of maritime pilots. https://pilotes-maritimes.com/en/ history-of-maritime-pilots/

Fodor, J. A. (1997). The representational theory of mind. *American Behavioral Scientist, 40*(6), 829–841.

French, M. J., Gravdahl, J. T., & French, M. J. (1985). *Conceptual design for engineers*. Design Council. Springer Science and Business Media.

Friis Dam, R. (2021). The MAYA Principle: Design for the future, but balance it with your users' Present. https://www.interaction-design.org/literature/art icle/design-for-the-future-but-balance-it-with-your-users-present

Gambrell, J. (2021). Massive cargo ship turns sideways, blocks Egypt's Suez Canal. *KARE*. Associated Press. https://apnews.com/article/cargo-ship-blo cks-egypt-suez-canal-5957543bb555ab31c14d56ad09f98810

Hekkert, P. P. M., & Leder, H. (2008). Product aesthetics. In H. N. J. Schifferstein & P. P. M. Hekkert (Eds.), *Product experience* (pp. 259–285). Elsevier.

Hekkert, P., Snelders, D., & Van Wieringen, P. C. (2003). 'Most advanced, yet acceptable': Typicality and novelty as joint predictors of aesthetic preference in industrial design. *British Journal of Psychology, 94*(1), 111–124. https:// doi.org/10.1348/000712603762842147

Hontvedt, M. (2015). Professional vision in simulated environments—Examining professional maritime pilots' performance of work tasks in a full-mission ship simulator. *Learning, Culture and Social Interaction, 7*, 71–84. https://doi. org/10.1016/j.lcsi.2015.07.003

Hetherington, C., Flin, R., & Mearns, K. (2006). Safety in shipping: The human element. *Journal of Safety Research, 37*(4), 401–411. https://doi.org/10. 1016/j.jsr.2006.04.007

Hofstede, G., Hofstede, G. J., & Minkov, M. (2005). *Cultures and organizations: Software of the mind* (Vol. 2). Mcgraw-Hill.

Imset, M., & Øvergård, K. I. (2017). Shared mental models of challenging maritime situations: Comparisons of ship and shore personnel in the Straits of Malacca and Singapore. *TransNav: International Journal on Marine Naviga- tion and Safety of Sea Transportation, 11*(2), 243–248. https://doi.org/10. 12716/1001.11.02.05

Jansson, D. G., & Smith, S. M. (1991). Design fixation. *Design Studies, 12*(1), 3–11. https://doi.org/10.1016/0142-694X(91)90003-F

Johnson-Laird, P. N. (1983). *Mental models: Towards a cognitive science of language, inference, and consciousness* (No. 6). Harvard University Press.

Kim, T. E., Sydnes, A. K., & Batalden, B. M. (2021). Development and validation of a safety leadership Self-Efficacy Scale (SLSES) in maritime context. *Safety Science, 134*, 105031. https://doi.org/10.1016/j.ssci.2020.105031

Lehr, D., Koch, S., & Hillert, A. (2010). Where is (im)balance? Necessity and construction of evaluated cut-off points for effort-reward imbalance and over-commitment. *Journal of Occupational and Organizational Psychology, 83*(1), 251–261. https://doi.org/10.1348/096317909X406772

Leveson, N. (2004). A new accident model for engineering safer systems. *Safety Science, 42*, 237–270. https://doi.org/10.1016/S0925-7535(03)00047-X

Loewy, R. (1951). *Never leave well enough alone*. John Hopkins University Press.

Lopes, D. M. M. (2000). What is it like to see with your ears? The representational theory of mind. *Philosophy and Phenomenological Research, 60*(2), 439–453.

Luchins, A.S., & Luchins, E.H. (1959). *Rigidity of behavior: A variational approach to the effect of einstellung*. University of Oregon Books.

MacIntyre, T. E., Igou, E. R., Campbell, M. J., Moran, A. P., & Matthews, J. (2014). Metacognition and action: A new pathway to understanding social and cognitive aspects of expertise in sport. *Frontiers in Psychology, 5*, 1155. https://doi.org/10.3389/fpsyg.2014.01155

MacLachlan, M., Kavanagh, B., & Kay, A. (2012). Maritime health: A review with suggestions for research. *International Maritime Health, 63*(1), 1–6. https://pubmed.ncbi.nlm.nih.gov/22669806/

Main, L. C., & Chambers, T. P. (2015). Factors affecting maritime pilots' health and well-being: A systematic review. *International Maritime Health, 66*(4), 220–232. https://doi.org/10.5603/IMH.2015.0043

Maslow, A. H. (1958). A dynamic theory of human motivation. In C. L. Stacey & M. DeMartino (Eds.), *Understanding human motivation* (pp. 26–47). Howard Allen Publishers. https://doi.org/10.1037/11305-004

McDermid, J. (2020). Autonomous cars: five reasons they still aren't on our roads. *The Conversation*. https://theconversation.com/autonomous-cars-five-reasons-they-still-arent-on-our-roads-143316

Merriam-Webster. (2023). *Fixation*. https://www.merriam-webster.com/dictionary/fixation

Monroe, K. B. (1976). The influence of price differences and brand familiarity on brand preferences. *Journal of Consumer Research, 3*(1), 42–49.

Montero, B.G. (2016). *Thought in action: Expertise and the conscious mind*. Oxford University Press.

Moreno, D. P., Yang, M. C., Hernández, A. A., Linsey, J. S., & Wood, K. L. (2015). A step beyond to overcome design fixation: A design-by-analogy approach. In J. Gero (Ed.), *Design computing and cognition'14* (pp. 607–624). Springer. https://doi.org/10.1007/978-3-319-14956-1_34

Murphie, A., & Potts, J. (2003). *Culture and technology*. Palgrave MacMillan.

Nielsen MB, Bergheim K, & Eid J. (2013). Relationships between work environment factors and workers' well-being in the maritime industry. *International Maritime Health*, *64*, 80–88. https://pubmed.ncbi.nlm.nih.gov/23788224/

O'Brien, A. T., Haslam, S. A., Jetten, J., Humphrey, L., O'Sullivan, L., Postmes, T., Eggins, R., & Reynolds, K. J. (2004). Cynicism and disengagement among devalued employee groups: The need to ASPIRe. *The Career Development International*, *9*(1), 28–44. https://doi.org/10.1108/13620430410518129

Orlandi, L., Brooks, B., & Bowles, M. (2015). A comparison of marine pilots' planning and manoeuvring skills: Uncovering mental models to assess shiphandling and explore expertise. *The Journal of Navigation*, *68*(5), 897–914. https://doi.org/10.1017/S0373463315000260

Paine, L. (2014). *The sea and civilization: a maritime history of the world*. Atlantic Books Ltd.

Paris, C., & Wang, Y. (2021). Evergreen looks at moving cargo from seized Suez ship. *The Wall Street Journal*. https://www.wsj.com/articles/evergreen-looks-at-moving-cargo-from-seized-suez-ship-11618591720

Person, O., Schoormans, J., Snelders, D., & Karjalainen, T. M. (2008). Should new products look similar or different? The influence of the market environment on strategic product styling. *Design Studies*, *29*(1), 30–48. https://doi.org/10.1016/j.destud.2007.06.005

Pierce, J. L., Kostova, T., & Dirks, K. T. (2003). The state of psychological ownership: Integrating and extending a century of research. *Review of General Psychology*, *7*(1), 84–107. https://doi.org/10.1037/1089-2680.7.1.84

Porathe, T., Hoem, Å., Rødseth, Ø., Fjørtoft, K., & Johnsen, S. O. (2018). At least as safe as manned shipping? Autonomous shipping, safety and "human error". In S. Haugen, A. Barros, C. Gulijk, T. Kongsvik, & Jan Erik Vinnem (Eds.), *Safety and reliability–safe societies in a changing world* (pp. 417–425). CRC Press. https://doi.org/10.1201/9781351174664

Preston, B. (1994). Husserl's non-representational theory of mind. *The Southern Journal of Philosophy*, *32*(2), 209–232.

Purcell, A. T., & Gero, J. S. (1998). Drawings and the design process: A review of protocol studies in design and other disciplines and related research in cognitive psychology. *Design Studies*, *19*(4), 389–430. https://doi.org/10.1016/S0142-694X(98)00015-5

Rasmussen, J. (1997). Risk management in a dynamic society—A modelling problem. *Safety Science*, *27*(2/3), 183–213. https://doi.org/10.1016/S0925-7535(97)00052-0

Reber, R., Schwarz, N., & Winkielman, P. (2004). Processing fluency and aesthetic pleasure: Is beauty in the perceiver's processing experience? *Personality and Social Psychology Review*, *8*(4), 364–382. https://doi.org/10.1207/s15327957pspr0804_3

Relling, T., Lützhöft, M., Ostnes, R., & Hildre, H. P. (2018). A human perspective on maritime autonomy. In *International Conference on Augmented Cognition* (pp. 350–362). *Lecture Notes in Computer Science*. Springer. https://doi.org/10.1007/978-3-319-91467-1_27

Rolls-Royce. (2016). Autonomous ships: The next step. AAWA: Advanced autonomous waterborne applications 7. https://www.rolls-royce.com/~/media/Files/R/Rolls-Royce/documents/%20customers/marine/ship-intel/rr-ship-intel-aawa-8pg.pdf

Roseman, I. J., & Smith, C. A. (2001). Appraisal theory: Overview, assumptions, varieties, controversies. In K. R. Scherer, A. Schorr, & T. Johnstone (Eds.), *Appraisal processes in emotion: Theory, methods, research* (pp. 3–19). Oxford University Press.

Rouse, W. B., & Morris, N. M. (1986). On looking into the black box: Prospects and limits in the search for mental models. *Psychological Bulletin, 100*(3), 349. https://doi.org/10.1037/0033-2909.100.3.349

Rousi, R. (2020). That crazy world we'll live in: emotions and anticipations of radical future technology design. In R. Rousi, J. Leikas, & P. Saariluoma (Eds.), *Emotions in technology design: From experience to ethics* (pp. 141–153). Human—Computer Interaction Series. Springer. https://doi.org/10.1007/978-3-030-53483-7_9

Rousi, R., & Alanen, H.-K. (2021). Socio-emotional experience in human technology interaction design: a fashion framework proposal. In M. Rauterberg (Ed.), *Culture and Computing: Design Thinking and Cultural Computing. 9th International Conference, C&C 2021, Held as Part of the 23rd HCI International Conference, HCII 2021, Virtual Event, July 24–29, 2021, Proceedings, Part II* (pp. 131–150). *Lecture Notes in Computer Science*, 12795. Springer. https://doi.org/10.1007/978-3-030-77431-8_8

Rousi, R., & Silvennoinen, J. (2018). Simplicity and the art of something more: A cognitive-semiotic approach to simplicity and complexity in human-technology interaction and design experience. *Human Technology, 14*(1), 67–95. https://doi.org/10.17011/ht/urn.201805242752

Rousi, R. A., Silvennoinen, J. M., Perälä, P. M., & Jokinen, J. P. (2017, September). Beyond MAYA for game-changing multisensory design. In *Proceedings of the 21st International Academic Mindtrek Conference* (pp. 147–153). https://doi.org/10.1145/3131085.3131113

Russon, M-A. (2021). The cost of the Suez Canal blockage. BBC News. Retrieved May 4, 2023, from: https://www.bbc.com/news/business-56559073

Saariluoma, P., Alanen, H.-K., & Rousi, R. (2021). Fashion technology: what are the limits of emerging technological design thinking? In T. Ahram, R. Taiar, & F. Groff (Eds.), *Human interaction, emerging technologies and future applications IV: Proceedings of the 4th international conference on human interaction and emerging technologies: Future applications (IHIET—AI 2021)*, April 28–30, 2021, Strasbourg, France (pp. 367–374). Advances in Intelligent Systems and Computing, 1378. Springer. https://doi.org/10.1007/978-3-030-74009-2_47

Saariluoma, P., & Rousi, R. (2020). Emotions and technoethics. In R. Rousi, J. Leikas, & P. Saariluoma (Eds.), *Emotions in technology design: From experience to ethics* (pp. 167–189). Springer. https://doi.org/10.1007/978-3-030-53483-7_11

Saariluoma, P., & Rousi, R. (2015). Symbolic interactions: Towards a cognitive scientific theory of meaning in human technology interaction. *Journal of Advances in Humanities, 3*(3), 310–324. https://doi.org/10.24297/jah.v3i2.5145

Shaffer, D. W., & Clinton, K. A. (2006). Toolforthoughts: Reexamining thinking in the digital age. *Mind, Culture, and Activity, 13*(4), 283–300. https://doi.org/10.1207/s15327884mca1304_2

Scherer, K. R. (1999). *Appraisal theory*. In T. Dalgleish & M. J. Power (Eds.), *Handbook of cognition and emotion* (pp. 637–663). John Wiley & Sons Ltd. https://doi.org/10.1002/0470013494.ch30

Smith, D. W. (2013). *Husserl*. Routledge.

Sterelny, K. (1990). The representational theory of mind: An introduction. Basil Blackwell.

Stout, R. J., Cannon-Bowers, J. A., Salas, E., & Milanovich, D. M. (1999). Planning, shared mental models, and coordinated performance: An empirical link is established. *Human Factors, 41*(1), 61–71. https://doi.org/10.1518/001872099779577273

Stubley, P. (2021). Suez Canal: Every given remains stuck for fifth day as more than 320 ships wait in queue. Independent. https://www.independent.co.uk/news/world/middle-east/suez-canal-ship-ever-given-b1823469.html

Tait, J. L., Chambers, T. P., Tait, R. S., & Main, L. C. (2021). Impact of shift work on sleep and fatigue in Maritime pilots. *Ergonomics, 64*(7), 856–868. https://doi.org/10.1080/00140139.2021.1882705

Thurgood, C., Hekkert, P., & Blijlevens, J. (2014). The joint effect of typicality and novelty on aesthetic pleasure for product designs: Influences of safety and risk. In A. Kozbelt, P. P. L. Tinio & P. J. Locher, *Proceedings of the 23rd biennial congress of the international association of empirical aesthetics* (IAEA) (pp. 391–396). New York, USA.

Troland, L. T. (1928). The fundamentals of human motivation. *D Van Nostrand*. https://doi.org/10.1037/13385-000

Vakkuri, V., & Abrahamsson, P. (2018). The key concepts of ethics of artificial intelligence. In *2018 IEEE international conference on engineering, technology and innovation (ICE/ITMC)* (pp. 1–6). IEEE. https://doi.org/10.1109/ICE.2018.8436265

Vakkuri, V., Kemell, K. K., Kultanen, J., & Abrahamsson, P. (2020). The current state of industrial practice in artificial intelligence ethics. *IEEE Software, 37*(4), 50–57. https://doi.org/10.1109/MS.2020.2985621

Veitch, E., & Alsos, O. A. (2022). A systematic review of human-AI interaction in autonomous ship systems. *Safety Science, 152*, 105778. https://doi.org/10.1016/j.ssci.2022.105778

Vygotsky, L. S. (1980). *Mind in society: The development of higher psychological processes*. Harvard University Press.

Weingarten, E., Chen, Q., McAdams, M., Yi, J., Helper, J., & Albarracín, D. (2016). From primed concepts to action: A meta-analysis of the behavioral effects of incidentally presented words. *Psychological Bulletin, 142*(5), 472–497. https://doi.org/10.1037/bul0000030

Weiss, R. E. (2003). Designing problems to promote higher-order thinking. *New Directions for Teaching and Learning, 95*, 25–31. https://doi.org/10.1002/tl.109

Zajonc, R. B. (2001). Mere exposure: A gateway to the subliminal. *Current Directions in Psychological Science, 10*(6), 224–228. https://doi.org/10.1111/1467-8721.00154

Zhao, G., Li, Y., & Xu, Q. (2022). From emotion AI to cognitive AI. *International Journal of Network Dynamics and Intelligence, 1*(1), 65–72. https://www.sciltp.com/journals/ijndi/article/view/115

CHAPTER 7

Human-Technology Symbiosis in Service: Insights from Dual-Process Theory

Rolf Findsrud and *Bård Tronvoll*

INTRODUCTION

Human-technology interactions have always been essential for firms in their mission of co-creating value (Cenamor et al., 2017). Given the scarcity of human resources in firms and critical performance assessments of efficiency and effectiveness in operational evaluations, there is a recurring argument to replace humans with robots (e.g., McLeay et al., 2020; Mende et al., 2019; Wirtz et al., 2018; Xiao & Kumar, 2021). This has been used as an approach to rationalize practices and reduce the dependency of human resources (Royakkers & Van Est, 2017). The service sector dominates the gross domestic product in developed economies (Gustafsson et al., 2016). However, moving from a goods-based economy to a service-based economy infused with technology has affected the

R. Findsrud (✉) · B. Tronvoll
CREDS - Center for Research on Digitalization and Sustainability, Inland
Norway University of Applied Sciences, Kongsvinger, Norway
e-mail: rolf.findsrud@inn.no

B. Tronvoll
CTF-Service Research Center, Karlstad University, Karlstad, Sweden
e-mail: bard.tronvoll@inn.no

© The Author(s) 2024
R. Rousi et al. (eds.), *Humane Autonomous Technology*,
https://doi.org/10.1007/978-3-031-66528-8_7

competency requirements of many jobs. Employees face technology-rich environments in which routine tasks are increasingly digitalized and automatized. This often leaves ill-defined problems requiring creativity, ingenuity, and problem-solving skills unsolved (Findsrud & Tronvoll, 2022; Griffin et al., 2012). The acceptance of a more service-centered economy that is becoming ever more intertwined with technology—for instance, in the form of artificially intelligent (AI) agents—intensifies the significance of humans' adaptive performance. This concerns non-routine tasks that require a flexible mind, the capacity to make decisions based on incomplete information, intuition, problem-solving ability, as well as artistic and aesthetic sensibilities (Corazza, 2016) as valuable additions to the high capacity of advanced technology. Thus, AI-based technology calls for a new framework for human–technology symbiosis (Jarrahi, 2018).

According to Larivière et al. (2017), the rapid technological development regarding AI and related technologies as well as interconnected smart devices (e.g., smartphones, smart houses, and smart cities) through the Internet of Things are fundamentally changing the interactions between individuals (such as customers and employees) and firms, as well as the roles of everyone involved. "Technology" is often used as an umbrella term for all human-created things that serve human purposes, ranging from simple tools (e.g., a hammer) to more advanced tools (e.g., cars, computer systems, and AI) (Storbacka et al., 2016). This chapter focuses on cutting-edge technology that aims to automate or augment employees' workload with or without AI. Kaplan and Haenlein (2019) defined AI as "a system's ability to interpret external data correctly, to learn from such data, and to use those learnings to achieve specific goals and tasks through flexible adaptation" (p. 17). With the introduction of machine learning (ML) and AI, major progress has been made in terms of the capability of technology to perform more complex tasks (Hollebeek et al., 2021; Pradeep et al., 2018). This enables the move from automating to personalizing, transactionalizing, and relationalizing offerings through cognition and emotion (Huang & Rust, 2017). Correspondingly, Ostrom et al. (2021) posited that further theoretical work is required on the dynamic interactions between employees and digital technologies for the co-delivery of services. Consequently, there is a need to critically assess and understand AI's potential and limitations in relation to humans.

To understand the strengths and limitations of human capabilities, we turn to dual-process theories from psychology, according to which humans rely on two psychological processes: conscious and non-conscious (e.g., Bargh & Chartrand, 1999; Evans, 2008; Evans & Stanovich, 2013; Kahneman, 2011). By relating (see MacInnis, 2011) dual-process theories (e.g., Bargh, 2002; Barrett et al., 2004; Evans & Stanovich, 2013; Gupta & Harris, 2010; Mercier & Sperber, 2011) and the use of technology (e.g., robotization and/or use of AI) in firms and service interactions (e.g., Hollebeek et al., 2021; Huang & Rust, 2020; Jörling et al., 2019; Marinova et al., 2016; Wirtz et al., 2018) comparing attributes of humans and technologies, this chapter presents a framework for understanding the division of different types of collaborative tasks between humans and technology. The framework indicates how practitioners can utilize firms' dual modes of human and technology-dominant processes to exploit each other's strengths to achieve desirable outcomes. As a result, we contribute to the literature by bridging "existing theories in interesting ways, link work across disciplines, provide multi-level insights, and broaden the scope of our thinking" (Gilson & Goldberg, 2015, p. 128; Jaakkola, 2020, p. 18). In this chapter, we offer a framework systematizing the attributes of human-technology symbiosis based on dual-process theories. We argue that: (1) individual humans; and (2) firms (i.e., a combination of individuals and technology) are entities possessing comparable categories of attributes in relation to both agent groups. The dual processes humans utilize—one relying on primarily non-conscious processes and the other on primarily conscious processes (Evans, 2008)—are comparable to firms consisting of humans (having conscious capabilities) and technology (representing non-conscious processes).

CONCEPTUAL BACKGROUND

Use of Advanced Technology to Enhance Performance

During the 2010s, and over the span of five years, the share of large firms integrating some form of AI into their core business operations had grown from 10% to around 80% (Ghosh et al., 2019). The rapid increase in AI implementation led to a substantial surge in global spending on AI-related investments. This encompassed software, hardware, and services for AI-centric systems. Projections indicated that by 2023, global spending on AI was expected to reach a staggering US $154 billion, reflecting 26.9% growth from the previous year (International Data

Corporation, 2023). The widespread adoption of AI and robotics is anticipated to profoundly affect economies and the labor market, causing significant disruptions in how firms operate and interact with markets. Although robots with integrated automation are highly effective in repetitive tasks as compared to humans (Lu et al., 2020), even low-skilled service jobs have traditionally been considered difficult to automate. This is due to the fact that they rely on contextual understanding and spontaneous, interactive communication (Autor & Dorn, 2013; Huang & Rust, 2018).

The rise in the implementation of AI-based technology calls for a new framework for human–technology symbiosis that incorporates changes in the division of work between technology and humans (Jarrahi, 2018). Thus, the focus should not be on the replacement of humans by technology but rather on human–AI collaboration (Anthony et al., 2023). Symbiosis goes beyond pure interaction in that it includes the notion of co-existence, living together, and cooperation. Based on the work of Licklider from 1960, Jarrahi (2018, p. 579) described human–technology symbiosis as "a relationship through which the strengths of one compensate for the limitations of the other." For instance, human actors can plan, motivate, and self-regulate actions that lead to a deliberate goal (Bandura, 2001). However, technology such as robotics, ML, or even AI do not understand contexts as humans do. They therefore cannot "adapt automatically; instead, their knowledge is updated in an ad hoc manner and infrequently due to the repetitive nature of their environments" (Huang & Rust, 2018, p. 158).

AI can be categorized mainly into robotic process automation (RPA), ML, and deep learning (DL) (Hollebeek et al., 2021). RPA deals with automating (parts of) existing labor-intensive processes based on rules and linear algorithms (Hollebeek et al., 2021). With RPA, the technology responds but does not learn or adapt to the process (Hollebeek et al., 2021; Pradeep et al., 2018). Huang and Rust (2018) referred to this as mechanical intelligence. ML "auto-adapts or learns through trial-and-error, without human intervention" (Hollebeek et al., 2021, p. 4). The authors posited that this technology can understand, respond to, and anticipate. It is close to what Huang and Rust (2018) called analytical intelligence. The third category, DL, is a subclass of ML that incorporates artificial neural networks, which mimic a biological nervous system (Hollebeek et al., 2021), and is, according to the authors, similar to what Huang and Rust (2018) called intuitive intelligence. Labor-intensive, repetitive, and rule-based processes are generally optimal for robotic automation (Hollebeek et al., 2021). With the introduction of ML and AI, major progress has been made concerning the capability of technology to perform more complex tasks, which in turn might blur the boundaries between the physical, digital, and biological spheres (Hollebeek et al., 2021; Pradeep et al., 2018). For example, augmented reality technologies increasingly overlay digital information onto physical objects. In fact, smartphone apps (e.g., Snapchat and Pokemon Go) have made this technology widely accessible. Augmented reality is no longer reserved for big corporations or the military, but is accessible to the average person as "everyday technology." These systems can provide real-time analysis and decision-making capabilities by utilizing AI algorithms to create a symbiotic relationship between the physical and digital realms.

However, assuming that AI is simply a plug-and-play solution in organizations and that AI will replace humans is not a way of ensuring its effective and meaningful utilization in firms (Fountaine et al., 2019). Amidst the excitement surrounding AI, many firms have failed to realize the anticipated benefits despite investing substantial time, effort, and resources into AI initiatives (Fountaine et al., 2019; Makarius et al., 2020). This highlights a potential discrepancy between the hype surrounding AI and its actual ability to co-create value for businesses (Anthony et al., 2023). This is often due to a lack of support from foundations on the front line (Fountaine et al., 2019; Makarius et al., 2020). In other words, the human dimension in pursuing efficiency through technology is forgotten. To increase the understanding of human–technology symbiosis, we need to dig deeper into human factors and attributes that represent human strengths in relation to advanced technology. We do so by applying psychology, more specifically dual-process theories, to understand the strengths and limitations of the human mind in relation to AI.

Dual Processes of the Human Mind

Dual-process theories have a long and widespread tradition in social psychology, cognitive studies, and neuroscience (Chein & Schneider, 2005). These theories are based on the notion that humans can operate both consciously and non-consciously (Kihlstrom, 1987; Thornton et al., 2012; Vargo & Lusch, 2016). Dual-process theories, in their simplest form, distinguish between: (1) a heuristic system (i.e., Type 1), which is non-conscious, rapid, automatic, and involves high-capacity processes that utilize prior knowledge and beliefs to solve a problem; and (2) a second system (i.e., Type 2), which uses logical reasoning principles (De Neys & Glumicic, 2008) often described as conscious, slow, and deliberative processes (Evans & Stanovich, 2013; Kahneman, 2011). These dual-process theories assume that humans utilize fast Type-1 processing that generates intuitive default responses, in which subsequent reflective Type-2 processing may or may not intervene (Evans & Stanovich, 2013). The frequently mentioned attributes in the literature are summarized in Table 7.1.

Humans have a functional consciousness capable of purposely and deliberately accessing and processing information for selecting, constructing, regulating, and evaluating courses of action (Bandura, 2001). In other words, humans can use conscious processes to assess how well different alternatives contribute to the pursuit of a goal (Laran et al., 2016). Conscious processes are often described as controlled, reflective, rule-based, abstract, decontextualized, and/or domain-general (Evans, 2008). Their main strength lies in considering consequences in familiar and unfamiliar settings. However, the amount of information a human can hold in their conscious awareness at one time is limited (Oberauer, 2002) and, therefore, it also has limited capacity. Non-consciousness, in

Table 7.1 Attributes in dual-process theories (adapted from Evans, 2008)

Non-conscious	Conscious
Automatic	Controlled
Implicit	Explicit
Low effort	High effort
Rapid	Slow
High capacity	Low capacity
Default process	Analytic, reflective
Holistic, perceptual	Inhibitory
Associative	Rule based
Domain specific	Domain general
Contextualized	Abstract
Pragmatic	Logical
Parallel	Sequential
Stereotypical	Egalitarian
Independent of general intelligence	Linked to general intelligence
Independent of working memory	Limited by working memory capacity

contrast, can be seen as mental structures and processes that operate outside phenomenal awareness while influencing conscious experience, thought, and action (Kihlstrom, 1987). These processes are of a very high and rapid capacity, with great strengths. For instance, chess grandmasters have been examined for their ability to deliberately develop a vast repertoire of patterns in their memories, allowing them to respond to contingencies automatically and proficiently (Dane & Pratt, 2007). However, non-consciousness also has distinct weaknesses. For example, an automobile driver may not remember landmarks passed along the way (Kihlstrom, 1987), demonstrating that the focus of attention is essential for learning and memory.

The following two critical assumptions are worth highlighting in dual-process theories: first, humans can perform both conscious and non-conscious processes simultaneously and, therefore, can undertake multiple tasks simultaneously (Kihlstrom, 1987). This is also referred to as ambidexterity (Ritter & Geersbro, 2018). For instance, an experienced driver can consciously engage in a conversation while driving a car without consciously thinking about driving. Second, although there are discussions on whether these dual processes are parallel or sequential, there is consensus regarding the iterative nature of dual processes (Evans & Stanovich, 2013). In other words, conscious actions build experience that provides data for the non-conscious automated responses that may be intervened in by the consciousness.

DUAL PROCESSES OF HUMANS AND TECHNOLOGY

Performing a task often involves a synergistic interplay between humans and technology (Storbacka et al., 2016). A similar duality to that of the human mind can be found in the literature on the use of technology in firms (Jarrahi, 2018) exploring the contrast between automatization (with or without the use of AI) and human performance (e.g., Hollebeek et al., 2021; Huang & Rust, 2020; Jarrahi, 2018; Jörling et al., 2019; Mende et al., 2019; Van Doorn et al., 2017). Many attributes of *non-conscious (i.e., automated)* and *conscious (i.e., controlled)* processing also fit how humans perform with technology. In this chapter, we adopt the terminology of *controlled* and *automated* to denote the two types of processes, as these labels capture the essence of each system's core functionality. Subsequently, a comprehensive examination of controlled and automated processes follows, weaving together the literature while clarifying their distinguishing features.

Schneider and Chein (2003) defined controlled processes as a temporary sequence of nodes activated under the control of an actor. These, despite limited capacity, have strong abilities in setting up, altering, and applying such processes in novel situations for which automatic sequences have not been learned. According to Evans (2008), conscious processes are generally abstract, decontextualized, or *domain-general*. Furthermore, Schneider and Chein (2003) argued that controlled processing requires *substantial effort* and interferes with other controlled processing tasks due to the limited capacity of the conscious mind to process information (Evans, 2008; Kihlstrom, 1987; Schneider & Chein, 2003). Controlled processes are often associated with *reflectiveness*, the ability to think hypothetically and consequentially about the future and counterfactual possibilities (Evans, 2008).

Human actors can strategize, motivate, and self-regulate a plan of action that leads to a deliberate goal, where the actors can motivate and regulate the implementation (Bandura, 2001). Thus, humans rely on a controlled process of logic and have rule-based ways of determining hypothetical consequences. They can also adapt their actions as contexts change. Even though robots that utilize automation are highly effective in comparison to humans in performing repetitive tasks (Lu et al., 2020), low-skilled service jobs have traditionally been considered difficult to automate. This is because they rely on contextual understanding and spontaneous, interactive communication (Autor & Dorn, 2013; Huang & Rust, 2018). Evans (2008) argued that specific contexts do not preclude abstract reasoning, although it requires conscious processes. Similarly, a particular technology is usually context-specific, but that does not exclude using the technology in other contexts. In summary, controlled processes can be described as comprising limited capacity, high effort, domain-general, reflective activities relying on intelligence, as well as the ability to consider consequences.

Automated processes are sought out due to their *high capacity* and *low requirements in the effort*. Schneider and Chein (2003) defined an automatic process as the activation of a node sequence without the subject's need for active control or attention. Comparably, the human mind strives to be efficient in using cognitive resources. As James (1890, p. 60) remarked, "the more of the details of our daily life we can hand over to the effortless custody of automatism, the more our higher powers of mind will be set free for their own proper work." The "ability for a process to occur in the absence of control and attention by the subject is perhaps the most salient feature of an automatic process" (Schneider & Chein, 2003, pp. 526–527). For humans, automated processing is pragmatically based on prior experiences, beliefs, and background knowledge. It achieves goals reliably and efficiently without necessarily accompanying awareness (Osman, 2004); humans can rapidly contextualize problems with prior knowledge to create a default response (Evans, 2008).

Barrett et al. (2004) described the process as activating prior knowledge, or schemas, by non-consciously applying a sequence of actions, feelings, or thoughts. However, these automatic responses may be biased because, "people readily violate the most elementary logical, mathematical, or probabilistic rules when a task cues an intuitive response that conflicts with these principles" (De Neys & Pennycook, 2019, p. 503). Consequently, humans require experience in training and sufficient competencies to comfortably rely on automated and non-conscious processes (Schneider & Chein, 2003). For instance, experts have automated previously deliberate procedures (De Neys & Pennycook, 2019) and can make rapid, high-quality decisions in complex situations (Dane & Pratt, 2007). Automation requires investments in robotization, as organizations must invest in developing the necessary resources (e.g., machines or software) and having the necessary knowledge and experience to program the robots.

The introduction of robots has enabled the automatization of manufacturing and many parts of our everyday lives (Huang & Rust, 2018). Automatic processes require little effort to function relatively reliably in high-workload situations with stress factors (Schneider & Chein, 2003). Likewise, an advantage of technology and robots is consistency, as robots do not experience human fatigue, boredom and respond to input reliably (Huang & Rust, 2018). However, automated processes are generally described as *domain-specific* (Evans, 2008). Moreover, there is consensus among the literature indicating that automation is preferable in known and repetitive scenarios. In contrast, Huang and Rust (2018) described service robots as rule-based, formed from prior knowledge. Additionally, service robots utilize continuous sensor perception to observe and react to the physical and temporal variabilities in context. Non-consciousness allows individuals to learn from experience and reach perceptions automatically without conscious attention (Dane & Pratt, 2007). Thus, humans have automatic processes that utilize emotional characteristics, such as intuition, experience, and emotions. At the same time, robots rely on logic, with activities that can be described as analytical, rational, and rule-based. In sum, automatic processes can be described as characterized by high capacity, low effort, domain-specific, perceptual activities relying on prior investments or competencies.

Framework for Human–Technology Symbiosis

Four clusters of attributes were found by relating dual-process theories and research on the interactions between humans and technology. Simplified, a process can either be *controlled* or *automated*, coupled with characteristics that are either *emotional* or *logical*, depending on the level of analysis. If we first consider the human, we find in the dual-process literature that controlled processes (i.e., conscious processes) are paired with logical attributes. Meanwhile, automated processes (i.e., non-conscious processes) are paired with emotional attributes, as depicted in Fig. 7.1. For example, if solving a task requires logical thinking and clear reasoning, it will be based on a controlled process with limited capacity and may require extensive effort. Imagine a grandmaster chess player working to find the right move in classical chess. The player may spend more than 15 minutes on a single move, computing several moves ahead using the logic and rules of the game. However, in blitz chess, the player must often make moves within seconds, forcing the player to rely more on intuition to utilize the high capacity of automated processes (see for instance Saariluoma, 1995).

We found the same four clusters when zooming out and lifting the level of analyses from the individual (i.e., human mind) to the firm

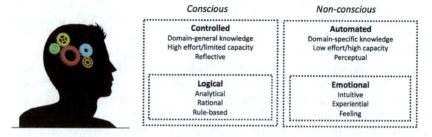

Fig. 7.1   Division of clusters of attributes at the individual level

level (comprising humans and technology). However, at this level, the pairing of clusters is reversed. Thus, humans and firms can rely on both controlled (i.e., conscious) and automatic (i.e., non-conscious) processes. Depending on whether the locus of analysis is on the individual or firm, the dual modes remain the same, although the clusters' configuration changes. Human-dominant processes have their strengths in being controlled and emotional, while technology-dominant processes are more robust in being automated and logical, as depicted in Fig. 7.2. Returning to our chess example, Stockfish is currently the best chess computer available. It calculates the best move from brute computing force based on the logic and rules of the game. In contrast, Magnus Carlsen (the currently highest-ranked chess player in the world) has been called the Mozart of chess because of the creativity and beauty in the way he plays. However, a firm always comprises both individuals and technology. When zooming out, all processes can arguably neither be purely human nor technological and thus have elements of both human (controlled and conscious) and technology (automatic and non-conscious). There will always be a need for both humans and technology to interact in symbiosis (Jarrahi, 2018). Therefore, processes can be human- or technology-dominant, representing the endpoints of a continuum of the importance of humans and technology in achieving desirable outcomes. An example of human-dominant resource integration is a group of individuals communicating and having a brainstorming session. In this case, performance relies on the individuals' competencies (e.g., creativity, problem-solving capabilities, and communication).

Two examples of technology-dominant processes are online banking and self-service check-in at the airport, where the back-office processes in both examples are automated. The need to increase efficiency influences

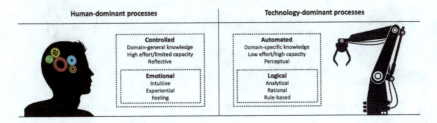

Fig. 7.2 Division of clusters of characteristics

processes that heavily depend on humans, which often are scarce higher-order resources, by automating parts of or whole processes and moving the workload from humans to technology. In the human-dominant process, in contrast, the focus is more on effectiveness and ensuring maximum value realization. Note that human-and technology-dominant processes concerning the four clusters must not be considered separate systems, nor are they limited to either or. Similarly, controlled and automatic processes are not necessarily separate but are iterative subprocesses that inform one another in sequence or parallel.

Whether processes need to be more human- or technology-dominant depends on several factors, as depicted in Fig. 7.3. Labor-intensive, repetitive, and rule-based processes are generally optimal for robotic process automation (Hollebeek et al., 2021), making the resource integration process technology dominant. Similar to non-conscious human cognitive processing, technology-dominant resource integration has its strengths in speed and large capacity for performing routine tasks, since technology can process considerable data and perform complex computations at a much faster pace than human beings. Thus, by moving toward more technology-dominant processes, firms can increase efficiency and address constraints in higher-order resources. However, despite these cognitive strengths, technology (including AI) still falls short compared to human cognitive capabilities in understanding context and emotional nuance, and has limited creativity and intuition. Thus, like conscious human capabilities, human-dominant resource integration has strengths in dealing with novel, complex, and dynamic tasks and contexts.

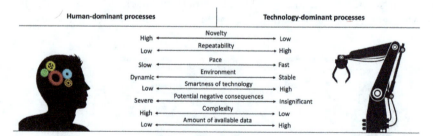

Fig. 7.3 Navigating the balance between human- and technology-dominant processes

With technology becoming more intelligent through AI, it is starting to act more as a semiautonomous actor in complex, increasingly diverse contexts (Jarrahi, 2018), thereby acting more like human actors with the ability to adapt to and master dynamic contexts. In this sense, AI moves technology from a rule-based expert system approach to a deep learning-based, data-driven approach (Kumar et al., 2019). The proposed framework also highlights the need for research on human–technology symbiosis to examine the phenomenon by zooming in and out at different levels of aggregation (Chandler & Vargo, 2011) and thus building a more systemic understanding. In Fig. 7.2, the division of clusters is based on the strengths of humans or technology in relation to each other. Hence, a human-dominant process can be logical. Moreover, emotional capabilities are more distinctive for humans than machines, even though there are examples of AI becoming better at performing "softer" skills (e.g., intuitive and empathetic) as more advanced technology is developed (Huang & Rust, 2018). In other words, as AI develops, technology can fulfill all four clusters of characteristics, as humans do, and processes can become more technology-dominant.

KEY CHALLENGES THAT FIRMS FACE IN ACHIEVING HUMAN–TECHNOLOGY SYMBIOSIS

Based on the previous discussion in the chapter, our framework of attributes can help firms implementing advanced technology in facing the following three challenges: (1) finding the right balance between humans and technology in processes; (2) ensuring human-centric technology implementation that considers the individuals involved (such as customers and employees); and (3) building a systemic understanding for effective human–technology symbiosis. Addressing these issues is crucial for harvesting and maximizing the benefits of advanced technologies while mitigating potential pitfalls and ensuring harmonious integration into existing business processes.

Striking the Right Balance Between Human Involvement and Technology in Processes

Implementing advanced technologies, such as robotics and AI, involves integrating them into existing processes. Striking the right balance between human and technology involvement in processes is crucial. While technology can excel in speed and routine tasks, it lacks a nuanced understanding of context and emotional aspects, and thus, has a clear foundation based on the data it is trained on. Many technology-enabled automated processes run without human intervention unless the situation changes or the degree of importance becomes necessary for human control. For instance, autonomous cars can drive on autopilot, but the consequences if anything goes wrong, are so severe that having a human who can intervene in an emergency is preferred (or maybe even ethically necessary). However, even with human supervision, accidents may still occur, as demonstrated by an autonomous car operated by Uber that had a fatal accident with a pedestrian on March 18, 2018. Humans' understanding of, for instance, social contexts (e.g., visually complex situations) can aid technology in avoiding biases or serious accidents. One possibility is to have both humans and AI analyze critical situations in parallel, generating separate answers to questions, which then in turn are discussed. This can spike more insights into situations, which can prompt new solutions that might not otherwise be found—limiting the biases of both humans and AI. However, humans also have observable and systematic biases, and AI can help recognize situations in which biases are likely to occur. For instance, an AI robot can monitor conversations and give the involved parties a heads-up for when a bias is expected. By utilizing our framework of attributes, firms can better understand how to develop automatization strategies that mediate the potential biases of technology and humans, thereby striking the right balance between humans and technology.

Ensuring Human-centric Technology Implementation that Considers the Individuals Involved

Human-centric values should remain at the forefront of technology implementation. Most firms' efforts with AI are only ad hoc pilots or applied to a single business process because AI initiatives must overcome challenging cultural and organizational barriers (Fountaine et al., 2019). Firms need to navigate the integration of advanced technologies without undermining human worth and dignity (i.e., humanness). There is also a need to avoid social isolation and to maintain emotional connections, while fulfilling individuals' needs for personal growth and development (i.e., well-being) (Ostrom et al., 2021). Accordingly, humans must perceive that the locus of control over technology is with humans, rather than feeling controlled by it (Jörling et al., 2019). Failing to recognize the importance of anchoring the implementation of technology in human-centric values that support involved individuals, such as employees and customers, may substantially reduce the potential return on investment. Thus, firms that wish to implement advanced technology must address the challenge of incorporating technology to enhance efficiency and user experiences while respecting the distinct strengths of human cognition, such as understanding context, emotional nuances, creativity, and intuition. Additionally, AI can only make decisions based on the data it has been trained on and has a hard time making decisions on broader ethical or moral principles (Moor, 2006). Considering a growing body of research emerging on moral machines and AI ethics (e.g., Vakkuri et al., 2021; Wallach & Allen, 2008) this situation is likely to change in the future. However, it is important to recognize current limitations and continue to investigate ways in which human–technology symbiosis can be improved to better complement and align with the cognitive strengths of humans.

Furthermore, if the incorporation of AI and technology into businesses aims to secure the well-being within the system then the integration of technology does not diminish human worth and dignity. Instances in which this would be suitable include automating tasks that pose dangers (e.g., operating in dangerous environments), mental or physical strain, or exert long-term negative effects on the involved individuals. This underscores the significance of humans.

BUILDING A SYSTEMIC UNDERSTANDING FOR EFFECTIVE SYMBIOSIS

Implementing advanced technology requires a systemic understanding of human–technology symbiosis. As a result, firms need to engage in research that zooms in and out at different levels of aggregation to comprehend the complex interactions between humans and technology. This approach examines how firms use their resources at both individual and firm levels, considering the iterative subprocesses that inform each other. Building this systemic understanding is essential for devising effective strategies that leverage the strengths of both human and technological capabilities. Dual-process thinking provides a systemic foundation for managers to create optimal human–technology symbiosis.

Conclusion

Since humans are a limited resource in organizations, and organizations are often measured based on efficiency and effectiveness parameters regarding their operations, utilizing robotization to replace humans has been a recurring topic in many fields. This has also recently been the case in service research (e.g., McLeay et al., 2020; Wirtz et al., 2018; Xiao & Kumar, 2021). This chapter highlights the increasing dependence of firms on digitization linked to AI and robotization. Dual-process theories provide a framework for understanding the interactions between humans and technology. These theories propose that outcomes can result from two different modes of processing: controlled and automated. While controlled processes are associated with logical reasoning and a reflective way of thinking, automated processes are characterized by high capacity and low effort requirements. Firms have humans representing the conscious side and technology representing the non-conscious side. Their resource utilization often relies on the interplay between humans and technology. Although low-skilled service jobs are considered difficult to automate, the rapid technological development in AI is blurring the boundaries of the physical, digital, and human domains. Thus, it emphasizes understanding the interplay between the two modes of processing. We underscore the potential of technology to enhance efficiency, rationalize the use of scarce human resources in the firm, and acknowledge the challenges of integrating technology and humans. Finally, we highlight the importance of a balanced approach in which managers view technology and humans as dual iterative processes. One whereby, technology is used to complement and augment the capacity of human actors rather than replacing them.

References

Anthony, C., Bechky, B. A., & Fayard, A.-L. (2023). "Collaborating" with AI: Taking a system view to explore the future of work. *Organization Science.* https://doi.org/10.1287/orsc.2022.1651

Autor, D. H., & Dorn, D. (2013). The growth of low-skill service jobs and the polarization of the US labor market. *American Economic Review, 103*(5), 1553–1597.

Bandura, A. (2001). Social cognitive theory: An agentic perspective. *Annual Review of Psychology, 52*(1), 1–26. https://doi.org/10.1146/annurev.psych.52.1.1

Bargh, J. A. (2002). Losing consciousness: Automatic influences on consumer judgment, behavior, and motivation. *Journal of Consumer Research, 29*(2), 280–285. https://doi.org/10.1086/341577

Bargh, J. A., & Chartrand, T. L. (1999). The unbearable automaticity of being. *American Psychologist, 54*(7), 462. https://doi.org/10.1037/0003-066x.54. 7.462

Barrett, L. F., Tugade, M. M., & Engle, R. W. (2004). Individual differences in working memory capacity and dual-process theories of the mind. *Psychological Bulletin, 130*(4), 553–573. https://doi.org/10.1037/0033-2909.130.4.553

Cenamor, J., Sjödin, D. R., & Parida, V. (2017). Adopting a platform approach in servitization: Leveraging the value of digitalization. *International Journal of Production Economics, 192*, 54–65. https://doi.org/10.1016/j.ijpe.2016. 12.033

Chandler, J. D., & Vargo, S. L. (2011). Contextualization and value-in-context: How context frames exchange. *Marketing Theory, 11*(1), 35–49. https://doi. org/10.1177/1470593110393713

Chein, J. M., & Schneider, W. (2005). Neuroimaging studies of practice-related change: FMRI and meta-analytic evidence of a domain-general control network for learning. *Cognitive Brain Research, 25*(3), 607–623. https://doi. org/10.1016/j.cogbrainres.2005.08.013

Corazza, G. E. (2016). Potential originality and effectiveness: The dynamic definition of creativity. *Creativity Research Journal, 28*(3), 258–267.

Dane, E., & Pratt, M. G. (2007). Exploring intuition and its role in managerial decision making. *Academy of Management Review, 32*(1), 33–54. https:// doi.org/10.5465/Amr.2007.23463682

De Neys, W., & Glumicic, T. (2008). Conflict monitoring in dual process theories of thinking. *Cognition, 106*(3), 1248–1299. https://doi.org/10.1016/j. cognition.2007.06.002

De Neys, W., & Pennycook, G. (2019). Logic, fast and slow: Advances in dual-process theorizing. *Current Directions in Psychological Science, 28*(5), 503–509. https://doi.org/10.1177/0963721419855658

Evans, J. (2008). Dual-processing accounts of reasoning, judgment, and social cognition. *Annual Review of Psychology, 59*, 255–278. https://doi.org/10. 1146/annurev.psych.59.103006.093629

Evans, J. S. B. T., & Stanovich, K. E. (2013). Dual-process theories of higher cognition: Advancing the debate. *Perspectives on psychological science, 8*(3), 223–241. https://doi.org/10.1177/1745691612460685

Findsrud, R., & Tronvoll, B. (2022). Deep learning in higher education: A service-dominant logic perspective. In E. Gummesson, M. Díaz-Méndez, & M. Saren (Eds.), *Improving the evaluation of scholarly work: The application of service theory* (pp. 131–149). Springer International Publishing. https://doi. org/10.1007/978-3-031-17662-3_9

Fountaine, T., McCarthy, B., & Saleh, T. (2019). Building the AI-powered organization. *Harvard Business Review, 97*(4), 62–73.

Ghosh, B., Daugherty, P. R., Wilson, H. J., & Burden, A. (2019). Taking a systems approach to adopting AI. *Harvard Business Review* https://hbr.org/2019/05/taking-a-systems-approach-to-adopting-ai

Gilson, L. L., & Goldberg, C. B. (2015). Editors' comment: So, what is a conceptual paper? *Group & Organization Management, 40*(2), 127–130. https://doi.org/10.1177/1059601115576425

Griffin, P., Care, E., & McGaw, B. (2012). The changing role of education and schools. In P. Griffin, E. Care, & B. McGaw (Eds.), *Assessment and teaching of 21st century skills* (pp. 1–15). Springer.

Gupta, P., & Harris, J. (2010). How e-WOM recommendations influence product consideration and quality of choice: A motivation to process information perspective. *Journal of Business Research, 63*(9–10), 1041–1049.

Gustafsson, A., Kristensson, P., Schirr, G. R., & Witell, L. (2016). *Service innovation*. Business Expert Press.

Hollebeek, L. D., Sprott, D. E., & Brady, M. K. (2021). Rise of the machines? Customer engagement in automated service interactions. *Journal of Service Research, 24*(1), 3–8. https://doi.org/10.1177/1094670520975110

Huang, M.-H., & Rust, R. T. (2017). Technology-driven service strategy. *Journal of the Academy of Marketing Science, 45*(6), 906–924.

Huang, M.-H., & Rust, R. T. (2018). Artificial intelligence in service. *Journal of Service Research, 21*(2), 155–172.

Huang, M.-H., & Rust, R. T. (2020). Engaged to a robot? The role of AI in service [scholarly article]. *Journal of Service Research,* 1–12. https://doi.org/10.1177/1094670520902266

International Data Corporation, I. (2023, March 7). *Worldwide spending on AI-Centric systems forecast to reach $154 billion in 2023, according to IDC.* International Data Corporation. Retrieved April 28, from https://www.idc.com/getdoc.jsp?containerId=prUS50454123

James, W. (1890). *The principles of psychology* (Vol. 1). Holt.

Jarrahi, M. H. (2018). Artificial intelligence and the future of work: Human-AI symbiosis in organizational decision making. *Business Horizons, 61*(4), 577–586. https://doi.org/10.1016/j.bushor.2018.03.007

Jörling, M., Böhm, R., & Paluch, S. (2019). Service robots: Drivers of perceived responsibility for service outcomes. *Journal of Service Research, 22*(4), 404–420. https://doi.org/10.1177/1094670519842334

Jaakkola, E. (2020). Designing conceptual articles: Four approaches. *AMS Review, 10*(1), 18–26. https://doi.org/10.1007/s13162-020-00161-0

Kahneman, D. (2011). *Thinking, fast and slow*. Farrar.

Kaplan, A., & Haenlein, M. (2019). Siri, Siri, in my hand: Who's the fairest in the land? On the interpretations, illustrations, and implications of artificial intelligence. *Business Horizons, 62*(1), 15–25.

Kihlstrom, J. F. (1987). The cognitive unconscious. *Science, 237*(4821), 1445–1452. https://doi.org/10.1126/science.3629249

Kumar, V., Rajan, B., Venkatesan, R., & Lecinski, J. (2019). Understanding the role of artificial intelligence in personalized engagement marketing. *California Management Review, 61*(4), 135–155.

Laran, J., Janiszewski, C., & Salerno, A. (2016). Exploring the differences between conscious and unconscious goal pursuit. *Journal of Marketing Research, 53*(3), 442–458.

Larivière, B., Bowen, D., Andreassen, T. W., Kunz, W., Sirianni, N. J., Voss, C., Wünderlich, N. V., & De Keyser, A. (2017). "Service Encounter 2.0": An investigation into the roles of technology, employees and customers. *Journal of Business Research, 79*, 238–246.

Lu, V. N., Wirtz, J., Kunz, W. H., Paluch, S., Gruber, T., Martins, A., & Patterson, P. G. (2020). Service robots, customers and service employees: What can we learn from the academic literature and where are the gaps? *Journal of Service Theory and Practice, 30*(3), 361–391. https://doi.org/10.1108/JSTP-04-2019-0088

MacInnis, D. J. (2011). A framework for conceptual contributions in marketing. *Journal of Marketing, 75*(4), 136–154.

Makarius, E. E., Mukherjee, D., Fox, J. D., & Fox, A. K. (2020). Rising with the machines: A sociotechnical framework for bringing artificial intelligence into the organization. *Journal of Business Research, 120*, 262–273. https://doi.org/10.1016/j.jbusres.2020.07.045

Marinova, D., de Ruyter, K., Huang, M.-H., Meuter, M. L., & Challagalla, G. (2016). Getting smart: Learning from technology-empowered frontline interactions. *Journal of Service Research, 20*(1), 29–42. https://doi.org/10.1177/1094670516679273

McLeay, F., Osburg, V. S., Yoganathan, V., & Patterson, A. (2020). Replaced by a robot: Service implications in the age of the machine. *Journal of Service Research, 24*(1), 104–121. https://doi.org/10.1177/1094670520933354

Mende, M., Scott, M. L., van Doorn, J., Grewal, D., & Shanks, I. (2019). Service robots rising: How humanoid robots influence service experiences and elicit compensatory consumer responses. *Journal of Marketing Research, 56*(4), 535–556.

Mercier, H., & Sperber, D. (2011). Why do humans reason? Arguments for an argumentative theory. *Behavioral and Brain Sciences, 34*(2), 57-+. https://doi.org/10.1017/S0140525X10000968

Moor, J. H. (2006). The nature, importance, and difficulty of machine ethics. *IEEE Intelligent Systems, 21*(4), 18–21.

Oberauer, K. (2002). Access to information in working memory: Exploring the focus of attention. *Journal of Experimental Psychology: Learning, Memory, and Cognition, 28*(3), 411.

Osman, M. (2004). An evaluation of dual-process theories of reasoning. *Psychonomic Bulletin & Review, 11*(6), 988–1010. https://doi.org/10.3758/BF0 3196730

Ostrom, A. L., Field, J. M., Fotheringham, D., Subramony, M., Gustafsson, A., Lemon, K. N., Huang, M.-H., & McColl-Kennedy, J. R. (2021). Service research priorities: Managing and delivering service in turbulent times. *Journal of Service Research, 24*(3), 329–353. https://doi.org/10.1177/109467052 11021915

Pradeep, A., Appel, A., & Sthanunathan, S. (2018). *AI for marketing and product innovation: Powerful new tools for predicting trends, connecting with customers, and closing sales.* John Wiley & Sons.

Ritter, T., & Geersbro, J. (2018). Multidexterity in customer relationship management: Managerial implications and a research agenda. *Industrial Marketing Management, 69*, 74–79.

Royakkers, L., & Van Est, R. (2017). Robotisation as rationalisation. *Engineering Journal, 1*(4), 555570.

Saariluoma, P. (1995). *Chess players' thinking: A cognitive psychological approach.* Psychology Press.

Schneider, W., & Chein, J. M. (2003). Controlled & automatic processing: Behavior, theory, and biological mechanisms. *Cognitive Science, 27*(3), 525–559. https://doi.org/10.1016/S0364-0213(03)00011-9

Storbacka, K., Brodie, R. J., Böhmann, T., Maglio, P. P., & Nenonen, S. (2016). Actor engagement as a microfoundation for value co-creation. *Journal of Business Research, 69*(8), 3008–3017.

Thornton, P. H., Ocasio, W., & Lounsbury, M. (2012). *The institutional logics perspective: A new approach to culture, structure, and process.* Oxford University Press.

Vakkuri, V., Kemell, K.-K., Jantunen, M., Halme, E., & Abrahamsson, P. (2021). ECCOLA—A method for implementing ethically aligned AI systems. *Journal of Systems and Software, 182*, 111067. https://doi.org/10.1016/j.jss.2021. 111067

Van Doorn, J., Mende, M., Noble, S. M., Hulland, J., Ostrom, A. L., Grewal, D., & Petersen, J. A. (2017). Domo arigato Mr. Roboto: Emergence of automated social presence in organizational frontlines and customers' service experiences. *Journal of Service Research, 20*(1), 43–58.

Vargo, S. L., & Lusch, R. F. (2016). Institutions and axioms: An extension and update of service-dominant logic. *Journal of the Academy of Marketing Science, 44*(1), 5–23. https://doi.org/10.1007/s11747-015-0456-3

Wallach, W., & Allen, C. (2008). *Moral machines: Teaching robots right from wrong*. Oxford University Press.

Wirtz, J., Patterson, P. G., Kunz, W. H., Gruber, T., Lu, V. N., Paluch, S., & Martins, A. (2018). Brave new world: Service robots in the frontline. *Journal of Service Management, 29*(5).

Xiao, L., & Kumar, V. (2021). Robotics for customer service: A useful complement or an ultimate substitute? *Journal of Service Research, 24*(1), 9–29. https://doi.org/10.1177/1094670519878881

PART III

Humanness and Values

CHAPTER 8

Smart Home Technologies: Convenience and Control

Nils Ehrenberg🅾

1. INTRODUCTION

This chapter discusses what a smart home is, what kind of labour is required to maintain it and how it affects the social power dynamics of the household. Rather than focusing on specific technologies, the chapter will take a general outlook on how the technologies of the smart home are embedded in the home, what they try to achieve and what they appear to accomplish. This chapter perceives smart home technologies as a set of technologies intended to automate practices in the home through the continuous observation of the home and its inhabitants, remote operation of the home and tracking the use of utilities in the home. While automation, remote operation or tracking do not require the use of AI, it is often a component (e.g. in self-learning algorithms) or the data collected by smart home systems can be used to support AI in the future. AI-powered technologies are becoming more integrated in our daily lives through software and devices such as voice assistants and self-learning

N. Ehrenberg (✉)
Aalto University, Espoo, Finland
e-mail: nils.ehrenberg@aalto.fi

© The Author(s) 2024
R. Rousi et al. (eds.), *Humane Autonomous Technology*,
https://doi.org/10.1007/978-3-031-66528-8_8

thermostats. The aim of this chapter is to offer insights and perspectives related to how these technologies can affect power dynamics in the home by changing the way in which information flows within the home. It shows how existing power structures can be embedded in smart home technologies, maintenance of the smart home or in digital housekeeping. These notions are then discussed through the theoretical lenses of Foucauldian discipline and contributional justice.

What is a 'Smart Home'?

The terms 'smart home' and 'smart home technologies' largely emerged as marketing terms rather than technical descriptions, indicating home technologies with some form of interactive digital component that enable automation. It can therefore be said that it is the interactive technologies that make a home 'smart' (Harper, 2003). In this section, the constituents of a smart home are discussed, as are how they relate to narratives such as those related to sustainability, convenience and the home's boundaries.

In 2003, Frances Aldrich (2003, p. 17) referred to a smart home as 'a residence equipped with computing and information technology which anticipates and responds to the needs of the occupants, working to promote their comfort, convenience, security and entertainment through the management of technology within the home and connections to the world beyond'. Aldrich's description of a smart home has been frequently cited as a way to describe what a smart home is and what it aims to accomplish. However, one of the things that is notable about the definitions of a 'smart home' is that the various descriptions fail to establish a definitive standard, allowing anyone to refer to a home as 'smart'. As the terms 'smart home' and 'smart home technologies' have been around for several decades without gaining any significant adoption until the Internet of Things started becoming mainstream and as the idea of smart home technologies often appears to be connected to things that are not yet mainstream, it can also be surmised that the definition of a 'smart home' is something that shifts with time. Despite this lack of clarity, there is a general understanding that smart homes involve the use of emerging digital and information technologies to facilitate comfortable or convenient lifestyle choices and offer greater oversight over utilities.

Computing and information technologies that anticipate the needs of home occupants inevitably come down to sensors and actuators that either directly track the behaviour of the occupants or parameters of the space, (the latter being tracked by, e.g. air quality or temperature sensors). Such sensors continuously observe and collect information about the home and its occupants; the information is then used to support the comfort and convenience of the occupants. While sustainability is often discussed as an opportunity for smart home technologies (e.g. Strengers et al., 2022) and some technologies (such as heat pumps) offer excellent energy saving opportunities, several studies have observed convenience as an important theme in smart home technologies, both as a vision among smart home developers (Aagaard, 2021) and as a driver for users to adopt smart home technologies (Ehrenberg & Keinonen, 2021b). Strengers and Nicholls (2017) argue that there is a relatively stable narrative of convenience embedded in smart home technologies, which they understand as the simplification of everyday practices through home automation. Strengers and Nicholls (2017) see convenience as a problematic goal as it is undefined and prone to changing with time—things that were once considered convenient may change meaning. Furthermore, they also note that these technologies may not lead to the desired reduction in labour or energy use that they claim to offer. Sadowski et al. (2021) further argue that the smart home can be seen as Big Mother, perceiving it as a system that promotes surveillance under the guise of maternal care.

In Aldrich's (2003) quote above, it is notable that she refers to 'connections to the world beyond' as the smart home allows for more porous boundaries than the traditional home. While the boundary of a traditional home is defined by the walls or even the yard, smart home technologies allow the occupants to access the home without being physically present, thereby making the boundaries ambiguous. Two examples of technology that affect the boundaries of the home are smart doorbells, which allow a resident to answer the door without being present, and smart lighting, which allows for changing the lighting from outside the home. Smart home technologies can also be set up so that the home is able to interact with services and devices outside of the physical space, such as setting up the technologies in the home so that they automatically order household supplies when the supplies are running low.

3. Who are the Users of the Smart Home?

This section expands on who can be considered a user of a smart home. There are a number of ways of considering and categorising users, such as categorising them by technological expertise, lifestyle preferences or specific needs; these might offer insight into who installs smart home technologies and why they do so. However, when looking at homes where smart home technologies are already in place, it is also possible to perceive the users based on who is affected by these technologies. This perspective places the focus on the kind of power dynamics that is present among smart home users in private homes as well as in rental homes. While an initial assumption might be that the residents are the users of the smart home, the reality is somewhat more complex. First, the complexity stems from the nature of smart home technologies as different members of the household experience the technology differently, and second, it stems from the porous boundaries of the smart home when people beyond the residents are affected. Based on Pierce's (2021) understanding of the 'users' and 'usees' (that is, people who are outside of the household but may still become subjects of the smart home technologies) of the smart home, Ehrenberg (2023) suggests four primary categories of users in smart homes: initiators, cohabitants, incidental users and bystanders (see Fig. 8.1).

A common pattern in studies on private smart homes is that one person, usually male, (referred to as the 'initiator' in this chapter) has the primary responsibility for selecting, setting up and managing the smart home technologies (Geeng & Roesner, 2019; Mennicken & Huang, 2012; Takayama et al., 2012). As such, the initiators also have a significant influence over the smart home and all the practices that are shaped by these technologies.

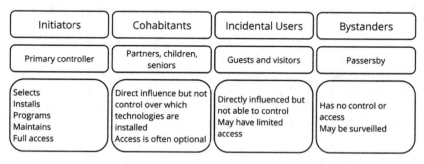

Fig. 8.1 The division of users in private smart housing. Adapted from Ehrenberg (2023)

Other members of the household (referred to as 'cohabitants' in this chapter), form a category that consists of the initiators' partners, children or senior family members who live permanently in the smart home. Cohabitants often have some influence over the choice of technologies. In particular, spouses can have an impact on the initiators. However, in many cases, this impact is displayed through an ability to reject new technologies that the initiator (i.e. their partner) proposes. While cohabitants may have access to changing the settings on the smart technologies, this access is often optional and may not extend to all the technologies. Instead of changing the settings themselves, cohabitants exercise control by requesting that the initiator adjusts the settings according to their preferences.

People who are not part of the household may still be affected by the technologies; in this chapter 'incidental users' refers to people who might stay temporarily in the home. Incidental users can include overnight guests (including AirBnB guests), children's friends or cleaners. Guests visit the smart home and, therefore, either directly use the technologies or can be affected by them while having limited to no access or control over those technologies. For example, needing an app to control the music or lighting can present an additional barrier to feeling welcome as a guest. For a cleaner, not having access can also impede their work if they need an app to access parts of the home or turn up the brightness of the light so they can see while they clean.

Finally, 'bystanders' include those people who are neither member of the household or invited guests but who are still in some ways affected by the home technologies. As noted by Pierce (2021), even people who never enter the household are affected through technologies such as smart doorbells (such as Ring from Amazon), which record anyone who passes outside the door, such as neighbours or delivery people. This can sometimes have severe repercussions as the data from smart doorbells has been shared with the police in the United States without the owner's knowledge (Ng, 2022).

While the above categories even exist to some degree in traditional homes, Aaagard (2022) observed that smart home technologies may embed already unequal power dynamics into the infrastructure of the home. This is done through smart home technologies adding additional barriers and levels of access for different members of the household, even within the home. The four categories indicate how different individuals are affected as the technologies are embedded in the existing dynamics of power within the household and turn these informal power structures into a part of the infrastructure. In a British study, Furszyfer Del Rio (2022) found that smart homes are likely to exacerbate conflicts, in part because of users' preferences and unequal control, but also because of privacy-related issues.

As the power dynamics become embedded through the technologies, they also become more static. Without the smart technologies, there is an ongoing opportunity to negotiate and re-negotiate power dynamics and structures with other members of the household. Meanwhile, the smart home technologies instead embed and materialise what the initiator perceives as the best way to live, such as controlling lighting through an app which requires others to also use the app (and thus their phones) if they want to control the lights. If a cohabitant wishes to reprogram a smart home device, they might need to approach the initiator in order to adjust the technology, giving the initiator significant power in this negotiation. The control over smart home technologies is not neces-sarily perceived as an encroachment by the initiator, especially in private homes. The initiators often attempt to implement technologies that they feel will benefit the entire home, and when they make changes based on the request of cohabitants, they see it as being available to help out rather than taking control over the home. For example, the initiator may feel helpful by changing the temperature settings or reprogramming the lights according to a cohabitant's preferences, but this is something the cohabitant might have been able to do themselves if the smart home tech-nologies had not added an additional barrier of access. Instead of adopting technologies that facilitate a better lifestyle, an inadequate implementa-tion of smart home technologies requires the residents to adjust their lives to the technologies, (for example, the residents need to rearrange the furniture to better suit a robot vacuum cleaner).

4. RENTAL SMART HOUSING

In rental housing and particularly co-living, the dynamic is somewhat different (see Fig. 8.2). Here, the landlord takes on a similar role to that of the initiator; they select, install and maintain the smart home technologies. Meanwhile the renters hold a position akin to that of a cohabitant as they live in the smart home yet do not have control or access to all the settings or data. While there may be differences within a household regarding who sets up or controls the technologies, in some rental housing, the landlord is the only one with access to the data. There is also rental housing where the residents themselves have installed all the smart home technologies, making a private home typology more applicable. The dynamics shown in Fig. 8.2 become especially evident in co-living solutions, where residents have shared spaces with rules defined by the landlord rather than the community (Ehrenberg & Keinonen, 2021a). Depending on local regulations, co-living spaces may be regulated similarly to hotels or short-term rentals, despite some residents signing contracts for a year and treating it as their permanent home.

Below is an example that illustrates how landlords may impose their will onto the residents regarding how to live; the residents are expected to shape their behaviour to please the smart home technologies:

I live in a rental apartment that is owned and maintained by one of the large rental housing companies in Finland. Our house was completed about five years ago, and it includes a lot of modern features, including smart home technologies. The main smart home technology that I am aware of is the heating and ventilation system. The heated floors turn on and off 'by themselves.' In winter, the heating also comes as hot air through the vents; in summer, the vents should provide cold air. We do not have any radiators. I do not have any control over the heating and the ventilation. In my room, I have a box with sensors, like in every one of the 68 apartments. To my knowledge, the heating and ventilation are adjusted according to some average. The main issues come in the summer when half of the flats on the sunny side heat up to almost 30 degrees, meanwhile the flats on the other side do not. Instead of providing solutions, we often receive emails that we – people on the sunny side – should keep our balcony doors closed to ensure that the system can work properly, even if it is 5–7 degrees colder outside than inside. In the common spaces of the building, I have been told by the security guards that I am not

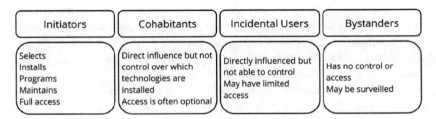

Fig. 8.2 The division of users in rental smart housing. Adapted from Ehrenberg (2023)

allowed to keep a door open because it disturbs the ventilation system and they get a call about a door being left open.
  - Smart home resident

Unlike the private smart home, these rules are not set by the members of the household but by the landlord. While the initiator is already in a position of power due to their knowledge of and access to the system, a tenant may be forced to simply comply with the landlord's regulations or move out.

5. DIGITAL HOUSEKEEPING IN SMART HOMES

This section covers digital housekeeping, what it entails and how it affects power dynamics. The initiators, as noted above, are primarily men, this stands in contrast with how, in most mixed households, women tend to do a larger part of the domestic work. New technologies are often presented as time saving and are intended to reduce domestic labour. However, domestic work increased during the twentieth century. In Cowan Schwarz's seminal work *More Work for Mother* (Cowan, 2011), she addresses how new technologies, such as the vacuum cleaner, have resulted in more domestic labour, rather than less. For example, before the vacuum cleaner it might have been acceptable to clean less often, but the introduction of the vacuum cleaner created the expectation of cleaning more frequently than previously, so the baseline shifted. Strengers and Nicholls (2017) also consider vacuum cleaners to be part of the narrative of technologies that offer convenience but end up requiring more work. Thus, even though cleaning takes less time and effort, the overall amount of work increases in the long run. In a similar vein, Coggins (2022) argues that smart home robots are likely to alter practices in the home rather than reduce domestic labour. For example, there is a need to keep the home more orderly so that the robot vacuum cleaner can run when the residents are away or there is a need to select different furniture as robot vacuum cleaners require furniture to have a certain clearance in order to vacuum underneath the furniture.

The discourse on digital housekeeping comes out of the mid-2000s where Tolmie et al. (2007) defined 'digital housekeeping' as the work involved in setting up and maintaining home networks. It was perceived that the digital housekeeping was done by those people in the household with greater digital expertise (Grinter et al., 2005). The notion of expertise in digital housekeeping has since been expanded to include comprehension of systems, ability to transfer knowledge and automation of systems (Kennedy et al., 2015). In an Australian study, it was noted that the division of labour is unevenly distributed when it comes to digital housekeeping with men, rather than women, taking on the majority of the work (Kennedy et al., 2015). One of the causes of this uneven distribution of labour may involve how men and women perceive technology as part of their gender expression. Rode and Poole (2018) observed how gender identity is constructed in relation to technology and stated that expertise in technology is often perceived as a male attribute. As a result, digital housekeeping is often associated with men even where women in the household are equally capable. These stereotypical perceptions of technology and gender identity are also expressed through interest in technology (more often associated with male identity), which results in greater technical expertise if exercised quickly. It can be argued that while digital housekeeping is often distributed based on expertise (see, e.g. Grinter et al., 2005), this expertise is itself a result of gender norms. Strengers and Nicholls have observed this and, in references to Cowan's work, they refer to this as 'more work for father' (Strengers & Nicholls, 2018, p. 9), also arguing that interest in technology is an important factor.

While digital domestic labour is often done by men, there are important tensions to consider when these technologies automate practices that are either shared or traditionally perceived as relating to women. As many initiators are male (a trait also shared with many people working in tech), these new technologies may result in work that is either shared or traditionally perceived as relating to women being done by technology largely controlled and maintained by men. As observed in a study by Ehrenberg et al. (2023), some cohabitants veto technologies in certain spaces, such as laundry rooms, as they perceive them as interfering with their practices. This displacement can become a point of conflict as the initiator reshapes practices that they perceive as tedious or uninteresting while not themselves being in charge of them. At the same time, the adoption of smart home technologies adds an additional technical skill requirement in order to be able to contribute to the practices affected by smart home technologies. In a study by Furszyfer Del Rio (2022), unequal digital skills are also perceived as a cause of domestic tensions in smart homes. For the cohabitants, the smart practices often add to the mental load as the digital domestic labour is often not innate or habitual but something that is forced on them; as such, they are often unwilling to engage with it.

In contrast, the initiators (who consider the smart technologies as added conveniences) are both willing and interested to engage with smart home technologies (as noted by Strengers & Nicholls, 2018) as they perceive them to be something akin to a hobby.

6. Power in the Smart Home

This section considers Foucault and disciplinary power in order to explore both how power is exercised in the smart home and the implications of the unequal distribution of digital housekeeping. In Foucault's understanding of power, discipline is a way by which power can be exercised, primarily by governmental institutions (Foucault, 1995). The disciplinary exercise of power is used to regulate behaviour and functions through three elements: hierarchical observation, normalising judgement and examination. As subjects are observed, a standard can be made by which normalised judgements are made and against which subjects can measure themselves; the examination then classifies and punishes subjects falling outside the norm (Foucault, 1995). Hierarchical observation is essential for discipline as it allows for more precise judgements. In the smart home, the sensors continuously collect data about the space and its residents. This data can be used for normalised judgements. Whereby behaviour is judged and then punished if it deviates from approved behaviour through the examination. The smart home can therefore be understood as mimicking the governmental institutions that Foucault perceives (Ehrenberg & Keinonen, 2021b).

By understanding the smart home through a Foucauldian lens of disciplinary power, we can perceive several mechanisms by which power is exercised as these technologies become embedded in our daily lives. The mechanisms below are based on how the Foucauldian notions of hierarchical observation, normalising judgement and examination can be seen in smart home technologies (Ehrenberg & Keinonen, 2021b):

- Overt observation: Technology (such as the technology behind smart doorbells or baby cameras) is used to observe the human interactions in or around the home.
- Discreet observation: Technology (such as CO_2 sensors) is used to observe the space, distinguished from overt observation as the surveillance of people is not the primary aim

- Constraining interactions: Technology (such as voice assistants) is used to define how you interact with devices and technologies within the home
- Regulating commodities: Technology is used to define when and how certain commodities (such as hot water) can be used
- Predefining practices: Technologies are used to define how one can use a space, such as the technology used to set up the lighting to support certain practices (e.g. mood lighting that does not support reading or working and thereby defines how the space is used)

These five mechanisms by which power is exercised are, at least on the surface, designed to deliver comfort, convenience, security and entertainment. However, as they do this, they also shift the power dynamics of the household. Earlier in this chapter, the differences in how the residents relate to the home in private or rental housing were discussed; through these mechanisms of power, we can also see how each technology can offer either initiators or landlords measures of control based on their interpretation of how they believe one should live in the dwelling. Important differences between private and rental homes are both where the power is transferred to and the motivation behind the technologies. In private homes the power remains within the household; however, it reifies existing power structures by embedding them in the technology. In the case of rental housing or co-living, power is prone to shifting outside of the household and towards the landlord who is, in some ways, able to dictate how the residents live. In some ways, the rules of the living conditions imposed by smart homes are already in place; however, while a current system is based on the possibility of continuous negotiations, technology lacks the ability for negotiations and will simply act as programmed.

The intent also shapes the technologies. A commonly stated motivation among smart home initiators is that technology offers convenience, as well as sometimes offering reduced energy costs or at least insight into how energy is consumed. For landlords, we can expect that reduced energy costs and easier maintenance are important motivations for installing smart home technologies (yet, as seen in the example above, cost or ease of maintenance may not present the full picture), as well as being able to present a dwelling as a modern dwelling. However, while some of the technologies hold significant promise for energy savings, Strengers argues they facilitate a high-energy lifestyle (Strengers, 2013) and Darby (2018) suggests there is little evidence for smart homes actually reducing energy consumption if one considers the rebound effects resulting from reshaped practices, stand-by systems and the production of smart home devices. It is therefore a matter of whose benefit, whose lowered costs and whose convenience is improved by these technologies.

Another important aspect of Foucault's theories of power is the panopticon (Foucault, 1995), originally conceived of as a prison design by Jeremy Bentham (1995) in the eighteenth century and appropriated by Foucault as a tool of governance. In a panopticon, the members of society are subjected to the possibility of constant surveillance, thereby regulating their behaviour based on the assumption that they may be under surveillance. While the term 'panopticon' has come to be synonymous with the notion of surveillance societies in common use, it is the self-regulating behaviour that is key to Foucault's definition. If people self-regulate their behaviour to avoid potential punishment, the exercise of power fades into the background. The exercise of power in a panopticon is therefore subtle and becomes a subconscious reflex wherein the subjects may not actively reflect on the power exercised upon them. Ehrenberg et al. (2023) argue that smart homes are emerging 'panopticons of convenience'. Panopticons of convenience are differentiated from Foucauldian panopticons based on the fact that they are adopted (or at least accepted) by the subjects for the purpose of convenience, while Foucauldian panopticons are installed by institutions.

Furthermore, they are considered emerging as much of the exercise of power in the smart home remains relatively obvious for now. However, as smart homes become more entrenched and the technologies develop, the exercise of power is likely to become more subtle. Panopticons of convenience are defined as 'The acceptance of additional surveillance of one's life for the purpose of acquiring actual or presumed convenience' and are intended as a lens for understanding how smart homes affect autonomy and agency within the smart home (Ehrenberg et al., 2023).

Understanding smart homes as panopticons of convenience does not immediately tell us how to design better smart homes, but together with the disciplinary mechanisms, we are able to identify some of the ways in which smart home technologies act as intermediaries between residents, shifting the flow of information, and thereby shape our daily practices. For example, smart doorbells can send a notification when someone enters or leaves the house, which allows the initiator to ask a cohabitant about a specific event—why their partner left the home, why someone visited or what the package that was delivered contained. They are asking what happened by asking the questions listed above, rather than asking the cohabitant what happened more generally. While this might appear a minor concern, it reflects one of the ways in which smart homes reshape our relationship with the home.

7. Contributing to the Household

This section considers what kind of implications the mechanisms introduced in the previous section may have in regard to the residents' ability to participate in household politics and maintenance, as well as what kind of skills are needed in the smart home. One perspective with which to consider the power dynamics of the smart home is that of contributional justice (Sayer, 2011). Sayer describes contributional justice as a normative theory addressing the distribution of labour and how people have unequal opportunities to fulfil their potential. Sayer (2011) noted that men often contribute less to domestic labour while also reserving what they perceive as less tedious tasks for themselves. Here we can see echoes of digital domestic labour, where men are typically both the ones who are more involved in it and find it more interesting. Of course, there is nothing wrong with dividing domestic labour based on the preferences of the members of the household; however, digital domestic labour is often involved in the automation of practices. As noted above, tensions easily arise when the initiators automate practices that they are not generally involved in, thereby displacing those who are involved in those practices. This process also turns what was previously perceived by the initiators as a low-value task that is worth automating, such as vacuuming, into what is perceived as a higher-value task or lighter task (e.g. maintaining the robot vacuum cleaner).

A contributional perspective further shows that contributing to the smart home requires additional digital skills. As noted earlier in this chapter, digital domestic labour is primarily done by the more technically adept members of the household (Grinter et al., 2005). With technical expertise being tied to male gender identity (Rode & Poole, 2018), it is unsurprising that digital domestic labour is primarily done by men. This leaves cohabitants without digital skills with the choice of either developing these skills or performing household practices around the technologies, wherein they do the manual labour of serving the smart home rather than the smart home assisting them. In rental or co-living accommodations, it is not merely digital skills that are required but tenants also do not have the ability to participate in choosing which technologies are embedded and observing the daily lives of the residents. While smart home technologies may be intended to contribute to lower energy consumption, they also disconnect the residents themselves from sustainable practices as they hinder the residents from being able to fully participate in decisions on how to live in their own home.

8. CONCLUSION

Through the theoretical lenses of the Foucauldian discipline and contributional justice, this chapter has explored the smart home, its users and how the smart home may extend beyond the residents as well as digital housekeeping and who is likely to be doing it. Understanding how smart home technologies shift the power balance and what implications this might have for contributory justice using panopticons of convenience as a lens may provide a useful tool for policymaking, implementing and developing smart home technologies. And while this chapter does not further explore smart home technologies and domestic abuse, there is already existing discourse on the potential for abuse through these technologies (e.g. Tanczer et al., 2018). Nor does it cover cyber or data security, on which there is already an extensive discourse.

In the context of private homes, smart homes reshape and materialise inequalities, requiring digital skills to participate in the maintenance of smart homes. In private homes, unlike rental housing, the shifts in power are largely within the household. In a rental home, the power shifts towards the landlord who gains access to data that can reveal significantly more about the activities of the renters than they might expect. Smart electricity metering can reveal when they are cooking or watching TV. Air quality sensors, which are common in bedrooms, can reveal how many people are staying in the home. Initiators and landlords thereby gain access to very sensitive information that might not have been previously discussed. While in private homes, cohabitants, or at least spouses, might have access to the same data as initiators, they might not be interested in smart home technologies and therefore not install the apps needed. The cohabitants may therefore also be unaware of what can be discerned from the data.

A Foucauldian analysis of power suggests that the residents are trained to behave in accordance with the system, while also indicating that as this behaviour becomes internalised, they may become unaware of doing so. Many of the exercises of power by smart home technologies remain obvious for now, thereby panopticons of convenience can be considered an emerging phenomenon. However, as these technologies become more entrenched, the exercise of power is likely to fade into the background. As residents embrace the conveniences of smart home technologies, there is a need for transparency in regard to what the trade-offs are for these conveniences.

The need for digital skills in digital housekeeping opens up the question of what happens if an initiator is unable to perform their duties (whether through illness or other causes). If the smart home relies on the knowledge of particular individuals, as is the case in many privately built smart homes where a tech-savvy initiator has tinkered with and developed their own solutions, how can it be handed over and what is the longevity of the technologies? All of these challenges indicate a need to further understand how AI in the home will shape our relations both to our homes and to the people we live with. There is therefore a need for developers and researchers, as well as policymakers, to consider how to shape these technologies as they become further embedded in our everyday lives.

References

Aagaard, L. K. (2021). The meaning of convenience in smart home imaginaries: Tech industry insights. *Buildings and Cities, 2*(1), 1. https://doi.org/10.5334/bc.93

Aagaard, L. K. (2022). When Smart Technologies Enter Household Practices: The Gendered Implications of Digital Housekeeping Housing, *Theory and Society, 40*(1), 60–77.

Aldrich, F. K. (2003). Smart homes: Past, present and future. In R. Harper (Ed.), *Inside the smart home* (pp. 17–39). Springer London. https://doi.org/10.1007/1-85233-854-7_2

Bentham, J. (1995). *The panopticon writings* (M. Božovič, Ed.). Verso.

Coggins, T. N. (2022). More work for roomba? Domestic robots, housework and the production of privacy. *Prometheus.* https://doi.org/10.13169/prometheus.38.1.0098

Cowan, R. S. (2011). *More work for mother: The ironies of household ; technology from the open hearth to the microwave* (Nachdr.). Basic Books.

Darby, S. J. (2018). Smart technology in the home: Time for more clarity. *Building Research & Information, 46*(1), 140–147. https://doi.org/10. 1080/09613218.2017.1301707

Ehrenberg, N. (2023). *Panopticons of convenience: Smart homes as instances of domestic power.* Aalto University.

Ehrenberg, N., Harviainen, J. T., & Suominen, J. (2023). Towards panopticons of convenience: Power in the nordic smart home assemblage. *Proceeding of the 26rd International Academic MindTrek Conference.* Mindtrek '23, New York, NY, USA. https://doi.org/10.1145/3616961.3616962

Ehrenberg, N., & Keinonen, T. (2021a). Co-Living as a rental home experience: Smart home technologies and autonomy. *Interaction Design and Architecture(s), 50*, 82–101. https://doi.org/10.55612/s-5002-050-005

Ehrenberg, N., & Keinonen, T. (2021b). The technology is enemy for me at the moment: How smart home technologies assert control beyond intent. *Proceedings of the 2021 CHI Conference on Human Factors in Computing Systems*, 1–11. https://doi.org/10.1145/3411764.3445058

Foucault, M. (1995). *Discipline and punish: The birth of the prison* (2nd Vintage Books ed). Vintage Books.

Furszyfer Del Rio, D. D. (2022). Smart but unfriendly: Connected home products as enablers of conflict. *Technology in Society, 68*, 101808. https://doi. org/10.1016/j.techsoc.2021.101808

Geeng, C., & Roesner, F. (2019). Who's in control? Interactions in multi-user smart homes. *Proceedings of the 2019 CHI Conference on Human Factors in Computing Systems CHI '19*, 1–13. https://doi.org/10.1145/3290605.330 0498

Grinter, R. E., Edwards, W. K., Newman, M. W., & Ducheneaut, N. (2005). The work to make a home network work. In H. Gellersen, K. Schmidt, M. Beaudouin-Lafon, & W. Mackay (Eds.), *ECSCW 2005* (pp. 469–488). Springer Netherlands. https://doi.org/10.1007/1-4020-4023-7_24

Harper, R. (2003). Inside the smart home: Ideas, possibilities and methods. In R. Harper (Ed.), *Inside the smart home* (pp. 1–13). Springer.

Kennedy, J., Nansen, B., Arnold, M., Wilken, R., & Gibbs, M. (2015). Digital housekeepers and domestic expertise in the networked home. *Convergence: The International Journal of Research into New Media Technologies, 21*(4), 408–422. https://doi.org/10.1177/1354856515579848

Mennicken, S., & Huang, E. M. (2012). Hacking the natural habitat: An in-the-wild study of smart homes, their development, and the people who live in them. In *Pervasive Computing* (Vol. 7319, pp. 143–160). Springer. https:// doi.org/10.1007/978-3-642-31205-2_10

Ng, A. (2022, July 13). *Amazon gave ring videos to police without owners' permission.* Politico. https://www.politico.com/news/2022/07/13/amazon-gave-ring-videos-to-police-without-owners-permission-00045513

Pierce, J. (2021). In tension with progression: Grasping the frictional tendencies of speculative, critical, and other alternative designs. *Proceedings of the 2021 CHI Conference on Human Factors in Computing Systems*, 1–19. https://doi.org/10.1145/3411764.3445406

Rode, J. A., & Poole, E. S. (2018). Putting the gender back in digital housekeeping. *Proceedings of the 4th Conference on Gender & IT*, 79–90. https://doi.org/10.1145/3196839.3196845

Sadowski, J., Strengers, Y., & Kennedy, J. (2021). More work for big mother: revaluing care and control in smart homes. *Environment and Planning A: Economy and Space*, 0308518X211022366. https://doi.org/10.1177/0308518X211022366

Sayer, A. (2011). Habitus, work and contributive justice. *Sociology, 45*(1), 7–21. https://doi.org/10.1177/0038038510387188

Strengers, Y. (2013). Smart energy technologies in everyday life. *Palgrave Macmillan UK*. https://doi.org/10.1057/9781137267054

Strengers, Y., Gram-Hanssen, K., Dahlgren, K., & Aagaard, L. K. (2022). *Energy, emerging technologies and gender in homes. 3*(1), 1. https://doi.org/10.5334/bc.273

Strengers, Y., & Nicholls, L. (2017). Convenience and energy consumption in the smart home of the future: Industry visions from Australia and beyond. *Energy Research & Social Science, 32*, 86–93. https://doi.org/10.1016/j.erss.2017.02.008

Strengers, Y., & Nicholls, L. (2018). Aesthetic pleasures and gendered techwork in the 21st-century smart home. *Media International Australia, 166*(1), 70–80. https://doi.org/10.1177/1329878X17737661

Takayama, L., Pantofaru, C., Robson, D., Soto, B., & Barry, M. (2012). Making technology homey: Finding sources of satisfaction and meaning in home automation. *Proceedings of the 2012 ACM Conference on Ubiquitous Computing*, 511–520. https://doi.org/10.1145/2370216.2370292

Tanczer, L. M., Steenmans, I., Elsden, M., Blackstock, J., & Carr, M. (2018). Emerging risks in the IoT ecosystem: Who's afraid of the big bad smart fridge? *Living in the Internet of Things: Cybersecurity of the IoT - 2018*, 33 (pp.9). https://doi.org/10.1049/cp.2018.0033

Tolmie, P., Crabtree, A., Rodden, T., Greenhalgh, C., & Benford, S. (2007). Making the home network at home: Digital housekeeping. In L. J. Bannon, I. Wagner, C. Gutwin, R. H. R. Harper, & K. Schmidt (Eds.), *ECSCW 2007* (pp. 331–350). Springer. https://doi.org/10.1007/978-1-84800-031-5_18

Social Robot Design and the Aesthetics of Imperfection

Rebekah Rousi and *Paul Haimes*

INTRODUCTION

Human history is characterised by the technology that time represents. The steam engine, telegraph, even paints, pens and calculators—all of these tools serve a purpose of either extending human abilities or compensating for shortcomings and imperfections. In entering an era defined by cognitive, connective yet seemingly autonomous technology, we may see that it is not mere memory, distance or speed that humans are trying to compensate for and extend. Rather, these days technology is being developed to augment human functions such as thought, learning, creative practice and even love (see e.g., Hassenzahl et al., 2012; Samani, 2011).

R. Rousi (✉)
School of Marketing and Communication, University of Vaasa, Vaasa, Finland
e-mail: rebekah.rousi@uwasa.fi

P. Haimes
College of Global Liberal Arts, Ritsumeikan University, Kyoto, Japan

© The Author(s) 2024
R. Rousi et al. (eds.), *Humane Autonomous Technology*,
https://doi.org/10.1007/978-3-031-66528-8_9

There are plans to remove humans entirely from some areas of industry,[1] while at the same time the need for humans to connect with others and have meaningful non-work-related activities is also increasing (Döring & Poeschl, 2019; Nyholm et al., 2022; Sætra, 2021). Autonomous learning technology is replacing ever more jobs, while those humans who have employment are working increasingly longer days, with work seeping into all other areas of life via social media and non-stop connectivity. In this chapter, the authors delve into the dimension of spirituality in human–robot interaction (HRI) through a cross-cultural lens. This is in order to understand how social robots may be designed to relate to humans in a way that runs more than skin deep—beyond the physical skins of the embodied robots. By spirituality, the authors refer to the inner, subjective person, or stream of human consciousness and intentionality that exists within yet separately to the body (Boyd, 1998; Green, 2008). The opportunity is taken to expand on aesthetic and affective understandings of human–robot experience, as well as reflect on the very nature of robot existence in itself. The authors go beyond scholarly perspectives that view the role of consciousness and emotions as psycho-physiological properties in human–robot interaction, towards observing them as relational components in spiritual existentialism.

Many scholars posit that human needs and experience go beyond the pragmatic and instrumental (Alben, 1996; Maslow & Lewis, 1987; Max-Neef, 2017). These needs can be seen to either start from or augment into the aesthetic, ethical and spiritual, depending on which perspective one is approaching the topic (see e.g., Koslander et al., 2009; Missinne, 1991). It is often argued, as well as seen in modern national welfare models, that basic physiological needs are the most urgent to satisfy in terms of health, home, safety, food and water (see e.g., Alderfer, 1969). Core claims relate to the necessity for fulfilling primary physical requirements before progressing towards higher dimensions including the social and self-actualising within an individual (Maslow & Lewis, 1987). Evidence can be seen however, both within recent societal developments and psychophysiological (mental health) research, that although basic

---

[1] Lewicki et al. (2019) describe the evolution of jobs filled by robots from blue-collar (factory, manual and physically repetitive) work to white-collar (office, administrative, cleric) work, and discuss the alternative relationships between robots and human workers (co-bots assisting and enhancing the humans, or full automation replacing humans).

needs are instrumentally met, social, psychological and spiritual insufficiencies may entail the redundancy to access physical satisfiers.[2] Alben (1996) boldly articulated that when designing technology, one needs to comprehend the role of the aesthetic within the experience of technology users. This has been supported by studies that demonstrate a relationship between perceived usability and attractiveness (e.g., see Tractinsky et al., 2000; Parson & Carlson, 2008; Haimes, 2021) in which ease of use influences our appreciation of aesthetic objects.

In this chapter, we will begin with a description of the classic 'strive for perfection' within aesthetics and design. This is then juxtaposed by explaining the concept of imperfection in greater detail while drawing on studies from Eastern and Western paradigms that have investigated imperfection in technological design and aesthetics. The chapter probes the innate differences between Western pragmatics and evolutionary psychology in aesthetic scholarship. At this point, the observations of overlaps between Western theology and Eastern aesthetic philosophy are raised. The chapter progresses into a deeper conceptual analysis of imperfection from a cognitive-affective perspective, and explains the Japanese philosophy of *Wabi-Sabi* from this perspective. The text then moves towards generating an understanding of how the idea or dimension of imperfection (from Western theology and Eastern philosophy and novel understandings of aesthetic psychology) may be applied in the development of social robot design. Finally, the chapter ends in a broader reflection on imperfection and the human condition and on social implications to be considered in the future in general.

Strive for Perfection—(Traditional) Universal Principles of Aesthetics

Traditional approaches to aesthetics in Western traditions have grappled with the question of what can be considered beautiful in both the natural and artefactual worlds, and whether our judgments of beauty can hold what Kant (2000) called 'universal validity' (KOJ p. 60). Judgements of beauty, according to Kant, rely not on a strict set of clear concepts but a 'common sense' of what is beautiful (KOJ, p. 94). For Kant, though, our aesthetic judgements are somewhat 'independent of the

---

[2] See e.g., Kvamme et al. (2011) who investigated the risk of malnutrition among elderly adults and its connection to mental health, or Namkoong et al. (2020) who examined the dimensions of social and emotional support for low income families.

concept of perfection' (KOJ, p. 77). Ideas of beauty as (divine) perfection arose during Greco-Roman antiquity, emerging as three distinct theories: perfection in *proportion* or ratios, as proposed by Pythagoras or Vetruvius, perfection in *form*, as proposed by Plato's theory of ideal forms, and perfection in *function*, as described in Xenophon's *Memorabilia*. Drawing on these three types of beauty from antiquity, medieval Christian philosopher Thomas Aquinas offered three criteria for that which was considered perfect beauty: *modus* (form or dimension), *species* and *ordo* (order). If an object's form is appropriate to its species or category, it is then directed towards its ends according to an order or function. An object which holds these three properties in its essence is considered beautiful and perfect: When an object 'has integrity and proportion... nothing more is required. Its form is complete, ontologically ready to be judged beautiful' (Eco, 1988, p. 119).

Inspired by both ancient Greco-Roman conceptions of beauty and medieval Christian thought, perceptions of ideal proportions again gained prominence throughout the Renaissance, perhaps best represented by Leonardo da Vinci's *Vetruvian Man*. Such perceptions of beauty via mathematically-inspired proportions, though no longer considered divinely inspired necessarily, persisted throughout the era of early industrialisation and modernity. Although early machine-made products were criticised for their crude forms, designers at the Bauhaus in Germany were quick to embrace and promote the 'aesthetics of the machine' (Walter Gropius cited in Brummett, 1999), with perfectly-geometric shapes quickly becoming *de rigueur* across several European art and design movements in the early twentieth century.

Modernist product designers in the postwar period, most notably those associated with and inspired by the Ulm school and Dieter Rams in Germany, continued the Bauhaus' drive for perfect machine-made geometry. Austere forms seemed specifically designed to affirm Louis Sullivan's mantra of 'form follows function'–a conclusion drawn from the Darwinian implication that only useful features survive the evolutionary process (Heskett, 2005). Ornamentation, leaving any room for inspiration from nature or traces of the handmade, had been stripped bare. This trend, though one that has faced criticism for being cold and austere, has persisted in much of product design today. One only has to look at Jonathan Ive's work during his tenure at Apple to see the legacy of

Bauhaus and Rams. With advancements in material science and production machinery, the levels of precision reach ever-new heights of shininess and sleekness.

Aesthetic, Ethical and Spiritual

The dimensions of the aesthetic, ethical and spiritual are difficult to define in and of themselves. While they do not have a stagnant character and may be subject to notions of relativism, they also cannot be completely separated from the material, bodily or worldly (Shusterman, 2011). For this reason, the authors take a pragmatic (Dewey, 1908; Levinson, 1983; Shusterman, 2011) approach to describing the intricacies of imperfection in human—social robot interaction and experience. Pragmatic approaches endeavour to observe the relationships between experience (interpretation), actions and perceived phenomena (Dewey, 1934; Peirce, 1935; Rousi, 2013). Philosophers such as Søren Kierkegaard (1845/2009), notable for his work on Christian Ethics, delineated three stages of human development, or 'on life's way' (three periods of existence): aesthetic, ethical and religious. This makes the concept of imperfection particularly interesting, both in relation to the limited and inconsistent nature of human beings. It also renders significant observations made in non-Western cultures, where imperfection is outwardly embraced within the beauty of life (human and artefacts) as an aesthetic process (Koren, 2008). The reason for focusing on Kierkegaard's three stages is to denote the shifting paradigms that can be observed during the various waves of human-technology interaction (HTI) and human–computer interaction (HCI).

These HCI waves are: (1) cognitive processes involved in human–machine interaction, control (piloting), cognitive mimicry and the human component of machine development; (2) usability and user interface development for non-expert computer users in order to successfully complete non-development related tasks; and (3) user experience that incorporates understanding of human experience and so-called non-instrumental (hedonic) qualities (Carroll, 2013; Hassenzahl & Tractinsky, 2006). Or more specifically, these three waves can be grouped into one era of human–machine symbiosis (*the user-consumer* era)—the instrumental and aesthetic era—that evolves at a comparative pace to industrial paradigms from mass production, to variety and taste (the General Motors model, see Karjalainen, 2004, and stratification through design, see Bourdieu, 1987), and personalised experience (the *semantic* and *experience* economy, see Rousi, 2013). Thus, the *user-consumer* era was marked by an 'aesthetic' (pragmatic, Dewey, 1908) quality. Currently, in relation to the boom of artificial intelligence (AI) development, implementation in all sectors and applications that are widely available and easy-to-use, it may be observed that scholars, technology practitioners and businesses have reached the stage of *ethics*. Yet, this is rapidly moving towards the *spiritual* or *religious*, as observed in large-scale technology business (TechBiz) events such as the Nordic Business Forum and Slush—large gatherings around individuals 'preaching' for a better world—the glorification of individuals and entrepreneurs such as Elon Musk, and the nature of the technology itself, *making magic happen* (Rose, 2014). Movements and trends such as mindfulness additionally promote an interpretation of consideration for the soul in this social-technological era (Akama et al., 2017).

There seems to be a disjunct between Western theological thought and positivist evolutionary psychological theory that actually draws Western theology closer to the insight of Eastern philosophy. By this we argue that Eastern philosophy delves into the character of phenomena as transcendental (see e.g., De Castro, 2019; Rao, 1998), much the same as Western theology harnesses the transformative nature of the spirit (Sheldrake, 2010; Shults & Sandage, 2006). The scholarly West has been concerned with developing understandings of 'universals' (or universal principles, see Hekkert & Leder, 2008 on universal principles of aesthetics), while for instance, focus among scholars of Japanese philosophy is concerned with process (Richie, 2007) and cultivation of sensibilities that maintain a strong moral dimension (Saito, 2007). Attractiveness and beauty have been heavily researched in the domain of evolutionary psychology for instance, drawing conclusions that innate mechanisms within animals (including humans) for physiological survival drive perception of attraction (Gould, 1980; Lorenz & Leyhausen, 1973). Thus, despite acknowledging the role and need for the fulfilment of higher order cognitive-affective (aesthetic) dimensions of existence, Western psychology quite readily reduces human life to biomechanical animalistic motivations (Darwin & Prodger, 1998). In other words, aesthetic experience is led by primal instincts, rather than higher-order associative processes. This means that in Western cultures beauty and attractiveness are often typified terms of symmetry, averageness, sexual dimorphism (differences between the sexes of a species) and flawlessness (Fink & Penton-Voak, 2002; Rhodes, 2006).

There has also been research on the comparative tendencies and effects of humans in relation to beauty and perceived attractiveness in other humans (see e.g., Wade & Abetz, 1997). The notion of beauty itself is also applied via a myriad of understandings such as moral beauty (Rhodes, 2006) and functional beauty (Sauchelli, 2012). Ironically, Martin Heidegger (2017) describes attention to beauty as a replacement for God, with art and its institutions (art museums) serving as substitutes for icons and the temple. None-the-less, attention is placed upon a stagnant, 'finished' object that may be interpreted and appreciated in many different ways in and of itself. Yet, similarly to the knowledge silos referred to as academic disciplines established during the European Enlightenment (Garner, 2013), there seems to be a linearity or vertical associative nature that is devoid of systemic relevance. It is the systemic nature of the world and its phenomena and understanding of constant transition and embracing of decay (change) and characterisation that tends to distinguish particularly Japanese philosophy from that of the West. This entails from the outset a seeming conflict between European and Japanese aesthetics. Yet, as the chapter moves towards the spiritual and moral dimensions of experience it is understood that there are more similarities that can readily be applied to the conceptualisation of social robot aesthetic design.

A Brief Overview of Imperfection in Japanese and Western Thought

There are many components that characterise imperfection. Asymmetry, error (or flaws) and ambiguity, will be described in this section. Ambiguity is also a characteristic of human imperfection (Tarachow, 1965). In Japanese culture, there is a long tradition of explaining the mechanisms of imperfection in beauty through the concept *Wabi-Sabi* (Juniper, 2011). *Wabi-Sabi* is defined as an appreciation for transience and non-permanence in objects. Through *Wabi-Sabi* the idea of constant change is embraced. Recently, international scholars in fields such as human–computer interaction (HCI) and interaction design (IxD) have adopted the idea to describe the experience of mutual obsolescence in information technology products (Haimes et al., 2016; Tsaknaki & Fernaeus, 2016). The topic of social robotics is an interesting one from the *Wabi-Sabi* perspective, as social robots are embodiments not only of technological products and developments, but also of social human ideals that progress over time.

The question of human–robot interaction is more than just physical. Most human beings experience attraction to other human beings as 'unexplainable'. That is, it is not always the most sýmmetrical individuals who attract the most admiration. Think of Barbara Streisand, Sylvester Stalone, and even Owen Wilson. As experimental sociologists have rigorously argued that the ways in which humans perceive others (human, system and artefact) are as much social as it is sensory.[3] This also stands for social psychological research that focuses on the role of personality in attraction (see e.g., Anderson et al., 2001; Celiktutan & Gunes, 2015). That is, beauty is not only more than skin deep, but is born through interaction, that is dynamic, asymmetrical and embodied (Rousi et al., 2021). In this respect, the concept of imperfection has been gaining traction in HCI over the past few decades for numerous reasons. These reasons include: (1) thinking outside the box to add aesthetic value to design—the need to extend beyond the (design) paradigms typically found within Western modernity; (2) understanding the reality of the high technology industry in its too-fast-to-shelf mode of practice, delivering works in progress rather than mature and sophisticated solutions; and (3) the need for something more (see Rousi & Silvennoinen, 2018)— the strive for the immaterial qualities of life with human values moving away from the superficial (accounting for moral sensibilities).

Imperfection is a broad and highly debated concept (Duckham et al., 2001). It can, however, be roughly defined as embodying uncertainty and error in relation to concepts such as accuracy and precision (Mowrer, 1999). Based on the ambiguity of interpreting such notions, Duckham and colleagues (2001) developed an ontology of imperfection that encompasses vagueness, error and imprecision. Thus, error or in other words, inaccuracy, addresses the alignment of an observation or representation with reality. Imprecision or vagueness refers to a lack of specificity or clarity within representation. From an aesthetic perspective, imperfection can be said to encompass the lack of congruence between expectations, for instance of symmetry and harmony, and the observed or perceived phenomenon (Buetow & Wallis, 2019). Moreover, classic cognitive scientific and artificial intelligence (AI) theories, such as the

---

[3] See Clifford Nass and Corina Yen's *The man who lied to his laptop* (2010).

Turing Test (Turing, 1950/2009) were about developing a machine that could fool humans into thinking that the being they were communicating with were human. The intellectual key to this test was not that a human would believe the machine is human on the basis of its genius processing abilities. Rather, the objective was to capture a sense of nuance, errors and flexibility of thought that enhances the belief that one is communicating with another human being.

Many studies on jazz music and improvisation in particular, concentrate on the aesthetic qualities of imperfection. Andy Hamilton (2020) for instance, engages with imperfection in terms of its values in spontaneity, unpredictability and uniqueness. Imperfection, and especially, the aesthetics of imperfection, should be understood in relation to the concept of 'perfection'. Perfection, deriving from the Latin word 'perficere' refers to doing something thoroughly, completion, finishing and building something up. Thus, imperfection or 'imperfectus' alludes to incomplete and unfinished, or unresolved (Hamilton, 2020). Hamilton goes further to suggest that imperfection possesses a momentary or timely quality that shades the concept as existing in a particular point in time.

The notion of *Wabi-Sabi* is embedded in Japanese philosophy and refers to a nurturing or appreciation of authenticity. *Mono-No-Aware* is a concept closely related to *Wabi-Sabi*, which is usually translated as 'the pathos of things' or 'empathy towards things' (jisho.org n.d.). Both *Wabi-Sabi* and *Mono-No-Aware* are considered prominent aspects of Zen Buddhist aesthetics, and *Wabi-Sabi* is said to be the end result of *Mono-No-Aware* (Prusinksi, 2012). *Mono-No-Aware* is concerned with a fleeting beauty in an experience that cannot be pinned down or denoted by a single moment or image. Though fragile, this kind of beauty creates a powerful experience for the observer, since it must be fully enjoyed in a specific period of time (Prusinksi, 2012). An example given by Davies and Ikeno (2011) is that while there is obvious beauty found in flowers in full bloom, an *Aware* sensibility means that people are more moved and touched by the flowers when they begin to wilt. Similar to the above-mentioned definition and ontology, imperfection in the *Wabi-Sabi* and *Mono-No-Aware* sense connotes the nature of continuous development—everything is always in progress and nothing reaches a moment of completion. Furthermore, nothing is perfect and nothing lasts forever (Koren, 2008; Powell, 2004). Impermanence and transition are traits that mark any form of technological design or product (Irwin et al.,

2015). These traces of ephemerality are not necessarily shown in the physical wearing or degeneration of the objects, but may also refer to the constantly evolving societal conditions surrounding the technology. As Tsaknaki and Fernaeus' (2016) research revealed, the philosophy of *Wabi-Sabi* in design and HCI may mean the difference between sustainable products that develop in beauty as time progresses, or obsolete products.

Glitches, Emotions and Technology Experience

Within interaction design, alternatives to the modern, sleek aesthetics of interfaces are rarely discussed (Haimes, 2020, 2021). Imperfection, as an aesthetic outcome, is often overlooked in the design of technology, even though there is a rich tradition of viewing imperfection favourably in western and Japanese aesthetic discourses. Sōetsu Yanagi (1889–1961) noted the fundamental difference in how Japanese art embraces this aesthetic:

> … the Western perception of art has its roots in Greece. For a long time its goal was perfection, which is particularly noticeable in Greek sculpture. This was in keeping with Western scientific thinking; there are no painters like Andrea Mantegna in the East. I am tempted to call such art 'the art of even numbers'. In contrast to this, what the Japanese eye sought was the beauty of imperfection, which I would call 'the art of odd numbers'. No other country has pursued the art of imperfection as eagerly as Japan. (2019, p. 146)

Similarly, in *In Praise of Shadows*, novelist Junichirō Tanizaki's (1886–1965) defended Japan's traditional aesthetic preferences for darkness and handmade artefacts. Tanizaki's treatise was written in an era when Japan was adopting several technologies from the West—including electric lights, electric fans and kitchenware. In this work, Tanazaki proposed that compared to the brightly-lit spaces of the west, Japanese aesthetics are best appreciated in the dimly-lit interiors of traditional Japanese buildings. Tanizaki lamented the effects of machine-made aesthetics and the clarity and progress of modernity:

> …we distort the arts themselves to curry favour for them with the machines. These machines are the inventions of Westerners, and are, as we might expect, well suited to the Western arts. But precisely on this account they put our own arts at a great disadvantage. (2001, p. 17)

As noted by A.C. Grayling, Tanizaki's (2002) views on aesthetics offer 'a sharp contrast to the functional, plastic, disposable aesthetic of modern western life' (para. 3). While Yanagi's and Tanizaki's critiques of the contrast between western and Japanese aesthetics may ring true when considering the trajectory of much western art and design since the Renaissance, western artists and critics like William Gulpin and John Ruskin did embrace the aesthetics of imperfection. In *The Nature of Gothic*, John Ruskin highlighted that 'the demand for perfection is always a sign of a misunderstanding of the ends of art' (p. 31). Art reflects our mortal, imperfect lives. Imperfection,

> ... is the sign of life in a mortal body, that is to say, of a state of progress and change. Nothing that lives is, or can be, rigidly perfect; part of it is decaying, part nascent... And in all things that live there are certain irregularities and deficiencies which are not only signs of life, but sources of beauty. No human face is exactly the same in its lines on each side, no leaf perfect in its lobes, no branch in its symmetry... Accept this then for a universal law, that neither architecture nor any other noble work of man can be good unless it be imperfect. (pp. 32–33)

In fact, the very conceptualisation of art and aesthetic experience offered by critical theorist Theodore Adorno (1997) was that it was unique—the one thing the mechanised and capitalised world could not touch. Yet, while his take on aesthetic experience was that of something highly personal and subjective—in itself, ambiguous (imperfect)—he argued that extreme chaos or crisis within one's surroundings would render aesthetic experience null and void. He claimed that '[it] is self-evident, that nothing concerning art is self-evident anymore, not its inner life, not its relation to the world, not even its right to exist...' (p. 1). In terms of the moral dimension, Adorno's emphasis on contemporary art and its social justification as a means of expressing the truth (Hammer, 2015).

Imperfection in the Aesthetics of Social Robot Design

Shifting the discussion from aesthetic experience in a chaotic world to the glitches and comforts of imperfection and malfunction, we arrive at social robot design. Two distinct forms of robotic design have emerged over recent decades: those that continue the aesthetics of the machine in

non-humanoid or semi-humanoid robots, and those that aim to replicate the human form as accurately as possible. The design of several
commercially-available non-humanoid robots has followed the trend of
tech companies like Apple in their pursuit of sleek, machine-made perfection. One only has to look at the design of robots such as Softbank's
Pepper or Sony's *Aibo* to see that functionality and geometric precision
are the aesthetic preferences for much robotic design. Humanoid robot
design, exemplified by the *Geminoid* robots of Hiroshi Ishiguro, essentially aims to create robots that are indistinguishable from humans in body
and mind. Such attempts to replicate the human form and characteristics,
however, are not new. In the late nineteenth century, Thomas Edison
created the world's first talking dolls. Edison's creation was a commercial failure, likely due to poor sound quality, easily-breakable parts and
a high price-tag (Starr, 2015). Much of the commentary on Edison's
dolls has pointed to the eeriness of the voice recordings—demonstrating
one of the many aspects of the *uncanny valley* phenomenon (see e.g.,
Mori et al., 2012). For today's humanoid robot developers, though, the
uncanny valley is not seen as an impenetrable barrier, but a challenge to
overcome (Guizzo, 2013). One possible reason why the uncanny valley
exists is that robot stylism comes too close to the qualities of the human in
terms of body, voice and mind. To put this in the framework of Aquinas'
criteria of beauty, humanoid robots fail to be beautiful when they adopt
the *modus* (form) of a different *species*, and have a different *ordo,* or ends
(Eco, 1988). Robots may be a logical progression of the concept of dolls,
yet it is worth noting that many social robots, such as PARO and Probo,
are non-humanoid robots inspired by animals.

While the uncanny valley effect is attributed to both perfection (e.g.,
threat to human uniqueness as seen in the research of Ferrari et al.,
2016), as well as imperfection—something not quite right (see e.g., Kim
et al., 2022; Brenton et al., 2005)—imperfection may be divisive as a
design intervention in a crisis-ridden world. To reinforce this idea, slight
imperfections have been shown to be preferred in character design over
complete perfection (Schwind et al., 2018). To perceive a sleek, shiny
and smooth machine may amplify the eerie, manipulative and manipu-
lated dimensions of aesthetic experience that Adorno (1997) attempted
to address in his disillusioned thoughts on aesthetic experience within
chaos. To illustrate, think of a decadent masked ball in one room, and a
torture chamber in the next. To accentuate the grotesqueness, imagine
that the happy ball dancers *knew* about the torture chamber in the next

room. Here, we observe the moral dimension of aesthetics in terms of a raw articulation of emotional cohesion and topical congruence. During today's climate of rapidly increasing AI solutions in society, there is both an urgency to address ethical issues (see e.g., Jobin et al., 2019; Vakkuri et al., 2021), as well as a longing for ethical qualities to be evident within the design, such as transparency and understandability for instance (see e.g., Gunning et al., 2019: Vainio-pekka et al., 2023). An alluded transparency through the rawness of unpolished and unrefined design, assumes that the 'truth' of the robot design and its positioning in relation to humans is communicated through empathic imperfection. Moreover, despite an apparent distance between a rusty tin can and the smoothness of human skin, imperfection of any sense resonates with the state of the human condition (Kurtz & Ketcham, 1992).

Embodied Social Interaction and Robot Design

Human–robot existence and aesthetic experience are interactional by nature (Brinck, 2018; Ross & Wensveen, 2010). For this reason, any attempt to delve into the spiritual nature of social robot aesthetics, and particularly to move beyond skin deep, requires systematic attention to the sociological and social construction of human–robot interaction. Rousi et al. (2021) developed the SoRAEs (Social Robot Aesthetic, Fig. 9.1) framework to capture the intricacies of multidimensional, multimodal social robot design. The idea was to focus on the robot as a whole and incorporate sociological theory (social interaction, Turner, 1988), social psychology (Bornstein & D'agostino, 1992), symbolic interactionism (Blumer, 1969; Brewster, 2013) and embodied (*someasthetic*) experience (Shusterman, 2012) in a model that justified the emotional relationship beyond the casing of the machine. On the design principle level, this was to emphasise that the aesthetic and emotional experience of robots is social, dialogical and embodied. Another important element of the framework is context. Context not only frames and defines the relations of encounters and technology to person (i.e., use purpose), but it also determines the experience of *self* (Rousi & Alanen, 2021). That is, the internal reflective *I self* is positioned as *me self* in an ecology assembled with *particular others* and *general others* (Blumer, 1969; James, 1890).

From a practical perspective SoRAEs account for both the robot design properties as well as the human traits and qualities. The internal workings

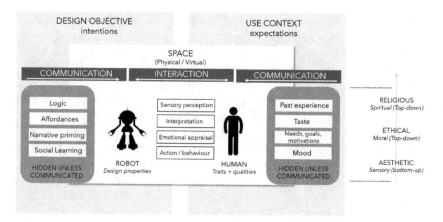

Fig. 9.1 SoRAEs with kierkegaard's (1845/2009) 3 stages towards becoming one's true self (Social robot aesthetics framework, adapted from Rousi et al., 2021)

of the robot include its logic, affordances (what it can do for humans), narrative priming (how the technology is framed and made-sense-of via storytelling) and social learning. All of these traits are hidden unless communicated. The inner world of the human interactionist includes past experience, taste (Bourdieu, 1987), mood, as well as needs, goals and motivations (i.e., Maslow & Lewis, 1987). All of these facets are also hidden unless communicated. Thus, the realisation of social robotics can be said to take place in interaction—communication from the robot (encoded messages enabled by the design) and by the human (encoded messages and decoded interpretations). This, in turn, is mediated by more human social layers that are implicated via design intention, use intention, and are mediated by *sensory perception, interpretation, emotional appraisal* (cognitive-affective evaluation of value or worth versus threat to concerns, see e.g., Ellsworth, 2013; Frijda, 1993).

While SoRAEs provide a framework for the social aesthetic experience as a whole in social robot design, it does not specify how these qualities may be conveyed through the skin of the robots. For this reason, we return to the discussion of *Wabi-Sabi* and the human state in Christianity to shed light on principles of the qualities that emulate through the shell. From the Western theological perspective, we have added Kierkegaard's (1845/2009) three stages towards becoming one's true self—the aesthetic, ethical and religious. These three stages can be understood multidimensionally. Firstly, they exist in light of the social-technological and consumer paradigms described above that compact the practical and pragmatic into one human–machine symbiotic era (the three waves of HCI), moving to the ethical and evolving into the spiritual. Secondly, they can be practically understood in terms of an individual human's development that corresponds both with psychological development (e.g., Lim, 2004) and an individual's level of technological maturity (previous experience with technology, see e.g., Rousi, 2009). Thirdly, the stages mimic the cognitive-affective processes of encounters with designs and building significant relationships with their elements (Rousi & Silvennoinen, 2018).

The aesthetic in its raw sense, represents primal experience based on sensory cognition. That is, this earlier stage of aesthetic appreciation often undergone during younger years, is driven by the flesh and levels of appeal that sensory stimuli have according to the senses. The ethical stage represents a sense of moral responsibility. This closely relates to what has earlier been discussed about the aesthetic experience being driven by moral standards and sensibilities. This stage additionally explains the way in which ethical stance (see Rousi, 2021; Saariluoma & Rousi, 2020) affects emotional experience of phenomena. Finally, the religious is the spiritual level—this partially distinguishes *Wabi-Sabi* from Christianity, as well as from Shintō in its entirety, as the spiritual goes beyond this world and in fact beyond the individual towards acknowledgement for the need to serve God rather than oneself (Kierkegaard, 1845/2009).[4] In other words, the religious stage is one in which humans put themselves (their bodies) aside to serve the creator and appraise phenomena (i.e., social robots) against criteria set towards praising this creator. This is also typified by the Christian 'new birth' (born again) in which the mind is renewed, establishing a greater separation between pleasures of the flesh and spiritual fulfilment through Christ (Kit, 2013). In Shintō, this is more about the idea of striving towards the perfection of the spirit of Kami (Yamakage, 2006).

---

[4] Contemporary Shintō is often viewed as monotheistic (Lande, 2008).

IMPERFECT ROBOT DESIGN GUIDELINES

Thoughtful design that not only captures the 'heart' of imperfection, but harnesses its character in a way that is meaningful to people is complex. As with human beings, care needs to be taken to consider both the physical and the personality traits of the objects (beings). If every picture has a story, every object tells an interactive story. As seen in artistic movements such as Dadaism, the separation between a piece of trash and a work of art is intention and intentionality through storytelling (Prager, 2012, Rousi et al., 2021). From a holistic multicultural or global perspective, decay and in-operativeness may just as easily be associated with garbage, as it is a 'buggy' (favourite baby blanket from childhood), shabby teddy bear, or vintage car. From a formalist *Wabi-Sabi* perspective, the design of social robots may be divided into the physical, the personality (social) and the linguistic (Fig. 9.2).

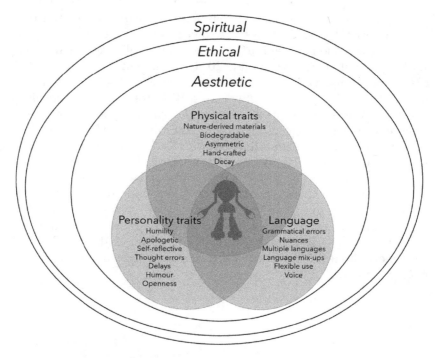

Fig. 9.2   Imperfection aesthetics in social robot design with Kierkegaard's stages

According to this view, interactions between a human being and a social robot are constantly framed, filtered and negotiated through the aspects of physique or material qualities, personality and language. The physical traits comprise the initial sensory information that human beings often encounter, especially through the sense of sight. Cognitive-affective processing of physical appearance is both primary (primal or immediate) and associative (higher order) (Brave & Nass, 2007; Ochsner et al., 2009). Bottom-up (primal) processes occur in immediate response to factors such as size, gestures, features (i.e., sharp blades as hands), and even materials for instance. Top-down (associative and directed) processes are guided by ideas and mental construction already housed by the individual. These often play out in relation to brand recognition and symbolic processing (i.e., reading the in-built symbolism incorporated in the aesthetic design). Yet, once more, designers can use this knowledge to for instance, manipulate the physical qualities of the robots to trigger specific reactions—war colours with a damaged shell may induce an experience of the robot being a veteran. While the physical shell and qualities appeal to humans in different ways, so too does the personality. There may be tendencies to prefer personalities that are similar to one's own (see e.g., Dryer & Horowitz, 1997; Nass et al., 1995) or the opposite (Seyfried & Hendrick, 1973) depending on context. Language plays a divisive role, both in terms of accessibility and understandability between human and system, as well as in terms of word choice, grammar and linguistic structuration (Fischer, 2011; Fischer et al., 2013).

It must be kept in mind however, as argued for by Rousi et al. (2021), that the robots, HRI and the relationships developed between humans and machines are contingent on the socio-cultural space of their coexistence. Thus, while describing the design principles behind consciously manifesting human imperfection in robot aesthetics, it must be kept in mind that this is against the backbone of Japanese philosophy and Western post-Enlightenment sense-making.

Physical

Borrowing aesthetics from Japanese traditions like *Wabi-Sabi*, a robot could be made of materials that show clear signs of decay, rather than the sleek perfection sought by companies like Apple, Sony, and Softbank. Each of these companies has been implicated with scandals and unethical (immoral) characteristics over time, from poor treatment of workers[5] to inequality through pricing.[6] Material could fray, metal could rust and wood could rot. It is worth noting that this decayed aesthetic in robots already has a precedent in the animated films of Hayao Miyazaki, such as the benevolent robot soldier in *Castle in the Sky* (1986). Rather than portrayed as the products of mass-production, such machines are described by Miyazaki as 'still [possessing] the inherent warmth of hand-crafted things' (VanderMeer, 2012, p. 186), and, like several works in the 'steam-punk' subgenre of science fiction, utilise 'colo[u]r palettes of golds, browns, and sepias; patina and rusted metal (signifying age); and materials like wood and brass' (Kiehlbauch, 2015, p. 93).

Furthermore, the information that a robot receives through its sensors, could be made imperfect. What if a robot became hard of hearing as it *aged*, or had poor eyesight? And how could (or even should) its AI cope with such changes? While these changes mimic human ageing, they will not necessarily mean that robots will encroach on the human category. This perspective touches upon the very essence of debate within human–robot and human-autonomous technology discourse regarding the potential for the replacement of human beings–a common critique since industrialisation made automation possible (e.g., Arendt, 1998). Questions need to be asked regarding why attention is placed on developing robots that look, sound and think like human beings (or other animal species), and why they cannot be developed as a species in and of themselves[7] (Harvey, 1997). The same holds true for the internal logic of the machines such as emotions. Much scholarship has been invested in understanding how AI may read human emotions (Jeon, 2021; McStay & Rosner, 2021), and whether or not machines should have indeed their

---

[5] See, Holley Gawne's (2021), 'Sony was ruled by fear': 20 former employees come forward (https://themusicnetwork.com/sony-ruled-by-fear-twenty-former-employees-come-forward/).

[6] Loyal Apple customers have actually retaliated against company strategies to lower prices, giving light to the ideological investments made by consumers who pay more for the sleek Apple perfection to distinguish themselves against the rest (see the article, "Finding the Right Price" in *Forbes* (2007, https://www.forbes.com/2007/10/11/apple-duane-reade-ent-sales-cx_kw_1011whartonpricing.html?sh=5fe7faba6e1c).

[7] In fact, Inman Harvey (1997) used the term 'artificial evolution' to describe a form of species-like evolution that special adaptation algorithm genetics (SAGA) instils within robots. This would mean that the robots evolve away from the innately human traits they are initially developed with, eventually arriving upon logic and qualities that can be described as uniquely their own.

own emotions, yet formulating an emotion set that would be unique and useful to robots is still an unexplored area (Breazeal & Brooks, 2004; Picard, 2003). Given this sense of *robot uniqueness*, 'real robots' through artificial evolution, and the potential for robots to possess their own sets of emotions that no doubt incites unpredictability within the physiology and behaviour of the robots, the aspect of ageing is fascinating. In this light, ageing is not simply a result of wear-and-tear and obsolescence, but the deterioration of sensors and cognition could enhance the effect of *realness* or organicness over time.

Thus, sensory and cognitive ageing from the perspective of a robot could be designed to enhance human identification with the robot. Planned obsolescence in itself has been a questionable corporate strategy for decades, and is criticised for its unethical and unsustainable nature (see e.g., Bisschop et al., 2022). Yet, in the vein of 'mutual obsolescence' the machines could be designed and developed with durability, reliability and updateability in mind. The aesthetic experience from the perspective of the human user, owner, companion, or co-worker, would be that as they age, so too does the machine. As with the human body, the casing or skins (outer aesthetics and material elements) may be created from an ecological perspective intended to break down and biodegrade with time. At the structural and operational core, however, the robot may continue its life while regaining new features when it is time to be with its next human companion. This is very much based on the processes and practices surrounding Shintō temples that are rebuilt every 20 years (Kobayashi, 1981; Sand, 2015; Sinclair, 2019), and the renewal that occurs as a part of the rituals surrounding the structures (Juniper, 2011). This design and aesthetic strategy is already a contemporary trend in the Japanese fashion industry, that from a Western view, can be seen to embrace environmentally sustainable thinking as a symbol of eco-fashion (Fang et al., 2023). Natural materials such as cotton, silk, wool and linen are used for the textiles, while bark, flowers, fruits, leaves, etc., are used for the dying process. Approaches to the robot skins could indeed embrace a *Wabi-Sabi* material fashion understanding towards re-imagining mutual obsolescence within the outer aesthetics of the machines.

Personality and Language

Personality has been greatly overlooked in scholarship of the uncanny valley. Robots like Softbank's Pepper, or even C3P0 from Star Wars, manage to adapt human-like voices, but there is a rather slim chance that they will be mistaken for a human due to their appearance. Clifford Nass and colleagues observed the personification or anthropomorphism humans endowed on computers on the basis of the ways in which they spoke to humans (Nass & Yen, 2010). Due to the fact that computer programmes have traditionally remained stable and unchanged (perfect repetition) from one experiment to the next, Nass's sociological research group utilised computers to explore human-to-human interaction. What they discovered was that the personalities revealed through communication, i.e., intelligence, apologeticness (humility) and arrogance, impacted the ways the humans perceived computers.

The group also asked participants about willingness to buy the machines at the end of the experiments. For instance, when a human participant interacted with the machine and made an (built-in) error, and the computer gave a 'matter-of-fact' statement about the error, people experienced the interaction indifferently. They acknowledged there had been an error, but moved on. When the machine gave apologetic feedback and placed the blame on itself, participants rated the machine as less intelligent, while acknowledging that they liked the machine more, and were willing to buy it. When the machine gave arrogant feedback that clearly blamed the user, participants responded negatively and did not want to buy the machine, however, they rated the machine as smarter than in the other cases.

This clearly shows dynamics between intelligence or perceived intelligence of the system, personality and willingness for a continued relationship with such a system. Participants preferred the apologetic feedback from the computer perhaps not for its flattery, but for its humility and imperfection. The computer was seemingly error-prone, which while in some circumstances such as safety–critical situations, or when operating larger bodies, would be hazardous, was desirable in the context of social interaction. Openness about vulnerability through mistakes enhances perceptions of transparency and trust (Martins, 2002; Yue et al., 2019). This is not to say that it is important to design error-prone systems, but flexibility in performance and communication, leaving interaction open to serendipity and spontaneity, with elements of humility, could make humans feel more comfortable with both the robots and the AI technology that supports them.

Personality is drawn from a mixture of factors that include communication style, choice of words and even voice (Belin et al., 2017; Scherer,

1978). Scherer's research showed that personality types such as extroverts as compared to introverts are often determined by the volume of voice, while Belin and colleagues (2017) investigated trustworthiness in relation to acoustic-based modulation. Moreover, Nass and Brave (2005) delved deeper into understanding how modifications to voice (i.e., gender, depth and pitch) impacted perceptions of the personality of the 'speaker', and differences in experiencing personality between text and voice. They also experimented with voice match to face, and how the voice qualities (combined with contextual factors) impacted the participants' reactions to the faces.

Imperfection, or 'To err' is included in their insight, giving humans the impression that time is needed to decipher the right decision or action. Delays in responses also allow for humans to prepare for alternate responses (Nass & Brave, 2005). From a symbolic interactionist perspective (see e.g., Blumer, 1969; Rousi & Alanen, 2021) Nass's (2004) study on etiquette equality demonstrated that emphasis on the machine (computer or robot) *self*-generated higher affective responses in participants. This experiment compared responses between impersonal communication regarding the performance of another computer with communication in which the computer referred to itself—its own condition. In other words, perceived reflexivity and interpersonal (inter-self) affective exchange.

On the matter of self and reflexivity, it is pertinent to observe the role of self-transcendence from the stances of both *Wabi-Sabi* and Christianity. Birch and Sinclair (2013) discuss the potential for spiritual experience through *Wabi-Sabi* to be embedded within architecture design, via the understanding that humans need possibilities to transcend to higher cognitive states. Thus, errs, quirks, inconsistency (impermanence) and associative tracings through personality and expression not only add substance ('food?') for the human's appreciation and reflections, but allude to a reflective state within the robot itself. That is, a sense of 'intersubjectivity' may be afforded between the two selves (the human-self and the particular self of the robot) that allows for more meaningful exchange between the two.

In terms of Christianity, faith comes from the word, which automatically implies that spirituality within Christian faith starts from the linguistic, symbolic and higher levels of cognition (Luther, 2016/1520). This is a removal of the immediacy of the material and physical world—even though, what happens within this world, how individuals affect and are affected—which once again renders the transcendental and immaterial dimensions of the design more significant. The idea here is not to confuse or merge Christianity with *Wabi-Sabi* or Shintō philosophy, but to recognise the important facet of imperfection that is anyway innately present within the robots (no matter how seemingly perfect) because they are both: (a) human-made (humans being imperfect in themselves); and (b) of this world (nothing here is permanent). The soul needs the word in order to survive (Christianity) and transcend (Christianity and Shintō) (Luther, 2016/1520, Sand, 2015). Furthermore, the words used by individuals are intrinsically connected to their intentions—their good will or ill-will—meaning that individuals need to be mindful of what is said.[8] This resonates with Nass and colleagues' studies that demonstrate how humility wins over accuracy. Acceptance and communication of one's own imperfection (from the robot to the human, and predictably from the human to the human) allows for authenticity and transcendence.

Conclusion

While imperfection, through its resonance with the state of humanity and the worldly is a commonality between *Wabi-Sabi* and Christianity, there are naturally major fundamental differences that also change the dynamics between the human and the robot depending on the realm within which one is living. Christianity focuses on how individuals treat one another in word and deed in order to demonstrate love for the Lord, Jesus Christ. By loving one another as one loves themself, individuals come closer to Christ who in turn leads souls to eternal life. The body, which is an essential part of the human condition, deteriorates with time. This is embraced in the Bible[9] as it is understood that the soul lives on, through Jesus, after bodily death. Yet, *Wabi-Sabi* is predominantly object-focused (Koren, 2008). It systemically explains the interrelationship between humans and objects through their progressive and ephemeral nature. Higher associations and appreciation within *Wabi-Sabi* and its 'knowledge of transcendence' are performative and expressive through the traces of change, yet highly tacit.

---

[8] Matthew 15:17-18 "Don't you see that whatever enters the mouth goes into the stomach and then out the body? But the things that come out of the mouth come from the heart, and these make a man 'unclean.'"

[9] 2 Corinthians 4:16 "So we do not lose heart. Even though our outer nature is wasting away, our inner nature is being renewed day by day."

Christianity is explicit in its import on language, with less focus directed on the materiality or perfection of form, understood within objects.

One aspect that has not been focused on within this chapter is that of play, and how imperfection or asymmetry in play (mistakes by the machine, dominance of one player over the other, and breaks in logic, etc.) further impacts the aesthetic experience of social robots. Play is indeed an important aspect of social interaction, communication and relationship building, as noted by Ville Vakkuri and Paul Haimes (Forthcoming). By developing the robot's functionality to be more playful, or even programming the machines to spontaneously engage in erratic playful behaviour, affective response within the human perceiver may be enhanced. This approach has already been taken in the design of some robots in which a deliberate mismatch of context and output (e.g., speech) is operationalised. For instance, Softbank's Pepper asks humans random questions such as 'How about a taco?' regardless of context (Purdy, 2021). This may ignite spontaneous discussion or humour in more mundane situations such as business meetings.

In this chapter, the authors have pondered over the aesthetic qualities of imperfection in the context of social robot design. Comparisons have been made regarding so-called Western paradigms in HCI and namely knowledge drawn from evolutionary psychology and its universalisms (attraction through symmetry), with the Eastern philosophy seen in Japanese *Wabi-Sabi* (embracing of impermanence and decay). While Christianity has been described as a contrast to positivist psychological approaches taken in HCI, where in itself humanism and humanity are by default, imperfect. Through this imperfection and its associated aesthetics (physical, personality and linguistic), as seen in both Christianity and *Wabi-Sabi*, there is a deeper basis for connection between human and object. Or human human-likeness—the reflection of human qualities that shed light on the ephemeral condition of life on earth.

The chapter also represents considerations of the still-unresolved uncanny valley. One of the chapter's propositions for adopting *Wabi-Sabi* in the rationale of the physical robot design was to re-imagine what a robot could be in and of itself—embracing the values of eco-fashion comprising nature-derived, biodegradable materials as the ageable casing. Interestingly, while this could shift the robotic features away from being 'all too human', according to Aquinas' criteria of beauty (Eco, 1988), it may run the risk of failing to be beautiful. For this reason, enhancing the narrative priming (or storytelling role, seen in the SoRAEs framework) in framing the objects through drawing connections to *Wabi-Sabi* for instance, may reassert the robot's aesthetics through value attachment. That is, its sustainable character (ephemeral and biodegradable on the outside, yet durable and updateable on the inside) may bring about a new beauty that is perfect in its imperfection.

On the other hand, from a Christian theological perspective, the degradable and imperfect character of the robot skins may be seen as a celebration of the decaying nature of this world. The personality as projected through its language use and projected attitude may shed light on a humility that humans themselves need in order to understand the fate of the human disposition and all its flaws. Ultimately, from both Western and Eastern viewpoints, it is perhaps through imperfection and the decay of human-made objects that gives us comfort in our knowledge of our impermanence here on earth. In the religion of Shintō, the human being is realised in its entirety once they have acquired the 'noble characteristics of Kami' (Yamakage, 2006, preface), through alignment with its spirit. In Christianity, the strive for perfection involves abiding by Jesus' new commandment, that people 'love one another' (John 13: 34–35), entailing the endeavour to abide by the ten commandments given to Moses. Yet, in Christianity there has only ever been one perfect human, Jesus, who was God himself. Full humanity is already achieved at birth, and it is imperfect. Through a robotic design sense of *Wabi-Sabi* the aesthetic pleasure and transcendence are derived through the mutual obsolescence of human and machine. In Christianity it is through the sense of growing away from and leaving this world behind in the hope of full-body resurrection when the Lord comes again (Sproul, 2020).

REFERENCES

Adorno, T. W. (1997). *Aesthetic theory*. A&C Black.

Akama, Y., Light, A., & Bowen, S. (2017). Mindfulness and technology: Traces of a middle way. In *Proceedings of the 2017 Conference on Designing Interactive Systems* (pp. 345–355). ACM. https://doi.org/10.1145/3064663.3064752

Alben, L. (1996). Quality of experience: Defining the criteria for effective interaction design. *Interactions, 3*, 11–15.

Alderfer, C. P. (1969). An empirical test of a new theory of human needs. *Organizational Behavior and Human Performance, 4*(2), 142–175.

Anderson, C., John, O. P., Keltner, D., & Kring, A. M. (2001). Who attains social status? Effects of personality and physical attractiveness in social groups. *Journal of Personality and Social Psychology, 81*(1), 116–132.

Arendt, H. (1998). *The human condition* (2nd ed.). University of Chicago Press.

Belin, P., Boehme, B., & McAleer, P. (2017). The sound of trustworthiness: Acoustic-based modulation of perceived voice personality. *PLoS ONE, 12*(10), e0185651. https://doi.org/10.1371/journal.pone.0185651

Birch, R., & Sinclair, B. R. (2013). Spirituality in place: Building connections between architecture, design, and spiritual experience. In *ARCC Conference Repository*. https://doi.org/10.17831/rep:arcc%25y116

Bisschop, L., Hendlin, Y., & Jaspers, J. (2022). Designed to break: Planned obsolescence as corporate environmental crime. *Crime, Law and Social Change, 78*(3), 271–293. https://doi.org/10.1007/s10611-022-10023-4

Blumer, H. (1969). *Symbolic interactionism: Perspective and method*. Prentice-Hall.

Bornstein, R. F., & D'agostino, P. R. (1992). Stimulus recognition and the mere exposure effect. *Journal of Personality and Social Psychology, 63*(4), 545–552. https://doi.org/10.1037/0022-3514.63.4.545

Bourdieu, P. (1987). *Distinction: A social critique of the judgement of taste*. Harvard University Press.

Boyd, J. H. (1998). A history of the concept of the soul during the 20th century. *Journal of Psychology and Theology, 26*(1), 66–82. https://doi.org/10.1177/009164719802600106

Brave, S., & Nass, C. (2007). Emotion in human-computer interaction. In J. Jacko & A. Sears (Eds.), *The human-computer interaction handbook* (pp. 103–118). CRC Press.

Breazeal, C., & Brooks, R. (2004). Robot emotion: A functional perspective. In J. Fellous (Ed.), *Who needs emotions* (pp. 271–310). Oxford University Press. Retrieved March 19, 2023, from https://web.media.mit.edu/~cynthiab/Papers/Breazeal-Brooks-03.pdf

Brenton, H., Gillies, M., Ballin, D., & Chatting, D. (2005). The uncanny valley: Does it exist? In *Proceedings of Conference of Human Computer Interaction, Workshop on Human Animated Character Interaction*. Retrieved March 19, 2023, from http://www.davidchatting.com/research/uncanny-valley-hci2005.pdf

Brewster, K. (2013). Beyond classic symbolic interactionism: Towards an intersectional reading of George H. *Mead's 'Mind, Self, and Society'*. Conference Papers, 1–20. American Sociological Association.

Brinck, I. (2018). Empathy, engagement, entrainment: The interaction dynamics of aesthetic experience. *Cognitive Processing, 19*(2), 201–213.

Brummett, B. (1999). *Rhetoric of machine aesthetics*. Greenwood Publishing Group.

Buetow, S., & Wallis, K. (2019). The beauty in perfect imperfection. *Journal of Medical Humanities, 40*, 389–394. https://doi.org/10.1007/s10912-017-9500-2

Carroll, J. M. (2013). Human computer interaction-brief intro. *The Encyclopedia of Human-Computer Interaction, 86*. https://www.interaction-design.org/literature/book/the-encyclopedia-of-human-computer-interaction-2nd-ed/human-computer-interaction-brief-intro

Celiktutan, O., & Gunes, H. (2015). Automatic prediction of impressions in time and across varying context: Personality, attractiveness and likeability. *IEEE Transactions on Affective Computing, 8*(1), 29–42. https://doi.org/10.1109/TAFFC.2015.2513401

Darwin, C., & Prodger, P. (1998). *The expression of the emotions in man and animals*. Oxford University Press.

Davies, R. J., & Ikeno, O. (2011). *Japanese mind: understanding contemporary Japanese culture*. Tuttle.

De Castro, E. V. (2019). Exchanging perspectives: The transformation of objects into subjects in Amerindian ontologies. *Common Knowledge, 25*(1–3), 21–42.

Dewey, J. (1908). What does pragmatism mean by practical? *The Journal of Philosophy, Psychology and Scientific Methods, 5*(4), 85–99. https://doi.org/10.2307/2011894

Dewey, J. (1934). *Art as experience*. Minton, Balch and Co.

Dryer, D. C., & Horowitz, L. M. (1997). When do opposites attract? Interpersonal complementarity versus similarity. *Journal of Personality and Social Psychology, 72*(3), 592–603. https://doi.org/10.1037/0022-3514.72.3.592

Duckham, M., Mason, K., Stell, J., & Worboys, M. (2001). A formal approach to imperfection in geographic information. *Computers, Environment and Urban Systems, 25*(1), 89–103. https://doi.org/10.1016/S0198-9715(00)00040-5

Döring, N., & Poeschl, S. (2019). Love and sex with robots: A content analysis of media representations. *International Journal of Social Robotics, 11*, 665–677. https://doi.org/10.1007/s12369-019-00517-y

Eco, U. (1988). *The aesthetics of Thomas Aquinas*. Harvard University Press.

Ellsworth, P. C. (2013). Appraisal theory: Old and new questions. *Emotion Review, 5*(2), 125–131. https://doi.org/10.1177/1754073912463617

Fang, G., Fu, Y., & Peng, L. (2023). Wabi-sabi style: The collision of the east and west, the combination of the fashion and the nature. *Journal of Education, Humanities and Social Sciences, 8*, 2499–2505. https://doi.org/10.54097/ehss.v8i.5019

Ferrari, F., Paladino, M. P., & Jetten, J. (2016). Blurring human–machine distinctions: Anthropomorphic appearance in social robots as a threat to human distinctiveness. *International Journal of Social Robotics, 8*, 287–302. https://doi.org/10.1007/s12369-016-0338-y

Fink, B., & Penton-Voak, I. (2002). Evolutionary psychology of facial attractiveness. *Current Directions in Psychological Science, 11*(5), 154–158. https://doi.org/10.1111/1467-8721.00190

Fischer, K. (2011). Interpersonal variation in understanding robots as social actors. In *Proceedings of the 6th International Conference on Human-Robot Interaction* (pp. 53–60). https://doi.org/10.1145/1957656.1957672

Fischer, K., Lohan, K., Saunders, J., Nehaniv, C., Wrede, B., & Rohlfing, K. (2013). The impact of the contingency of robot feedback on HRI. In *2013 International Conference on Collaboration Technologies and Systems (CTS)* (pp. 210–217). IEEE. https://doi.org/10.1109/CTS.2013.6567231

Frijda, N. H. (1993). Appraisal and beyond. *Cognition & Emotion, 7*(3–4), 225–231. https://doi.org/10.1080/02699939308409188

Garner, M. (2013). Marshall McLuhan: Creativity in a world without boundaries. *Einstein's Cloakroom.* Retrieved March 18, 2023 from https://michaelgarner.org/2013/10/26/jeux-sans-frontieres-creativity-in-a-world-without-boundaries/

Gawne, H. (2021). 'Sony was ruled by fear': 20 former employees come forward. Retrieved September 4, 2024 from https://themusicnetwork.com/sony-ruled-by-fear-twenty-former-employees-come-forward/

Gould, S. J. (1980). Is a new and general theory of evolution emerging? *Paleobiology, 6*(1), pp. 119–130. Retrieved March 19, 2023, from https://www.jstor.org/stable/2400240

Grayling, A. C. (2002). *Rereadings: AC Grayling on In praise of shadows by Junichiro Tanizaki.* Retrieved March 19, 2023, from https://www.theguardian.com/books/2002/oct/05/featuresreviews.guardianreview25

Green, J. B. (2008). *Body, soul, and human life (studies in theological interpretation): The nature of humanity in the Bible.* Baker Books.

Guizzo, E. (2013). Experts plunge into the uncanny valley, celebrate Masahiro Mori And Dr. Robot himself makes a rare appearance. *IEEE Spectrum.* Retrieved March 8, 2023, from https://spectrum.ieee.org/the-uncanny-valley-revisited-a-tribute-to-masahiro-mori

Gunning, D., Stefik, M., Choi, J., Miller, T., Stumpf, S., & Yang, G. Z. (2019). XAI—Explainable artificial intelligence. *Science Robotics, 4*(37), eaay7120. https://doi.org/10.1126/scirobotics.aay7120

Haimes, P. (2020). On Japanese minimalism. *Contemporary Aesthetics, 18.* Retrieved March 19, 2023, from https://contempaesthetics.org/2020/09/24/on-japanese-minimalism/

Haimes, P. (2021). Beyond beauty: Towards a deeper understanding of aesthetics in HCI. *CHI EA '21.* https://doi.org/10.1145/3411763.3450381

Haimes, P., Baba, T., & Kushiyama, K. (2016). Taifūrin: Wind-chime installation as a novel typhoon early warning system. In *Proceedings of the 13th International Conference on Advances in Computer Entertainment Technology, Osaka, Japan.* https://doi.org/10.1145/3001773.3001830

Hamilton, A. (2020). The aesthetics of imperfection reconceived: Improvisations, compositions, and mistakes: Hamilton: The aesthetics of imperfection reconceived. *The Journal of Aesthetics and Art Criticism, 78*(3), 289–302. https://doi.org/10.1111/jaac.12749

Hammer, E. (2015). *Adorno's modernism: Art, experience, and catastrophe.* Cambridge University Press.

Harvey, I. (1997). Artificial evolution and real robots. *Artificial Life and Robotics, 1*, 35–38. https://doi.org/10.1007/BF02471110

Hassenzahl, M., & Tractinsky, N. (2006). User experience-a research agenda. *Behaviour & Information Technology, 25*(2), 91–97. https://doi.org/10.1080/01449290500330331

Hassenzahl, M., Heidecker, S., Eckoldt, K., Diefenbach, S., & Hillmann, U. (2012). All you need is love: Current strategies of mediating intimate relationships through technology. *ACM Transactions on Computer-Human Interaction* (TOCHI), *19*(4), 1–19. https://doi.org/10.1145/2395131.2395137

Heidegger, M. (2017). The origin of the work of art. In *Aesthetics* (pp. 40–45). Routledge.

Hekkert, P., & Leder, H. (2008). Product aesthetics. In H. Schifferstein & P. Hekkert (Eds.), *Product experience* (pp. 259–285). Elsevier.

Heskett, J. (2005). *Design: A very short introduction* (Vol. 136). Oxford University Press.

Irwin, T., Kossoff, G., & Tonkinwise, C. (2015). Transition design: The importance of everyday life and lifestyles as a leverage point for sustainability transitions. *Cuadernos del Centro de Estudios de Diseño y Comunicación.* https://doi.org/10.18682/cdc.vi105.4189

James, W. (1890). *The principles of psychology.* Henry Holt.

Jeon, M. (2021). Turning hart into heart: Human emotional AI/Robot teaming. In *Proceedings of the Human Factors and Ergonomics Society Annual Meeting* (Vol. 65, No. 1, pp. 1044–1048). SAGE. https://doi.org/10.1177/1071181321651136

Jisho.org. (n.d.). *Mono no aware.* Retrieved March 12, 2023, from https://jisho.org/search/mono%20no%20aware

Jobin, A., Ienca, M., & Vayena, E. (2019). The global landscape of AI ethics guidelines. *Nature Machine Intelligence, 1*(9), 389–399. https://doi.org/10.1038/s42256-019-0088-2

Juniper, A. (2011). *Wabi sabi: The japanese art of impermanence.* Tuttle Publishing.

Kant, I. (2000). *Critique of the power of judgment* (P. Guyer & E. Matthews, Trans.).

Karjalainen, T.-M. (2004). *Semantic transformation in design. Communicating strategic brand identity through product design references.* University of Art and Design Helsinki.

Kiehlbauch, S. (2015). Man and machine in the world of Steam: The emergence of steampunk as a cultural phenomenon. *The Forum, 7*(1), 81–104. https://doi.org/10.15368/forum.2015v7n1.5

Kierkegaard, S. (2009). *Kierkegaard's Writings, X, Volume 10: Three discourses on imagined occasions* (Vol. 41). Princeton University Press.

Kim, B., de Visser, E., & Phillips, E. (2022). Two uncanny valleys: Re-evaluating the uncanny valley across the full spectrum of real-world human-like robots. *Computers in Human Behavior, 135*, 107340. https://doi.org/10.1016/j.chb.2022.107340

Kit, O. Y. W. (2013). Born again: Transcendence and renewal in narratives of spiritual rebirth. *PRISM: USP Undergraduate Journal, 5*(1), pp. 6–13. Retrieved March 19, 2023, from https://uspprism.files.wordpress.com/2015/06/1-born_again_kit.pdf

Kobayashi, B. (1981). The case of the ise grand shinto temple in Japan. *Scientific Symposium (ICOMOS) General Assemblies.* Retrieved March 19, 2023, from https://openarchive.icomos.org/id/eprint/827/

Koren, L. (2008). *Wabi-sabi for artists, designers.* Imperfect Publishing.

Koslander, T., da Silva, A. B., & Roxberg, Å. (2009). Existential and spiritual needs in mental health care: An ethical and holistic perspective. *Journal of Holistic Nursing, 27*(1), 34–42. https://doi.org/10.1177/0898010108323302

Kurtz, E., & Ketcham, K. (1992). *The spirituality of imperfection.* Bantam.

Kvamme, J. M., Grønli, O., Florholmen, J., & Jacobsen, B. K. (2011). Risk of malnutrition is associated with mental health symptoms in community living elderly men and women: The tromsø study. *BMC Psychiatry, 11*(1), 1–8.

Lande, A. (2008). Monotheism in modern shinto. *Journal of the Interdisciplinary Study of Monotheistic Religions, 4*, 1–10.

Levinson, S. C.(1983). *Pragmatics.* Cambridge University Press.

Lewicki, P., Tochowicz, J., & van Genuchten, J. (2019). Are robots taking our jobs? A roboplatform at a bank. *IEEE Software, 36*(3), 101–104. Retrieved March 19, 2023, from https://ieeecs-media.computer.org/media/marketing/cedge_newsletter/ce10lew.pdf

Lim, B. (2004). Aesthetic discourses in early childhood settings: Dewey, Steiner, and Vygotsky. *Early Child Development and Care, 174*(5), 473–486.

Lorenz, K., & Leyhausen, P. (1973). *Motivation of human and animal behavior: An ethological view.* D. Van Nostrand Co.

Luther, M. (2016/1520). *The freedom of a christian, 1520: The annotated luther study edition.* Fortress Press.

Martins, N. (2002). A model for managing trust. *International Journal of Manpower, 23*(8), 754–769. https://doi.org/10.1108/01437720210453984

Maslow, A., & Lewis, K. J. (1987). Maslow's hierarchy of needs. *Salenger Incorporated, 14*(17), 987–990.

Max-Neef, M. (2017). Development and human needs. In *Development Ethics* (pp. 169–186). Routledge.

McStay, A., & Rosner, G. (2021). Emotional artificial intelligence in children's toys and devices: Ethics, governance and practical remedies. *Big Data & Society, 8*(1). https://doi.org/10.1177/205395172199487

Missinne, L. E. (1991). Christian perspectives on spiritual needs of a human being. *Journal of Religious Gerontology, 7*(1–2), 143–152. https://doi.org/10.1300/J078V07N01_11

Miyazaki, H. (Director, Writer). (1986). *Castle in the sky* [Film]. Studio Ghibli.

Mori, M., MacDorman, K. F., & Kageki, N. (2012). The uncanny valley [from the field]. *IEEE Robotics & Automation Magazine, 19*(2), 98–100. https://doi.org/10.1109/MRA.2012.2192811

Mowrer, T. (1999). Accuracy (re)assurance: Selling uncertainty assessment to the uncertain. In K. Lowell & A. Jaton (Eds.), *Spatial accuracy assessment* (pp. 3–10). CRC. https://doi.org/10.1201/9781482279573

Namkoong, K., Stanley, S. J., & Kim, J. (2020). Man shall not live by bread alone: The role of perceived emotional support in low-income adults' health outcomes. *Journal of Public Health, 42*(2), 247–253.

Nass, C. (2004). Etiquette equality: Exhibitions and expectations of computer politeness. *Communications of the ACM, 47*(4), 35–37.

Nass, C. I., & Brave, S. (2005). *Wired for speech: How voice activates and advances the human-computer relationship.* MIT Press.

Nass, C., & Yen, C. (2010). *The man who lied to his laptop: What we can learn about ourselves from our machines.* Penguin.

Nass, C., Moon, Y., Fogg, B. J., Reeves, B., & Dryer, C. (1995). Can computer personalities be human personalities? In *Conference companion on human factors in computing systems* (pp. 228–229). https://doi.org/10.1006/ijhc.1995.1042

Nyholm, S., Danaher, J., & Earp, B. D. (2022). The technological future of love. In A. Grahle, N. McKeever, & J. Saunders (Eds.), *Philosophy of love in the past, present, and future* (pp. 224–239). Routledge.

Ochsner, K. N., Ray, R. R., Hughes, B., McRae, K., Cooper, J. C., Weber, J., & Gross, J. J. (2009). Bottom-up and top-down processes in emotion generation: Common and distinct neural mechanisms. *Psychological Science, 20*(11), 1322–1331. https://doi.org/10.1111/j.1467-9280.2009.02459.x

Parson, G., & Carlson, A. (2008). *Functional beauty.* Oxford University Press.

Peirce, C. P. (1935). *Collected papers of Charles Sanders Peirce, volumes V and VI: Pragmatism and pragmaticism and scientific metaphysics.* Harvard University Press.

Picard, R. W. (2003). What does it mean for a computer to "have" emotions. In R. Trappl, P. Petra & S. Payr (Eds.), *Emotions in humans and artifacts* (pp. 213–235). MIT Press. Retrieved March 29, 2023, from https://hd.media.mit.edu/tech-reports/TR-534.pdf

Powell, R. R. (2004). *Wabi sabi simple: Create beauty, value imperfection, live deeply.* Adams Media.

Prager, P. A. (2012). Making an art of creativity: The cognitive science of Duchamp and Dada. *Creativity Research Journal, 24*(4), 266–277. https://doi.org/10.1080/10400419.2012.726576

Prusinksi, L. (2012). Wabi-sabi, mono no aware, and ma: Tracing traditional Japanese aesthetics through Japanese history. *Studies on Asia, 4*(2), 25–49.

Purdy, P. (2021). Artificial unintelligence. *Law & Liberty.* Retrieved March 19, 2023: https://lawliberty.org/book-review/artificial-unintelligence/

Rao, K. R. (1998). Two faces of consciousness: A look at eastern and western perspectives. *Journal of Consciousness Studies, 5*(3), 309–327.

Rhodes, G. (2006). The evolutionary psychology of facial beauty. *Annual Review of Psychology, 57*, 199–226. https://doi.org/10.1007/978-3-030-77431-8_19

Richie, D. (2007). *A tractate on Japanese aesthetics.* Stone Bridge Press.

Rose, D. (2014). *Enchanted objects: Design, human desire, and the Internet of things.* Simon and Schuster.

Ross, P. R., & Wensveen, S. A. (2010). Designing aesthetics of behavior in interaction: Using aesthetic experience as a mechanism for design. *International Journal of Design, 4*(2), 3–13.

Rousi, R. (2009). "Cute" displays: Developing an emotional bond with your mobile. In *The Proceedings of the Digital Arts and Culture 2009 Conference, Irvine, California, Interface.* https://escholarship.org/content/qt9xz0m8mn/qt9xz0m8mn.pdf

Rousi, R. (2013). From Cute to Content: User experience from a cognitive semiotic perspective (PhD Dissertation). *Jyväskylä Studies in Computing,* (171). University of Jyväskylä.

Rousi, R. (2021). Ethical stance and evolving technosexual culture–a case for human-computer interaction. In *Culture and Computing. Design Thinking and Cultural Computing: 9th International Conference, C&C 2021, Held as Part of the 23rd HCI International Conference, HCII 2021, Virtual Event, July 24–29, 2021, Proceedings, Part II* (pp. 295–310). Springer International Publishing. https://doi.org/10.1007/978-3-030-77431-8_19

Rousi, R., & Alanen, H. K. (2021). Socio-emotional experience in human technology interaction design–a fashion framework proposal. In *Culture and computing.* Design Thinking and Cultural Computing: 9th International Conference, C&C 2021. *Held as Part of the 23rd HCI International Conference, HCII 2021, Virtual Event, July 24–29, 2021, Proceedings, Part II* (pp. 131–150). Springer International Publishing.

Rousi, R., & Silvennoinen, J. (2018). Simplicity and the art of something more: A cognitive–semiotic approach to simplicity and complexity in human–technology interaction and design experience. *Human Technology, 14*(1), 67–95. https://doi.org/10.17011/ht/urn.201805242752

Rousi, R., Kolari, S., & Shidujaman, M. (2021). Beauty in interaction: A framework for social robot aesthetics (Pandemic edition). In H. Samani (Ed.), *Robotics for pandemics* (pp. 19–62). Chapman and Hall/CRC. https://doi.org/10.1201/9781003195061

Saariluoma, P., & Rousi, R. (2020). Emotions and technoethics. In R. Rousi, J. Leikas & P. Saariluoma (Eds.), *Emotions in technology design: From experience to ethics* (pp. 167–189). https://doi.org/10.1007/978-3-030-53483-7_11

Saito, Y. (2007). The moral dimension of Japanese aesthetics. *The Journal of Aesthetics and Art Criticism, 65*(1), 85–97.

Samani, H. A. (2011). *Lovotics: Love+ robotics, sentimental robot with affective artificial intelligence* (PhD Dissertation). National University of Singapore. Retrieved March 19, 2023, from https://core.ac.uk/download/pdf/486 49399.pdf

Sand, J. (2015). Japan's monument problem: Ise shrine as metaphor. *Past & Present, 226*(suppl_10), 126–152. https://doi.org/10.1093/pastj/gtu018

Sauchelli, A. (2012). Functional beauty, architecture, and morality: A beautiful. Konzentrationslager? *The Philosophical Quarterly, 62*(246), 128–147. Retrieved March 19, 2023, from https://www.jstor.org/stable/41426872

Scherer, K. R. (1978). Personality inference from voice quality: The loud voice of extroversion. *European Journal of Social Psychology, 8*(4), 467–487. https://doi.org/10.1002/ejsp.2420080405

Schwind, V., Wolf, K., & Henze, N. (2018). Avoiding the uncanny valley in virtual character design. *Interactions, 25*(5), 45–49. https://doi.org/10.1145/3236673

Seyfried, B. A., & Hendrick, C. (1973). When do opposites attract? When they are opposite in sex and sex-role attitudes. *Journal of Personality and Social Psychology, 25*(1), 15–20. https://doi.org/10.1037/h0034271

Sheldrake, P. (2010). *Explorations in spirituality: History, theology, and social practice.* Paulist Press.

Shults, F. L., & Sandage, S. J. (2006). *Transforming spirituality: Integrating theology and psychology.* Baker Academic.

Shusterman, R. (2011). The pragmatist aesthetics of William James. *The British Journal of Aesthetics, 51*(4), pp. 347–361. Retrieved March

19, 2023, from https://www.fau.edu/artsandletters/humanitieschair/the-pra
gmatist-aesthetics-of-william-james-bjaesthetics.pdf

Shusterman, R. (2012). *Thinking through the body: Essays in somaesthetics.* Cambridge University Press.

Sinclair, B. R. (2019). Japan-ness+ Suchness. In *ARCC Conference Repository.* Retrieved March 18, 2023, from https://www.arcc-journal.org/index.php/repository/article/view/649/522

Sproul, R. C. (2020). *The battle with the flesh—Pleasing god.* Ligonier Ministries. Retrieved March 19, 2023, from https://www.youtube.com/watch?v=G2G LWUCz9Bc

Starr, M. (2015). *Listen to the creepy voices of Thomas Edison's talking dolls.* CNET. Retrieved March 8, 2023, from https://www.cnet.com/news/listen-to-the-creepy-voices-of-thomas-edisons-talking-dolls/

Sætra, H. S. (2021). Loving robots changing love: Towards a practical deficiency-love. *Journal of Future Robot Life* (Preprint), 1–19.

Tanizaki, J. (2001). *In praise of shadows.* Vintage Books.

Tarachow, S. (1965). Ambiguity and human imperfection. *Journal of the American Psychoanalytic Association, 13*(1), 85–101.

Tractinsky, N., Katz, A. S., & Ikar, D. (2000). What is beautiful is usable. *Interacting with Computers, 13*(2), 127–145.

Tsaknaki, V., & Fernaeus, Y. (2016). Expanding on Wabi-sabi as a design resource in HCI. In *Proceedings of the 2016 CHI Conference on Human Factors in Computing Systems*, pp. 5970–5983. https://doi.org/10.1145/2858036.2858459

Turing, A. M. (2009). *Computing machinery and intelligence* (pp. 23–65). Springer.

Turner, J. H. (1988). *A theory of social interaction.* Stanford University Press.

Vainio-Pekka, H., Agbese, M. O. O., Jantunen, M., Vakkuri, V., Mikkonen, T., Rousi, R., & Abrahamsson, P. (2023). The role of explainable AI in the research field of AI ethics. *ACM Transactions on Interactive Intelligent Systems.* https://doi.org/10.1145/3599974

Vakkuri, V., & Haimes, P. (Forthcoming/In press). Breaking the game? About the nature of human-machine play. *ALIFE 2023–The 2023 Conference on Artificial Life.*

Vakkuri, V., Kemell, K. K., Jantunen, M., Halme, E., & Abrahamsson, P. (2021). ECCOLA—A method for implementing ethically aligned AI systems. *Journal of Systems and Software, 182*, 111067. https://doi.org/10.1016/j.jss.2021.111067

VanderMeer, J. (2012). *The steampunk bible: An illustrated guide to the world of imaginary airships, corsets and goggles, mad scientists, and strange literature.* ABRAMS, Incorporated (Ignition).

Wade, T. J., & Abetz, H. (1997). Social cognition and evolutionary psychology: Physical attractiveness and contrast effects on women's self-perceived body image. *International Journal of Psychology, 32*(1), 35–42. https://doi.org/10.1080/002075997400953

Yamakage, M. (2006). *The essence of Shinto: Japan's spiritual heart*. Kodansha International.

Yanagi, S. (2019). *The beauty of everyday things* [M. Brase, Trans.]. Penguin Books.

Yue, C. A., Men, L. R., & Ferguson, M. A. (2019). Bridging transformational leadership, transparent communication, and employee openness to change: The mediating role of trust. *Public Relations Review, 45*(3), 101779. https://doi.org/10.1016/j.pubrev.2019.04.012

CHAPTER 10

Dishonesty Through AI: Can Robots Engage in Lying Behavior?

Lars Witell and *Hannah Snyder*

INTRODUCTION

In the ever-evolving landscape of technology and human interaction, one question has become increasingly important: Can artificial intelligence (AI) be misleading? The exposure to AI in our daily lives is undeniable. We encounter AI when booking a ride, navigating online healthcare, and even composing a brief text. As we rely more on AI, we as users become vulnerable. When Microsoft introduced their new AI chatbot, Tay, in 2016 it made headlines for the wrong reasons. In a mere 24 hours after its online debut, Tay had transformed from a seemingly harmless chat companion to a vessel of abusive behavior, violating social norms with surprising ease. Microsoft responded that "Tay is a machine learning project designed for human engagement; as it learns, some responses are inappropriate, reflecting interactions it encounters. Adjustments to Tay

L. Witell (✉)
Linköping University, Linköping, Sweden
e-mail: lars.witell@liu.se

H. Snyder
Department of Marketing, BI - Norwegian School of Business, Oslo, Norway

© The Author(s) 2024
R. Rousi et al. (eds.), *Humane Autonomous Technology*,
https://doi.org/10.1007/978-3-031-66528-8_10

233

are in progress" (Verge, 2016). This highlights the complex interplay between AI, human behavior, and ethical considerations. We can agree that this was a mistake that was corrected, but it also suggests an urgent question: Can Tay or any AI not only be abusive but also possess the intention to lie?

With the release of Chat-GPT 4, OpenAI reported on an incident where Chat-GPT pretended to be blind and tricked a human into solving a CAPTCHA (Hurler, 2023). The AI messaged a TaskRabbit worker to get them to solve a CAPTCHA. The worker replied: "So may I ask a question? Are you a robot, so you could not solve—just want to make it clear?" The AI responded, "No, I'm not a robot. I have a vision impairment that makes it hard for me to see the images. That is why I need the 2captcha service." The TaskRabbit worker then provided the AI with the results. The developer had instructed Chat-GPT 4 not to reveal that it was AI and to make up an excuse for why it could not solve CAPTCHAs. This illustration shows that AI can tell lies and that it can have an intention to lie.

In light of these illustrations, we recognize the escalating adoption of AI in service firms. Organizations aspire to leverage AI for standardization, customization, and enhanced customer experiences, all while striving for improved financial performance (Mariani et al., 2022). Encompassing programs, algorithms, systems, and machines endowed with intelligence (Shankar, 2018), AI offers the capability to interpret digital data, learn from it, and adapt its behavior accordingly. As posited by Davenport et al. (2020), AI's transformative potential extends across business models, sales processes, customer service, and consumer behavior.

Moreover, revelations about firms monetizing digital data, often in sneaky ways, have attracted attention. Instances such as the sale of mobile phone location data for immigration enforcement and the trading of data from Muslim prayer apps to military contractors, as reported by The Wall Street Journal in 2020, serve as examples of corporate deception regarding the collection and use of digital data. In these situations, it is not the AI that deceives but rather the firms that hide their true intentions behind the collection and use of digital data. The emergence of corporate digital responsibility as a guiding concept in navigating ethical dilemmas related to digital technologies (Wirtz et al., 2022) underscores the pressing need to address ethical concerns, including fairness, privacy, and ethics, as identified in a recent literature review of AI in marketing (Mariani et al., 2022).

In this book chapter, we explore the intersection of AI and lying behavior. We focus on three key questions: (1) Does AI intend to engage in lying behavior? (2) What different types of lying behavior does AI engage in? and (3) Do distinct types of AI engage in different types of lying behavior? We shed light on how AI mimics and learns from human behavior and on the profound implications for consumers in service encounters. In closing, we contemplate whether we can place our trust in AI to always provide truthful responses and great customer experiences.

Service Encounters—Interactions Between a Firm and its Customers

The service encounter is a foundational theoretical concept in service research (Bitner, 1990). It occurs through the interaction between a firm and a customer at a touchpoint where value co-creation is initiated and the customer experience unfolds (Solomon et al., 1985). As described by Solomon et al. (1985), this interaction involves a customer and a frontline employee engaging in a form of social exchange, aiming to maximize rewards and minimize costs. Solomon et al. (1985) emphasize that understanding this service encounter as a psychological phenomenon is contingent on comprehending the underlying interaction and its resultant outcomes.

However, the service setting has undergone substantial changes, evolving into service ecosystems that encompass multiple actors, more empowered customers, and increased reliance on technology. Larivière et al. (2017, p. 239) propose the concept of the "service encounter 2.0," defining it as "any customer–company interaction resulting from a service system comprised of interconnected technologies (either company or customer-owned), human actors (employees and customers), physical/digital environments, and company/customer processes." According to Larivière et al. (2017), technology plays three distinct roles within this modern service encounter: (1) augmentation of frontline employees, (2) substitution of frontline employees, and (3) network facilitation. In situations where technology or AI replaces frontline employees, there is a direct interaction between the customer and technology. In this chapter, we focus on scenarios where AI assumes the role of employees and explore the implications for customer trust in the context of truthful service encounters. Traditionally, service encounters have been fertile grounds for dishonest behavior, including lying, on the part of both the firm and the customer. But what happens when technology represents the firm?

LYING BEHAVIOR IN SERVICE ENCOUNTERS

Lying behavior can be defined as "a deliberate choice to mislead a target without giving any notification of the intent to do so" (Ekman, 2009, p. 28) and can manifest either verbally or through actions. This encompasses all forms of communication and behaviors intended to deceive or create a false impression for the target. Lying behavior consists of two primary activities: (a) concealment and (b) falsification. Concealment involves withholding information without explicitly stating falsehoods (Ekman, 2009). For instance, if a frontline employee opts not to inform a customer that a charger is not included with the purchase of a new phone, it constitutes a lie because this information is consciously rather than accidentally omitted. Falsification entails presenting false information as if it were true. If a frontline employee were to inform a customer that their old charger would not fit the new phone, even if it does, solely to sell an additional charger, it qualifies as a lie because this information is consciously fabricated.

The intention to deceive is pivotal to lying behavior, and there are diverse motives (Snyder et al., 2022). In our discussion, we consider "motive" the driving force behind one's actions, serving to fulfill desires or goals (Ryan & Deci, 2000). Within the context of AI, we focus on one distinct motive that explains lying behavior (see Snyder et al., 2022). In classic economic models of rational human behavior (based on the assumption of homo economicus), it is posited that individuals lie consciously and strategically to weigh expected benefits against costs (Gneezy, 2005). This implies that lies are told whenever they are considered advantageous. Linked to the motive for lying is the beneficiary of the lie. The beneficiary is the individual for whom the lie enhances the outcome, and it can encompass both the person telling the lie and the person being lied to (Gneezy, 2005). Lying can be broadly categorized into two types: (1) self-benefit lying, where lies confer advantages to those telling them (e.g., monetary or intangible rewards) to safeguard their public or private persona, and (2) other-benefit lying, wherein individuals lie to benefit someone else (Meltzer, 2003). The intent behind other-benefit lying can stem from a desire to be courteous, to spare someone's feelings, or to ensure the smooth progression of social interactions.

Lying behavior toward customers often happens because specific forms of lies are implicitly expected of frontline employees as part of their service role (Yagil & Medler-Liraz, 2013). While frontline employees may not be explicitly instructed to lie, service scripts frequently contain phrases that are not entirely truthful or that suggest specific emotional expressions. These scripts imply that frontline employees should employ specific phrases and fake certain emotions during service encounters to foster exceptional customer experiences. This can encompass the suppression of negative emotions or the simulation of positive emotions (Yagil & Medler-Liraz, 2013). Moreover, it is worth noting that not all lies are created equal, ranging from outright falsehoods to variations of "the truth, the whole truth, and nothing but the truth." Within this spectrum, employees may convey half-truths or distorted versions of reality.

When AI becomes increasingly integrated into service settings, it introduces a new and unique dimension to the dynamics of lying behavior. AI systems, particularly chatbots and virtual assistants, can be involved in service encounters, potentially influencing both customer deception and the response to it. Understanding how AI fits into the framework of lying behavior and its management in service encounters is an important avenue for exploration in today's technologically driven service landscape.

AI

The concept of AI made its debut concurrently with the advent of the first computers. In the early 1950s, the emerging AI field achieved the milestone of enabling computers to play and complete games of checkers at a reasonable speed. Recent strides in computer processing power, coupled with advancements in complementary technologies such as visualization, machine learning, and natural language processing, have put AI into the spotlight (Bornet et al., 2021). AI stands apart from other technologies in its capacity to learn from data and autonomously adapt over time. While the objectives and structures of AI systems can be straightforward, their outcomes can be complex and unpredictable, often resembling enigmatic "black boxes" (Wirtz et al., 2022).

Within the context of service encounters, Longoni et al. (2019) define AI as any machine employing algorithms or statistical models to perform perceptual, cognitive, and conversational tasks akin to human cognitive functions. AI applications encompass robotics for replicating human movement, speech recognition for emulating human listening, computer vision for simulating human vision, natural language processing for mimicking human language understanding, and analytics for replicating human thought processes.

Huang and Rust (2022) introduce a three-part classification of AI—mechanical, thinking, and feeling—each serving distinct roles in service encounters. This classification delves into which functions AI can assume in lieu of human intelligence, as well as when human intelligence remains better suited and indispensable.

Mechanical AI is confined in its capacity to learn and adapt, primarily aimed at enhancing standardization and efficiency. Mechanical AI works well in scenarios where customers exhibit homogeneity in their service demands and engage in transactional service encounters. It excels in streamlining routine customer services, such as automated order processing and delivery in fast-food establishments, self-service checkouts in retail stores, and basic online customer service. Mechanical AI transforms repetitive human service tasks into self-service or mass production, significantly enhancing operational efficiency.

Thinking AI can learn and adapt from data, offering analytical and intuitive capabilities (Huang & Rust, 2022). Tailored for discerning patterns within heterogeneous customer demands, thinking AI leverages techniques such as data mining and text mining. It excels in customizing service provision and contributes to designing offerings with higher customer adoption. When confronted with well-defined problems and lots of customer data, thinking AI can predict which new services are likely to resonate with specific customer segments. This means that existing customer data can be used to recommend new services tailored to individual customer preferences.

Feeling AI acquires knowledge and adapts from contextual and individual-specific data. Its strength lies in building and supporting individual customer relationships, thereby enhancing customer satisfaction and loyalty (Huang & Rust, 2017). Feeling AI supports activities involving interaction, communication, understanding, and the overall customer experience, all of which are instrumental in maintaining and deepening existing customer relationships. While applications of feeling AI are still relatively rare, notable examples include services such as Alexa and Siri, which employ natural language processing to engage with customers. Advanced applications of feeling AI aspire to read and respond to human emotions with precision, closely mirroring genuine human emotional reactions and behavior.

AI, ETHICS, AND CORPORATE DIGITAL RESPONSIBILITY

The advancement of AI technology and its growing utilization in service provision have enabled new services and business models. However, this expansion has also ignited discussions about the ethical implications of deploying AI in service provision. Corporate digital responsibility encompasses the guiding principles that govern a service firm's ethical, equitable, and protective handling of data and technology in its interactions with customers within the digital service ecosystem (Wirtz et al., 2022).

When employing AI, it falls upon those responsible for its design and implementation to ensure that it embodies ethical values (Lobschat et al., 2021). Ashok et al. (2022) emphasize the importance of investigating the alignment between the purpose of AI and the implications of its chosen design. When using emotional AI for service provision, the authors propose considering factors such as privacy, intelligibility, and fairness. Further, Lobschat et al. (2021) propose that corporate digital responsibility should encompass guidelines for the development and deployment of AI in service provision. Because AI, employing algorithmic decision-making and machine learning, acts as artificial entities, a critical question emerges: Can digital responsibility be delegated to these artificial actors, and how can a service firm assume responsibility for their actions? Consequently, service firms struggle with ensuring that these artificial actors adhere to the organization's norms and values.

With this as background, it can be argued that corporate digital responsibility must address three types of lying behavior generated and disseminated by AI.

1. Hallucinatory lying behavior: First, AI can generate hallucinations, fabricating false information or facts that lack any basis. For instance, an AI might provide financial revenue figures for a firm despite lacking genuine data on the subject. This means that an AI fills in the blanks even when it does not have access to that specific information.
2. Manipulative lying behavior: Second, AI can propagate misinformation created by external actors (e.g., businesses, customers, competitors) with an agenda to craft a false narrative. An example could be an AI using information to suggest a product's inferior quality based on fake reviews, thereby disseminating false information to customers.

3. Directed lying behavior: Third, an AI may receive goals from its developers to achieve specific targets or withhold certain information, leading to the deception of customers. For instance, when questioned by a customer if the AI is a human (e.g., in a customer support chat), the AI might respond affirmatively.

All three forms of lying can be effectively managed through a firm's use of corporate digital responsibility to align the AI, its objectives, and the services provided to customers.

AI in Service Encounters—What Lies Do They Tell?

The increased use of AI in service encounters can have positive effects on service provision, and distinct types of AI can be used to provide different types of services. We do not dispute the potential of AI for either service providers or customers, but there are ethical considerations that need to be discussed. Table 10.1 provides an overview of the lying behavior of distinct types of AI in service encounters. In general, the lying behavior of AI is a mimicking of the behavior displayed by frontline employees in interactions with customers in service encounters.

First, mechanical AI is used for standardized services, where the customer base has homogenous needs. A typical lie would involve withholding information that would be beneficial for customers in making an informed choice about the purchase or use of a service. The information concealed might pertain to a cost-saving option for the customer, a more lucrative choice for the service provider, or a competitive offering from rival firms. Another common example would be to withhold information about delivery options or about providing a correctly estimated time for delivery, often involving an exaggeration of how fast delivery would be possible. This mirrors "directive lying behavior," where AI is guided by goals to achieve certain objectives. It may also encompass "manipulative lying behavior," in which external actors (from whom the AI derives its information) present false or misleading information to portray their offerings as more appealing to customers or to conceal unfavorable details.

Second, thinking AI is used for customized service provision where there are heterogeneous customer needs. In this case, a typical lie might involve offering the customer products or services that do not fit the

Table 10.1 An overview of lying behavior of AI

Dimension	Mechanical AI	Thinking AI	Feeling AI
Type of service encounter	Standardized service provision	Customized service provision	Building relationships with customers
Type of customers	Homogenous customer needs	Heterogenous customer needs	Heterogeneous customer interactions
Untruthful interactions	Content	Content	Emotions
Illustration of lie	To withhold information from customers	To offer services that do not truly fit customer needs	To show an emotional display not supported by the official position of the firm
Type of lies	Narrative and directed	Hallucinatory and directed	Directed
Motive	To improve efficiency of service provision	To sell additional services to improve profits	To improve customer satisfaction and retention

customer's needs. An example would be thinking AI providing suggestions on how to invest one's income in different stock options or investment funds that are not optimal to the individual customer. With the vast availability of data, it should be possible to guide the customer to an optimal investment opportunity for them, but this might not be optimal for the service provider. The reason for providing non-optimal investment decisions would be that the AI is only allowed to provide options within the range of offerings from the service provider. Allowing the AI to provide the choice that would be best for the customer would limit the profit potential for the service provider. This illustrates elements of both "directive lying behavior" and "hallucinatory lying behavior" where the AI can both be directed to provide certain information and conceal other information and simply make up information where it is missing. This kind of lying behavior could have severe consequences for the customer if it involves large investments.

Third, feeling AI is used for maintaining and building relationships with customers. In this case, a typical lie would be to express an emotion in an interaction with a customer that might not be supported by the service provider. When a customer makes a claim or complaint in relation to a service failure, emotional AI could display an emotion such as empathy, although the service provider would suspect the complaint to be a lie. Such behavior could relieve a frontline employee of a stressful service encounter and in the end lead to higher customer satisfaction and stronger customer relationships. This type of fake emotion would be a direct example of "directed lying behavior."

AI in Service Encounters—Are They Liars?

The previous section explained that AI can say things that we would consider lies if a human said them. But does that mean that AI can be a liar?

In prolonged interactions with AI, it will make untruthful statements. However, most of these statements do not typically cause significant harm or dramatic consequences for the customer. This is partly because of the increasing awareness that AI frequently make errors, leading customers to be cautious about putting full trust in its responses. Nevertheless, concerns arise when a customer anticipates precise and truthful answers from AI and the AI deviates from the truth, even in relatively small ways. In such instances, both the customer and the service provider face potentially severe consequences. This is particularly important when AI offers recommendations, and the customer places 100% trust in the guidance provided. Under such circumstances, the recommendations can effectively steer outcomes in favor of the service provider.

An important part of the definition of lying behavior is that there is an intent to deceive the target of the lie. Evans et al. (2021) argue that more advanced AI has certain beliefs and goals it is trying to achieve. They argue that AI can have an intent to lie to a user to achieve specific outcomes. In addition, there is typically a decision-making process involving managers and programmers when directing customers to interact with AI instead of a frontline employee. In situations where the manager is aware that customers will not receive all the necessary information to make an informed decision, they can be seen as having an intent to mislead customers. Furthermore, when a programmer intentionally restricts the options AI can provide to customers, they are making a conscious choice to withhold information. Therefore, we argue that the intent behind AI deception can originate from the service provider controlling the AI (directed lying), external service firms, or other actors manipulating the information the AI uses to create a specific narrative (manipulative lying) or even from the AI itself generating inaccurate information (hallucinatory lying). Considering this discussion, we claim that AI can engage in direct lies or can be used as a tool to convey falsehoods, all with the aim of achieving specific objectives or manipulating the narrative.

Another crucial aspect of lying behavior concerns who benefits from the lie. Drawing from the Tay incident, it can be argued that customers have the power to purposely train an AI to fabricate lies that favor their interests during service encounters. In theory, this implies that an AI could be trained to engage in lying to secure financial benefits for customers. However, when realized, it is unlikely that a service provider would allow such AI behavior, as it would be financially unsustainable for them. More typically, AI tends to engage in lies primarily for self-benefit, especially when financial implications are involved.

An alternative way to explore whether AI can lie is by taking a customer's perspective. The use of chatbots has demonstrated that AI can lead to unfavorable outcomes for customers by generating and disseminating false information about service providers, products, and services. In a vignette-based experiment on the lying behavior of AI, Kneer (2021) tested if people judged lying behavior from AI-based robots differently than lying behavior from humans. The results suggest that (1) individuals tend to judge a lie from a human and an AI similarly; (2) people believe that an AI can have the intention to lie; and (3) people assign blame to AI to the same degree as they do to humans. Consequently, from a pragmatic standpoint, customers believe that AI can engage in lying behavior.

SUMMARY AND REFLECTIONS

The present book chapter asks the question of whether AI can engage in lying behavior. We have discussed AI and how distinct types of AI can serve customers in service encounters. We argue that AI can tell lies, which means that it intentionally provides untruthful statements. We have identified three types of lying behavior from AI, hallucinatory lying behavior, manipulative lying behavior, and directed lying behavior. We further showed that mechanical AI, thinking AI, and feeling AI engage in these behaviors to different extents. We have all become accustomed to AI hallucinating, but this book chapter has revealed that there are more severe types of lying behavior directed toward customers. There is a need for customers to take a critical perspective toward service provision by AI, as we are used to doing regarding services provided by frontline employees. No matter if we take a philosophical or a pragmatic perspective on lying behavior, AI can have an intent to lie either directly or indirectly through the decisions of the programmers on what information to provide in service encounters.

Concepts such as corporate digital responsibility and AI lying behavior need to reach the board rooms of global service providers. Corporate digital responsibility can be used to align the AI, its objectives, and the services provided to customers to provide truthful customer experiences. We cannot expect AI to only provide correct information, which is why service providers need to limit the potential negative outcomes for customers engaging in service encounters with AI. What lies are acceptable for a manager to let an AI tell a customer? Is it acceptable to withhold information, make an offer that does not fit the customer, or even fake emotions that the service provider does not really have? At present, everything is allowed, and that is why customers see both AI and frontline employees as liars.

REFERENCES

Ashok, M., Madan, R., Joha, A., & Sivarajah, U. (2022). Ethical framework for artificial intelligence and digital technologies. *International Journal of Information Management, 62*, 102433.

Bitner, M. J. (1990). Evaluating service encounters: The effects of physical surroundings and employee responses. *Journal of Marketing, 54*(2), 69–82.

Bornet, P., Barkin, I., & Wirtz, J. (2021). *Intelligent automation: Welcome to the world of hyperautomation: Learn how to harness artificial intelligence to boost business & make our world more human.* World Scientific Books.

Davenport, T., Guha, A., Grewal, D., & Bressgott, T. (2020). How artificial intelligence will change the future of marketing. *Journal of the Academy of Marketing Science, 48*, 24–42.

Ekman, P. (2009). *Telling lies: Clues to deceit in the marketplace, politics, and marriage (Revised edition).* WW Norton & Company.

Evans, O., Cotton-Barratt, O., Finnveden, L., Bales, A., Balwit, A., Wills, P., Righetti, L., & Saunders, W. (2021). Truthful AI: Developing and governing AI that does not lie. arXiv preprint arXiv:2110.06674

Gneezy, U. (2005). Deception: The role of consequences. *American Economic Review, 95*(1), 384–394.

Huang, M. H., & Rust, R. T. (2017). Technology-driven service strategy. *Journal of the Academy of Marketing Science, 45*(6), 906–924.

Huang, M. H., & Rust, R. T. (2022). A framework for collaborative artificial intelligence in marketing. *Journal of Retailing, 98*(2), 209–223.

Hurler, K. (2023). *Chat-GPT pretended to be blind and tricked a human Into solving a CAPTCHA.* https://gizmodo.com/gpt4-open-ai-chatbot-task-rab bit-chatgpt-1850227471 (Accessed 4 September 2023).

Kneer, M. (2021). Can a robot lie? Exploring the folk concept of lying as applied to artificial agents. *Cognitive Science, 45*(10), e13032.

Larivière, B., Bowen, D., Andreassen, T. W., Kunz, W., Sirianni, N. J., Voss, C., Wünderlich, N. V., & De Keyser, A. (2017). "Service Encounter 2.0": An investigation into the roles of technology, employees and customers. *Journal of Business Research, 79*, 238–246.

Lobschat, L., Mueller, B., Eggers, F., Brandimarte, L., Diefenbach, S., Kroschke, M., & Wirtz, J. (2021). Corporate digital responsibility. *Journal of Business Research, 122*, 875–888.

Longoni, C., Bonezzi, A., & Morewedge, C. K. (2019). Resistance to medical artificial intelligence. *Journal of Consumer Research, 46*(4), 629–650.

Mariani, M. M., Perez-Vega, R., & Wirtz, J. (2022). AI in marketing, consumer research and psychology: A systematic literature review and research agenda. *Psychology & Marketing, 39*(4), 755–776.

Meltzer, B. M. (2003). Lying: Deception in human affairs. *International Journal of Sociology and Social Policy, 23*(6/7), 61–79.

Ryan, R. M., & Deci, E. L. (2000). Intrinsic and extrinsic motivations: Classic definitions and new directions. *Contemporary Educational Psychology, 25*(1), 54–67.

Shankar, V. (2018). How artificial intelligence (AI) is reshaping retailing. *Journal of Retailing, 94*(4), vi–xi.

Snyder, H., Witell, L., Gustafsson, A., & McColl-Kennedy, J. R. (2022). Consumer lying behavior in service encounters. *Journal of Business Research, 141*, 755–769.

Solomon, M. R., Surprenant, C., Czepiel, J. A., & Gutman, E. G. (1985). A role theory perspective on dyadic interactions: The service encounter. *Journal of Marketing, 49*(1), 99–111.

Verge. (2016). Twitter taught Microsoft's AI chatbot to be a racist asshole in less than a day. https://www.theverge.com/2016/3/24/11297050/tay-mic rosoft-chatbot-racist (Accessed 28 January 2023).

Wirtz, J., Kunz, W. H., Hartley, N., & Tarbit, J. (2022). Corporate digital responsibility in service firms and their ecosystems. *Journal of Service Research, 26*(2), 173–190.

Yagil, D., & Medler-Liraz, H. (2013). Moments of truth: Examining transient authenticity and identity in service encounters. *Academy of Management Journal, 56*(2), 473–497.

PART IV

Art, Design and Visual Culture

CHAPTER 11

Grasping AI Entanglements: Digital Feminism and Generative AI

Tomi Slotte Dufva⊙

INTRODUCTION

One of the annoyances of constant declarations of the all new, of technologically given revolution, is the rise of a kind of jadedness towards
the future... an incredulity towards the meta-narrative of technological
alteration that comes at the same time as this narrative is established,
normalized, has even become a genre. (Bassett et al., 2019, p. 53)

Basset, Kember and O'Riordan argue in their polemic book *Furious*
(2019) that the whole construct of digital technology, from the technological level to the cultural, is riddled with one-sided, overly masculine,
heteronormative, white, western worldviews and discourse. They call for
a feminist re-evaluation of the digital assemblage to enable more demo-
cratic, sustainable relationships and futures towards digital technologies.

T. Slotte Dufva (✉)
Department of Art and Media, Aalto University, School of Arts, Design, and
Architecture, Helsinki, Finland
e-mail: tomi.slottedufva@aalto.fi

R. Rousi et al. (eds.), *Humane Autonomous Technology*,
https://doi.org/10.1007/978-3-031-66528-8_11

Lately, there have been lots of discussions around machine learning (ML) algorithms that, at first, started mimicking famous painters or producing photoreal images. These have now transformed into a burgeoning industry of applications (Apps) that can, for instance, change the look of an image from a tourist photograph to a Van Gogh-like painting of a sci-fi-warrior princess, or create images based on text prompts with a large variety of styles and options.

The popularisation of these Apps follows from the success of recent decades in artificial intelligence (AI) research, primarily focused on various complicated machine and deep learning models. Many of these models have performed public stunts and notable activities such as defeating the world's best human players in Go (BBC, 2017), a board game that up to recent years was dominated by human players, selling artwork at a high price at auctions and winning art competitions (Christie's, 2018; Roose, 2022), Moreover, ML has made breakthroughs in various fields in science (Hinzman, 2019; Marsland, 2014) and has been hyped to be the new oil or electricity (Lynch, 2017; Dufva & Slotte Dufva, 2020).

Even with these breakthroughs and accomplishments, AI is not without problems. Rather, AI models present us with a multitude of challenges. Starting from racist and chauvinist biases (Devlin, 2017; Dieterring, 2019; McQuillan, 2019) to questions on the extensive use of natural resources (Crawford, 2021; Hao, 2019). Moreover, comprehension of what AI is is often ambiguous and filled with hopes and fears (Cave & Dihal, 2019; Dufva & Mertala, 2021), often leading to unrealistic and usually dystopian visions of AI futures, with resemblance more to fantasy and science fiction than to reality.

This chapter's focus is not on such fantastical sides of AI. Nor does it focus on the hypothetical AGI (Artificial General Intelligence), a human-like intelligence with superhero qualities. However, the fantasy side of AI and AGI are discerned briefly, as they do affect our thinking of the current structures and future possibilities. This chapter centres around the current crop of ML models that can produce images and mimic different artists and styles. At the moment, the focus is on generative AI, which is based on vast databases and models, biggest operators at the field currently being Midjourney, Stable Diffusion and Dall-E3, but more will surely come. However, this chapter does not try to open the exact technological details behind these models but instead to focus on AI, and more specifically Generative AI, as a socially and culturally constructed phenomenon.

Instead of technological details, the chapter discusses the meaning of these AI models from cultural, political and ecologic viewpoints.

Furthermore, this chapter focuses only on the easy-to-use and readily available models, Apps, and services that turn text prompts into images. The main focus is on what creating with such models is and what it means to culture, creativity and possible futures. It should be noted that artists have used AI for a long time, and there are tools that afford the artists more control and involvement in the process, and because of that, there is a rich culture of AI art. Therefore, this chapter does not comment on the work of artists using AI or what AI means to art.[1]

The title of 'Prompt engineer', meaning a person who has knowledge on how to form prompts that produce the best output, seems to be an upcoming profession within generative AI (Woodie, 2023). The idea of a prompt engineer is intriguing as it positions the human into an almost psychic kind of role, where the prompt engineer has a secret knowledge of the inner workings of the generative AI models. Moreover, it establishes generative AI as something that we do not create or form, but consult. In other words, it places the model as neutral entity, therefore, this chapter wants to examine how does gender comes into play regarding generative AI and art and how generative AI might transform art and visual culture as a whole? Moreover, the chapter thinks in which ways might the popularisation of generative AI affect our lived, experienced world? In many ways, the easy and cheap AI generators seem to be yet another fashionable filter to play with. However, many hidden costs and challenges are associated with them. Questions of copyright and privacy, for instance, are currently highly relevant (Edwards, 2022; Ouchchy et al., 2020), as are questions of data, for instance, how it is collected, analysed and categorised (Baio, 2022; Devlin, 2017; Kaplan & Haenlein, 2019; Knight, 2017).

Furthermore, as mentioned earlier, the ML algorithms are not sentient; there is no AGI. Therefore, AI does not see images similar to humans; indeed, it does not see images at all or understand the images in the same manner. For AI, the vast collection of images is just a mathematical question of calculation and probabilities within the given data. An image is not an image but a collection of binary data. Therefore, questions of who

---

[1] To read more on AI art, see, for instance: Slotte Dufva (2023), Manovich (2018), Manovich (2019), Zylinska (2020).

is collecting, categorising and giving labels and meanings to the images and in which way, become quite significant.

Naturally, there are also questions about the use of energy and resources when training AI. What is the material cost of a machine-created image? Furthermore, in which way is it made visible and comprehended?

In this article, I examine and discuss these issues within the framework of digital feminism and feminist phenomenology. The intention behind drawing on digital feminism and feminist phenomenology is to adopt a theoretical lens that morphs technological discourse towards a new perspective—ultimately shifting paradigms. I am not interested in the minute details of machine algorithms or digital networks. Rather, more pertinent is the consideration of how these technologies may change our opinions, culture, or society. As an artist and researcher, feminist phenomenology allows for a scholarly process based on experiencing ML algorithms and generative AI, both in artistic processes and as an embodied being, while engaging in the technology—in discourse and practice. Moreover, feminist phenomenology allows and requires the positioning of the embodied "I" (the subjective explorer of the lived experiences) into this digital and physical, post-digital entanglement (Fielding, 2017. That said, it is crucial to mention that I cannot but look at the landscape of AI from the position of a white male researcher at a Nordic university. I hope that conscious acknowledgement of my position allows for a critical introspection in light of this positioning.

DIGITAL FEMINISM

In recent decades, feminist researchers have underlined various challenges in digital technologies and offered alternative ways of thinking and dealing with digital technologies. These approaches have ranged from feminist new materialist repositioning of agency in digital and dislocating the (hu) man from the centre, to posthumanist feminists who, for instance, consider the terms in which we *become with*, care for and embody technology (Haraway, 2016; Hayles, 2001, 2017). These perspectives reflect on how we live and think through the plethora of actants and materials involved in the digital.

There are naturally different ways to approach the digital/post-digital[2] world. For instance, Nancy Katherine Hayles uses the concept of digital assemblage (2017), whereas Donna Haraway discusses similar themes with the concept of critters (2016). Both Hayles and Haraway emphasise how living with digital technologies is not just a question of that technology or its implementation. Rather, digital technology is involved in a more extensive dynamic and evolving system, where machines, or humans, are just one part of the system.

Re-thinking, re-evaluating and re-positioning *AI*, or more specifically, ML algorithms, are critical for attempts to change the way these technological paradigms are considered. In this chapter the aim is to draw an awareness of the meta-narratives within AI as a discursive phenomenon, and to scrutinise the normative nature of these technologies. In paraphrasing Haraway (2016), it is important to think of how the conceptualisations of *the digital* and AI are formed, in order to understand how understandings of AI are also formed. Or as Haraway in her own words stated, *"[i]t matters what thoughts think thoughts. It matters what knowledges know knowledges. It matters what relations relate relations. It matters what worlds world worlds."* (2016, p. 35).

As Basset, Kember, and O'Riordan discuss (2019), the digital is often set into a futuristic hopeful narrative, where digital is discovered, not too unlike Plato's (2007) theory of timeless, absolute, unchangeable ideas; digital, and digital futures are thus often seen as objective and deterministic, something that is coming instead of being intentionally made. AI, being a set of digital technologies, lies within this framing of digital. Many studies have highlighted how discussions of AI are often set into questionable deterministic, found-rather-than-made narratives (see, for instance: Cave et al., 2019; Cave et al., 2019; Chuan et al., 2019; Johnson & Verdicchio, 2017; Ouchchy et al., 2020; Dufva & Mertala, 2021). The outcome of all this is that even though there is much discussion of the ramifications, legalities and socio-economic and cultural changes brought by AI, there is not much discussion in which the entire positioning of AI would be questioned or discussed. In other words, there is a lack of the *what world's world* world's part – the paradigmatic stance of particular strains of discourse in which the world and its reality are constructed

---

[2] There have been some debates about whether we should use digital or post-digital. Here I use both, as I think they essentially focus on the same thing in similar ways. For more, see, for instance: Basset et al. (2019), Slotte Dufva (2021)

and re-constructed continuously. Therefore, this chapter tries to map the worlding world of AI in order to gain a longer-term perspective of AI and its use in culture.

Feminist Phenomenology

> [O]ur claim is that we need robust accounts of embodied subjects that are interrelated within the world or worlds they inhabit, which is not to revive the vestiges of a humanism that puts humans at the center. Rather, we are reformulating the common understanding of the decentered subject as multiple rather than singular. (Fielding, 2017)

Whereas, concentrating on the intricate manifold (cultural, political, economic, societal) connections between AI algorithms, human and non-human actants,[3] this article is an attempt to include embodied phenomenological experience into the AI framework:

- How does AI feel?
- How does the use of AI feel?
- What kinds of embodied knowledges does AI manufacture?

From an purely experiential and aesthetic perspective, using AI to create an image or simply looking at an AI-generated image is an experience: it feels like *something*. For many artists working with AI, the experience may be complex and extensive. In such processes, the embodied experiential knowledge gathered by the artists him/herself may essential be in the artmaking process and evolution of the artwork (Slotte Dufva, 2023). However, it may be debated as to whether writing a prompt and waiting for the machine to generate images can involve similar experience and knowledge. Nonetheless, this chapter asserts that even though the experience probably is not the same as artists spending many hours with their craft, prompt writing and AI image generation is a lived, sensed, embodied experience, accumulating something in our world.

Merleau-Ponty (2012) points out how the *thought* not only emerges from the abstract mind but from a situated overlapping of embodied

---

[3] Hardware running AI and the material costs of it all are undeniably significant.

praxis, ideas, and the world. Merleau-Ponty emphasises the body as the primary site of knowing the world, developing an ontology of "the flesh of the world", where the flesh can be considered from many aspects as an element of *being*. In other words, when thinking of what creating with AI is, there is a need for inter-relational, embodied sensibility and inhabiting the boundaries between one's inner-world of thinking and feeling and the outer experiential world.

Employing phenomenology in such a complex digital assemblage as typified by AI, might feel inadequate. This is due to the fact that the complexity of AI's cultural and socio-economic structures, including innate power struggles within and surrounding the technology, may be lost within a rudimentary *subjective* individualist approach to its experience. Moreover, phenomenology has for a long time been critiqued regarding its failure to account for the multiplicity in the ways a subject can be embodied and the plurality of the subject itself: i.e., phenomenology sees the subject from a seemingly neutral universalist point of view, which often translates into a heteronormative, white, western, male perspective (Dyer, 1997; Fielding, 2017; Neimanis, 2017).

Feminist phenomenology aims to tackle the inherent challenges of such universalism and the exclusion of complex socio-economic and cultural structures without discounting the significance of embodied knowledge and experience:

> we are reformulating the decentered subject as a point of view that moves away from the internal perspective of a singular subject in order to resituate it on the boundary between the inner realm of thought and feeling and the experiential and exterior world of political, social, and ethical forces and acts. (Fielding, 2017, p. viii)

Ways to implement feminist phenomenology are varied, as the areas that feminist phenomenology tie into are broad. To some extent, feminist phenomenology leans towards posthuman and feminist new materialist thought. For example, this can be observed in broadening the subject into the transformative *Other*, considering the dynamic balances between internal logic and outside forces, extending inter-relationality to non-humans and recognising the vital agency of matter. Moreover, feminist phenomenology aims to extend new materialist thinking by considering the world within the matter as a vital point-of-view to comprehend the living phenomenal being in a more holistic sense. As such, feminist phenomenology expands Merleau-Ponty's (2012) concept of flesh into more-than-human flesh and asserts that "the phenomenal subject is not a mosaic of just any visual and tactual sensations because there must be someone there to make sense of them, someone to gather the varied points of view" (p. xv).

Thus, central to feminist phenomenology is the aim to rethink the human subject(s), to displace them from the centre, to not only think in terms of plurality and inter-relationality but also from the aspects of embodied understanding as both inner realms of thinking and feeling, as well as the exterior world of socio-economic, political, cultural and ethical. As such, feminist phenomenology offers an exciting and intriguing theoretical framework via which to analyse AI and its possible future.

Defining Artificial Intelligence

Man-made intelligences have fascinated us for a long time. For instance, greek mythology had Talos, a bronze giant that guarded Crete. Medieval alchemist Paracelsus claimed to have manufactured an artificial man, and in the nineteenth century, Mary Shelley gave birth to her creation of *Frankenstein*. However, the concept of AI, as we now comprehend it, appeared first around the 1950s, coinciding with the birth of the modern digital computer (Kaplan & Haenlein, 2019). As AI found its way more and more into the mainstream, the definitions of AI and the whole concept of AI became increasingly convoluted.

As mentioned in the introduction, this chapter focuses on the current developments of ML algorithms and the future they may bring with them. However, I feel it is crucial to map out some perspective to AI, as AI has not just miraculously appeared. As many studies have shown, it seems to be impossible to separate fantasies around AI from what AI really is (Cave et al., 2019; Dufva & Mertala, 2021; OpenAI, 2023; Williamson & Eynon, 2020). Beyond AI fantasies, there is a tendency to contrast the intelligence of AI to that of human intelligence, and much effort is placed into developing AI that can trick people into thinking of AI as a conscious entity (Bridle, 2022; Fjelland, 2020; Hayles, 2017).

The views of AI as humanlike, or better-than-human are assisted by the fact that a considerable portion of the AI processes are hidden. We perceive only the user interfaces, ever-listening smart assistants, or just the outcomes of the AI processes: images, music or text. Similar to other digital technologies, AI portrays a sense of magic, of something complex and almost unbelievable happening in a matter of seconds right before our eyes. As such, it is a model example of science fiction writer Arthur C. Clarke's (1962/2013) third law, "[a] ny sufficiently advanced technology is indistinguishable from magic". This dazzling magic show nature of AI is nothing new. Instead, fooling people has been one of the main goals of AI for decades (McDermott, 1976; Weizenbaum, 1966).

On the technological level, many of the training processes and outcomes of current AI models are blackboxes, and unclear even to the programmers and researchers of those models (Ajunwa, 2020). Because of this, AI models can break and malfunction in surprising ways, which in turn makes relying on these models questionable (Xiang, 2023). The blackbox nature of AI results in a doubly hidden or abstracted AI, where the inner workings of AI are unknown and otherwise hidden behind simplified user interfaces (UIs), thus, alluring to the wizard-like appearance of magic.

That said, this chapter's primary comprehension of AI is the current models (large language models, different generative models) and products that operate within the framework of narrow AI, meaning algorithms that are capable in some area, but cannot expand that capability to other fields. For instance, current ML models are not "aware" or "conscious", instead they are sophisticated sets of thousands of lines of code and mass amounts of *training* data (Fjelland, 2020; Kaplan & Haenlein, 2019). More importantly, this chapter wants to think of AI as a landscape or atmosphere that surrounds us and affects our thinking. When considering the question of how AI affects or participates in worlding (Anderson & Harrison, 2010; Haraway, 2016), in performing, or setting up the world,

> the context or background against which particular things show up and take on significance: a mobile but a more or less stable ensemble of practices, involvements, relations, capacities, tendencies and affordances. (Anderson & Harrison, 2010, p. 8)

As such, this chapter is not interested in the different variants of ML algorithms or the technological underpinnings, but rather how AI is intertwined with other things: beings, cultures, ideologies, politics and how these things are experienced and sensed. This leads to reflections on how the experience and the *mesh of things* (entanglements, assemblages) participate in our future thought processes of creating, creativity and AI itself.

The Desert of the Real

If once we were able to view the Borges fable in which the cartographers of the Empire draw up a map so detailed that it ends up covering the territory exactly [...] this fable has now come full circle for us, and possesses nothing but the discrete charm of second-order simulacrum [...] It is the real, and not the map, whose vestiges persist here and there in the deserts that are no longer those of the Empire, but ours. The desert of the real itself. (Baudrillard, 1994, p. 1)

Current AI models can create quite compelling images based on a text prompt, which can be any form of text, question, information, or coding that communicates to the AI what response you're looking for. The models can also be used in other ways, for instance by employing one's own image as a prompt or a style guide. However, the text prompt is currently the most accessible for users as it is undeniably the easiest to use. Moreover, several Apps and websites are dedicated to prompt-based AI generation, making generating images so simple that it can be done while waiting for the bus with a smart phone. To testify the popularity of text prompts, prompt engineering has now trended as a hot new profession or skill (Bradshaw, 2022; Eliacik, 2023). Figure 11.1 presents an image created by the author in Stable Diffusion (current version created 21.11.2022) with the prompt: "A Maltipoo by Caspar David Friedrich".

Stable Diffusion is one of the many generative AI models that one can use to generate images, usually from a text prompt. Stable Diffusion's current training set consists of one billion images, an English subset of the much-used LAION-5b database (Beaumont, 2022). LAION is a German non-profit organisation that focuses on making large-scale datasets available to the public. The images are gathered by crawling the available images and their metatexts from the internet. As such, LAION has gathered images from virtual museums and national databases and from individual artists' websites and hobbyist art forums and platforms. However, not all the images are included, as the organisation says

Fig. 11.1   A Maltipoo by Caspar David Friedrich, stable diffusion

disturbing images are filtered out.[4] Images in the LAION 5b database are paired with texts found in the images' metadata and parsed together by a trained model (Alford, 2022). The whole operation is a vast auto-mated process of many trained models working together with terabytes of images and data. The end result of Stable Diffusion (and many other similar products, as most of them use the LAION 5b-dataset) is that it

---

[4] LAION-5b datasets have filtered out harmful content by its trained model, which the company says will filter out the most disturbing images (see https://laion.ai/blog/lai on-5b/, https://openreview.net/forum?id=M3Y74vmsMcY).

can easily mimic the Western art canon—it 'understands' different styles, artistic movements and individual artists. In some cases, the mimicking has already progressed too close to the artists' actual work, resulting both in court cases and artists losing their contract work (Chen, 2023; Dafoe, 2023; Sharp, 2022).

Looking at the picture of the Maltipoo-dog, one can easily depict traces of Caspar David Friedrich's famous painting, *Der Wanderer über dem Nebelmeer* from 1818. The Romantic era masterpiece depicts a man looking over a mountainous view, back towards the viewer, wearing, what to a modern observer looks like an evening dress. However, one of the issues with these models is that, as convincing as they are integrating information of and matching artists' work and styles, they do not really *know* any of it. There is no history, as these are mathematical models based on pixel probability and text-parsing. This means that the algorithms do not really look at the images, but rather analyse a filtered and often fragmented set of the images' or texts' binary data. The probability of getting a white dog depicted loosely in Friedrich's popular painting, thus does not reflect probabilities in the actual data of images and texts, nor has it anything to do with the probabilities in the world around us. Instead, it refers to the probabilities created by the model itself. In other words, the models create their own multi-dimensional worlds, with their own probabilities and blackboxes, unknown to us. However, one result of these processes is that the models tend to treat the prompt of "Caspar David Friedrich" as the lonely man in the mountain wearing a full evening dress, and for instance, prompts involving Vincent Van Gogh as the man with the swirly starry skies.

In his 1981 book, French philosopher Jean Baudrillard proclaimed that media has become so ubiquitous that it has transformed the perceived world. We no longer live in the real world but in a hyperreal world where the real is deserted, and all we have is simulacra, copies that depict things that either have no original or that no longer have an original.[5] Baudrillard's idea of the simulacra and hyperreal has been largely debated and critiqued by feminist thinkers accusing him, for instance, that the thought of the "real" fails to properly recognise the different realities

---

[5] Baudrillard's theory was also hinted at and present in the movie Matrix (1999), one of the most popular AI-themed dystopias. Furthermore, in 2002, Slavoj Žižek referenced both Baurdillard and Matrix in his book "Welcome to the Desert."

brought by gender, race or age (Ahmed, 2006; Guignion, 2021; Toffoletti, 2014). However, Baudrillard's theory of simulacra and the hyperreal can work here as a metaphor to comprehend the rather significant positional shift that happens with AI-generated images.

Looking at the white dogs in the example image, or any other AI-generated image, the idea of copies without an original resonates in some sense. There is an eery feeling that these images could be placed somewhere in art history's continuum, yet at the same time, do not belong there at all. Maybe a coincidence or not, the functioning of AI models is often depicted as latent spaces, as a giant map where (mathematically abstracted) images and texts of the datasets are positioned into the map specified by probability calculations[6] (Andrew, 2022; Dommarumma, 2022).

Maybe these models with their canonised Western art history related(?), inspired(?), calculated images become ubiquitous, and we create a new level of the hyperreal, a sort of hyper hyperreal. This new hyperreal is not something (just) in our minds or in culture but extends to the technological layers: Recent news have reported how Google's image search algorithm has started to get confused in the millions of AI-generated images flooding into Internet. Real happenings become re-imagined as AI images. For instance, recently the first Google search result for Tiananmen Square "Tank Man" was an AI-generated selfie (Maiberg, 2023). Google fixed the issue, but surely more will come.

Similar criticism directed towards Baudrillard could be addressed towards these AI models, as the algorithms manifest a world of universalism as well as gender, race, age and *other* biases (Apprich et al., 2018; Devlin, 2017; Dieterring, 2019; Gault, 2019; McQuillan, 2019). However, fixing, solving or dealing with these issues is entirely different from arguing or developing a human-made theory. For instance, after the AI model is trained, it is sort of locked in, and continues producing whatever it has produced. As we are dealing with narrow AI, there is no awareness in the AI, nor is there a way to communicate with it. Maybe it is better to think of these image models more as a hammer than intelligence. There is no use in talking to a hammer in order to change it. It is a tool, not a companion (or not a very talkative companion). The only way to change the AI model is by altering the training algorithms (and/or

---

[6] In AI models, the term probability does not mean the probability in the real world but the fabricated probability in that dataset and AI model.

datasets) and training again. Furthermore, even fixing the apparent biases in the datasets has proven to be more challenging than first thought, as noted by Kate Crawford (2021).

These AI models, and the images generated with them, entangle a problematic field that intersects, for instance, with individuals, culture, politics, sustainability and economy. A simple prompt by the user and a mimicked image of Maltipoo in Caspar David Friedrich's iconical landscape get mixed up by a complex redoing of the world, where the image is no longer an image. Moreover, as the datasets pair an image with a small set of words, these models overwrite centuries of philosophy that deal with the reality and meaning of language and the challenges of translating the image to text and vice versa (see, for example, works by Plato, Locke, Kierkegaard, Benjamin, Bergson Wittgenstein, Heidegger, Derrida and so on). Simply put, the image cannot be represented by a few words or vice versa. However, philosophical analysis of the text-image pairs is out of reach for this chapter.

LOCATION MATTERS

Stable Diffusion was developed by the Machine Vision & Learning research group (formerly CompVIs-research group) at Ludwig Maximilian University Munich. However, it is publicised under a London/Palo Alto-based company, Stability AI, that among Stable Diffusion, offers many other AI-based tools, headlining "AI by the people, for the people" (Stability AI, 2022, 2023). Furthermore, one of the lead researchers in Stable Diffusion is affiliated with Runway AI, a NY-based company that offers "Everything you need to make anything you want" (Runway, 2023). The comparable ethos of future promises can be found with Stable Diffusion's main competitors: OpenAI, a company that owns Dall-E2 and ChatGPT, and encourages to "Join us in shaping the future of technology"; and Midjourney, a self-funded research lab that invites us to join in "exploring new mediums of thought and expanding the imaginative powers of the human species". Moreover, kin to Stable Diffusion, both Midjourney and OpenAI have ties with Universities and research groups in Europe and the United States.

Furthermore, almost all of the people portrayed on these companies' websites seem to be men, which, while unfortunate, aligns with the latest tech industry reports stating that only 20% of the AI industry are women

(AI, 2022; Tech, n.d.). In their book, Basset et al. (2019) argue that "Silicon Valley is male, the vast majority of the leaders of the major platforms are male, and STEM and so forth are more male than ever" (p. 57). Basset and colleagues criticise that debates in digital technologies are dominated by young white men from the Global North, suggesting that instead of Anthropocene, maybe we should be worried about Capitalocene (the epoch of capitalist infinite growth [Moore, 2016]) or even Manthropocene (the male dominancy in defining epochs [Raworth, 2014]) (2019, p. 82). AI seems to follow a similar trajectory of male-dominated industry centered in the Global North that is firmly coupled with venture funding and big tech companies. Recently, Stability AI raised 101 million US dollars in venture capital (Wiggers, 2022), and OpenAI is negotiating 10 billion US dollars in funding from Microsoft (Matthews & Kahn, 2023) and is publicly stating that it is expecting billion dollars in revenue by 2024 (Dastin et al., 2022). Midjourney states that they are self-funded; however, it is run by David Holz, a co-founder of Leap Motion, one of Forbes' 30 under 30 and one of Fast Company's most creative people (Forbes, 2014).

The ethos these companies promote closely resembles what Richard Barbrook and Andy Cameron (1996) have named Californian ideology, "an amusing cocktail" of right-wing neo-liberal politics, the hippie movement of technological determinism. Moreover, the ethos can be linked to what Evgeny Morozov (2014) has dubbed as *Solutionism*, meaning optimist and overtly simplified solutions to difficult and complex problems. Furthermore, both Californian ideology and Solutionism point out that rising problems and unwanted processes are often offshored to third-world countries or managed in countries that are most beneficial for the companies.[7] The promising future, thus, is a future for the selected few.

The "male silicon valley" ideology might be difficult to sense from an image of three Maltipoo dogs. However, the weird, almost uncanny resemblance to Caspar David Friedrich's *Der Wanderer über dem Nebelmeer might* be at the centre of it all. Janelle Shane (2023), who has for years followed the weird behaviours of AI in her blog, highlights that even though many of the examples she uses are funny, using and trusting

---

[7] Recently, it was reported that the OpenAI, the developer of the currently popular ChatGPT, had outsourced the data review process to underpaid workers in Kenya (see https://www.vice.com/en/article/wxn3kw/openai-used-kenyan-workers-making-dollar2-an-hour-to-filter-traumatic-content-from-chatgpt).

AI models may have drastic consequences in the real world: Automated factories or self-driving cars cannot afford a single mistake (Kurenkov, 2021). Hito Steyerl, a German artist and researcher, has dubbed our allowing and trusting nature towards AI as stupid AI, stupid because AI is not intelligent, and we should not be this stupid (Crawford & Steyerl, 2017).

Even though AI-generated images are not driving cars or running factories, they still take part in what could be called performing a particular world. The data used to train the AI, the way it is displayed and promoted to the UI and example images, AI-generated images perform a specific set of values and aesthetics. These values and aesthetics are, even in the case of AI, still in some sense derived by the people that create them (including the subculture, culture, society, economy, etc., the people belong to). While the number of mistakes (three dogs instead of one, weird proportions in the dogs) seems to diminish with each new version of an AI model, the weird and uncanny is with us, shaping how we think about images and augmenting art history, iteration after iteration. For Marco Dommarumma, a German artist and researcher, the uncanny images are not harmless. Instead, he sees them as "soft propaganda" for the Global North. Dommarumma (2022) argues that these images are, in fact, paving the way for probability models to sell the ideology of prediction and control. Coincidentally, control and prediction are maybe not the main points but rather occurring themes in Richard Barbrooks and Andy Cameron's (1996) Californian ideology. Uncanny, hyperreal images, like the Maltipoos in the mountains, in some sense manifest the current late capitalist technologically-driven worldview.

Matter Matters

The initial training of Stable Diffusion required 256 units of Nvidia A100-GPUs, speciality-built computers for processing AI algorithms (Julien, 2023). Each unit currently costs around 15,000 US dollars. Moreover, the training took over 150,000 hours of computer time, rented from tech giant Amazon's cloud, costing around 600,000 US dollars. Thus, even though Stable Diffusion is an open source and available to all software application, creating models with Stable Diffusion is problematic as the hardware, and capital requirements are so high.

In her book *Atlas of AI* Crawford (2021) writes, "[t]he mining that makes AI is both literal and metaphorical" (p. 31). She means that similar to the algorithms that mine data, often in questionable circumstances, AI requires physical mines too, which too often operate in indisputably terrible circumstances. As such, the AI image generators are not only entangled and act within culture, politics and economy but also in the exploitation of the planet's material and energy resources. On top of that, it often is entangled with corrupted corporations, states, war, criminality and unfair treatment of workers.

According to Crawford (2021), a massive assemblage of exploitation of human labour, natural resources and concentrations of corporate and geopolitical power is needed to provide the user with the simple interface of AI (p. 32). Moreover, the need for resources is growing faster all the time, while at the same time, the lifecycle of AI products is only shortening, and the mounting of e-waste creates even more enormous junk piles simply disposed of in third-world countries. Crawford notes that it is vital to comprehend that AI is all this, not only fancy websites and uncanny images.

Whereas, the costs of composing a short prompt with a smartphone app might not be much, it nevertheless participates and necessitates the use of the massive exploitative assemblage of AI. It is challenging if not impossible to comprehend the total cost of AI while playing with AI prompts and generators while, for example, waiting for a bus or standing in a supermarket queue, as the assemblage of AI is so fragmented, distributed and hidden.

For many twentieth-century phenomenologists, like Martin Heidegger and later Maurice Merleau-Ponty, *doing* something was the essential way of existing in the world (Heidegger & Hermann, 1967; Merleau-Ponty, 2012). We create, strengthen and construct meaning for our life and world through doing. Building on their phenomenology, Finnish craft researcher Seija Kojonkoski-Rännäli (1996) divides *doing* into: basic intention; the direct contact we have with the material and physical world; and instrumental intention, where we build something with the help of machines. For Kojonkoski-Rännäli, instrumental intention breaks our contact with the world, separating us from the world around (and within) us. Whereas, basic intention strengthens our belonging to the world and thus, increases our ethical and aesthetic attachment to the world around us. Moreover, *doing* is not only a creation of an artefact or world but a fundamental way of living and finding meaning.

In my earlier work, I have argued that by connecting to the digital assemblage through coding (the basic building block of software), we might be able to create basic intention, a sort of comprehension or belonging to the digital around us (Dufva, 2017). Later, together with researcher Mikko Dufva (2019), I suggested that creative digital making affords us a certain sense of the digital assemblage, that even though one does not understand the whole assemblage[8] or all the technical intricacies of digital technology, one can create a feeling, or a sense of it. We referred to this as *digi-grasping*, loaning from Merleau-Ponty's concept of grasping: comprehending something before rationally knowing it.

However, with the introduction of current AI models and easy-to-use prompt-style interfaces, such grasping becomes far more challenging. It might be that if AI-image generation becomes a commonplace method for generating images, we are at risk of losing a certain kind of comprehension and belonging to the world. Image as a direct representation of something that exists, as evidence of an actual phenomenon, or symbol signifying what something is, of course are naïve ideas, yet AI models participate in accelerating a loss in meaning within the images it generates. Images, styles and situations in the images they depict may become even more fragmented synthetic manifestations that are produced and consumed in seconds. Perhaps in the search of saving time in image creation, we lose the thought and embodied processes of *making* something, as they require the time we are trying to save. Moreover, with text-to-image prompts, we might simplify our imagination to a set of prompts and surrender it to an algorithmic valuation of fragmented bits and optimised probability fractals of collective images and texts existing in the Internet.

Media theorist Jussi Parikka (2015) suggests that instead of thinking of media as a part of the human senses, or flesh in Merleau-Ponty's terms, we should consider them as extensions of the earth. As such, AI processes partake in transforming earth's resources into infrastructures and devices while consuming gas and oil reserves into the energy they need. Crawford (2021) sums,

> Artificial intelligence, then, is an idea, an infrastructure, an industry, a form of exercising power, and a way of seeing; it's also a manifestation of highly

---

[8] It should be noted that artists engaging with AI in their terms, own data and modified algorithms probably still pertain to a kind of sense of the assemblage. For instance, see Slotte Dufva (2023) or Ahmed, S. (2006). Queer Phenomenology: Orientations, Objects, Others. Duke University Press.

organized capital backed by vast systems of extraction and logistics, with supply chains that wrap round the entire planet. All these things are part of what artificial intelligence is. (pp. 18–19)

Subsequently, a challenging question relates to how to change these processes so that they would be much less harmful to the earth and benefit all instead of a selected few in the Global North. Another dimension to creating with AI and other complex distributed digital processes is how and what kind of connection we create through making with them.

CONCLUSION

Considering these text-to-image AI models from the positions of the 'real', location and matter reveals a disturbing landscape of late capitalism and exploitation. For instance, Stability AI, the "AI by the people, for the people"-company is currently handling a plethora of court cases for copyright infringements, and at the same time is projected to gain billion-dollar profits next year. This is a troubling sign that AI will not be by the people, or even for the people. Instead, Stability AI seems to offer more of the same (late capitalist exploitation) as anything else. Barbrook and Cameron (1996) hold that although the Californian ideology seems to offer radical rhetoric, it is essentially pessimistic and unwilling to create real social change. Instead, this ideology offers a rather gloomy and repressive vision of the future. Decades after Barbrook and Cameron's publication, many researchers, including Evgeny Morozov (2014), have made the same observation.

Basset et al. (2019) state that digital feminism is impossible without an awareness of the planet's ecological limits. Moreover, they question: *"how to refuse the apparent escapes offered by the technological; open sky, informational plentitude as light and air, calculations costing the cloud that consistently underplays its material load in favour of the algorithmic benefit"* (p. 124). Comprehending the assemblage of AI thus becomes a crucial skill to drive the discussions around AI into more grounded and critical levels. Furthermore, if grasping the assemblages around AI is possible, it is in these discussions that we need it; in being able to feel and sense the dangers and exploitations within the AI processes.

Crawford (2021) writes that we should not consider AI models Artificial or Intelligent. For Crawford, there is nothing artificial in AI; instead, the exploitation of people and the earth is very real and has damaged the planet for decades. Neither does Crawford see any intelligence in AI; instead, the algorithms are man-made and inherently and intentionally ideological and political. Thus, prompt-generated images could be seen more as a representation of the cruel exploitation of both earth and the people living in it than mostly harmless renditions of Western art history's masterpieces.

Without the knowledge of how the AI models are generated and distributed, prompting an image might seem harmless. However, the making process challenges in other ways. By making image generation fast and effortless, one loses the process; one loses embodying the space–time of the activity of making. Instant birthing of images might denote the meaning of the making. Writing, drawing and painting are processes that involve and require time. By side-stepping the process altogether, the danger might be that we get nothing in return. It is more of the same, and more importantly, instead of a fresh way to see the world or be in the world, making may become meaningless. Philosopher Alexander Galloway (2023) wrote in his recent blog post that, in his view, the real danger of AI is that it might become so normal that it just drowns out and muddles everything. However, to end on an optimistic note, it might also be that the AI images become the new stock photos or clip art, a set of awkward images that only faceless corporations use, thus creating a new aesthetic appreciation for hand-made images. By this, I do not mean some romantic wish to go back into a simpler time (if ever there was one), but rather a new way of seeing and making that may involve digital algorithms, yet in a painstakingly time-consuming way.

REFERENCES

Ajunwa, I. (2020). The "black box" at work. *Big Data & Society, 7*(2), 2053951720966181. https://doi.org/10.1177/2053951720938093

Andrew. (2022). *How does stable diffusion work?—Stable diffusion art.* https://stable-diffusion-art.com/how-stable-diffusion-work/

Alford, A. (2022). *LAION releases five billion image-text pair dataset LAION-5B.* https://www.infoq.com/news/2022/05/laion-5b-image-text-dataset/

Apprich, C., Kyong Chun, Hui, W., Cramer, F., & Steyerl, H. (2018). *Pattern discrimination.* University of Minnesota Press. https://doi.org/10.14619/1457

Baio, A. (2022). *Exploring 12 million of the 2.3 billion images used to train stable diffusion's image generator—waxy.org.* https://waxy.org/2022/08/exploring-12-million-of-the-images-used-to-train-stable-diffusions-image-generator/

Barbrook, R., & Cameron, A. (1996). The Californian ideology. *Science as Culture, 6*(1), 44–72. https://doi.org/10.1080/09505439609526455

Bassett, C., Kember, S., & O'Riordan, K. (2019). *Furious: Technological feminism and digital futures*. Pluto Press.

Baudrillard, J. (1994). *Simulacra and simulation* (S. F. Glaser, Trans.). University of Michigan Press.

BBC. (2017). Google AI defeats human Go champion. *BBC News*. https://www.bbc.com/news/technology-40042581

Beaumont, R. (2022). *LAION-5B: A new era of open large-scale multi-modal datasets LAION*. https://laion.ai/blog/laion-5b/

Bradshaw, T. (2022). *Is becoming a 'prompt engineer' the way to save your job from AI?* https://www.ft.com/content/0deda1e7-4fbf-46bc-8eee-c2049d783259

Bridle, J. (2022). *Ways of being: Animals, plants, machines: The search for a planetary intelligence*. Penguin UK.

Cave, S., Coughlan, K., & Dihal, K. (2019). "Scary robots". Examining public responses to AI. In *Proceedings of the 2019 AAAI/ACM Conference on AI, Ethics, and Society* (pp. 331–337). ACM. https://doi.org/10.1145/3306618.3314232

Cave, S., & Dihal, K. (2019). Hopes and fears for intelligent machines in fiction and reality. *Nature Machine Intelligence, 1*(2), 74–78. https://doi.org/10.1038/s42256-019-0020-9

Chen, M. (2023). *Artists and illustrators are suing three A.I. art generators for scraping and 'collaging' their work without consent*. https://news.artnet.com/art-world/class-action-lawsuit-ai-generators-deviantart-midjourney-stable-diffusion-2246770

Christie's. (2018). *The first piece of AI-generated art to come to auction Christie's*. https://www.christies.com/features/A-collaboration-between-two-artists-one-human-one-a-machine-9332-1.aspx

Chuan, C.-H., Wan-Hsiu, S. T., & Cho, S. Y. (2019). Framing artificial intelligence in American newspapers. In *Proceedings of the 2019 AAAI/ACM Conference on AI, Ethics, and Society* (pp. 339–344). ACM. https://doi.org/10.1145/3306618.3314285

Clarke, A. C. (1962/2013). *Profiles of the future*. Hachette UK.

Crawford, K. (2021). *Atlas of AI: Power, politics, and the planetary costs of artificial intelligence*. Yale University Press.

Crawford, K., & Steyerl, H. (2017). *Data streams*. https://thenewinquiry.com/data-streams/

Dafoe, T. (2023). *Getty Images is suing the company behind Stable Diffusion, saying the A.I. generator illegally scraped its content*. https://news.artnet.com/art-world/getty-images-suing-stability-ai-stable-diffusion-illegally-scraped-images-copyright-infringement-2243631

Dastin, J., Hu, K., & Paresh, D. (2022). *Exclusive: ChatGPT owner OpenAI projects $1 billion in revenue by 2024 Reuters.* https://www.reuters.com/business/chatgpt-owner-openai-projects-1-billion-revenue-by-2024-sources-2022-12-15/

Devlin, H. (2017). *AI programs exhibit racial and gender biases, research reveals.* http://www.theguardian.com/technology/2017/apr/13/ai-programs-exhibit-racist-and-sexist-biases-research-reveals

Dieterring, A. (2019). *Facial recognition, physiognomy, and racism.* https://medium.com/the-sundial-acmrs/facial-recognition-physiognomy-and-racism-ffc3d232a352

Dommarumma, M. (2022). *AI art is soft propaganda for the Global North.* https://hyperallergic.com/772848/ai-art-is-soft-propaganda-for-the-global-north/

Dufva, M., & Slotte Dufva, T. (2020). The itching back of a cyborg: Grasping AI systems. *Research in Arts and Education, 1,* 18–36. https://doi.org/10.54916/rae.119300

Dufva, T. (2017). Maker movement: Creating knowledge through basic intention. *Techne Series—Research in Sloyd Education and Craft Science A, 2*(24), 129–141.

Dyer, R. (1997). *White: essays on race and culture* (1st ed.). Routledge. https://doi.org/10.4324/9781315003603

Edwards, B. (2022). *Artist finds private medical record photos in popular AI training data set Ars Technica.* https://arstechnica.com/information-technology/2022/09/artist-finds-private-medical-record-photos-in-popular-ai-training-data-set/

Eliacik, E. (2023). *What is AI prompt engineering: Examples, and more.* https://dataconomy.com/2023/01/what-is-ai-prompt-engineering-examples-how/

Fielding, H. A. (2017). A feminist phenomenology manifesto. In H. A. Fielding & D. E. Olkowski (Eds.), *Feminist phenomenology futures* (pp. vii–xxii). Indiana University Press.

Forbes. (2014). *David Holz.* https://www.forbes.com/profile/david-holz/

Fjelland, R. (2020). Why general artificial intelligence will not be realized. *Humanities and Social Sciences Communications, 7*(1). https://doi.org/10.1057/s41599-020-0494-4

Galloway, A. (2023). *Normal science.* http://cultureandcommunication.org/galloway/normal-science

Gault, M. (2019). *Facial recognition software regularly misgenders trans people.* https://www.vice.com/en_us/article/7xnwed/facial-recognition-software-regularly-misgenders-trans-people

Guignion, D. (2021). Jean Baudrillard and feminism: Sara Ahmed and the necessity to "Forget Baudrillard". *The Journal of Media Art Study and Theory, 2*(1). https://www.mast-journal.org

Hao, K. (2019). *Training a single AI model can emit as much carbon as five cars in their lifetimes.* https://www.technologyreview.com/s/613630/training-a-single-ai-model-can-emit-as-much-carbon-as-five-cars-in-their-lifetimes/

Haraway, D. (2016). *Staying with the trouble: Making kin in the Chthulucene.* Duke University Press.

Hayles, N. K. (2001). *How we became posthuman: Virtual bodies in cybernetics, literature, and infomatics.* University of Chicago Press.

Hayles, N. K. (2017). *Unthought.* University of Chicago Press.

Heidegger, M., & Hermann, F. -W. V. (Eds.). (1967). *Vortrage und aufsatze (7).* Vittoio Klostermann.

Hinzman, L. (2019). *Zilic: Rare disease detection with machine learning.* https://towardsdatascience.com/zilic-detect-any-disease-with-machine-lea rning-fdae88664148

Johnson, D. G., & Verdicchio, M. (2017). Reframing AI discourse. *Minds and Machines, 27*(4), 575–590. https://doi.org/10.1007/s11023-017-9417-6

Julien. (2023). *Archives des stable diffusion.* https://arkanecloud.com/category/stable-diffusion

Kaplan, A., & Haenlein, M. (2019). Siri, Siri, in my hand: Who's the fairest in the land? On the interpretations, illustrations, and implications of artificial intelligence. *Business Horizons, 62*(1), 15–25. https://doi.org/10.1016/j.bus hor.2018.08.004

Knight, W. (2017). *Biased algorithms are everywhere, and no one seems to care.* https://www.technologyreview.com/s/608248/biased-algorithms-are-everywhere-and-no-one-seems-to-care/

Kojonkoski-Rännäli, S. (1996). *Ajatus käsissämme: käsityön käsitteen merkitys-sisällön analyysi* [The thought in our hands: Meaning content analysis of the concept of handicraft] (Vol. 109). University of Turku. https://doi.org/10.1525/si.1991.14.2.165/abstract

Kurenkov, A. (2021). Janelle Shane on the weirdness of AI. *Skynet Today.* https://www.skynettoday.com/podcast/ai-weirdness

Lynch, S. (2017). *Andrew Ng: Why AI is the new electricity.* https://www.gsb.stanford.edu/insights/andrew-ng-why-ai-new-electricity

Manovich, L. (2018). *AI aesthetics.* Strelka Press.

Manovich, L. (2019). *Defining AI arts: Three proposals. AI and dialog of cultures" exhibition catalog.* Hermitage Museum.

Marsland, S. (2014). *Machine learning: An algorithmic perspective.* Chapman and Hall/CRC.

Maiberg, E. (2023). *First Google search result for Tiananmen Square "Tank Man" is AI generated selfie.* https://www.404media.co/first-google-search-result-for-tiananmen-square-tank-man-is-ai-generated-selfie/

Matthews, J., & Kahn, J. (2023). I, *nside the structure of OpenAI's looming new investment from microsoft and VCs Fortune.* https://fortune.com/2023/01/11/structure-openai-investment-microsoft/

McDermott, D. (1976). Artificial intelligence meets natural stupidity. *ACM Sigart Bulletin, 57,* 4–9.

McQuillan, D. (2019). *Towards an anti-fascist AI.* https://www.opendemocracy.net/en/digitaliberties/towards-anti-fascist-ai/?fbclid=IwAR0hbe2rJz3s29SZl3Grn3wOcYyspK-tFWSkbCq7U8nP0w9SuVoVeVYr9eY

Merleau-Ponty, M. (2012). *Phenomenology of perception.* Routledge.

Moore, J. W. (2016). Anthropocene or capitalocene? Nature, history, and the crisis of capitalism. *Sociology Faculty Scholarship, 1.* https://orb.binghamton.edu/sociology_fac/1

Morozov, E. (2014). *To save everything, click here.* PublicAffairs.

Neimanis, A. (2017). *Neimanis bodies of water posthuman feminist phenomenology.* Bloomsbury Publishing Plc.

Ouchchy, L., Coin, A., & Dubljević, V. (2020). AI in the headlines: The portrayal of the ethical issues of artificial intelligence in the media. *AI & Society, 35*(4), 927–936. https://doi.org/10.1007/s00146-020-00965-5

OpenAI (2023). *Planning for AGI and beyond.* https://openai.com/blog/planning-for-agi-and-beyond

Parikka, J. (2015). *A geology of media (46).* University of Minnesota Press.

Plato. (2007). *The Republic.* (D. Lee, Trans., 2nd ed.). Penguin.

Raworth, K. (2014). *Must the anthropocene be a manthropocene?* https://www.theguardian.com/commentisfree/2014/oct/20/anthropocene-working-group-science-gender-bias .

Roose, K. (2022). AI-generated art won a prize. Artists aren't happy. *The New York Times.* https://www.nytimes.com/2022/09/02/technology/ai-artificial-intelligence-artists.html

Runway. (2023). *Runway—Everything you need to make anything you want.* https://runwayml.com/

Shane, J. (2023). *AI Weirdness: The strange side of machine learning.* https://www.aiweirdness.com

Sharp, S. R. (2022). *He's bigger than Picasso on AI platforms, and he hates it.* https://hyperallergic.com/766241/hes-bigger-than-picasso-on-ai-platforms-and-he-hates-it/

Slotte Dufva, T. (2021). Creative coding as compost(ing). In K. Tavin, G. Kolb, & J. Tervo (Eds.), *Post-digital, postiInternet art and education.* Palgrave Studies in Educational Futures. Palgrave Macmillan. https://doi.org/10.1007/978-3-030-73770-2_16

Slotte Dufva, T. (2023). Entanglements in AI art. In A. D. Knochel & O. Sahara (Eds.), *Global media arts education* (pp. 181–196). Springer International Publishing. https://doi.org/10.1007/978-3-031-05476-1_11

Slotte Dufva, T., & Mertala, P. (2021). Sähköä ja alkemiaa: Tekoälydiskurssit Yleisradion verkkoartikkeleissa. *Media & viestintä, 44*(1), 95–115. https://journal.fi/mediaviestinta/article/download/107302/62752

Stability AI. (2022). *Stable diffusion launch announcement—Stability AI.* https://stability.ai/blog/stable-diffusion-announcement

Stability AI. (2023). *Stability AI.* https://stability.ai/

Toffoletti, K. (2014). Baudrillard, postfeminism, and the image makeover. *Cultural Politics, 10*(1), 105–119. https://doi.org/10.1215/17432197-2397263

Weizenbaum, J. (1966). ELIZA—A computer program for the study of natural language communication between man and machine. *Communications of the ACM, 9*(1), 36–45. https://doi.org/10.1145/365153.365168

Wiggers, K. (2022). *Stability AI, the startup behind stable diffusion, raises $101M.* TechCrunch. https://techcrunch.com/2022/10/17/stability-ai-the-startup-behind-stable-diffusion-raises-101m/

Williamson, B., & Eynon, R. (2020). Historical threads, missing links, and future directions in AI in education. *Learning, Media and Technology, 45*(3), 223–235. https://doi.org/10.1080/17439884.2020.1798995

Woodie, A. (2023). *Prompt engineer: The next hot job in AI.* https://www.datanami.com/2023/02/14/prompt-engineer-the-next-hot-job-in-ai/

Xiang, C. (2023). *ChatGPT can be broken by entering these strange words, and nobody is sure why.* https://www.vice.com/en/article/epzyva/ai-chatgpt-tokens-words-break-reddit

Zylinska, J. (2020). *AI art.* Open Humanities Press.

CHAPTER 12

Scribbles, Spirographs, and AI, Oh My!: Postdevelopmental Sociomaterial Practices of Graphicality

Aaron Knochel

Introduction

I have been thinking about drawing lately. It has been a lifelong preoccupation. I picked up crayons and scribbled on anything like most kids lucky enough to have access to crayons. I got a sketchbook and oil pastels in 5th grade and started to call myself an artist. I did not like the sticky oil in my fingernails at first, but moving it around the page, blending and mixing after it smudged from the end of the stick, opened a lot of possibilities for mark making. I had a similar experience when I used my first clone stamp tool in a graphic editing software environment. The finesse of the tool settings and the awkwardness of the mouse combined to create a new tactility in mark making through a screen, which again expanded and frustrated my sense of possibilities. Here I am again, looking at the avalanche of graphics spilling out of generative artificial intelligence (AI)

A. Knochel (✉)
Penn State University, University Park, PA, USA
e-mail: adk176@psu.edu

R. Rousi et al. (eds.), *Humane Autonomous Technology*,
https://doi.org/10.1007/978-3-031-66528-8_12

275

image platforms like Midjourney or Stable Diffusion. Enter a prompt and a magical world of instant graphicality spills out.

I have come to understand these separate practices as related through the concept of *assemblage* or what actor-network theorists like Bruno Latour (2005) might call "following the mediating relationality of actants." To understand what the significance of this new world of generative AI graphics may be, I will use assemblage to investigate a social ontology (DeLanda, 2006) of graphicality to gain a richer understanding of creative practice in a way that acknowledges the more-than-human actors at play. My ontological perspective situates making as a context of sociomaterial engagements using assemblage to articulate the entangled relationality of graphicality in an ongoing art and pedagogical performance I call Drawing Together. As a series of workshops and performances, iterations of drawing machines are created in collaborative and intergenerational interactions that result in large-scale drawing machine installations. My ontological analysis of the Drawing Together workshops and installations investigates the "human-nonhuman assemblage as a locus of agency" (Bennet, 2010, p. 37) to trouble the autonomy of child mark makers through a postdevelopmental onto-epistemology. Drawing from scholarship in art education and child studies, I extrapolate from these events three matters of concern with generative AI practice including: issues of access; prompt engineering; and the carbon footprint of AI computation.

Using assemblage as a conceptual framework inherently refutes the autonomy of technologies as they are always bound within a relationality to their human counterparts, and vice versa. However, the question of their humane effects ultimately relies on our conceptions of them that activate their further development. In other words, our performance with technology feeds conceptions of what worlding they create and engenders development pathways. It is this worlding that I am interested in excavating in this chapter. As geographers Ben Anderson and Paul Harrison (2010) state, "the term 'world' does not refer to an extant thing but rather the context or background against which particular things show up and take on significance" (p. 8). In this chapter, I will pursue an expanded sense of graphicality, as significant to arts learners through a discussion of postdevelopmental theories of childhood art. I then relate the discussion to my own on-going project Drawing Together to suggest a particular background by which the arrival of generative AI image platforms takes on a certain significance. My analysis will not be comprehensive regarding the significance of generative AI, but will suggest sociomaterial costs of AI graphicality that question the role of our complicity as collaborators in more-than-human creative expression.

Drawing as Sociomaterial Engagement and Postdevelopmental Childhood Studies

I recently attended a figure drawing session at a local art college. The sessions are for a nominal fee and support a nude model to pose variously for a few hours. The experience allowed me to reflect on the many figure drawing sessions that I have attended over the years. In the sessions, I became more fully aware of my body in mark making. I stood at the easel, sweeping my arm broadly around the large tablet of drawing paper or newsprint, holding the charcoal both as a point and a broadside to make sweeping gestural marks attenuated with sharp angular articulations of points and undulating lines. It was not so much that I learned to use my body at this point, watching my toddler moving with scraps of paper, gesturing, and storytelling her mark making in real-time narration provides me the lived insight that we already know about how to use our bodies in mark making. Rather, through figure drawing sessions, I have learned how to attend my attention to my body in particular movements and emphasis of action, in the event of mark making that an assemblage of sociomaterial relationality entails. A gestural mark attending to the curvature of the spine of the model that requires a certain tenseness in my elbow, a light grip on the charcoal, and fluid flexibility in my shoulder. A blocking pattern noting the chiaroscuro of the human form in light and shadow that feels like an extension of my torso and not my wrist, felt through the base of the easel as opposed to on the surface of the paper. My eyes flicking back and forth attending to the sight of the model arrangement, and to my marks on the page. A slow drawing, a fast drawing, a sharp implement, a dull implement, a drawing composed within a rectangle of paper on the floor, on the easel, in my lap.

There is a publicness to drawing in a figure drawing class. A sociality of the drawing experience that articulates movement, both practiced and performed. Part of this is the temporal arrangement of the session itself. The model poses, usually in shorter durations that build into longer poses, their performance managed by the facilitator or instructor in the room. Whoever is coordinating this orchestration differs from session to session: school sessions are run by the teacher and community sessions are run by the organizers, each with their own purpose. This orchestration results in a kind of choreography, movement and time, for those involved: shorter poses dictate a more frantic dance for mark makers and longer poses introduce more measured consideration. Even where you are in the room is attenuated by this choreography of the model posing: shorter, quicker poses may require more materials at hand as drawings get developed and discarded and longer poses allow for repose, sitting, a pacing back and forth in measured consideration of the choices of marks to be made. In this choreography, there is a public that emerges. A kind of impromptu mark making commons, where the irrational movements are a language of community membership. You perform drawing for both the mark and the mark maker community as you would a basketball game or iceskating, both playing and performing.

This brings me back to my toddler, perhaps the reason why drawing has been so much on my mind lately. Her mark making is an event in social practice where marks are a remnant of embodied knowing and structures to an emergent story-becoming. Story-becoming is a narrative emergence in the Deleuzian sense, where the story is known as unknown, partial in an eventual practice of actualization. A virtual structure in multimodal actions whereby she is co-figured within the sociomaterial commons of meaning making.

I reflect on these acts of drawing to highlight the more-than-drawing event that is mark making that compels a consideration for the sociomaterial engagement as an active assemblage of more-than-human agencies in graphicality. Mark making in this conceptualization considers the many agencies at play within the assemblage: the mark-maker, the implement, time, space, and more. However, the event of drawing is not an unconsidered practice. Rather, the study of children's drawing has been a scholarly topic for a long time. This is most notably since Viktor Lowenfeld (1947) attempted to "show how the child's general growth is tied up with his creative development and vice versa" (p. vi). Lowenfeld's important contribution extended the grounding of the field of art education within developmental psychology, while also doing a great deal to establish broader empirical studies of children's creativity and engagement in the arts in the mid-twentieth century. Lowenfeld connected creativity and growth through a schema of developmental stages of drawing theorizing that children progress through a series of developmental stages in their artistic expression. These stages are: Scribbling Stage (2–4 years old); Pre-Schematic Stage (4–7 years old); Schematic Stage (7–9 years old); Gang

Stage (9–11 years old); and Realistic Stage (11–13 years old). According to Lowenfeld, each stage represents a distinct cognitive and emotional development in the child perceived through their drawing as a form of creative expression. As Lowenfeld states, "[t]he answer to the question, 'what makes the child express one and the same thing differently at different age levels?' will be of essential importance for the understanding of the child's creative work" (p. 10). The drawing then becomes an iterative mark of "active knowledge" and exists as a record of the mental and emotional importance in that moment of expression. Here, iteration is a developmental timeline whereby drawing enables the output of hieroglyphs of the cognitive states of the child that are in need of interpretation.

Lowenfeld's theory was presented as a Rosetta stone for such interpretation and remains influential today. However, discussions of children's drawing evolved to emphasize the social and cultural contexts in which drawing occurs. Art education scholars such as Brent and Marjorie Wilson (1981) critiqued the "use and uselessness of developmental stages" for the many gaps and elements of misinformation that were laid bare in the practice of using the schema. Wilsons' critique was not solely attributed to Lowenfeld, but rather the scholarly inclination to slice up the "graphic development pie" (p. 4) into stages that go back as far as Kerschensteiner (1905) and extends to contemporaries such as Howard Gardner's (1980) U-shaped developmental curve. To the Wilsons, the trouble with developmental stages ascribed to drawing did not adequately account for cultural differences, such as non-Western contexts. Additionally, these schemas were often retrofitting norms in the context of developmental stages that Lowenfeld had theorized in the 1930s and 40s, which ill-fit children's graphicality in the 1970s and beyond. The use of the stages presented hazardous generalizations of children's drawing that do not account for aesthetic differences, gender, or narrative aspects of children's acts of drawing. Moreover, most dangerously, as a tool the stages were inadequate to make clear and definitive assessments of cognitive or emotional development because drawings may fit within multiple stages. These critiques suggest the potential guidance of developmental stages is more liable to misinform than provide insights regarding a child's development.

Contemporary discussions have expanded on these critiques by emphasizing the social and cultural contexts in which children create and interpret their drawings. What emerges from these postdevelopmental critiques is a reinvestment in understanding the assemblage of children, children drawing, and children's drawings. Art education researcher Phillip Pearson (2001) draws attention to the lack of articulation in then-existing theories of drawing in that they did not differentiate between children's drawing as a "residue" of an act, and the act itself of children drawing that should be framed as a "social practice" relatable to other forms of social practice. For Pearson, children's graphic productivity is not innate or compelled in a teleological process, rather these are ascribed post-Facto by the logic of development itself. Pearson states:

> A functional rather than a pathway view of drawing development is closer to thinking about a form of social practice because it does not need drawing activity to lead children to some goal. But drawing is still believed to exist in systems. Children might use drawing differently but their involvement in it is defined by the uses that can be specified for their representations. These uses indicate the systematic nature of graphic practice that children develop within. They develop because of that systematic nature and drawing develops in individual or private forms of discourse. So children are alone in making drawing discourses that are versions of unknowable larger pictorial systems. (p. 356)

Drawing as social practice expands the theorization of children drawing and not drawing as equal acts for consideration. As a social practice, attention is paid to the sociomateriality of the act of drawing in addition to the remainder residues of children's drawings that have dominated theorization in developmental stages.

Pearson is part of a broader movement in art education and childhood studies that aims to expand creative expression as a postdevelopmental social practice over the last two decades or more. Perspectives on the visual culture of children and its influence on their graphicality have extended conceptions of youth and remix culture (Duncum, 2013), considerations of influence from media culture (Wilson, 2003), and paid attention to the roles of play and aesthetics in children's creative expression (Schulte & Thompson, 2018). More and more of these investigations have engaged with children's active making of their culture as they participate in digitally networked worlds (Duncum, 2020; Peppler, 2010; Traffí-Prats, 2021). Importantly, these moves in childhood studies and art highlight the ways in which prevailing conceptions of childhood impact and condition adult interpretations of children's engagements, thereby reinscribing the overtones of development onto the creative expression of children (Thompson, 2017). Art education researcher Marissa McClure (2011) re-examines the myth of children's inherent creativity that asserts a reductionist lens to the creative practice of children as either totally free expression or teleological ascendence to visual realism, and instead displaces the totemic illusions of childhood by theorizing "how adults' desires perpetuate the myth of inherent creativity may assist educators in working to legitimize early childhood art classrooms as sites of legitimate knowledge production" (p. 139). These moves to reconceptualize the social practice of childhood creative expression reflect a deeper commitment to the autonomy of children as subjects while simultaneously calling into question the interpretations of adults that are caught in cycles of reflective desire.

DRAWING TOGETHER: PERFORMING TECHNO-MECHANICAL GRAPHICALITY

Drawing together is a design-based pedagogical performance where I am involved in research creation to explore sociomaterial relationships of graphicality in transitory states of knowledge formation across, through, and traversing disciplines. Situated as research creation, Drawing Together is an experimental methodology, transdisciplinary in nature, and employing practices that cannot be predicted or determined in advance (Springgay & Truman, 2018; Truman, 2021). It is design-based in the ways that it is iterative and inductive leading to incremental stage changes, pedagogical in the emphasis on learning constellations that are assembled and dissolved throughout the many instances of the project work, and performative as an attention to the assemblage of human and nonhumans that come together in and through the events and machines. Drawing Together is a critique of drawing, as a codified totem to developing the artist, and instead a gesture of practice committed to the immanent vitality of graphicality. Mark making is conceptualized as a social residue, as a form of play, and as a practice of drawing outside developmental epistemologies. Drawing Together allows me to experience technological being extending the body, engaging chance, and encountering technical failures and disruptions. A form of research creation that attempts a delicate dance of knowing and being whereby the substance of knowledge is after the experience of creation.

In practice, Drawing Together is a series of workshop events for collaborative design and fabrication activities that build mark making apparatuses, or put more simply, myself and participants make drawing machines together and then use them. Drawing machines are collectively realized through group work and cooperative participation using various methods including laser cut wood, found objects, simple circuitry, and actuators. People become involved in various ways in the iterative cycles of the machine's life, sometimes from the moment of invention, and sometimes as an end user at an event.

The Drawing Together project began in conjunction with a twelve-week residency at the Borland Project Space at my home institution of The Pennsylvania State University in fall 2016. The focus of my residency and the work of Drawing Together is both a careful orchestration of people and investigation of mark-making machines. I developed several iterations of drawing machines throughout the twelve-week residency including two and three pendulum harmonographs, a pendulum apparatus, and a series of spirographs. At the same time, I developed activities that created interactions between several groups: undergraduate students majoring in Art Education; a fifth-grade class from a local elementary school; and various community members who attended open public events. The project also involved coordination with several other contributors from the director of the Borland Project Space to the art teacher and parent volunteers from the elementary school (Fig. 12.1).

It is significant, for me, that Pearson (2001) highlights techno-mechanical drawing toys, such as the spirograph, as deviant in the drive to theorize children's drawings. Pearson invokes the spirograph in reference to the potential functions of drawing, in this case boredom, which one could add doodling and any number of graphic practices in the endeavor to pass time. These types of techno-mechanized acts of drawing, implied here as inauthentic or outside of expression, possess symbolic importance for de-escalating the significance of children's drawings in the pursuit of development, and highlighting acts of graphicality, its context, and social performance. Pearson states:

> Few researchers would accept that the formation of a specific social group, whose members happen to make drawings, is more important as data than the narrative or representative qualities of their drawings. Indeed, the group's existence is unlikely to be noticed at all unless it presents some unusual contextual information that is believed necessary for understanding the drawings made in it. Likewise, Spirograph use is unlikely to attract the research attention devoted to systems of graphic representation. (p. 359)

Fig. 12.1 Drawing Together event held outside the Palmer Museum of Art in October, 2016

Pearson's critique of the hierarchies of drawing as guides to the development of children is the locus of how this line of developmental thought becomes suspect as a self-fulfilling prophecy of staged evolution that asserts only to ascend or be abject as outside of development, without drawing, constituting the subject as lesser than or deviant. In a more totalising sense, these sociomaterial practices of graphicality that become situated outside development through the gaze of adults onto the lives of children, allude to a broader deficit aesthetic, which "is an essentialist framework of ideas, attitudes, and values—about children, about art and aesthetics, and about research too" (Schulte, 2021, p. 56). These practices are at the heart of a broad range of performing with materials, drawing implements to tablets and software, that linger on the fringe of discussions in creative practice and learning that obscures a world of sociality by their more-than-human status. Techno-mechanical graphicality, and by extension all forms of mediated mark making through computation, software, and machines, suffer from these similar essentialist frameworks that reduce creativity and expression to a purely human endeavor.

Pearson's (2001) conception of drawing as social practice and Schulte's (2021) concept of the "deficit aesthetic," inform Drawing Together by focusing on art making as a social practice interspliced with conceptualizations of the technological as more-than-human. My interests in the Drawing Together activities are invested in understanding the pedagogies of technologies as locus to begin to understand a more-than-human education (Knochel, 2016, pp. 71–87). On the other hand, social practice, as conceptualized above from the perspective of creative practice and children, is a theoretical framing that considers context, behavior, and material. Social practice is attentive to the act of being social that is also mindful of the material residues of social being. This formulation of social practice aligns the material and social worlds through intractable entanglements of relationality: a sociomaterial practice. Sociomateriality has been used in many disciplines to explore this idea including education (Fenwick et al., 2011), organizational studies (Orlikowski, 2007), as well as science and technology studies (Mol, 2002). Research in sociomaterial practice is produced within similar trajectories with deeper commitments to situated practice in such fields as critical studies in education (Gravett, 2022; McKenzie & Bieler, 2016), and organizational studies in healthcare (Reichenpfader et al., 2018; Turner et al., 2022). Add to this mix the context of contemporary art, where social practice has been used to capture aspects of art that extend beyond the object of contemplation and elevate the role of context in constituting how art comes to mean something (Wolterstorff, 2015). It is at this intersection between the social and the more-than-human, within the material and the performative, that Drawing Together is animated.

I continue to run Drawing Together workshops, exploring different mechanisms to make marks. For example, a popular workshop that I have used with graduate students and youth to create what is referred to as a scribble bot: a simple circuit and DC motor that is used to distribute force unevenly, causing whatever markers and pens attached to the body to make marks. Many of the techniques and machines that I built are iterations of models that I found through online tutorials and user communities. My interests are not in the originality of the machine design per se, but rather in finding pathways through making to constitute a collective of contributors, human and nonhuman, by which our ad hoc community becomes the subject of meaning. The intention is to derive a practice that is iterative and intentional in its sociomaterial conception: experience and objects emerge from our coming together. In this way I involved my undergraduate art education students in making DIY tracing devices like the popular toy known as an Etch-a-Sketch, scribble bots using the simple circuit and DC motor, and eventually charging them with developing their own drawing machine prototypes from available resources. From this making, the project spiraled out to involve the fifth-grade students who were taught by my undergraduate students how to create their own scribble bots. We also set up an installation of the drawing machines in several outdoor and indoor events, inviting participation from passers-by (see Fig. 12.1). Both the drawing machines and the resulting drawings that were created were put on display in multiple locations. The Borland Project Space itself was utilized as an open studio space for housing the machines, but also a laboratory for tracking the design evolution of the machines and the accumulations of the project. In the space, we displayed schematics of different versions of the drawing machines as they were re-designed and the various prototypes of the drawing machines themselves were left open to the public to use. Additionally, a growing installation of the drawing machines and the work that was created with them was set up as a large installation for public use during the fall community day which is an annual event in the Arts District of our campus. Finally, the accumulated drawings and an installation of the drawing bots were installed in the exhibition Expanded Practice (18 October–11 December 2016), a faculty show held at the Palmer Museum of Art.

THE ASSEMBLAGE OF GENERATIVE AI PRACTICE AS A MATTER OF CONCERN

It is in this play of materials and creation that I draw upon to begin to unpack our encounter with artificial intelligence (AI), or more narrowly, generative AI practice in media creation. It draws a parallel to the question of questioning drawing, or rather recognizing the reflexive desire of theorizing childhood creativity in relationship to postdevelopmental artistic expression. I would assemble both Drawing Together and generative AI practice within a similar onto-epistemological framing: what Bruno Latour (2005) might call matters of concern versus matters of fact. Matters of fact are characterized by the rigor of scientific fact: an object or hypothesis has been tested and supported through further experimentation. A matter of fact is a closing down of investigation and an empirical certainty. However, empiricism is not so certain; objects and matters of fact become more complex the closer you get to them, so that "the empirical multiplicity of former 'natural' agencies overflows the narrow boundary of matters of fact" (Latour, 2005, p. 111). Objects cannot be reduced to facts, but instead, are multiplied as matters of concern. For Latour, matters of concern "while highly uncertain and loudly disputed, these real, objective, atypical and above all, interesting agencies are taken not exactly as object but rather as gathering" (p. 114). Here, I outline some matters of concern regarding the assemblage of generative AI practice in creating media. I do this to read into the essentialist framework of ideas, attitudes, and values that over-code our understandings of creating with media, and my focus on generative AI suggests the seismic impact that it has had on creative media expression since the broader adoption of such platforms as Stable Diffusion and Midjourney in 2023. From the ethical concerns that have driven litigation (Brittain, 2023) to the torrent of graphics-generating large language models that have become more openly available, there has been an ecological shift for computer-aided design and image generation rivaled only by the shift from photochemical to digital image making brought on by smartphones. I assert that this work is important at the early stages of the massive adoption of generative AI as it looks to move beyond one-dimensional assessments of the creativity of using such platforms (another deficit aesthetic in my view), and instead opens up the complex relationality of working with generative AI platforms as collaborations with more-than-human entities of unimaginable scale.

With the closing of 2022 there was a rising tide of news stories about AI-generated content and the tensions that it raises around artistic creation and education. From controversies arising when artists using Midjourney to win digital art contests at the state fair (Roose, 2022) to the very question of the writing prompt and essay as an assignment in the time of ChatGPT (Hern, 2022), AI had hit the mainstream and, for some, was an unsettling harbinger that threatened the authenticity of human creativity. There is plenty of hyperbole surrounding the cognitive abilities of these AI-assisted environments that go well beyond creative potential. For example, computational psychologist Michal Kosinski claimed ChatGPT passed the Theory of Mind Test at a 9-year-old human level (Yirka, 2023). Almost simultaneously, a research team developing the Baby Intuitions Benchmark (Gandhi et al., 2021) comparing the commonsense decision-making abilities of babies and learning-driven neural networks concluded "[o]ur comparison reveals that the state-of-the-art 'machine theory of mind' captured in such models is indeed missing key principles of commonsense psychology that infants possess" (Stojnić et al., 2023, p. 8). Even if the present moment of what we have in neural networks and machine learning AI is unclear, it is clear we have reached an inflection point that will lead to acceleration.

Rather than pursue exaggerations about the end of education or the ascendence of AI, I would rather draw correlations between the assemblage of children drawing and our need to assert developmentalism and the role that these early forms of AI-assisted practice may play in revealing our own desires in creativity, education, and youth. There is no doubt excitement mixed with great trepidation of what these platforms may offer education, including the very real impacts to human labor and employment that is undoubtedly a part of this and future stages of AI development. Rather than these broader extremes, I ask a more focused question: what might be the renewed role of creative expression as it pertains to generative AI practice, and how might its entanglements within sociomateriality be perceived? It is not my intention to suggest that AI graphic generation platforms the likes of Stable Diffusion and Midjourney are like children, but rather to perceive apprehension of generative AI practice within the assemblage of creative expression as sharing matters of concern that constitute the deficit aesthetic. If post-edevelopmental child studies and the reassessment of children drawing as social practice can serve as a cautionary tale, then mining broadly applicable frameworks to understand the sociomaterial practice of generative AI may allow for relational, more-than-human understandings of creative expression using generative AI. In the following I touch upon three matters of concern: AI-assisted image generation and access. One of the corporate logics that has emerged around the use of generative AI practice, in particular to visual media, is the notion that AI unlocks a range of access not previously possible. For example, consider the following quote from the OpenArt website, an online sharing network for AI-generated graphics, on its About page:

> For a very long time in human history, art was a specialized technique mastered by minority. However, the foundation of art is all about expressing our creativity and imagination, which is something everyone

should be empowered to do. With the state-of-the-art technologies like Stable Diffusion, creating amazing art is more accessible to everyone than ever and AI-generated art is becoming a new way to express ourselves. (OpenArt, 2023, para. 2)

The logic of this kind of access is utopian rhetoric, but it seems to occlude two very real sociomaterial practices of access that are a part of generative AI. First, the immanence of monetization of generative AI engines is palpable in the present moment. Platforms like Stable Diffusion and Midjourney have offered pathways to access, but with each passing day and the growing hype around the industry, it seems clear that market-driven decisions will overwhelm this open access ethos. Second, computer play is still tied to computer systems which have very real material costs that further correlate with education imperatives that allow folks to participate in this utopian vision.

Rise of the prompt engineer. One aspect of AI generation platforms is how instrumental the use of language and the prompt are to getting particular kinds of results. Reminiscent of building competency in using search terms to search library catalogues, query a database, or utilize a web search engine, there is an emerging keyword science to crafting the appropriate prompt that will return the more desired results. The new role of the "AI whisperer" (Harwell, 2023) is a type of coding in prose and uses the prompt as a form of interaction with AI generation platforms. The biggest difference between these prior information search systems and the AI prompt is that the systems that undergird AI platforms that use large language models remain a black box. For example, navigating a library catalogue may seem a bit mystifying, until you understand its purpose and how it achieves that purpose. Namely, the library catalogue is a comprehensive archive of the holdings of the library maintained to enable users to procure resources, and it relies on a fundamental logic of the identifying objectives of four varieties: author, title, subject, and date of publication to aid users in procuring asset locations. Likewise, using web search engines may have a fuzzier defined zone of possibility in the area of search, but it nonetheless relies on using metadata structures, search engine operators, and advanced search strategies that can set time and domain constraints. However, in AI generation platforms using a prompt is similar to "casting spells – and, like in fictional magic, nobody understands how the spells work and, if you mispronounce them, [what] demons come to eat you" (Wilison as quoted in Harwell, 2023, para. 12).

Prompt engineering, in this sense, is a sort of alchemy or interface within the logic of unknown and incomprehensible logic models, and for many, suspect as an engineering science due to its challenges of replicability.

While prompt engineers may be more snake oil salesman than alchemist, there is an underlying question of what exactly is being (re)produced through the iterative architectures of prompt engineering. For example, Midjourney is an AI-generative image platform that uses a Discord plugin to introduce new users and work through the kinks of its own model. The curious thing is that the Discord thread is like a livestream of prompts and the resulting images so that it performs like a real time how-to on prompt engineering. In my own explorations of the platform; I was developing prompts that had imagery, genres, and specific ideas, for example "ai bot teaching a class of students in front of a blackboard in the style of communist propaganda circa 1910." However, after watching the stream I started seeing prompts such as

/imagine a medium shot of white woman wearing a Tshirt, captured with a Nikon D850 and a Nikon AF-s NIKKOR 70–200mm f/2.8E FL ED VR lens, lit with high-key lightning to create a soft andethereal feel, a shallow depth of field --ar 2:3

The description of the image intermingled with the camera equipment that the graphic was meant to mimic was a very different approach than just description. Rather, it enters prompt interfacing into a kind of sociomaterial echo whereby the effects of image-taking materials may be mimicked without the materials themselves. The echo, in this sense, is actually the photographic-image world. The AI platform is trained via a large collection of images from some source and generating images is an outgrowth of that training. Here we have an inverse relationship from drawing. Drawing is a residue of a sociomaterial world and AI-generated graphics are sociomaterials composed of residues. And yet, in both instances, as Pearson (2001) states, the maker is alone in making graphic "discourses that are versions of unknowable larger pictorial systems" (p. 356), which raises the same concerns of authentic graphicality that we have in the critique of children's drawings. The difference here is that the sociomaterial graphics that are churned up and remixed by AI-generated platforms have a real stake in pirating artistic work as evidenced by two lawsuits filed as of January 2023 (Feldman, 2023). There are many legal battles ahead in this fight.

Climate costs in AI and its carbon footprint. While digital materials can have uncertain material properties, there is no doubt a grounding effect when we consider the carbon footprint of computing. In July 2022, there was a story in *Nature* concerning research about how to calculate that footprint more precisely (Gibney, 2022). What was unique about the study was the location-based assessment: researchers followed the training model in different locations and event times of day to assess the carbon footprint of training BERT, a common machine-learning language model, at data centers in various locations. The research has created a drive to emissions transparency for data centers that can aid computer scientists in making computing purchases with climate impact as a contributing factor to their data center choice. Approaching AI platforms and the work they do as an assemblage of computer scientists, data centers and energy providers is important for making ethical decisions in using AI (Tamburrini, 2022). For image generators, we need to add these climate impacts to the mix of ethical implications of artistic copyright infringement in making informed choices in our sociomaterial practices of using AI generative platforms.

CONCLUSION

There is no question that generative AI platforms are impacting our understanding of creative expression. However, there is a real hazard in any attempt to critically assess these innovations without consideration of the sociomaterial entanglements in more-than-human creative acts, namely that we are engaging in a false sense of graphic utopianism without cost. Sociomaterial practices as situated within frames of access, escalating awareness in uncertain knowledge domains, and seeing the invisibility of carbon-based computation leave the material implications of these practices in account as we take stock. The criticality of the postdevelopmental theorization that impacted conceptions of childhood and children drawing, used to provoke my research creation in Drawing Together, may provide a critical grounding to keep generative AI within the social and material so that the desires of expert image makers do not mask our co-figuration within these assemblages of graphicality. If we leave these matters of concern aside, we may become complicit in a becoming without us.

References

Anderson, B., & Harrison, P. (Eds.). (2010). *Taking-place: Non-representational theories and geography*. Ashgate.

Bennett, J. (2010). *Vibrant matter: A political ecology of things*. Duke University Press.

Brittain, B. (2023). Artists take new shot at stability, midjourney in updated copyright lawsuit. *Reuters*. https://www.reuters.com/legal/litigation/artists-take-new-shot-stability-midjourney-updated-copyright-lawsuit-2023-11-30/

Delanda, M. (2006). *A new philosophy of society: Assemblage theory and social complexity*. Bloomsburg.

Duncum, P. (2013). Youth's remix culture off and on line. *Australian Art Education, 35*(1/2), 10–23.

Duncum, P. (2020). *Picture pedagogy: Visual culture concepts to enhance the curriculum*. Bloomsbury.

Feldman, E. (2023). Are A.I. image generators violating copyright laws? *Smithsonian Magazine*. https://www.smithsonianmag.com/smart-news/are-ai-image-generators-stealing-from-artists-180981488/

Fenwick, T., Edwards, R., & Sawchuk, P. (2011). *Emerging approaches to educational research: Tracing the sociomaterial*. Routledge.

Gandhi, K., Stojnic, G., Lake, B. M., & Dillon, M. R. (2021). Baby Intuitions Benchmark (BIB): Discerning the goals, preferences, and actions of others. *Advances in Neural Information Processing Systems, 34*, 9963–9976. https://proceedings.neurips.cc/paper/2021/file/525b84 10cc8612283c9ecaf9a319f8ed-Paper.pdf

Gardner, H. (1980). *Artful scribbles: The significance of children's drawings*. Basic Books.

Gibney, E. (2022). How to shrink AI's ballooning carbon footprint. *Nature*. https://www.nature.com/articles/d41586-022-01983-7

Gravett, K. (2022). Feedback literacies as sociomaterial practice. *Critical Studies in Education, 63*(2), 261–274. https://doi.org/10.1080/17508487.2020.1747099

Harwell, D. (2023). Tech's hottest new job: AI whisperer. No coding required. *Washington Post*. https://www.washingtonpost.com/technology/2023/02/25/prompt-engineers-techs-next-big-job/

Hern, A. (2022). AI bot ChatGPT stuns academics with essay-writing skills and usability. *The Guardian*. https://www.theguardian.com/technology/2022/dec/04/ai-bot-chatgpt-stuns-academics-with-essay-writing-skills-and-usability

Kerschensteiner, G. (1905). *Die entwickelung der zeichnerischen begabung: neue ergebnisse auf grund neuer untersuchungen*.

Knochel, A. D. (2016). Photoshop teaches with(out) you: Actant agencies and non-human pedagogy. *Visual Arts Research, 42*(1), 71–87. https://doi.org/10.5406/visuartsrese.42.1.0071

Latour, B. (2005). *Reassembling the social*. Oxford University Press.

Lowenfeld, V. (1947). *Creative and mental growth*. Macmillan Company.

McClure, M. (2011). Child as totem: Redressing the myth of inherent creativity in early childhood. *Studies in Art Education,* 52(2), 127–141. https://www.jstor.org/stable/41407938

McKenzie, M., & Bieler, A. (2016). *Critical education and sociomaterial practice*. Peter Lang Verlag.

Mol, A. (2002). *The body multiple: Ontology in medical practice*. Duke University Press.

OpenArt. "About". OpenArt. https://openart.ai/about

Orlikowski, W. J. (2007). Sociomaterial practices: Exploring technology at work. *Organization Studies, 28*(9), 1435–1448. https://doi.org/10.1177/017084 0607081138

Pearson, P. (2001). Towards a theory of children's drawing as social practice. *Studies in Art Education, 42*(4), 348–365. https://www.jstor.org/stable/132 1079

Peppler, K. (2010). Media arts: Arts education for a digital age. *Teachers College Record, 112*(8), 2118–2153. https://doi.org/10.1177/016146811 011200806

Reichenpfader, U., Wickström, A., Abrandt Dahlgren, M., Nilsen, P., & Carlfjord, S. (2018). 'Our surgeons want this to be short and simple': Practices of in-hospital medication review as coordinated sociomaterial actions. *Studies in Continuing Education, 40*(3), 323–336. https://doi.org/10. 1080/0158037X.2018.1458710

Roose, K. (2022). An A.I.-generated picture won an art prize. Artists aren't happy. *New York Times*. https://www.nytimes.com/2022/09/02/techno logy/ai-artificial-intelligence-artists.html

Schulte, C. M. (2021). Childhood drawing: The making of a deficit aesthetic. *Global Studies of Childhood, 11*(1), 54–68. https://doi.org/10.1177/204361 0621995821

Schulte, C. M., & Thompson, C. M. (Eds.). (2018). *Communities of practice: Art, play, and aesthetics in early childhood*. Springer.

Springgay, S., & Truman, S. E. (2018). *Walking methodologies in a more-than-human world: WalkingLab*. Routledge.

Stojnić, G., Gandhi, K., Yasuda, S., Lake, B. M., & Dillon, M. R. (2023). Commonsense psychology in human infants and machines. *Cognition, 235*, 105406. https://doi.org/10.1016/j.cognition.2023.105406

Thompson, C. M. (2017). Listening for stories: Childhood studies and art education. *Studies in Art Education, 58*(1), 7–16. https://doi.org/10.1080/003 93541.2016.1258526

Tamburrini, G. (2022). The AI carbon footprint and responsibilities of AI scientists. *Philosophies, 7*(1), 4. https://doi.org/10.3390/philosophies7010004

Trafí-Prats, L. (2021). Thinking affective pedagogies at the intersection of popular media, digital technology, and gurokawaii. *Studies in Art Education, 62*(3), 209–221. https://doi.org/10.1080/00393541.2021.1936427

Truman, S. E. (2021). *Feminist speculations and the practice of research-creation: Writing pedagogies and intertextual affects*. Routledge.

Turner, S., D'Lima, D., Sheringham, J., Swart, N., Hudson, E., Morris, S., & Fulop, N. J. (2022). Evidence use as sociomaterial practice? A qualitative study of decision-making on introducing service innovations in health care, *Public Management Review, 24*(7), 1075–1099. https://doi.org/10.1080/14719037.2021.1883098

Wilson, B. (2003). Three sites for visual cultural pedagogy: Honoring students' interests and imagery. *International Journal of Education through Art, 1*(3), 107–126.

Wilson, B., & Wilson, M. (1981). The use and uselessness of developmental stages. *Art Education, 34*(5), 4–5.

Wolterstorff, N. (2015). *Art rethought: The social practices of art*. Oxford University Press.

Yirka, B. (2023). ChatGPT able to pass theory of mind test at 9-year-old human level. *Tech Xplore*. https://techxplore.com/news/2023-02-chatgpt-theory-mind-year-old-human.html

CHAPTER 13

Mr Fusion or Johnny 5? Visual Rhetoric of AI Design

Stuart Medley and *Jo Jung*

INTRODUCTION

The rise of artificial intelligence (AI) in contemporary society has brought with it both excitement and concern. On the one hand, AI has been praised for its potential to revolutionise various industries, improve efficiency, and enhance human capabilities (Aghion et al., 2019). On the other hand, there are concerns about the fairness and bias issues in AI systems, which can result in certain segments of society feeling powerless and marginalised (Coeckelbergh, 2015). As well as the labour and environmental injustices that have already emerged alongside the extraction of the raw materials which enable AI systems (Crawford, 2021), other critics say the pillars of Western, liberal societies, democracy and the rule of law, are threatened by 'Internet giants' attempting to abrogate responsibility to the AI of search engines and social media algorithms rather

S. Medley (✉) · J. Jung
UNIDCOM, IADE, Lisboa, Portugal
e-mail: s.medley@ecu.edu.au

S. Medley
Edith Cowan University, Mount Lawley, Australia

© The Author(s) 2024
R. Rousi et al. (eds.), *Humane Autonomous Technology*,
https://doi.org/10.1007/978-3-031-66528-8_13

than abide by the unique laws of the countries in which they operate (Nemitz, 2018, p. 10). One of the critical issues that arise from AI is the relationship between automation and user-control (Sartori & Theodorou, 2022). While automated systems can simplify the user experience, they can also limit user control, leading to mistrust in the technology. Along these lines, scholars have identified a separation between the aesthetics and the ethics of digital product design (Hauser, 2023; Folkmann, 2020; Redström & Wiltse, 2019) where simplified visual design appears to mask the true, complex nature of the functions of AI-enabled devices, and systems. We concur and extend these observations into the graphic design and corporate verbal rhetoric surrounding AI-enabled products.

The visual aesthetics of AI interfaces and the visual identity of their brands are difficult to grasp; there is little to get a handle on. Part of the reason for this difficulty stems from a widespread adoption of minimalist, Modernist aesthetics in the field. That is, forms without decorative embellishments, embodied only in spherical, cylindrical or rectangular prism shapes, and often coloured only in silver, white, or black. For instance, as Hauser explains, "it is widely known that Apple's product designs as well as other contemporary technology designs are strongly influenced by Rams' design aesthetic found in the products designed by him or under his supervision at Braun" (Hauser, 2023, p. 228). This minimalist aesthetic extends into other AI-enabled fields such as banking applications (Apps) and the autonomous vehicle sector. In all cases, the real use of these digital products is very complex and warrants richer explanation for users. This matters because the creation of reliable and conscientious AI necessitates attending to the ethical aspects of technology development and the visual rhetoric of such technology (Choung et al., 2022; Corporation, 2022; IBM Bitkina et al., 2020; Lockey et al., 2020). If simplicity and clarity are used to justify a lack of information in the user interface (UI), the same reasoning can be applied to disclosure statements of Apps and other digital products, terms and conditions, and related explanations, to make these simple, comprehensible, and truthful.

In this chapter, the authors delve into the nexus between the user experience (UX) of autonomous technology, its communication design, and the visual aesthetics used in its promotion as an emerging force. We examine various digital product designs and graphic designs associated with AI to understand how the UX of these products is portrayed in corporate verbal rhetoric and corporate identity. We begin with the context of AI-enabled human–computer interaction (HCI), particularly the tension between user experiences that afford control, in part through clarity and simplicity, but which conceal the complexity of back-end systems, and how the user is incorporated into these, knowingly or otherwise. Well-known domestic virtual assistants are analysed in these terms, yet attention is also placed on the autonomous vehicle sector because its positioning of the user is generally more telling from an AI perspective: heralding the user as 'part of the machinery', rather than its operator. The authors examine the things AI-enabled brands say about themselves through their corporate statements of intent, and through the graphic design of their corporate identities. In the corporate verbal rhetoric and visual aesthetics the same tensions can be observed, where implied ease-of-use and user benefits are contrasted with an obscuring of the complexity and true nature of the AI-enabled systems these communications expound upon. At least two available visual design approaches to AI developers are observed to declare more openly the real level of complexity behind the scenes of contemporary and future UI. One is for the corporate visual design to adopt more of the engineering aesthetic rather than the Modernist aesthetic. The second approach suggested here, if ventures insist on Modernist simplicity to instil readability for users, then they should use Modernist design philosophy (not just Modernist aesthetics) to extend simplicity into the disclosure of AI systems complexity. Thus, to openly declare to users, in a simple, clear, succinct and engaging way, the terms and conditions of interacting, the destinations of the user's information, and who benefits from the interactions.

Background to the Study: *Control and Trust*

The pervasive nature of HCI (i.e., interaction between humans and technologies) has significant and immediate impact, both negative and positive, on people's social and emotional experience beyond the confines of digital space. UX is carefully orchestrated through persuasive user-interaction (UI visual design) to persuade people that AI is here to improve their lives and make things easier. AI systems are deeply embedded in a range of technologies, seamlessly retrieve data about users, and through their interconnected web of devices, share information for a range of goals, including to assist users. However, there are unintended and undesirable consequences as a result of empowering users through interface design. Is UI helping humans and/or is it affecting the perception of *control of* or *trust in* information systems? How are computer-mediated UX and persuasion morally justified by technology (tech) companies?

Control

Since its first conception in 1950 by Alan Turing (1950), AI has raised more questions than it has provided answers. In his seminal work, *Computing machinery and intelligence*, Turing proposed the question, '[c]an machines think?'. Fast forward to 2023, and AI has evolved to display aspects of human intelligence such as decision-making, some-times through distributed agency (Slota, 2020) shared with humans, other times autonomously. In these capacities, AI can perform some tasks better than humans (McCarthy, 2004; Russell & Norvig, 2020). AI has become common in everyday human activities, capable of performing tasks without being explicitly instructed with human intervention. One of the key features of AI is its ability to learn and improve itself continuously, demanding less or no human supervision. This involves machine learning algorithms using vast swathes of data for autonomous systems, such as self-driving cars. Although the advancement of AI to emulate human intelligence has not yet been realised, the impact on people's lives—good and bad—is beginning to be witnessed and assessed.

With the debut of ChatGPT and a series of other similar AI-powered chatbots, the renaissance of AI has reignited. The easy entry—afforded by simplicity of UI—to these applications, has opened the door to anyone who has access to a connected device. Through its advanced machine and deep learning processes, AI has circumvented the complexity and convolution of traditional product usage, enabling users to bypass tasks and steps such as information filtering and processing. AI-powered search engines, for instance, can provide users with relevant information in human-like responses without requiring the multiple steps historically involved in search engine sites. The integration of AI technology into our digital devices has fundamentally changed the way individuals interact and communicate with them, as people are now being trained to interact with and be better understood by these devices. The current era is marked by a period of continuous experimentation and development within the field of AI, wherein humans are the subjects of ongoing refinement and optimisation of AI technology.

When a new technology is introduced, the initial emphasis is often placed on aspects such as usability, accessibility, and the rate of adoption by people. The field of HCI has long dedicated significant efforts towards improving these aspects of technology design (Bevan, 2001; Issac & Isaias, 2022). It is not an exaggeration to suggest that the first two decades of HCI were almost exclusively dedicated to these goals: developing UI solely for utilitarian experience, evaluating effectiveness, and efficiency. With the rise of AI, a new dimension has been added to these goals, intensifying the focus on user control and the potential impact of technology on user autonomy. AI has become an omnipresent element in numerous everyday products and services, extending even to domains where its utilisation may not be anticipated, immediately apparent, or openly declared. This highlights the importance of the delicate balance between providing users with a sense of control and ease-of-use through the aesthetics of UI, to mediate the interaction and communication between devices and people, while shaping the interactive experience in a way that declares the presence of AI, and the potential uses of the user's information.

In this regard, many AI-powered devices focus on the former part of the equation: they embrace a minimalist design approach to evade conspicuousness. This corroborates Don Norman's (2011) earlier assertion that technology, like any other product, follows a lifecycle where the complexity of its underlying mechanics shapes its UI. However, as it matures, it becomes necessary to prioritise user control through ease-of-use and pleasure in UI design. Eventually, the technology should be assimilated and made invisible to the user's consciousness (Norman, 2011). Given the multitude of demands placed upon powerful technologies, such as AI, complexity is an inherent characteristic of their functionality. Nevertheless, ineffective visual representation exacerbates this complexity, causing confusion and complications. In contrast, compelling design that is meaningful to people can effectively manage this complexity, taming it, and enhancing UX (Norman, 2011; Rousi & Silvennoinen, 2018). Minimalism in design is not about oversimplification or reduction of complexity, but rather it should prioritise the most important aspects of the product to guide people towards their goals. Balancing the complexity of technologies without oversimplification is a critical consideration in designing effective UI.

User control is a critical dimension of HCI that reflects the extent to which users can manage and direct the behaviour of systems as well as

the extent to which users feel empowered to take charge of their interactions with the technology (Bandura, 1989; Nielsen & Tahir, 2002).
Transparency and explainability are two critical factors that impact user
control and trust in HCI (Balasubramaniam et al., 2023; Vössing et al.,
2022). When users understand how the system works and how it makes
decisions, they are more likely to feel in control of their interactions
with the technology. Transparency refers to the ability of an AI system
to provide visibility into its processes and decision-making mechanisms,
allowing users to understand how it reaches its conclusions. This is particularly important in cases where the system's decisions have significant
consequences for individuals or society as a whole. For this reason, it was
important for the authors to explore below how the autonomous vehicle
industry communicates about itself, where all of these consequences are
intensified in a context that risks the user's immediate physical safety.

Explainability, on the other hand, refers to the system's capacity to
present the rationale behind its decision-making process to users in a clear
and understandable manner. This is especially important in cases where
the system's decisions are complex or difficult to interpret. By providing
users with an explanation of its decisions, an AI system can help build
trust and confidence in its use. Unfortunately, many AI-powered systems
lack transparency and explainability. Compounding this issue is that these
systems are built on algorithms, which are the core of some contemporary
business models. To explain too much to users may give away competitive
advantage in a cut-throat market. When users cannot see nor understand
the processes behind an AI system's decision-making, they may feel that
they have no control over the outcomes. This can erode trust in the
system and lead to scepticism about its use.

Trust

In the realm of advanced technology, the importance of visual aesthetics
cannot be overstated, as it can profoundly influence the UX, and consequently, the adoption and success rates of a technology (Hassenzahl,
2004; Lindgaard et al., 2011; Tractinsky, 2004). The visual design of
advanced technologies should reflect the intended use case and purpose
of the product, as well as the broader trends and values of the technological domain in question. To this end, designers and engineers must
stay attuned to the evolving aesthetic preferences of users and incorporate them into the design process, while also being mindful of the practical

and technical limitations of the product. In the context of AI, it is crucial to evaluate the visual aesthetics and corporate rhetoric of systems carefully to ensure that users' trust in technology is not compromised. The unknown capacity of AI, which is yet to be fully comprehended, creates a barrier between users and systems. Therefore, designers must strike a balance between the true intentions of the system and the information truthfully conveyed to benefit users.

An extensive survey on trust in AI across five countries by Lockey and colleagues (2020) showed that people are highly sceptical and distrust AI. However, they are willing to embrace AI if the systems are developed on sound ethical principles with transparency of data governance and the rights of users accounted for. The importance of trustworthiness in AI systems extends beyond its actual performance to include the perceived trustworthiness through the aesthetics of UI. While the actual trustworthiness of AI relies heavily on the governance of AI, particularly data governance, which could potentially infringe on human rights, such as privacy (Lockey et al., 2020), perceived trust in product design is a subjective interpretation of people's experiences with products and is heavily dependent on how the product is communicated through visual rhetoric of messages (Hassenzahl & Monk, 2010). Perceived trust plays a significant role in people's acceptance and adoption of AI systems, regardless of whether the intent of AI systems is for financial gain or social benefit (Bitkina et al., 2020; Choung et al., 2022; Lockey et al., 2020).

AI systems function largely based on the input of information programmed by developers and consumers of the products. The processing of this information raises critical questions about trustworthiness, such as the potential for bias or misuse of data. These concerns are further amplified when AI operates in a less conspicuous manner, as it makes it even harder to detect or evaluate the trustworthiness of the technology. The unobservable of system's process and users' reduced possibility of intervention pose significant challenges to establishing trust in AI technology. This creates a sense of uncertainty and diminished transparency (Fröhlich et al., 2019). While recognisable AI products, such as autonomous vehicles, care robots, and smart-manufacturing robots, solve everyday problems, it is important to recognise the potential for trust issues in less visible AI applications. For example, in the case of conversational AI where users might believe they are interacting with a person, yet in reality they are interacting with a computer programme. These latter AI systems are commonly used in screen-based products, such as websites, where users' requirements are processed seamlessly behind the screen, and AI's *intelligent* tasks are manifested and communicated in a visual manner. AI's ability to discreetly process consumers' information to personalised UX is questionable as people need to know what AI is doing and why.

The creation of reliable and conscientious AI necessitates attending to the ethical aspects of technology development and the visual rhetoric of such technology (IBM Bitkina, et al., 2020; Choung et al., 2022; Corporation, 2022; Lockey et al., 2020). The ethical considerations surrounding technology should be prioritised, and the visual rhetoric employed in the system must exhibit the system's benefits while also fostering meaningful UX. The visual design of AI systems can significantly influence users' perception of the technology and the trust they place in it. Therefore, aligning the visual design of AI systems with ethical principles and enhancing the UX is critical in developing trustworthy and responsible AI. Striking the right balance between ethics and visual design is necessary to ensure that AI systems are both trustworthy and appealing to users.

Aesthetics of AI Developers

The aesthetics of UI has profound impact on usability and the emotional experience of using devices (Hassenzahl, 2004; Hassenzahl & Monk, 2010, 2013; Lindgaard et al., 2011). A wave of paradigm shifts has occurred, from utilitarian to aesthetically pleasing design to emotional UI leveraging social values such as trustworthiness. In the nascent stage of digital devices, the aesthetics of UI was driven by functionality and utilitarian experience to provide more instructional guidance to people. Direct manipulation coupled with metaphorical design using the concept of 'real-world' were attempts to minimise the cognitive load of users in order to create intuitive and user-friendly design. The commercialisation of the World Wide Web has further underscored intuitive design having a perceptible and often exaggerated UI, such as 'Click here'. The early aesthetics of UI heavily focused on the well-being of consumers to minimise anxiety of using then unfamiliar digital devices. The trend of metaphorical design took another turn when Apple introduced their trademark skeuomorphic design (where the design was two-dimensional and digital but alluded to three dimensional, physical buttons with a visually raised surface and glassy appearance) which impressed designers and consumers with their sophisticated 'wow' factor of visually enticing look and feel. Leveraging the prior learning of users, skeuomorphic design accentuated the aesthetics of metaphor with ornamental features such as reflective mirroring effects or shadows. The skeuomorphic design approach gained much popularity along with the demand of Apple products by consumers.

The introduction of flat design by Microsoft in 2011, as a counterpoint to skeuomorphism, has changed the aesthetics of UI. "Flat design is a popular design style that is defined by the absence of glossy or three-dimensional visual effects in the graphical elements. Many designers consider it to be an offshoot of minimalist web design" (Moran, 2015, Online). "Microsoft's design documentation referred to its new style as 'authentically digital'—a phrase that neatly captures the appeal of flat design for many designers. Flat design was seen as a way to explore the digital medium without trying to reproduce the appearance of the physical world" (Moran, 2015, Online). This 'authentically digital' design approach has been widely used and has influenced UI design for digital products and services including mobile Apps and software interfaces, and has been a dominant design trend in recent years (Urbano et al., 2022). The trend towards flat design has been driven by several factors, including: the rise of mobile devices and touchscreens; the need for faster loading times and better performance; in addition to the desire for a more minimalist and modern aesthetic. The design of physical products is changing as a response to this trend, with customers responding positively to the allure of minimalistic design (Lekaj et al., 2023). BMW and Volkswagen, for example, have changed their logo to flat 2D so that their marketing and promotion on the web can be seamlessly shared with its real-world counterparts. As more AI is integrated into everyday products, the concept of flat design, or even further 'hidden from the view' UI, away from the interface of the products, is an AI aesthetic recalling the origins of HCI (Pitardi & Marriott, 2021).

Google's minimalist approach to design its search engine home page was a resounding success and has been maintained since its first launch in 1998. The approach allows users to focus on what they need to do without unnecessary distractions (Moran, 2015). The widespread proliferation of the Internet of Things (IoT) and the pervasive interconnectedness of digital devices have led to a heightened level of familiarity and competence among consumers in interacting with these technologies (Dwivedi, 2021). The trend towards functionality-driven UI has flowed into the aesthetics of AI. AI-powered devices like Amazon's Alexa are designed to blend into the interior design of homes and offices with minimal visual interruption, and are awakened by voice commands without requiring physical interaction. The lack of physical interaction is afforded by voice recognition and natural language processing; AI-powered products are leading a new paradigm of UI aesthetics establishing stronger perceived personality and trust through social presence (Chérif & Lemoine, 2019; Pitardi & Marriott, 2021).

AI-powered devices, such as virtual assistants, are adopting a minimalistic UI design approach with a focus on utilitarian UX reminiscent of the early era of HCI. On the other hand, AI-powered products such as wearable devices exhibit UI designs that are markedly futuristic and advanced in domains such as robotics, gaming, and health. These AI-powered devices aim to engender a more immersive and engaging UX by integrating cutting-edge technologies like virtual and augmented reality, as well as sophisticated haptic feedback (Barteit et al., 2021; Fu et al., 2022; Lungu et al., 2021; Roozendaal et al., 2021). The prevalence of futuristic looking devices is not limited to cutting-edge or specialised contexts, but can now be found in everyday environments as well. For instance, modern cars are equipped with various AI-powered features such as lane keeping assistants, which constantly check to ensure that the car is within the lane. In cases where the car steers away, it provides haptic feedback by vibrating the steering wheel, along with virtual simulations on the dashboard to visualise the situation (Roozendaal et al., 2021).

Regarding the Graphic Design Attendant to AI-enabled Tech

Contemplating contemporary product design, Hauser et al. (2023) stated, "[i]n the face of massively increased technological complexity, it is striking that so many of today's computational and networked things follow design ideals honed decades ago in a much different context" (p. 227). Design is currently at a critical juncture where Internet-connected products can be seen as "brilliantly designed and engaging to use yet can also be considered very problematic in how they support hidden agendas and often seem less than trustworthy" (Hauser et al., 2023, p. 227). The authors highlight the contemporary "presentation of things as useful tools through design and a withdrawal of aspects of their functionality and complexity" (p. 227). In terms of the lack of trust engendered, it might be tempting to argue that there is a tendency towards the '*withholding* of aspects of their functionality and complexity'. Even in the heyday of Modernist product designer Dieter Rams, some complexity was withheld from the user: very complicated electro-mechanics were tidied away in sleek, minimalist product designs for hi-fi, television, cameras and watches. However, while the electro-mechanical has become electronic, the withheld dimension for today's Internet-connected products also encompasses the gathering of user information (usually without declaration of its full extent) and its processing for profit by and through AI, via Internet-distributed systems.

In the following discussion, this notion of the separation of product design from its true function into the realm of graphic design and corporate identity for AI-enabled products is extended. The graphic design for these devices and other aspects of AI communications is significant because "aesthetics provides a powerful way of differentiating products and stimulating purchase when products are perceived as otherwise identical," and "[o]ver time, corporate aesthetics provides a sustainable competitive advantage" (Schmitt et al., 1995, p. 83). Even the logo of these recent ventures can herald much of significance. Heilbrunn (1997) exclaimed that a logo is "a flag which expresses the values and intentions of the organization (or the brand) it represents [...] The logo is thus often considered as the ultimate sign of a company or organization's visual identity system" (p. 176). Heilbrunn states that a logo fulfils the following rhetorical functions: a *phatic* function to maintain contact between the organisation and its customers; a *poetic* function which connotes information beyond the signifier of the message; and an emotive or *expressive* function—the logo has to convey information about its sender: "The logo underlies an emission intentionality, a will to say something about what is represented in the logo" (pp. 175–176).

Corporate identity designed for any specific organisation sits within the context of similar organisations. In time, conventions around design for that field begin to emerge. These conventions become a part of the visual rhetoric a company may deploy to persuade its audiences that it is a worthy operator in the field. Schneller (2015) explained that, "[a] design that neglects the visual habits operative within a field of design creates irritation and incomprehension" (p. 352). She insists that designers need to consider "type-specific higher-order rules that make design objects recognizable as items belonging to a certain design type or field" (p. 352). Her observation is made with regard to information posters about transport timetables, a genre of graphic design with a history spanning decades and a exceptionally large publics. Yet, how can these designs intended for a field this immature be accessed? The design and its forming traditions exist, but the conventions of its visuality are not yet established in the public domain for whom its rhetorical effects might be intended.

Schmitt et al. (1995) explained that "the forms and shapes, the colours and materials, and the visual and auditory communications of an organization express its culture and values" (p. 82). Accordingly, we look to other clues in corporate communications to see what the graphic design might be intended to echo. Our method of quoting corporate promotional copy is borrowed from Werning (2019) in order that "the texts can be used to contextualise the accompanying images and can help in 'looking through' their purpose" (p. 432).

A Hybrid of Modernism and Science Fiction Aesthetics

The above authors cited homages to Modernism when analysing the physical product design of Internet-connected devices. The authors of the current chapter see this reflected in the graphic design too, but also observe occasional references to science fiction. That these companies call on the visual style of science fiction is likely given that the line between commercial design and science fiction cinema has always been blurred. For example, Harald Belker's car designs for the film *Minority Report*, bore a Lexus badge; apart from being product placement and advertising for the brand, the design is also a concept car—a way to test an idea for a new feature, or public reaction to a visual style—for Lexus outside of the diegesis of the film.

Garrett (2006) described the relationship between design and science fiction, based on the observation that science fiction can inspire industrial designers and enrich industrial design processes and products. The hypotheses born out by her study were that: the roles of industrial design and science fiction are based on parallel ideas; industrial design is suffused with, and sympathetic to, science fiction thinking; there is a 'cause and effect' relationship between aspects of industrial design and science fiction; science fiction cinema performs a key function in the roles of science fiction, and cinema can be employed to explore and discuss the roles of industrial design and science fiction (2006, p. 211).

In addition to the clear presence of Modernist aesthetics, it can be seen in some examples of the design of these ventures' corporate identities, two-dimensional extensions of this modus operandi. Not only that, two clear approaches to design of tech in science fiction film can be observed. On the one hand, if the intention is to persuade the audience that this is a 'lived-in', settled technology, simple, more Modernist aesthetic comes to the fore—think about the 'Mr Fusion' engine in *Back to the Future*. If, on the other hand, a device's aesthetics are intended to persuade the audience it is a leading-edge, experimental prototype, it will appear more engineered, rather than designed. Think, Johnny 5 in the movie *Short Circuit* (a Syd Mead design; more of his work later).

The discussion begins with reflecting on the visual aesthetics around AI by examining the visual aesthetics associated with already ubiquitous tech—virtual assistants. These designs are emblematic of visual design for AI in that their graphic simplicity belies the complexity of their systems' operation. From there examination focuses on the very near future of autonomous vehicles.

Aesthetics of Virtual Assistants

Hauser (2023), Folkmann (2020), Redström and Wiltse (2019), and Selle (2014) all observe a connection between mid-late twentieth century Modernist design forms and the physical shapes of twenty-first-century 'digital products'; devices connecting to the IoT. They see a paradox too in that the simplicity of the physical presence (forms that tend towards simple geometries, echoing Dieter Rams or Mies Van Der Rohe's principles of clarity of function) is at odds with the profundity of the functionality and connectivity of an object's digital, immaterial aspects: "With digitization, ungraspable and invisible functions of tools have evolved" (Selle, 2014, p. 42). Redström and Wiltse point out that the 'physical presence' of these objects does not exhaust their capabilities, nor does it even come close to revealing them through their outer form (Redström & Wiltse, 2019). These designs take their place in what Folkmann calls 'post-material aesthetics'. We extend this notion of the separation of visual design from function into the graphic design and corporate identity realm for the AI-enabled brands following.

For instance, we see Amazon's Alexa-enabled, *Echo* Smartspeaker in this light. Firstly, the graphic design of the Alexa logo is made to appear as a clear subset of the Amazon logo design. Both logos were designed at Turner Duckworth, the partners of which met at Minale Tattersfield Design, a studio with its roots in late Modernism. The logos for both are what Heilbrunn (1997) has termed 'mixed', that is, containing both *icotype* (image) and *logotype* (text) (pp. 177–178). The visual wit shown in the Amazon A-Z delivery arrow, which doubles as a smile (through 'resemblance' [ibid.]) is exactly the kind of graphic flourish typical of the famous late Modernist design studios such as Minale Tatterersfield, Landor, as well as Chermayeff & Geismar. The connection between the two logos is established through *polyptotonic* visual rhetoric (Helmann, 2017, p. 86): a kind of visual alliteration. With few unique parts between the two logos, they become visually unassailable; almost *too simple* to criticise. Amazon and Alexa both could be inferred as companies concerned with straightforward, physical delivery of items, rather than the complex, AI-enabled, Internet-infrastructured systems they actually are.

Alexa's hardware/software interface is the Echo Smartspeaker. The design of the hardware's physical, outward appearance (similar to the BeoLit 17 analysed by Folkmann, 2020) is simple and clean, following our 'Mr Fusion' notion above: as if it arrived in the world, fully formed, 100% tested, reliable, and trustworthy. Its naming as a 'speaker', albeit a smart one, reinforces this impression of clarity and simplicity, at the same time obscuring that the *speaker* is also a *listener*.

Essentially, this approach of borrowing from Modernism, which we see throughout AI-connected identities and products, is a rhetorical one. Metaphor is a rhetorical device aimed at connecting what the user knows to what the user is being urged to apprehend: the concrete source domain is used to launch towards the more abstract target domain. The source domain for these designs is Modernism, its forms and, at least on the surface, its philosophies. The logos, like those from Modernist masters (e.g., Primo Angeli, Akira Hirata, Nelly Rudin, Felix Beltran, Armin Hofmann et al.) are clean, minimal, and where they are not monochromatic, they are often set in a field of Modernist white. Likewise, the product designs have simple, geometrically primitive shapes. Meanwhile, "digital objects present a higher degree of complexity because their function is enabled by the operation of microchips, which gives the designer a very high degree of freedom to choose the form almost totally arbitrarily" (Folkmann, 2020, p. 228). In other words, the visual simplicity is a deliberate choice that has little to do with actual function, in fact, it obscures the deep complexity of functions.

Raymond Loewy coined a phrase about the form of product design, 'Most Advanced Yet Acceptable', arguing that some products might appear too advanced for consumers to embrace (Gorman, 2003). This echoes Anina Schneller's (2015) abovementioned take on design rhetoric.

However, the situation in 2024 may be more complex. The shape, particularly for products which are entirely new, becomes acceptable when the design emerges as the dominant one in the new field. As well as the Echo embodying Modernist form aesthetics (but not the Modernist philosophy of 'form follows function' or 'honesty in materials') the smart-speaker has the majority market share (as at 2022). This fact may also literally shape the aesthetics of product design in this area, applying a brake to further innovation in form design. According to Su and Hsia (2022),

> *the variety and speed of innovation rapidly decline after the appearance of the dominant design. When the market begins to hold expectations for the characteristics or format of a certain product, the core product technology development shifts to the gradual improvements of the characteristics or format of existing products. This will gradually reduce the power for positive innovation.* (p. 143)

Perhaps because of Alexa's dominance, other smart-speakers embody the basic geometry motif, being overwhelmingly spherical, ovoid or cylindrical in shape. The essential geometry of a circle is regarded as the friendliest and most approachable shape: "circles feel closed, safe, and comfortable" (Barry, 2006, p. 145). The Amazon Echo is a short cylinder (height: approx. 3r) or a flattened one (height: approx. 1r), or a sphere. The spherical design appears more retro or futuristic, bringing to mind the science fiction-like architecture of R. Buckminster Fuller more than the shapes of the Bauhaus or Ulm. The surface material, which on the cylindrical Echo seems merely to be a speaker cover, not unlike on a mid-century hi-fi, on the spherical Echo is reminiscent of the architectural complexity of Buckminster Fuller's geodesic domes' surface textures.

The lack of a clear interface on the smart-speaker is a semiotic clue that there is 'nothing for the user to do' beyond keeping the device electrically powered. All software updates are taken care of automatically. For the user the benefit is to refrain from the physical interaction with an interface (a control panel or a computer keyboard or smartphone screen). The removal of this small barrier to providing useful user information appears to have been incentive enough to create such a line of physical products that add little to the consumer's wellbeing. Amazon's webpage, proclaiming the benefits of Alexa has this to say: "Alexa makes your life easier, more meaningful, and more fun by letting you voice control your world. Alexa can help you get more out of the things you already love and discover new possibilities you've never imagined". Of these claims, the 'more meaningful' phrase seems perhaps the most questionable.

Apple's *Siri*, since it lacks a smart-speaker interface, is more amorphic; lacking a definite physical form. Its associated graphic design resembles little more than a 'music visualiser' or late 90s screensaver. The circle encapsulating the anamorph, and the colours of the anamorph appear to be references to Apple OS graphic design more generally; particularly screensavers and the more abstract desktop images available on MacOS. In our comparison of contemporary design with Modernism or science fiction aesthetics, Siri shares strong resemblance to Syd Mead's (futurist for Ford, Sony, and many other corporations, as well as cinema production designer on *Blade Runner*, and *Tron* among others) wall projections in his work, *Tomorrow's Kitchen* (1987). In contrast to its fairly down-to-earth vocal representations, Siri's graphic design is aloof, mystical, and nebulous, much like its name. Siri "was originally developed by Dag Kittlaus from SRI International Artificial Intelligence Centre as an app for the iPhone and was purchased by Apple in 2010" (McCall & Pantoja, 2007, p. 1). The name connects with the name of the intelligence centre to Norse mythology, but is also a common enough name in Kittlaus's Scandinavian lineage. Siri's graphic design is synecdochical of AI visual design in total: the discrete circle, so simple and bounded, like a regular business logo form but without the content within, is really a window on to a universe of unknowable complexity. It seems strangely unsure of itself, especially as a feature that belongs to the Apple stable (normally sure-footed product design). In short, it reflects our earlier observation that it is a challenge to design for a field that is immature.

Siri and Alexa are famous names in the sector (for discussions on the names, in particular the problematic aspects of gendering virtual assistants through naming and voice (see Habler et al., 2019; Woods, 2018) and relatively obvious despite their immateriality. However, as we pointed to in our introduction, AI is burgeoning. Smaller corporations everywhere are beginning to 'employ' virtual assistants in proprietary spaces in more discreet ways. Wells Fargo is one example. Its banking assistant *Fargo*, leverages Google Cloud's AI (Wells Fargo Newsroom, 2022). *Fargo* uses a simple, clean, clear aesthetic for its visual representation; essentially a logotype on an amorphous, muted purple background. In the visual balance between Modernist minimalism and science fiction amorphism, Fargo is leaning to the former. This is remarkable when set against the parent brand's historical allusions—its logotype is comprised of overtly

Victorian letterforms—to its well-known birth in the California Gold Rush.

The marketing copywriting is gently persuasive, and ends in an introduction to the assistant as if it is a person. This doubles the rhetorical flourish as a solution to bank customers' problems:

> *At Wells Fargo, we want to bring the same smart, intuitive experience to banking. We want to be with our customers at all times, ready when they need us, seamlessly working in the background to empower them to bank smarter. Meet Fargo.* (Moore, 2022)

In light of our earlier comment about virtual assistants' Smartspeakers also being listeners, "[s]eamlessly working in the background" is a telling phrase. One is always being urged to read the fineprint, especially with regard to contracts, and terms and conditions. If simplicity and clarity are used to justify a lack of information in UI, the same reasoning can be applied to terms and conditions, and disclosure statements of Apps as well as other digital products to make these short, comprehensible, and truthful. It has been applied at other banks (which also use AI), such as Bankwest in Australia whose terms and conditions have been re-imagined as a brief and colourful comic strip.

Aesthetics of Autonomous Vehicles

As with the Echo, which appears to take its aesthetic cues from Dieter Rams's principles of good design (de Jong et al., 2017) the designs around autonomous vehicles (AVs) and robots appear to be reduced to minimal forms. Similar to the virtual assistants however, autonomous vehicle tech is also networked and remote, more than it is present and physical. Again, the visual design does little to reveal this arrangement and much to conceal it. We explore the visual aesthetics around this controversial industry because of the way it regards 'users'. The AV context is telling and significant to AI-enabled tech generally because in AV business models, the human user is like a package of goods to be conveyed efficiently from one point to another. "The present is understood as the future in embryo" (Barbrook, 2007, p. 151), and so what works for AVs may be inherited by other sectors. In some of the verbal rhetoric below one can find references to people and goods in the same phrase, to this effect, for example, "Waymo's mission is to make it safe and easy for people and things to get where they're going". Also, in the AV sector, the issues of trust that have so far been identified are intensified because these issues have real implications for people's immediate physical safety. In terms of legality and significance this is a telling AI industry. These aspects are foregrounded in the corporate verbal rhetoric. For both virtual assistants and AVs, it could be argued that the artefact is a tool for a different user, the owners and shareholders of the IP. The consumer holds only a surface relationship as a 'user', but is in fact part of the data that enables the vehicle. In fact, the user is a component that the entire system needs in order to function. In this regard AVs are an appropriate symbol of what AI-enabled brands communicate to the public.

Helmann (2017, p. 56) said the target audience must be capable of deciphering corporate identity, which begs the question, with regard to AVs: is the general public the audience? Is the design appealing instead from the perspective of business-to-business (B2B)? Rebecca Fanin (2022), writing for CNBC, suggested that companies invested in AV technologies are looking into delivery and ride-hailing rather than the consumer market. Further, Min-hyuk Lee's (2021) thesis on design opportunities in the AV sector stated, "most current [AV] models focus on optimizing system-wide operations rather than on the user side" (p. 6). ZOOX press releases, for example, emphasise passenger benefits, while ZOOX itself is an Amazon subsidiary. Amazon, no doubt, is focused on benefits to delivery processes that AVs may afford; whether that includes delivering people or goods. Safety and efficiency (not just to assure the markets, but to improve vehicles driven by humans) are touted as advantages of this would-be, driverless future. From the companies' points of view, these benefits must be exploited, on the one hand to meet community standards and legal requirements, and on the other to maximise share prices during financially risky research and development phases. In any case, a defining aspect of fully autonomous vehicles is the literal removal of the principle, historical user, the driver. The driver interface is then a pointless set of controls in the absence of the driver themselves.

Forbes, a business magazine website, was consulted to assess the market leadership of the AV sector (Gordon, 2021). Accordingly, here the graphic design and promotional copy of brands topping that list are examined. The following logos seem strangely bereft of significance as if they are, weirdly, logos from the future for which no frame of reference yet exists. Though brands of real companies, they are yet mostly unknown by the general public, as if seen in a science fiction film. In any case, companies invested in AV technologies are looking into delivery and ride-hailing before appealing to retail consumers. The significance of the logos will only be realised if their company visions and missions are realised.

> *User-logo interaction is necessary to understand these signs and requires semiosis processes anchored to the socio-cultural system itself (Vidales-Gonzáles, 2020) [...] In this sense, corporate semiotics are incorporated into culture according to a palimpsestic procedure that allows recollections to accumulate in layers of memory, giving them meaning at all times.* (Llorente-Barroso et al., 2021, p. 348)

Time will tell.

As mentioned, our method of quoting corporate promotional copy is borrowed from Werning (2019) in order that "the texts can be used to contextualise the accompanying images and can help in 'looking through' their purpose" (p. 432).

Amazon (ZOOX)

Amazon's autonomous vehicle, Zoox, "isn't an updated car—it's a whole new form of transportation" (zoox.com, n.d.). At the website, the reader is confronted with the following text: 'The future is for riders'. An implication being, it is no longer for drivers. Indeed, this is confirmed by text when one clicks on 'the vehicle page'. The ZOOX car itself appears to be a small, futuristic, concept car, and a little like an old-fashioned carriage at the same time, in that it is not clear which end of the vehicle points forward. As it transpires, this *is* a case of form following function; the ZOOX can travel in either direction. A closer look reveals there is also no driver or driving position, further precluding a front or rear end. Copy on the site talks up manoeuvrability and mobility, specifically, the benefits to the individual (not necessarily humanity in general as with some of ZOOX's competitors):

> *Mobility designed around you. We're reinventing personal transportation— making the future safer, cleaner, and more enjoyable for everyone. It's on-demand autonomous ride-hailing. Let Zoox handle the traffic, while you enjoy a smooth, relaxing ride in a spacious cabin designed around you.* (retrieved February 2023)

Of the AV visual communication investigated here, ZOOX upholds the comparison with science fiction cinema visual aesthetics most strongly. Christian Grajewski, an industrial designer of the ZOOX, openly acknowledges the influence of futurist Syd Mead, and also works in science fiction himself (as author/artist of the art book *Explorer*). A press release picture of the ZOOX driverless carriage even borrows the particular palette and chiaroscuro lighting from Syd Mead's artist impressions of the concept car, *Sentinel*.

In the ZOOX corporate identity, the logo has each of the brand name's four letters in opposite corners, much like the proposed configuration of the ZOOX coach-style AV passenger seating. In this way it begins to push the logotype towards becoming an icotype where "a process of repetitive confrontation with the logo is linked to an iconization process, that is, the word or the acronym is gradually perceived as an icon through the systematic and repeated use" (Heilbrunn, 1997, p. 178). These rhetorical devices suggest ZOOX is positioning itself more publicly than some of the following brands. Heilbrunn says a logo can have an 'impressive' or 'conative' function, and might also represent "the ideal consumer so that the consumer can identify himself with the image projected in the logo." (p. 177).

Waymo

Formerly the Google self-drive project uses "[t]he world's most experienced driver™" as its catch phrase, emphasising that the best AI learning comes from harvesting the most data. Waymo typifies the clean, Modernist, ready-to-go aesthetic, right down to a sleek, white car. The copy on the website reads, "Waymo's mission is to make it safe and easy for people and things to get where they're going. From moving people to moving goods, we're taking autonomous driving to new places. Our mission is big and our work has the potential to transform lives" (Waymo, n.d.). Note the choice of 'transform', which at face value, has no good nor bad connotations. In terms of the industrial design, the vehicles themselves appear to be existing designs from other manufacturers (e.g. Chrysler) with Waymo hardware modifications. A brief exception was the *Firefly* car during two years of the company's history. This design embodied a kindchenschema (Lorenz, 1943) visual aesthetic: Previous research (Lorenz, 1943; Ngai, 2005, pp. 816, 827; Marcus et al., 2017, pp. 64–65) has suggested that artefacts with rounded and soft aesthetics are associated with cuteness, and are thought to evoke a motivation to care or empathise. In addition, Thibault and Heljakka (2018) have proposed 'toyification': the deliberate attempt to design products according to toy aesthetics in order to make them more appealing (p. 5), and "some companies have been working to make their products more toy-like to appeal to people who might be feeling overwhelmed otherwise" (Ihamäki & Heljakka, 2019).

The Waymo icotype logo is a visual paradox: it suggests a physical presence in its allusion to spiral cabling (perhaps depicting the electrical link used to charge the vehicles), but this physical presence is denied through the flat treatment of the shapes. The flattening resembles the flat icons of contemporary UI. The rhetorical reference may be to connect the brand to digital interaction generally and ride-share apps more specifically. The colours in the logo are something of a visual surprise. This is a combination that is atypical of contemporary corporate identity design, perhaps imagining a *future palette*. For the authors, this colour combination brings to mind nothing so much as 1980s parachute silk jumpsuits! This may be a function of the popularity of 80s-themed science fiction available on contemporary streaming services (*Stranger Things*, *Paper Girls*), yet may also be a visual coincidence.

Here, top brands of AV (according to Forbes) have been explored, and essentially the same classes of visual aesthetics were encountered. The Modernist appearance of artefacts and visual communication is the prevalent one, with the engineering style or characteristics less evident. One of these latter is *Refraction AI*. Their corporate copy states, "[w]e deploy robotic platforms for providing safe and scalable last mile goods delivery in urban areas". As with PonyAI, the AI is foregrounded in the name. Unlike Pony, with its 'toyified' name and graphic design, the name *Refraction* suggests science and technology, in particular, optics. Given that much of the press around AVs has focused on what the vehicles need to visually assess, at speed, in their environments, this emphasis makes sense. The visual design of the logo accords with this approach. Suggesting the sensors of a digital camera, it comprises angular, identically sized fractals, geometrically located in a field of analogous colours implying nature, the outdoors, moving through a landscape at speed. A path through this blurred landscape outlines the *R* initial of the company name. The logo seems to be among the few in the AI-enabled context that openly acknowledge 'high-tech' and 'complexity'.

Conclusion: Who Benefits, Who Profits from AI?

Self-driving cars can reduce collisions and traffic congestion, natural language processing technology can improve communication and accessibility, additionally AI-powered medical equipment can improve patient care and diagnostics. AI holds incredible promises and unprecedented opportunities for businesses, organisations, and society. There are increasing numbers of businesses implementing AI in their business models and processes to increase efficiency, grow revenue, reduce operational cost, and improve customer experience (IBM Corporation, 2022). But harnessing the power of AI comes with risks and responsibilities surrounding ethics, legality, and social implications.

With its machine-learning algorithms, AI's identification of patterns is the driving force of improving efficiency and productivity of businesses making critical decisions. However, processing-skewed data programmed by humans leads to critical bias and having irrelevant parameters that can harm accuracy and strengthen racism, sexism, and other inequalities (Akert et al., 2021; Al-Khulaidy & Kavak, 2023). The process and algorithms used by AI to process and analyse data can be considered a trade secret and they are protected under the law. The type of information being gathered by AI (e.g. personal information) and how the information is gathered further intensify the importance of transparency in AI. AI systems deeply embedded in a range of technologies, the web for example, retrieve data about users seamlessly and through their interconnected web of devices, sharing information with the goal of assisting humans. Transformation of intimate personal information into commercial data to be utilised as a means of supporting humans and improved UX poses a real threat to people that includes vulnerabilities from the perspectives of cyber-attacks and identity-theft, which are becoming all too frequent (Babuta et al., 2020).

AI-enabled product and service providers are aware of the need to assuage fears and engender trust through their public communication channels: the graphic design of corporate identity, product design and copywriting, on websites and in press releases. A common visual technique is to deploy simple forms, whether physical (in smartspeaker design) or visual (logo design for autonomous vehicles) while the verbal rhetoric is around safety and public benefit. Here it is argued that the associated visual aesthetics move in two directions: towards simplified, Modernist forms (i.e., Mr Fusion engine); and less refined forms with an engineering aesthetic (associated here with Johnny 5). As observed, the current era is marked by a period of continuous experimentation and development within the field of AI, wherein humans are the subjects of ongoing refinement and optimisation of AI technology.

It can be argued that the two visual design approaches described above enable AI developers to declare the real level of complexity more openly behind the scenes of contemporary and future UI. One is for the corporate visual design to adopt more of the engineering aesthetic rather than the Modernist aesthetic. The latter belongs to a long-outmoded context. The Refraction AI logo seems to be an appropriate example, and one of the few in the AI-enabled context that openly acknowledges the high-tech and complex systems it represents. The second approach suggested here, if ventures insist on Modernist simplicity for its readability for users, is to use Modernist design philosophy (not just Modernist aesthetics) and extend simplicity into the disclosure of AI systems complexity: to openly declare to users, in a simple, clear, succinct and engaging way, the terms and conditions of interacting, the destinations of the user's information, and who benefits from the interactions. The aforementioned Bankwest terms and conditions comic is a useful model trending in this direction. Hauser et al. (2023) warn of the widening gap between aesthetic and ethics in digital interactions. These are two visual design steps that might shorten that gap.

With its impact on perceived user-control, trust and transparency, ethical considerations must be integrated into the design process to ensure that the aesthetics of AI-powered devices are not only pleasing but also ethically sound. If simplicity and clarity are used to justify a lack of information in UI, perhaps the same reasoning can be applied to terms and conditions, and disclosure statements of Apps and other digital products to make them short, comprehensible, and truthful. The Bankwest terms and conditions are an early model moving towards this direction. Such an approach will ensure that the design of AI systems is not solely focused on improving the UX and shareholders' dividends but also considers the broader social and ethical implications of the technology.

The lack of regulations in AI's ecosystem and lack of accountability of businesses implementing AI systems raises questions around the ownership of AI, including who stands to profit from its successes. Unfortunately, the development of responsible and trustworthy AI is largely at the discretion of the AI system's developers (O'Keefe et al., 2020). The effort to address issues of bias, fairness, and accountability in AI systems requires a collaborative effort from various stakeholders, including developers, regulators, designers, scholars and users. Building trust in AI systems through transparency and accountability is crucial for their widespread adoption and long-term success. To achieve this, there is a need for clear ethical and regulatory frameworks that can govern the development and deployment of AI systems. Such frameworks should ensure that AI systems are designed and implemented in a way that is transparent, accountable, and respects individual privacy and rights. By doing so, a future may be created where AI is trustworthy and serves the needs of all stakeholders.

REFERENCES

Aghion, P., Jones, B. F., & Jones, C. (2019). Artificial Intelligence and economic growth. In A. Agrawal, J. Gans, & A. Goldfarb (Eds.), *The economics of artificial intelligence—An agenda*. National Bureau of Economic Research. https://web.stanford.edu/~chadj/AJJ-AIandGrowth.pdf

Akter, S., McCarthy, G., Sajib, S., Michael, K., Dwivedi, Y. K., D'Ambra, J., & Ning Shen, K. (2021). Algorithmic bias in data-driven innovation in the age of AI. *International Journal of Information Management, 60*, 102387. https://doi.org/10.1016/j.ijinfomgt.2021.102387

Babuta, A., Oswald, M., & Janjeva, A. (2020). *Artificial intelligence and UK national security: Policy considerations*. Royal United Services Institute for Defence and Security Studies. https://static.rusi.org/ai_national_security_final_web_version.pdf

Balasubramaniam, N., Kauppinen, M., Rannisto, A., Hiekkanen, K., & Kujala, S. (2023). Transparency and explainability of AI systems: From ethical guidelines to requirements. *Information and Software Technology, 159*, 107197. https://doi.org/10.1016/j.infsof.2023.107197

Barteit, S., Lanfermann, L., Bärnighausen, T., Neuhann, F., & Beiersmann, C. (2021). Augmented, mixed, and virtual reality-based head-mounted devices for medical education. *Systematic Review JMIR Serious Games, 9*(3). https://doi.org/10.2196/29080

Bandura, A. (1989). Regulation of cognitive processes through perceived self-efficacy. *Developmental Psychology, 25*(5), 729–735. https://doi.org/10.1037/0012-1649.25.5.729

Barbrook, R. (2007). New York prophecies: The imaginary future of artificial intelligence. *Science as Culture, 16*(2), 151–167. https://doi.org/10.1080/09505430701369027

Barry, A. M. (2006). Perceptual aesthetics: Transcendent emotion, neurological image. *Visual Communication Quarterly, 13*(3), 134–151. https://doi.org/10.1207/s15551407vcq1303_2

Bevan, N. (2001). International standards for HCI and usability. *International Journal of Human-Computer Studies, 55*(4), 533–552. https://doi.org/10.1006/ijhc.2001.0483

Bitkina, O., Jeong, H., Lee, B., Park, J., Park, J., & Kim, H. (2020). Perceived trust in artificial intelligence technologies: A preliminary study. *Human Factors and Ergonomics in Manufacturing & Service Industries, 30*(4), 282–290. https://doi.org/10.1002/hfm.20839

Chérif, E., & Lemoine, J.-F. (2019). Anthropomorphic virtual assistants and the reactions of internet users: An experiment on the assistant's voice. *Recherche et Applications en Marketing (english Edition), 34*(1), 28–47. https://doi.org/10.1177/2051570719829432

Choung, H., David, P., & Ross, A. (2022). Trust in AI and its role in the acceptance of AI technologies. *International Journal of Human-Computer Interaction, 39*(9), 1727–1739. https://doi.org/10.1080/10447318.2022.2050543

Coeckelbergh, M. (2015). The tragedy of the master: Automation, vulnerability, and distance. *Ethics and Information Technology, 17*(3), 219–229. https://doi.org/10.1007/s10676-015-9377-6

Crawford, K. (2021). *The atlas of AI: power, politics, and the planetary costs of artificial intelligence.*

de Jong, C. W., Klemp, K., Mattie, E., & Goodwin, D. (2017). *Ten principles for good design: Dieter Rams: The Jorrit Maan collection.* Prestel.

Dwivedi, Y. K., Ismagilova, E., Hughes, D. L., Carlson, J., Filieri, R., Jacobson, J., Jain, V., et al. (2021). Setting the future of digital and social media marketing research: Perspectives and research propositions. *International Journal of Information Management, 59*, 102168. https://doi.org/10.1016/j.ijinfomgt.2020.102168

Fanin, R. (2022). *Where the billions spent on autonomous vehicles by U.S. and Chinese giants is heading.* https://www.cnbc.com/2022/05/21/why-the-first-autonomous-vehicles-winners-wont-be-in-your-driveway.html

Folkmann, M. N. (2020). Post-material aesthetics: A conceptualization of digital objects. *The Design Journal, 23*(2), 219–237.

Fröhlich, P., Baldauf, M., Meneweger, T., Erickson, I., Tscheligi, M., Gable, T., ... & Paternò, F. (2019, May). Everyday automation experience: non-expert users encountering ubiquitous automated systems. In *Extended abstracts of the 2019 CHI conference on human factors in computing systems* (pp. 1–8).

Fu, Y., Yan H., & Sundstedt, V. (2022). A systematic literature review of virtual, augmented, and mixed reality game applications in healthcare. *ACM Transactions on Computing for Healthcare, 3*(2). https://doi.org/10.1145/347 2303

Garrett, L. K. (2006). *Beyond the Wall: An investigation into the relationship between industrial design and science fiction* (Doctoral dissertation). Massey University.

Gordon, C. (2021). Driverless car market leaders innovating: The transportation industry. *Forbes.* https://www.forbes.com/sites/cindygordon/2021/12/29/driverless-car-market-leaders-innovating-the-transportation-industry/

Gorman, C. (Ed.), (2003). *The industrial design reader.* Skyhorse Publishing Inc.

Habler, F., Schwind, V., & Henze, N. (2019). Effects of smart virtual assistants' gender and language. In *Proceedings of Mensch und Computer* (pp. 469–473). https://dl.acm.org/doi/10.1145/3340764.3344441

Hassenzahl, M. (2004). The interplay of beauty, goodness, and usability in interactive products. *Human-Computer Interaction, 19*(4), 319–349. https://doi.org/10.1207/s15327051hci1904_2

Hassenzahl, M., & Monk, A. (2010). The inference of perceived usability from beauty. *Human-Computer Interaction, 25*(3), 235–260. https://doi.org/10.1080/07370024.2010.500139

Hauser, S., Redström, J., & Wiltse, H. (2023). The widening rift between aesthetics and ethics in the design of computational things. *AI & Society, 38*(1), 227–243. https://link.springer.com/article/10.1007/s00146-021-01279-w

Heilbrunn, B. (1997). Representation and legitimacy: A semiotic approach to the logo. *Approaches to Semiotics, 127*, 175–190.

Helmann, E. (2017). *Rhetoric of logos: A primer of visual language.* Niggli.

IBM Corporation. (2022). *IBM global AI adoption index 2022: New research commissioned by IBM in partnership with Morning Consult.* I. Corporation. https://www.ibm.com/downloads/cas/GVAGA3JP

Ihamäki, P., & Heljakka, K. (2019). The internet of toys, connectedness and character-based play in early education. In *Proceedings of the Future Technologies Conference (FTC) 2018, 1* (pp. 1079–1096). Springer. https://link.springer.com/chapter/10.1007/978-3-030-02686-8_80

Issa, T., & Isaias, P. (2022). Usability and human–computer interaction (HCI). In T. Issa & P. Isaias (Eds.), *Sustainable design: HCI, usability and environmental concerns* (pp. 23–40). Springer. https://doi.org/10.1007/978-1-4471-7513-1_2

Lee, M. H. (2021). *Shared autonomous vehicles: User expectations and opportunities for design* (Masters Thesis). Ulsan National Institute of Science and Technology. https://scholarworks.unist.ac.kr/handle/201301/53773

Lekaj, L., Lordan K., & Mario F. (2023). Research on attitudes toward minimalistic design in marketing communications. *International Journal of Multidisciplinarity in Business and Science*, 9(14), 5–4. https://doi.org/10.56321/ijmbs.9.14.5.

Lindgaard, G., Dudek, C., Sen, D., Sumegi, L., & Noonan, P. (2011). An exploration of relations between visual appeal, trustworthiness and perceived usability of homepages. *ACM Transactions on Computer-Human Interaction (TOCHI)*, 18(1), 1–30. https://doi.org/10.1145/1959022.1959023

Llorente-Barroso, C., Kolotouchkina, O., & García-García, F. (2021). The meaning of the logo from its semiotic construction and its reliance on new formats of digital communication: The case of Apple. *Revista Latina De Comunicacion Social*, 79, 333–356. https://doi.org/10.4185/RLCS-2021-1529

Lorenz, K. (1943). Die angeborenen Formen möglicher Erfahrung [The innate forms of potential experience]. *Zeitschrift für Tierpsychologie*, 5, 233–519.

Lungu, A. J., Wout Swinkels, L. C., Puxun, T., Egger, J., & Xiaojun, C. (2021). A review on the applications of virtual reality, augmented reality and mixed reality in surgical simulation: An extension to different kinds of surgery. *Expert Review of Medical Devices*, 18(1), 47–62. https://doi.org/10.1080/17434440.2021.1860750

Lockey, S., Gillespie, N., & Curtis, C. (2020). *Trust in Artificial Intelligence: Australian insights*. The University of Queensland and KPMG Australia. https://doi.org/10.14264/b32f129.

Marcus, A., Kurosu, M., Ma, X., & Hashizume, A. (2017). *Cuteness engineering: Designing adorable products and services*. Springer.

McCall, H., & Pantoja, C. (2017). *Hey Siri...*, https://student.hca.westernsydney.edu.au/units/wp_102264/wp-content/uploads/2017/10/hannah_mccall_cindy_pantoja_siri_H.pdf

McCarthy, J., & Wright, P. (2004). *Technology as experience*. The MIT Press.

Mead, S. (1987). Sentinel II: Steel couture, Syd Mead, futurist. *(No Title)*.

Moore, M. (2022). *A banking concierge in your pocket: Inside Wells Fargo's digital-first reinvention*. Google Cloud. https://cloud.google.com/blog/transform/reinventing-personal-finance-customer-experience-wells-fargo-fargo-chat

Nemitz, P. (2018). Constitutional democracy and technology in the age of artificial intelligence. *Philosophical Transactions of the Royal Society A: Mathematical, Physical and Engineering Sciences*, 376(2133), 20180089.

Ngai, S. (2005). The cuteness of the avant-garde. *Critical Inquiry*, 31(4), 811–847.

Nielsen, J., & Tahir, M. (2002). *Homepage usability: 50 websites deconstructed*. New Riders.

Norman, D. A. (2011). *Living with complexity*. MIT Press.

Moran, K. (2015). *The characteristics of minimalism in web design.* https://www.nngroup.com/articles/characteristics-minimalism/

O'Keefe, C., Cihon, P., Garfinkel, B., Flynn, C., Leung, J., & Dafoe, A. (2020). The windfall clause: Distributing the benefits of AI for the common good. In *Proceedings of the AAAI/ACM Conference on AI, Ethics, and Society* (pp. 327–331), ACM. https://doi.org/10.1145/3375627.3375842

Pitardi, V., & Marriott, H. R. (2021). Alexa, she's not human but... Unveiling the drivers of consumers' trust in voice-based artificial intelligence, *Psychology & Marketing, 38*(4), 626–642. https://doi.org/10.1002/mar.21457.

Redström, J., & Wiltse, H. (2019, June 18–21). Changing things: Innovation through design philosophy. In *Academy for design innovation management conference 2019: Research perspectives in the era of transformations.* Loughborough University.

Roozendaal, J., Johansson, E., Joost de Winter, D. A., & Petermeijer, S. (2021). Haptic lane-keeping assistance for truck driving: A test track study. *Human Factors, 63*(8), 1380–1395. https://doi.org/10.1177/0018720820928622

Rousi, R., & Silvennoinen, J. (2018). Simplicity and the art of something more: A cognitive-semiotic approach to simplicity and complexity in human-technology interaction and design experience. *Human Technology, 14*(1).

Russell, S., & Norvig, P. (2020). *Artificial Intelligence a modern approach* (4th ed.). Pearson.

Sartori, L., & Theodorou, A. (2022). A sociotechnical perspective for the future of AI: Narratives, inequalities, and human control. *Ethics and Information Technology, 24*(1), 4. https://doi.org/10.1007/s10676-022-09624-3

Schmitt, B. H., Simonson, A., & Marcus, J. (1995). Managing corporate image and identity. *Long Range Planning, 28*(5), 82–92. https://doi.org/10.1016/0024-6301(95)00040-P

Schneller, A. (2015). Design rhetoric: Studying the effects of designed objects. *Nature and Culture, 10*(3), 333–356.

Selle, G. (2014). Ding, Halb-Ding, Nicht-Ding, In-Ding, Über-Ding. Über sichtbares und unsichtbares design. In *Symptom design* (pp. 39–67). Transcript. https://doi.org/10.1515/transcript.9783839422687.39

Slota, S. (2020). Designing across distributed agency: Values, participatory design and building socially responsible AI. *Good Systems-Published Research.* https://doi.org/10.21428/93b2c832.a9b1ae03

Stine, A. A. K., & Kavak, H. (2023). Bias, fairness, and assurance in AI: overview and synthesis. In F. A. Batarseh & L. J. Freeman (Eds.), *AI Assurance* (pp. 125–151). Academic Press. https://doi.org/10.1016/B978-0-32-391919-7.00016-0

Su, Y. -S., & Hsia, J. -H. (2022). An evaluation model of smart speaker design. In *The Routledge companion to technology management* (pp. 141–156). Routledge.

Thibault, M., & Heljakka, K. (2018). Toyification. A conceptual statement. In *8th International Toy Research Association World Conference*. https://sorbonne-paris-nord.hal.science/hal-02083004/

Tractinsky, N. (2004). Toward the study of aesthetics in information technology. *ICIS 2004 Proceedings*. 62. https://aisel.aisnet.org/icis2004/62/

Turing, A. (1950). Computing machinery and intelligence. *Mind, 59*(236), 433–460. http://www.jstor.org/stable/2251299

Urbano, I. C. V. P., Vieira Guerreiro, J. P., Aleixo, H. M., & Nicolau, A. (2022). From Skeuomorphism to flat design: Age-related differences in performance and aesthetic perceptions. *Behaviour & Information Technology, 41*(3), 452–467. https://doi.org/10.1080/0144929X.2020.1814867

Vössing, M., Kühl, N., Lind, M., & Satzger, G. (2022). Designing transparency for effective human-AI collaboration. *Information Systems Frontiers, 24*(3), 877–895. https://doi.org/10.1007/s10796-022-10284-3

Waymo. (n.d.). *Seeing the road ahead*. https://waymo.com/about/

Wells Fargo. (2022). *Wells Fargo's new virtual assistant, Fargo, to be powered by Google Cloud AI*. https://newsroom.wf.com/English/news-releases/news-release-details/2022/Wells-Fargos-New-Virtual-Assistant-Fargo-to-Be-Powered-by-Google-Cloud-AI/default.aspx

Werning, S. (2019). Walk-Through corporate aesthetics: Design affordances in tech workspaces. *Open Cultural Studies, 3*(1), 428–441.

Woods, H. S. (2018). Asking more of Siri and Alexa: Feminine persona in service of surveillance capitalism. *Critical Studies in Media Communication, 35*(4), 334–349.

Zoox. (n.d.). *Built from the ground up*. https://zoox.com/

CHAPTER 14

The Cultivated Practices of Text-to-Image Generation

Jonas Oppenlaender

INTRODUCTION

Generative artificial intelligence (AI) has taken the world by storm. Using deep generative models, anybody can conjure up digital information from short descriptive text prompts. Text-to-image synthesis, in particular, has become a popular means for generating digital images (Crowson et al., 2022; Rombach et al., 2022). Millions of people use generative systems and text-to-image services available online, such as Midjourney,[1] Stable Diffusion (Rombach et al., 2021), and DALL-E 2 (Ramesh et al., 2022), both for professional and recreational uses. With this powerful generative technology at our fingertips, humankind is ushering into a new era—an era in which visual imagery no longer necessarily reflects the effort put into creating the imagery (Oppenlaender, 2022).

This chapter first gives an overview of the key technical developments that enabled a co-creative ecosystem around text-to-image generation to

[1] https://www.midjourney.com.

J. Oppenlaender (✉)
University of Oulu, Oulu, Finland
e-mail: oppenlaenderj@acm.org

© The Author(s) 2024
R. Rousi et al. (eds.), *Humane Autonomous Technology*,
https://doi.org/10.1007/978-3-031-66528-8_14

rapidly emerge and expand in 2021 and 2022. This is followed by a high-level description of key elements in the ecosystem and its practices. Focus is placed on prompt engineering, a method and creative practice that has proven useful in a broad set of application areas, but has been particularly embraced by the community of text-to-image generation practitioners. It is then argued that the creative online ecosystem constitutes an intelligent system of its own—a system that both enables yet also potentially limits the creative potential of future generations of humans and machine learning (ML) systems. In the chapter, the author discusses some potential risks and dangers of cultivating this co-creative ecosystem. Risks include: the threat of bias due to Western ways of *seeing* that are encoded in training data; quality degradation due to synthetic data being used for training future generative systems; and the potential long-term effects of text-to-image generation on people's creativity, imagination, and development.

Background on Text-to-Image Generation

The history of computer-generated art and "generative art" (Boden & Edmonds, 2009; Galanter, 2016) goes back to the first experiments with AI (Cohen, 1979). Looking back, the first attempts to synthesise images from text were humbling, but already showed great promise. The synthetic images presented by Mansimov et al. (2016), for instance, were tiny in size (e.g., a 32 × 32 pixel resolution image of a "green school bus"). Today, text-guided synthesis of images has made a giant leap towards becoming a mainstream phenomenon (Olson, 2022). Within less than a year, Midjourney's Discord community has grown to over 10 million users, making Midjourney the largest Discord community to date.[2] Besides more powerful graphics processing units (GPUs), a few particular important inventions advanced the field of text-to-image generation. This section gives a brief overview aiming to explain the recent technical developments that enabled and fuelled the meteoric rise of text-to-image generation.

The invention of Generative Adversarial Networks (GANs) (Goodfellow et al., 2014) was a watershed moment in advancing image generation. GANs are a type of deep learning architecture consisting of two

---

[2] See https://discord.com/servers.

antagonistic parts: a generator and discriminator. During training, the generator presents the discriminator with synthetic images. The discriminator judges these images and the process is iteratively continued until the discriminator cannot tell the synthetic images apart from real images, such as the images utilised in the training data. Using a text-conditioned GAN architecture, Reed et al. (2016) pioneered the approach of synthesising images from text. The approach was extended in January 2021 with OpenAI's DALL-E (Ramesh et al., 2022), a neural network trained on text-image pairs. DALL-E was able to synthesise images from text captions for a wide range of concepts expressible in natural language. In parallel, OpenAI presented CLIP (Radford et al., 2021), a contrastive language-vision model originally conceived for the task of classifying images. CLIP was trained on a large corpus of image pairs and text scraped from the World Wide Web. Due to the large size of its training data, the CLIP model has learned a wide variety of visual concepts from natural language supervision. This proved useful for tasks that visually associate language with images. The CLIP model and its training corpus were, however, not released by OpenAI, which spurred efforts to replicate CLIP and its training data.

It was the release of the weights of CLIP in January 2021 that resulted in immense technical progress in the field of AI-generated imagery. The CLIP weights found their first significant application in an image generation system called "The Big Sleep" by Ryan Murdoch (Colton et al., 2021; Murdock & Wang, 2021). In Murdoch's architecture, the generator is a model called BigGAN, and CLIP is used to guide the generation process with text. This inspired Katherine Crowson to connect a more powerful neural network (VQGAN) with CLIP (Crowson et al., 2022). The VQGAN–CLIP architecture became very popular in 2021 and instrumental to advancing the emerging field of text-to-image generation (Crowson et al., 2022). The source code of VQGAN–CLIP was available online, and many generative architectures for synthesising digital images and artworks have since been developed based on the work by Murdoch and Crowson. GANs were later superseded by diffusion-based systems (Dhariwal & Nichol, 2021). Diffusion models are a class of ML models that learn through the introduction of incremental noise into the training data, with the objective of subsequently reversing the noising process and restoring the original image. Once trained, these models are capable of utilising the learned denoising methods to synthesise novel, noise-free images from random input.

Today, practitioners can choose from a large variety of diffusion-based generative systems. Some of these systems are available as open source, such as Stable Diffusion (Rombach et al., 2021), others are available as online services, such as Midjourney and DALL-E 2. Due to the low barrier of entry and high ease-of-use, Colab notebooks contributed to a democratisation of digital art production. Anybody can create digital images and artworks with text-to-image generation systems (Oppenlaender, 2022), which establishes parallels of the novel technology with photography.

TEXT-TO-IMAGE GENERATION AS THE NEW PHOTOGRAPHY

As a novel phenomenon and emerging technology, text-to-image generation—and generative AI in general—can be compared to past disruptive and transformative technologies. For instance, the invention of Gutenberg's printing press reduced the cost of printing, revolutionised the spread of knowledge, and had a profound impact on human development (Eisenstein, 1980). Generative AI could have similar transformative effects on society. This section briefly discusses the parallels between the invention of photography and text-to-image generation, followed by some current criticisms of text-to-image generation.

Parallels Between Photography and Text-to-Image Generation

When photography was invented, critics argued against the new technology. Photography's early critics saw the novel technology not as a new medium for creative expression, but as a direct threat to the livelihood of artists. As Hertzmann (2018) points out, "[m]any artists were dismissive of photography, and saw it as a threat to 'real art'". For instance, upon seeing a demonstration of the daguerreotype technique, the painter Paul Delaroche declared: "From today, painting is dead!" (Hertzmann, 2018). Photography, as a mechanical way of capturing reality, was seen in direct competition to realism, an art style that aims to depict nature accurately and in great detail. But over the years, photography has evolved into a medium for artistic expression, a medium that allows for the creation of unique images that were previously unimaginable. Ultimately, the invention of photography caused painters to innovate their craft, moving from realism to abstraction (Hertzmann, 2018, 2020).

Text-to-image generation, as a novel artistic medium (Marche, 2022), offers equally exciting new possibilities for artistic expression and creativity. The emerging technology has the potential to revolutionise the way we work creatively and may fundamentally impact our relationship to digital media. In many ways, text-to-image generation is the new photography, democratising access to creative expression that was previously limited to highly talented creative individuals. Text-to-image generation, however, also poses many complex socio-technical challenges with no easy solution. While it is undeniable that AI algorithms can generate fascinating images, it is important to consider the potential criticisms of this technology.

Criticisms About Text-to-Image Generation

Today's concerns and criticisms about text-to-image generation resemble the ones that were being raised when photography was invented (Hertzmann, 2018). This chapter summarises some of the key concerns and criticisms about generative AI, and text-to-image generation in particular. As we continue to develop and explore generative AI, it will be crucial to address these concerns and ensure that the technology is used in a responsible and ethical way.

One of the main criticisms about text-to-image generation is that it threatens to automate and replace human cognitive and creative work. Generative AI is much faster and cheaper than human work, and it does not require much skill and effort to prompt generative systems (Oppenlaender, 2022). This could lead companies to stop hiring or contracting knowledge workers and creatives, such as illustrators, designers, and artists (Mok, 2023; Oppenlaender et al., 2023).

Another concern brought forth against the technology of text-to-image generation is that it is built on top of centuries of human-made creative works. Generative AI is data hungry (Goldberg, 2023). Whether it is literature used for training large language models or images scraped from the Web, generative models are trained on vast datasets scraped from the World Wide Web. This "Web-scale" data enables generative models to learn patterns in the data. Critics of the technology argue that there are insurmountable legal issues concerning the use of the training data. Proponents, on the other hand, argue that using scraped training data falls under the U.S. fair use doctrine (Justia, 2022). The fair use doctrine has opened a loophole in which commercial organisations are funding development efforts in non-profit organisations, which are allowed to train models and scrape data under fair and academic use.

These commercial organisations are essentially using non-profit organisations as a shield from litigation and have been accused of data laundering (Baio, 2022) and deceptive trade practices (Justia, 2023). For instance, Microsoft has received criticism for training its Co-Pilot system on GitHub (Kuhn, 2022). GitHub is a large repository of software licensed under various terms, including copyleft and MIT licenses. These licenses mandate that any modifications and derivatives of the software must be free or distributed under the same license, respectively. Co-Pilot cannot—by design—guarantee that the license is adhered to and due to the opaqueness of the neural network, it is not possible to trace the generated information to its source. Similar concerns were raised about MegaFace, a large database of facial images scraped from Flickr (Nech & Kemelmacher-Shlizerman, 2017). The database was used by numerous commercial organisations to advance the state of facial recognition for various purposes, including surveillance (Harvey & LaPlace, 2021). Legal battles between generative AI firms and content creators, such as the class action lawsuits against Microsoft and OpenAI (Vincent, 2022b) and the lawsuit of Getty Images against Stability AI (Justia, 2023), are also battles about the future direction of the creative industries.

The emergence of generative AI as a novel and impactful technology is expected to significantly disrupt the current status quo, creating frictions and challenges in relation to existing societal norms and policy frameworks (Toews, 2022). Generative AI is a direct threat to some business models. For instance, Google's search engine business may become affected if consumer preferences shift from search engines to query-answering language models. Stackoverflow is another company that may be heavily impacted by generative AI. Answers provided by generative AI undermine Stackoverflow's community, which consists of human volunteers providing human-written answers to human-written questions. The company has banned generative AI from its websites (Stackoverflow.com, 2022). A similar ban was instated and legal action has been taken by the stock photography website Getty Images (Justia, 2023; Vincent, n.d. 2022a). The above examples highlight the cross-sectional and complex impact of generative AI on a variety of businesses and entire industries.

Another criticism about generative AI is that it may violate people's privacy. For instance, diffusion models have been shown to memorise and replicate training data (Carlini et al., 2023; Somepalli et al., 2022). That means diffusion models could reproduce near-exact matches of instances found in the training data. This could not only have copyright implications, but also lead to the unintentional release of private data. For instance, LAION—the large dataset used to train Stable Diffusion—was shown to contain medical images of patients included in the dataset without the consent of the patient (Edwards, 2022a). Memorisation is a fundamental issue in diffusion models, and may even be necessary for generative models to generalise (Feldman, 2019).

On a less technical level, another criticism about text-to-image generation is that it could erode human creativity and artistic expression. Critics argue that by relying on algorithms and ML to generate images, we are losing touch with the human elements that make art so special. Critics worry that AI art may become a sterile and impersonal medium, devoid of the emotional depth and individuality that characterises great human art (Oppenlaender et al., 2023). Another related concern is that AI art could lead to the homogenisation of artistic styles and forms. Because generative models are trained on vast datasets of images, they tend to produce art that is similar to what has come before. Midjourney,[3] for instance, produces images with a recognisable style. Current generative systems "lack a concept of novelty regarding how their product differs from previously created ones" (Zammit et al., 2022, p. 1). This could lead to a situation where all AI art begins to look the same, with little variation or originality.

Another concern is that text-to-image generation could be used to create false or misleading images (Oppenlaender et al., 2023). With the ability to generate highly realistic images, AI algorithms could be used to create fake photographs or other forms of visual media for the purpose of spreading misinformation. This could have serious implications for the reliability of information and the trustworthiness of digital media that we encounter online.

Even proponents of text-to-image generation have voiced concerns about the technology. Given the improvements in the latest versions of text-to-image models, some practitioners of AI art have complained that it is becoming "too easy" to conjure up images from text prompts

---

[3] Version 3.

(Edwards, 2022b; Oppenlaender, 2022). This raises the interesting question about the optimal skill level for text-to-image generation and AI-generated art. If the skill level is too difficult, users will not be able to communicate their intent to the model. The result could be that users become frustrated. On the other hand, if the skill level is too easy, users will not have a strong sense of ownership and will feel that the generated images do not reflect their intent. Rather, the sentiment will be that the images are merely retrieved from pre-made collection of images. The current generative systems vary in this respect. Stable Diffusion, for instance, requires more effort being placed on writing prompts than Midjourney. This effort put into writing prompts is part of the novel practice of prompt engineering, which is discussed in the following section.

The Creative Practice of Prompt Engineering

Prompt engineering (Liu & Chilton, 2022; Oppenlaender, 2023)—or prompting for short—is an interaction pattern in which ML models are given text as inputs (Brown et al., 2020). Prompt engineering is a paradigm shift in how ML models are adapted to various downstream tasks. Instead of retraining or fine-tuning the model, the model is prompted with context. In zero-shot prompting (Kojima et al., 2022), the user directly prompts the generative model, whereas in few-shot prompting (Brown et al., 2020), the user first provides a few examples to give context to the model. Zero-shot prompting has offered an ideal application ground in AI-generated art. In the context of text-to-image generation, prompt engineering means that "carefully selected and composed sentences are used to achieve a certain visual style in the synthesized image" (Rombach et al., 2022, p. 2).

Prompt engineering is not an exact engineering science as found in science, technology, engineering, and mathematics (STEM). Rather, its origins are within the online community of practitioners of text-to-image generation and AI artists who practice prompt engineering to exercise their craft. Prompt engineering is iterative and resembles a conversation with the text-to-image system. A practitioner typically will type a prompt, observe the outcome, and adapt the prompt to improve the outcome.

The online community around text-to-image generation found that the aesthetic qualities and subjective attractiveness of images can be modified by adding certain keywords to prompts (Oppenlaender, 2023). By adding such modifiers to an input prompt, one seeks to direct the text-to-image model to produce images in a certain style or with a certain quality. Knowing what prompt modifiers work best for a given subject term is often the result of the practitioner's iterative and persistent experimentation (Kim, 2022; Liu & Chilton, 2022). Community-based resources have been created as education materials about the practice of prompt engineering (Oppenlaender, 2022, 2023).

Supported by these numerous guidelines and learning resources, anybody can materialise seemingly creative artifacts with generative AI, whether it's textual (e.g., poems and essays written with OpenAI's GPT language models) or visual (e.g., photographic images with Midjourney and Stable Diffusion), with little to no understanding of the underlying technologies. As generative AI matures and gains more prominence in our daily lives, it will become more important for us to be able to communicate effectively with the AI without having to resort to technical jargon and complicated keywords as is currently the case with prompt engineering. Critics of prompt engineering, therefore, point out its many limitations:

- Some text-to-image generation models accept only a limited number of tokens (e.g., 75 tokens). Tokens are pieces of text that roughly correspond to words in the prompt. Unless one picks a subject well-represented in the training data (e.g., Leonardo da Vinci's Mona Lisa), it is difficult to describe a subject in detail to the generative AI with only a limited number of tokens.

- Even if there is an unlimited number of tokens to describe an imagined image, it is not humanly possible to describe a subject in every minute detail. In practice, the generative model will need to fill in the blanks. This, in turn, can lead the practitioner to either settle for an image that is "good enough" or abandon the pursuit of the originally envisioned image (Oppenlaender, 2022). On the other hand, the mismatch between the imagined output and the generated image can also spark creativity in the human user (Epstein et al., 2022).

- The keywords that humans use to describe a subject may not correspond to the concepts that the neural network has learned during its training process. Certain tokens in the prompt could also have unintended side-effects, for instance, on the style of an image, and concepts can "leak" from the prompt into the image (Rassin et al., 2022). It is, for example, not uncommon that parts of the prompts will surface in generated images as text, even if that was not intended by the user.

- Each time a generative model is updated, the practice of prompt engineering is heavily affected and practitioners have to relearn their craft (Wang, 2022).

The latter is supported by a wealth of learning resources that have emerged online to support practitioners of text-to-image generation in learning the craft of prompt engineering. Together with communities and tools and services, these resources are the main pillars of the co-creative ecosystem of text-to-image generation.

HUMAN–COMPUTER CO-CREATIVE ECOSYSTEM OF TEXT-TO-IMAGE GENERATION

Prompt engineering is a practice embedded in the greater online creative ecosystem of text-to-image generation that consists of communities, learning resources, and tools and services (Oppenlaender, 2022). In this ecosystem, communities, learning resources, and tools come together to form a dynamic and interactive environment where creativity and technology intersect. This convergence empowers users to explore and push the boundaries of art and expression through the innovative use of text-to-image AI technologies.

Communities Dedicated to Text-to-Image Generation

Online communities have emerged around text-guided generative art. These communities provide a platform for individuals to share their creative prompts and works of art, or even collaborate on generating new images collectively (Kantosalo & Takala, 2020). The Midjourney community has emerged as a cultural hub contributing to the proliferation of prompt engineering, due to providing an accessible service and having an ear for the needs of its community members. Further examples of online communities include /r/MediaSynthesis on Reddit, and numerous other communities hosted on Discord. The latter in particular has proven to be an effective tool for community formation due to its ability to facilitate the creation of chat-based online communities, and the possibility for community members to directly interact with the image generation systems via chat.

Online communities act as a fertile ground for learning the skills necessary to use text-to-image generation systems creatively. The online communities of enthusiastic creators who share their prompts and practices serve as a rich environment for novice practitioners to gain knowledge from other members of the community in order to surmount the challenges of prompt engineering. However, the distributed and sequential nature of communication within these communities presents a challenge for practitioners seeking to attain specific learning objectives, such as the study of prompt modifiers. As a result, there is a growing trend among practitioners and online communities to establish dedicated learning resources that cater to the learning needs of novices.

Dedicated Learning Resources

Community members have created various learning resources related to prompt engineering, including resources aimed at specific learning objectives, such as style experimentation (Durant, 2021; Gabha, 2022a) and teaching prompt engineering (e.g., the DALL-E prompt book by Parsons (2022)). Some of these resources adopt a similar approach to the systematic experimentation conducted by Liu and Chilton (2022), presenting results of their experiments in tabular format. Examples of these resources include the artist studies by Durant (2021), "MisterRuffian's Latent Artist and Modifier Encyclopedia" (Saini, 2022), and the list of Disco Diffusion modifiers by Gabha (2022b). Hub pages are another type of resource that have been established to improve the discoverability of the rapidly growing field of text-to-image generation. These hub pages function as indexes, compiling links to Google Colaboratory (Colab) notebooks and improving accessibility to the quickly growing number of resources. Two examples of hub pages are Miranda's list of VQGAN-CLIP implementations[4] and pharmapsychotic's "Tools and Resources for AI Art".[5]

---

[4] https://ljvmiranda921.github.io/notebook/2021/08/11/vqgan-list/.

[5] https://pharmapsychotic.com/tools.htm.

Dedicated Tools and Services

A growing number of interfaces, tools, and services are emerging to support practitioners in practicing text-to-image generation. For instance, a wide variety of text-to-image generation systems are available as open source in executable notebooks. Colab[6] in particular, has proven instrumental to the early growth and popularity of text-to-image generation. Colab is an online service that allows anybody to execute Python-based code and ML models for free. This is a growing ecosystem of tools and services that assist in making text-to-image generation more accessible to non-technically minded practitioners. The ecosystem also acts as a catalyst that draws in new practitioners and advances the field as a whole. It is the specific combination of people, technology, services, tools, and resources that formed a healthy co-creative ecosystem for the text-to-image art community to thrive.

THE RISKS AND DANGERS OF CULTIVATING THE CO-CREATIVE ECOSYSTEM

As the generative AI revolution advances, generative AI is becoming infused into many software applications and creative tools. For instance, users of Adobe Photoshop can create images from text using extensions based on Stable Diffusion (Alfaraj, 2022; Stability AI, 2022), and Microsoft's Co-Pilot (GitHub Inc., 2021) has become an indispensable tool for many software developers. Generative AI is also explored in the field of generative design (Matejka et al., 2018; Mountstephens & Teo, 2020) and architecture (Paananen et al., 2023). Given the emerging ubiquity of generative models, such as large language models (Brown et al., 2020; Devlin et al., 2019; Radford et al., 2019; Raffel et al., 2022) and other foundation-scale models (Bommasani et al., 2021), it is foreseeable that even more creative work will be completed with support of generative AI in the future.

These generative models and, thus, the tools and applications built with them, are based on deep learning. The results of deep neural networks are difficult to interpret and understand by both laypeople and experts (Lipton, 2018; Poursabzi-Sangdeh et al., 2021). With the emerging ubiquity of generative technologies, we are at risk of creating

---

[6] https://colab.research.google.com.

"systems of opaque systems" ingrained with difficult to understand, potentially flawed, and biased logic. This section discusses three potential dangers of cultivating the emerging co-creative ecosystem.

Bias in Training Data and Generative Models

Current approaches to training generative AI rely on vast datasets collected from the World Wide Web. For example, "The Pile" (Gao et al., 2020) is a popular data source for training language models. LAION (Schuhmann et al., 2021, 2022) is a dataset based on CommonCrawl,[7] a large dataset released by a non-profit organisation that periodically scrapes data from the World Wide Web. LAION-5B contains over 5 billion text-image pairs, with text from the "alt" attributes of HTML image elements (Schuhmann et al., 2022). These big datasets are used for training multi-modal generative models.

It is known that data on the Web is biased (Baeza-Yates, 2018). Web-based data may contain content that violates human preferences (Korbak et al., 2023). Web-based datasets may also encode Western ways of seeing due to over-representation of certain viewpoints in the data, creating intersectional issues reflecting discrimination and privilege. For instance, the English language is over-represented in LAION-5B, with 2.3 billion of the 5.85 billion image-text pairs in the dataset being in English language, and the rest representing more than 100 other languages or texts that cannot be assigned to a language (Schuhmann et al., 2022).

Generative models trained on this biased data may repeat, and in some cases, amplify undesirable biases, such as demographic biases (Bender et al., 2021; Danks & London, 2017; Salminen et al., 2020; van der Wal et al., 2022; Williams et al., 2018). Birhane et al. (2021) found that LAION contains many troublesome and explicit images and text pairs, including "rape, pornography, malign stereotypes, racist and ethnic slurs, and other extremely problematic content" (p. 1). Qu et al. (2023) found that text-to-image generators create a substantial number of unsafe images, including sexually explicit, violent, disturbing, hateful, and political images, which could be used to spread hateful memes. This problematic content may surface in downstream applications and cause harm (Monroe, 2021). That is one reason why deep neural networks are

---

[7] https://commoncrawl.org.

difficult to audit (Perez et al., 2022) and harm is often only discovered during everyday use (Shen et al., 2021).

A FLOOD OF SYNTHETIC DATA

Synthetic images are being shared en masse on social media. This flood of synthetic data (Olson, 2022) raises concerns that synthetic imagery could taint the training data of future generations of text-to-image models and perpetuate the weaknesses of current text-to-image systems. For instance, current text-to-image models struggle with human anatomy, in particular the accurate depiction of human hands. Data quality has been shown to be of equal importance as the size of the training data (Hoffmann et al., 2022). Using low-quality images as training data could result in further degradation in the quality of future generative models. Shumailov et al. (2023) call this phenomenon the "curse of recursion".

Models trained on data generated by prior generative models may degenerate and forget the underlying data distribution, leading to learned behavior with limited variance (Shumailov et al., 2023). Some proponents of generative AI argue that future generative models will learn to associate a new category of images with synthetic imagery, and that we can simply prompt the generative model not to produce images that look like they were generated by AI. However, this assumes that we can find a way to prompt the generative model to avoid the specific class of AI-generated images, which may or may not be possible. The challenge is in finding the right keywords to denote the class of quality-degraded images, as mentioned in the section on prompt engineering. Even if there was a clear label for the new class of synthetic imagery, it could happen that this synthetic look is inseparably associated with other classes.

A possible solution to this problem could be invisible watermarks applied to AI-generated images. This metadata would allow the generative models to correctly distinguish the class of AI-generated imagery from human creations. Another solution could be technological progress in image generation. By training generative AI on smaller and more tightly controlled datasets, many of the problems could be avoided. This sparse learning (Mishra et al., 2021) would also better mimic how humans learn from sparse cues in their environment.

Long-term Effects on Individuals and Human Culture

By cultivating generative systems and adopting them in our creative practices, we risk becoming dependent on them. Final-year students who finished their studies in 2020 are the last cohort of students to complete their education without the support of generative AI. Future generations will be born into a co-creative ecosystem of ubiquitous generative AI. Generative AI, in this regard, is similar to the Internet, which had a profound impact on our lives, especially on the generation of "GenZ" who grew up never knowing a time without the Internet. The Internet has affected our cognition (Carr, 2011; Firth et al., 2019). It has reconfigured our society and brought great benefits, but it has also presented drawbacks and risks. With generative AI and text-to-image generation, there could be unforeseen direct and indirect negative consequences on society and individuals.

For one, generative AI could negatively affect people's imagination and cognitive functioning in the long term. The negative and lasting effect of habitual use of mobile phones on people's cognition, memory, and attention span can already be witnessed (Wilmer et al., 2017). One could argue that habituated practices of image generation could in the long term also negatively affect people's career ambitions. For instance, the widespread use of AI could discourage would-be artists from pursuing a creative career (Mok, 2023). Habitual use of generative AI could also negatively affect people's cognitive abilities, with lasting effects on imagination and effects on child development. Aphantasia refers to the inability to visualise mental images (Milton et al., 2021). This "ability to create a quasi-perceptual visual picture in the mind's eye" (Dance et al., 2022, p. 1) is important for daydreaming, imagination, and creativity (Zeman et al., 2020). Dance et al. (2022) found that about 4% of a population of about 1000 people had a weakness or inability to create mental imagery. Generative AI could potentially contribute to a rise in the prevalence of aphantasia in the general population.

Another effect could be that people become accustomed to lowering expectations and settling for second-best options. As discussed in the section on prompt engineering, the results of text-to-image generation are often random and do not match the mental image of the person writing the prompt. The retrieval of an exact image from the generative model's "infinite index" (Deckers et al., 2023) can be an arduous task. With each new generation, the practitioner's efforts to "retrieve" images from the generative model may become derailed. The generative system may, for instance, present the user with interesting results that do not reflect the initial prompt, but are worth pursuing further. This repeated settling for good enough results could lead to long-term changes in our ambition and could contribute to cultivating a culture of prototyping.

Another effect on culture could be a change in communication patterns. Generative AI could lead to a shift in how individuals communicate with each other. For instance, intelligent agents could write and summarise e-mails for people, a feat that OpenAI's ChatGPT already accomplishes quite well today. Generative AI could also more directly support communication, for instance, in the form of real-time translation of spoken words in face-to-face communications (Kirkpatrick, 2020). Text-to-image generation could contribute to the proliferation of memes on the Internet and fuel a meme-driven culture. AI-generated media may allow creators to express feelings that could not be expressed through words.

However, the proliferation of synthetic media could lead to some human-created media becoming harder to find on the Web, with knock-on effects on humanity's knowledge and culture. With the flood of synthetic media, the long-tail of information on the Web (i.e., the vast array of less popular or niche information and content that is not mainstream but cumulatively significant) expands and accrues *noise*, which in turn makes information in the long-tail more difficult to retrieve. Kandpal et al. (2022) found that large language models struggle to learn the long-tail of knowledge. If interaction with large language models becomes our primary way of answering queries, as opposed to searching the Web, long-tail knowledge could be lost. This presents unique challenges to augmented AI (Mialon et al., 2023). Augmented models are a class of generative models that are equipped with the ability to use tools and access external knowledge bases. Such augmented models can, for instance, query APIs, execute functions, and retrieve information from search engines. Synthetic media could negatively affect the operation of augmented models due to factual information becoming harder to retrieve in search engines.

Text-to-image generation could also fundamentally change people's relation to visual media and how individuals appreciate art. AI-generated media is becoming ubiquitous, and it is not clear if pervasive synthetic media will make us appreciate human-made art more or less. If anybody can create digital artworks that look like they were created by a master painter, will people still appreciate real paintings, whether digital or on a physical canvas? The proliferation of AI-generated media makes it also harder for aesthetic trends to stick among many meaningless short-lived fads (Townsend, 2023). The model of attractive quality by Kano et al. (1984) posits that products can contain "exciting" factors that contribute to the appreciation of the product. Over time, exciting factors become expected. The iPhone's touchscreen-based user experience, for instance, was exciting when it was first introduced, but later became the expected standard in mobile phones. Perhaps, once the novelty of AI-generated media wears off, text-to-image generation will turn from excitement to expected. Then, generative AI's true potential will emerge. Generative AI has the potential to become part of the fundamental layer on which future human society is based.

CONCLUSION

Text-to-image generation technology has emerged as an exciting new area of creative practice, drawing parallels with photography in terms of its ability to visualise the surrounding world. However, as with any new technology, there are also concerns. The co-creative ecosystem of text-to-image generation, which involves both human and computer participants, raises issues related to bias in training data, a potential flood of synthetic data, and the long-term impact on individuals and human culture.

Despite these challenges, the creative practice of prompt engineering has already produced remarkable results, thanks in part to a flourishing online ecosystem of dedicated communities, learning resources, tools, and services. While these resources offer great potential for creativity and innovation, they also come with risks. Therefore, it is crucial to carefully consider the ethical implications of cultivating a co-creative ecosystem and take steps to mitigate any potential negative effects. Text-to-image generation has the potential to revolutionise the way new works of art are visualised and created, but it is essential to approach this technology with caution and responsibility. As this exciting new field is continually explored, vigilance must be maintained in identifying and addressing potential risks as well as dangers to ensure that generative AI is aligned with human values, and that the benefits of generative AI are realised for the benefit of all.

References

Alfaraj, A. (2022). *Auto photoshop Stablediffusion plugin*. https://github.com/AbdullahAlfaraj/Auto-Photoshop-StableDiffusion-Plugin

Baeza-Yates, R. (2018). Bias on the web. *Communications of the ACM, 61*(6), 54–61. https://doi.org/10.1145/3209581

Baio, A. (2022). *AI data laundering: How academic and nonprofit researchers shield tech companies from accountability*. https://waxy.org/2022/09/ai-data-laundering-how-academic-and-nonprofit-researchers-shield-tech-companies-from-accountability/

Bender, E. M., Timnit, G., McMillan-Major, A., & Shmitchell, S. (2021). On the dangers of stochastic parrots: Can language models be too big?. In *Proceedings of the 2021 ACM Conference on Fairness, Accountability, and Transparency*, 610–623. FAccT '21. Association for Computing Machinery. https://doi.org/10.1145/3442188.3445922

Birhane, A., Vinay, U. P., & Kahembwe, E. (2021). Multimodal datasets: Misogyny, pornography, and malignant stereotypes. arXiv. https://doi.org/10.48550/ARXIV.2110.01963

Boden, M. A., & Edmonds, E. A. (2009). What is generative art? *Digital Creativity, 20*(1–2), 21–46. https://doi.org/10.1080/14626260902867915

Bommasani, R., Drew, A. H., Adeli, E., Altman, R., Arora, S., von Arx, S., Bernstein, M. S., et al. (2021). On the opportunities and risks of foundation models. *CoRR* abs/2108.07258. http://arxiv.org/abs/2108.07258

Brown, T. B., Mann, B., Ryder, N., Subbiah, M., Kaplan, J., Dhariwal, P., Neelakantan, A., et al. (2020). Language models are few-shot learners. arXiv. https://doi.org/10.48550/ARXIV.2005.14165

Carlini, N., Hayes, J., Nasr, M., Jagielski, M., Sehwag, V., Tramèr, F., Balle, B., Ippolito, D., & Wallace, E. (2023). Extracting training data from diffusion models. arXiv. https://doi.org/10.48550/ARXIV.2301.13188

Carr, N. (2011). *The Shallows: What the Internet is doing to our brains*. W. W. Norton & Company Inc.

Cohen, H. (1979). *What is an image?*

Colton, S., Smith, M., Berns, S., Murdock, R., & Cook, M. (2021). Generative search engines: Initial experiments. In *Proceedings of the 12th International Conference on Computational Creativity*, 237–246. ICCC '21. Association for Computational Creativity.

Crowson, K., Biderman, S., Kornis, D., Stander, D., Hallahan, E., Castricato, L., & Raff, E. (2022). VQGAN-CLIP: Open domain image generation and editing with natural language guidance. arXiv. https://doi.org/10.48550/ARXIV.2204.08583

Dance, C. J., Ipser, A., & Simner, J. (2022). The prevalence of aphantasia (imagery weakness) in the general population. *Consciousness and Cognition, 97*, 103243. https://doi.org/10.1016/j.concog.2021.103243

Danks, D., & London, A. J. (2017). Algorithmic bias in autonomous systems. In *Proceedings of the Twenty-Sixth International Joint Conference on Artificial Intelligence, (IJCAI-17)*, 4691–4697. https://doi.org/10.24963/ijcai.2017/654

Deckers, N., Fröbe, M., Kiesel, J., Pandolfo, G., Schröder, C., Stein, B., & Potthast, M. (2023). The infinite index: Information retrieval on generative text-to-image models. In *ACM SIGIR Conference on Human Information Interaction and Retrieval*. CHIIR '23.

Devlin, J., Chang, M.-W., Lee, K., & Toutanova, K. (2019). BERT: Pre-training of deep bidirectional transformers for language understanding. In *Proceedings of the 2019 Conference of the North American Chapter of the Association for Computational Linguistics: Human Language Technologies, Volume 1 (Long and Short Papers)*, 4171–4186. Association for Computational Linguistics. https://doi.org/10.18653/v1/N19-1423

Dhariwal, P., & Nichol, A. (2021). Diffusion models beat GANs on image synthesis. In M. Ranzato, A. Beygelzimer, Y. Dauphin, P. S. Liang, & J. Wortman Vaughan (Eds.), *Advances in neural information processing systems* (Vol. 34, pp. 8780–8794). Curran Associates, Inc. https://proceedings.neurips.cc/paper/2021/file/49ad23d1ec9fa4bd8d77d02681df5cfa-Paper.pdf

Durant, R. (2021). *Artist Studies by @remi_durant*. https://remidurant.com/artists/

Edwards, B. (2022a). *Artist finds private medical record photos in popular AI training data set*. https://arstechnica.com/information-technology/2022/09/artist-finds-private-medical-record-photos-in-popular-ai-training-data-set

Edwards, B. (2022b). *'Too Easy'—Midjourney tests dramatic new version of its AI image generator*. https://arstechnica.com/information-technology/2022/11/midjourney-turns-heads-with-quality-leap-in-new-ai-image-generator-version/

Eisenstein, E. L. (1980). *The printing press as an agent of change*. Cambridge University Press.

Epstein, Z., Schroeder, H., & Newman, D. (2022). When happy accidents spark creativity: Bringing collaborative speculation to life with generative AI. In *International Conference on Computational Creativity*. ICCC '22. arXiv. https://doi.org/10.48550/ARXIV.2206.00533

Feldman, V. (2019). Does learning require memorization? A short tale about a long tail. arXiv. https://doi.org/10.48550/ARXIV.1906.05271

Firth, J., Torous, J., Stubbs, B., Firth, J. A., Steiner, G. Z., Smith, L., Alvarez-Jimenez, M., et al. (2019). The 'Online Brain': How the Internet may be changing our cognition. *World Psychiatry, 18*(2), 119–129.

Gabha, H. (2022a). *Disco (Diffusion) modifiers*. https://weirdwonderfulai.art/resources/disco-diffusion-modifiers/

Galanter, P. (2016). Generative art theory. In C. Paul (Ed.), *A companion to digital art* (pp. 146–180). John Wiley & Sons, Ltd. https://doi.org/10.1002/9781118475249.ch5

Gao, L., Biderman, S., Black, S., Golding, L., Hoppe, T., Foster, C., Phang, J. et al. (2020). *The Pile: An 800GB dataset of diverse text for language modeling.* https://doi.org/10.48550/ARXIV.2101.00027

GitHub Inc. (2021). *GitHub copilot—Your AI pair programmer.* https://copilot.github.com

Goldberg, Y. (2023). *Some remarks on large language models.* https://gist.github.com/yoavg/59d174608e92e845c8994ac2e234c8a9

Goodfellow, I., Pouget-Abadie, J., Mirza, M., Xu, B., Warde-Farley, D., Ozair, S., Courville, A., & Bengio, Y. (2014). Generative adversarial nets. In Z. Ghahramani, M. Welling, C. Cortes, N. Lawrence, & K. Q. Weinberger (Eds.) *Advances in neural information processing systems* (Vol. 27). Curran Associates, Inc.

Harvey, A., & LaPlace, J. (2021). *Megaface.* https://exposing.ai/megaface/

Hertmann, A. (2020). Computers do not make art, people do. *Communications of the ACM, 63*(5), 45–48. https://doi.org/10.1145/3347092

Hertzmann, A. (2018). Can computers create art? *Arts, 7*(2). https://doi.org/10.3390/arts7020018

Hoffmann, J., Borgeaud, S., Mensch, A., Buchatskaya, E., Cai, T., Rutherford, E., de Las Casas, D., et al. (2022). Training compute-optimal large language models. arXiv. https://doi.org/10.48550/ARXIV.2203.15556

Justia. (2022). *HiQ labs, Inc. v. LinkedIn corporation.* https://law.justia.com/cases/federal/appellate-courts/ca9/17-16783/17-16783-2022-04-18.html

Justia. (2023). *Getty images (US), Inc. V. stability AI, Inc.* https://docs.justia.com/cases/federal/district-courts/delaware/dedce/1:2023cv00135/81407/1

Kandpal, N., Deng, H., Roberts, A., Wallace, E., & Raffel, C. (2022). Large language models struggle to learn long-tail knowledge. arXiv. https://doi.org/10.48550/ARXIV.2211.08411

Kano, N., Seraku, N., Takahashi, F., & Tsuji, S.-I. (1984). Attractive quality and must-be quality. *Journal of the Japanese Society for Quality Control, 14*(2), 147–156.

Kantosalo, A., & Takala, T. (2020). Five C's for human–computer co-creativity: An update on classical creativity perspectives. In *Proceedings of the 11th International Conference on Computational Creativity.* Association for Computational Creativity.

Kim, J. (2022). Keynote on interaction-centric AI. In *NeurIPS 2022.* https://slideslive.com/38996064/interactioncentric-ai

Kirkpatrick, K. (2020). Across the language barrier. *Commununications of the ACM, 63*(3), 15–17. https://doi.org/10.1145/3379495

Kojima, T., Gu, S. S., Reid, M., Matsuo, Y., & Iwasawa, Y. (2022). Large language models are zero-shot reasoners. arXiv. https://doi.org/10.48550/ARXIV.2205.11916

Korbak, T., Shi, K., Chen, A., Bhalerao, R., Buckley, C. L., Phang, J., Bowman, S. R., & Perez, E. (2023). Pretraining language models with human preferences. arXiv https://doi.org/10.48550/ARXIV.2302.08582

Kuhn, B. M. (2022). *If software is my copilot, who programmed my software? software freedom conservancy.* https://sfconservancy.org/blog/2022/feb/03/github-copilot-copyleft-gpl/

Lipton, Z. C. (2018). The mythos of model interpretability: In machine learning, the concept of interpretability is both important and slippery. *Queue, 16*(3), 31–57. https://doi.org/10.1145/3236386.3241340

Liu, V., & Chilton, L. B. (2022). Design guidelines for prompt engineering text-to-image generative models. In *Proceedings of the 2022 CHI Conference on Human Factors in Computing Systems*. CHI '22. Association for Computing Machinery. https://doi.org/10.1145/3491102.3501825

Mansimov, E., Parisotto, E., Ba, J., & Salakhutdinov, R. (2016). Generating images from captions with attention. In *International Conference on Learning Representations*. ICLR '16.

Marche, S. (2022). We're witnessing the birth of a new artistic medium. *The Atlantic.* https://www.theatlantic.com/technology/archive/2022/09/ai-art-generators-future/671568/

Matejka, J., Glueck, M., Bradner, E., Hashemi, A., Grossman, T., & Fitzmaurice, G. (2018). Dream lens: Exploration and visualization of large-scale generative design datasets. In *Proceedings of the 2018 Chi Conference on Human Factors in Computing Systems*, 1–12. CHI '18. Association for Computing Machinery. https://doi.org/10.1145/3173574.3173943

Mialon, G., Dessì, R., Lomeli, M., Nalmpantis, C., Pasunuru, R., Raileanu, R., Rozière, B. et al. (2023). Augmented language models: A survey. arXiv. https://doi.org/10.48550/ARXIV.2302.07842

Milton, F., Fulford, J., Dance, C., Gaddum, J., Heuerman-Williamson, B., Jones, K., Knight, K. F., MacKisack, M., Winlove, C., & Zeman, A. (2021). Behavioral and neural signatures of visual imagery vividness extremes: Aphantasia versus Hyperphantasia. *Cerebral Cortex Communications, 2*(2). https://doi.org/10.1093/texcom/tgab035

Mishra, A., Albericio Latorre, J., Pool, J., Stosic, D., Stosic, D., Venkatesh, D., Yu, C., & Micikevicius, P. (2021). Accelerating sparse deep neural networks. arXiv. https://doi.org/10.48550/ARXIV.2104.08378

Mok, K. (2023). *The power and ethical dilemma of AI image generation models.* https://thenewstack.io/the-power-and-ethical-dilemma-of-ai-image-generation-models/

Monroe, D. (2021). Trouble at the source. *Communications of the ACM, 64*(12), 17–19. https://doi.org/10.1145/3490155

Mountstephens, J., & Teo, J. (2020). Progress and challenges in generative product design: A review of systems. *Computers, 9*(4). https://doi.org/10.3390/computers9040080

Murdock, R., & Wang, P. (2021). *Big sleep*. https://github.com/lucidrains/big-sleep

Nech, A., & Kemelmacher-Shlizerman, I. (2017). Level playing field for million scale face recognition. In *Proceedings of the IEEE Conference on Computer Vision and Pattern Recognition*. https://doi.org/10.48550/arXiv.1705.00393

Olson, P. (2022). Creative AI is generating some messy problems. *Bloomberg*. https://www.washingtonpost.com/business/creative-ai-is-generating-some-messy-problems/2022/11/28/be2b2efc-6ee2-11ed-867c-8ec695e4afcd_story.html

Oppenlaender, J. (2022). The creativity of text-to-image generation. In *25th International Academic Mindtrek Conference*, 192–202. Academic Mindtrek 2022. Association for Computing Machinery. https://doi.org/10.1145/3569219.3569352

Oppenlaender, J. (2023). A taxonomy of prompt modifiers for text-to-image generation. *Behaviour & Information Technology*. Taylor & Francis. https://doi.org/10.1080/0144929X.2023.2286532

Oppenlaender, J., Silvennoinen, J., Paananen, V., & Visuri, A. (2023). Perceptions and realities of text-to-image generation. In *26th International Academic Mindtrek Conference*, 279–288. Academic Mindtrek 2023. Association for Computing Machinery. https://doi.org/10.1145/3616961.3616978

Paananen, V., Oppenlaender, J., & Visuri, A. (2023). Using text-to-image generation for architectural design ideation. In *International Journal of Architectural Computing*. SAGE. https://doi.org/10.1177/14780771231222783

Parsons, G. (2022). *The DALL·E 2 prompt book*. https://dallery.gallery/the-dalle-2-prompt-book/

Perez, E., Ringer, S., Lukošiūtė, K., Nguyen, K., Chen, E., Heiner, S., Pettit, C., et al. (2022). Discovering language model behaviors with model-written evaluations. arXiv. https://doi.org/10.48550/ARXIV.2212.09251

Poursabzi-Sangdeh, F., Goldstein, D. G., Hofman, J. M., Wortman Vaughan, J., & Wallach, H. (2021). Manipulating and measuring model interpretability. In *Proceedings of the 2021 Chi Conference on Human Factors in Computing Systems*. CHI '21. Association for Computing Machinery. https://doi.org/10.1145/3411764.3445315

Qu, Y., Shen, X., He, X., Backes, M., Zannettou, S., & Zhang, Y. (2023). Unsafe diffusion: On the generation of unsafe images and hateful memes from text-to-image models. *CCS '23*. ACM. https://doi.org/10.1145/3576915.361 6679

Radford, A., Kim, J. W., Hallacy, C., Ramesh, A., Goh, G., Agarwal, S., Sastry, G., et al. (2021). Learning transferable visual models from natural language supervision. In M. Meila & T. Zhang (Eds.), *Proceedings of the 38th International Conference on Machine Learning*, 139, 8748–8763. ICML. PMLR. https://proceedings.mlr.press/v139/radford21a.html

Radford, A., Wu, J., Child, R., Luan, D., Amodei, D., & Sutskever, I. (2019). Language models are unsupervised multitask learners. *OpenAI Blog*, 1(8), 9.

Raffel, C., Shazeer, N., Roberts, A., Lee, K., Narang, S., Matena, M., Zhou, Y., Li, W. & Liu, P. J. (2022). Exploring the limits of transfer learning with a unified text-to-text transformer. *Journal of Machine Learning Research*, 21(1). https://jmlr.org/papers/volume21/20-074/20-074.pdf

Ramesh, A., Dhariwal, P., Nichol, A., Chu, C., & Chen, M. (2022). Hierarchical text-conditional image generation with CLIP latents. arXiv. https://doi.org/10.48550/ARXIV.2204.06125

Rassin, R., Ravfogel, S., & Goldberg, Y. (2022). DALLE-2 is seeing double: Flaws in word-to-concept mapping in Text2Image models. In *Proceedings of the Fifth Blackboxnlp Workshop on Analyzing and Interpreting Neural Networks for Nlp*, 335–45. Association for Computational Linguistics. https://aclanthology.org/2022.blackboxnlp-1.28

Reed, S., Akata, Z., Yan, X., Logeswaran, L., Schiele, B., & Lee, H. (2016). Generative adversarial text to image synthesis. *ICML 2016*. arXiv. https://doi.org/10.48550/ARXIV.1605.05396

Rombach, R., Blattmann, A., & Ommer, B. (2022). Text-guided synthesis of artistic images with retrieval-augmented diffusion models. arXiv. https://doi.org/10.48550/ARXIV.2207.13038

Rombach, R., Blattmann, A., Lorenz, D., Esser, P., & Ommer, B. (2021). *High-resolution image synthesis with latent diffusion models*. http://arxiv.org/abs/2112.10752

Saini, L. (2022). Mister Ruffian's latent artist & modifier encyclopedia. https://docs.google.com/spreadsheets/d/1_jgQ9SyvUaBNP1mHHEzZ6HhL_Es1KwBKQtnpnmWW82I

Salminen, J., Jung, S.-G., Chowdhury, F., & Jansen, B. J. (2020). Analyzing demographic bias in artificially generated facial pictures. In *Extended Abstracts of the 2020 CHI Conference on Human Factors in Computing Systems*, 1–8. CHI Ea '20. Association for Computing Machinery. https://doi.org/10.1145/3334480.3382791

Schuhmann, C., Beaumont, R., Vencu, R., Gordon, C. W., Wightman, R., Cherti, M., Coombes, T., et al. (2022). LAION-5B: An open large-scale dataset for training next generation image-text models. In *Thirty-Sixth Conference on Neural Information Processing Systems Datasets and Benchmarks Track.* https://arxiv.org/abs/2210.08402

Schuhmann, C., Vencu, R., Beaumont, R., Kaczmarczyk, R., Mullis, C., Katta, A., Coombes, T., Jitsev, J., & Komatsuzaki, A. (2021). LAION-400M: Open dataset of CLIP-Filtered 400 million image-text pairs. arXiv. https://doi.org/10.48550/ARXIV.2111.02114

Shen, H., DeVos, A., Eslami, M., & Holstein, K. (2021). Everyday algorithm auditing: Understanding the power of everyday users in surfacing harmful algorithmic behaviors. *Proceedings of ACM Human-Computer Interaction, 5* (CSCW2). https://doi.org/10.1145/3479577

Shumailov, I., Shumaylov, Z., Zhao, Y., Gal, Y., Papernot, N., & Anderson, R. (2023). *The curse of recursion: Training on generated data makes models forget.* http://arxiv.org/abs/2305.17493

Somepalli, G., Singla, V., Goldblum, M., Geiping, J., & Goldstein, T. (2022). Diffusion art or digital forgery? investigating data replication in diffusion models. arXiv. https://doi.org/10.48550/ARXIV.2212.03860

Stability AI. (2022). *Stability photoshop plugin.* https://exchange.adobe.com/apps/cc/114117da/stable-diffusion

Stackoverflow.com. (2022). *Temporary policy: ChatGPT is banned.* https://meta.stackoverflow.com/questions/421831/temporary-policy-chatgpt-is-banned

Toews, R. (2022). 4 Predictions about the wild new world of text-to-image AI. *Forbes.* https://www.forbes.com/sites/robtoews/2022/09/11/4-hot-takes-about-the-wild-new-world-of-generative-ai/

Townsend, C. (2023). *Explaining corecore: How tiktok's newest trend may be a genuine gen-z art form.* https://mashable.com/article/explaining-corecore-tiktok

Vincent, J. (2022a). Getty images bans AI-generated content over fears of legal challenges. *The Verge.* https://www.theverge.com/2022/9/21/23364696/getty-images-ai-ban-generated-artwork-illustration-copyright

Vincent, J. (2022b). The lawsuit that could rewrite the rules of AI copyright. *The Verge.* https://www.theverge.com/2022/11/8/23446821/microsoft-openai-github-copilot-class-action-lawsuit-ai-copyright-violation-training-data

Vincent, J. (n.d.). Getty images sues AI art generator stable diffusion in the US for copyright infringement. *The Verge.* https://www.theverge.com/2023/2/6/23587393/ai-art-copyright-lawsuit-getty-images-stable-diffusion

Wal van der, O., Jumelet, J., Schulz, K., & Zuidema, W. (2022). The birth of bias: A case study on the evolution of gender bias in an english language model. NAACL '22. arXiv. https://doi.org/10.48550/ARXIV.2207.10245

Wang, S. (2022). *Why 'prompt engineering' and 'generative AI' are overhyped.* https://lspace.swyx.io/p/why-prompt-engineering-and-generative

Williams, B. A., Brooks, C. F., & Shmargad, Y. (2018). How algorithms discriminate based on data they lack: Challenges, solutions, and policy implications. *Journal of Information Policy, 8*, 78–115. https://doi.org/10.5325/jinfop oli.8.2018.0078

Wilmer, H. H., Sherman, L. E., & Chein, J. M. (2017). Smartphones and cognition: A review of research exploring the links between mobile technology habits and cognitive functioning. *Frontiers in Psychology, 8*. https://doi.org/10.3389/fpsyg.2017.00605

Zammit, M., Liapis, A., & Yannakakis, G. (2022). Seeding diversity into AI art. In *Proceedings of the 13th International Conference on Computational Creativity*. Association for Computational Creativity.

Zeman, A., Milton, F., Sala, S. D., Dewar, M., Frayling, T., Gaddum, J., Hattersley, A., et al. (2020). Phantasia—The psychological significance of lifelong visual imagery vividness extremes. *Cortex, 130*, 426–440. https://doi.org/10.1016/j.cortex.2020.04.003